Dora Marsden and Early Modernism

Studies in Literature and Science

published in association with the
Society for Literature and Science

Titles in the series

Transgressive Readings: The Texts of Franz Kafka and Max Planck
by Valerie D. Greenberg

A Blessed Rage for Order: Deconstruction, Evolution, and Chaos
by Alexander J. Argyros

Of Two Minds: Hypertext Pedagogy and Poetics
by Michael Joyce

The Artificial Paradise: Science Fiction and American Reality
by Sharona Ben-Tov

Conversations on Science, Culture, and Time
by Michel Serres with Bruno Latour

Genesis by Michel Serres

The Natural Contract by Michel Serres

*Dora Marsden and Early Modernism: Gender,
Individualism, Science* by Bruce Clarke

Dora Marsden and Early Modernism

Gender, Individualism, Science

Bruce Clarke

Ann Arbor

THE UNIVERSITY OF MICHIGAN PRESS

Copyright © by the University of Michigan 1996
All rights reserved
Published in the United States of America by
The University of Michigan Press
Manufactured in the United States of America
⊗ Printed on acid-free paper

1999   1998   1997   1996   4   3   2   1

A CIP catalogue record for this book is available from the British Library.

Library of Congress Cataloging-in-Publication Data

Clarke, Bruce, 1950–
    Dora Marsden and early modernism : gender, individualism, science
/ Bruce Clarke.
        p.   cm. — (Studies in literature and science)
    Includes bibliographical references and index.
    ISBN 0-472-10646-5 (hardcover : acid-free paper)
    1. Marsden, Dora, b. 1882. 2. Women editors—Great Britain—
Biography. 3. Women authors, English—20th century—Biography.
4. English periodicals—Great Britain—History. 5. Feminism—Great
Britain—History. 6. Literature and science—Great Britain—
History. 7. e-uk. I. Title. II. Series.
PN5123.M345C57   1995
324.6'2'092—dc20
    [B]   95-40679
                                                                  CIP

for Donna

Acknowledgments

I want to thank the late Mrs. Elaine Bate, Dora Marsden's niece, for her warm hospitality when I visited her in Prestatyn, Wales, in 1985 to read the Marsden papers for the first time. Her kindness and high spirits will be missed by all who knew her. My profound thanks are also due to Miss Jane Lidderdale and Mrs. Mary Nicholson, for their generous help, and to Mike Weaver for his guidance early in the project. Jean F. Preston, former Curator of Manuscripts at the Princeton University Library, and Robert Bertholf, of the Poetry/Rare Books Room at SUNY/Buffalo, made my stays comfortable and productive. The American Council of Learned Societies provided a 1985 grant-in-aid and a 1990 travel grant for international meetings; Texas Tech University awarded a 1987–88 State Organized Research Fund grant and a 1990 faculty development leave. Working with LeAnn Fields, Eve M. Trager, and Ellen McCarthy of the University of Michigan Press has been a pleasure.

For manifold forms of aid and encouragement, I would also like to express my gratitude to Charles Altieri, Wendell Aycock, Sherry Ceniza, Hugh Crawford, Doug Crowell, Keith Cushman, Paul Delany, David Downing, Rachel Blau DuPlessis, Arthur Efron, Richard Frye, Les Garner, Sandra Gilbert, N. Katherine Hayles, Linda Henderson, Christopher Heywood, David Leon Higdon, David Kadlec, M. Jimmie Killingsworth, A. Walton Litz, Norwood Pratt, Robert Markley, Martin Rosenberg, Robert Salter, John Samson, Marcella Sherman, Jeffrey Smitten, and Joel Weinsheimer. And thanks to the students of my 1992 seminar on Anglo-American literary modernism for giving the project a strong final push.

Earlier versions of some material in this work have appeared as "D. H. Lawrence and the *Egoist* Group," *Journal of Modern Literature* 18:1 (Winter 1992); "Dora Marsden and the *Freewoman*: Anarchism and Literature," *Works and Days: Essays in the Socio-Historical Dimensions of Literature and the Arts* 10:1 (Spring

1992); and "Dora Marsden's Egoism and Modern Letters: West, Weaver, Joyce, Pound, Lawrence, Williams, Eliot," *Works and Days* 2:2 (Fall 1984).

Grateful acknowledgment is made to the following.

J. T. Caldwell for permission to print an unpublished letter of Guy Aldred.

Cambridge University Press for permission to reprint excerpts from D. H. Lawrence, *A Study of Thomas Hardy and Other Essays,* ed. Bruce Steele, copyright © the Estate of Frieda Lawrence Ravagli 1985; and from D. H. Lawrence, *Women in Love*, ed. David Farmer et al., copyright © the Estate of Frieda Lawrence Ravagli 1987.

Alister Kershaw for permission to print unpublished letters of Richard Aldington.

The Manuscripts Division, Department of Rare Books and Special Collections, Princeton University Libraries, for permission to publish excerpts from the correspondence in the Dora Marsden Collection.

Miss Jane Lidderdale, O.B.E., for permission to reprint unpublished letters of Miss Harriet Shaw Weaver to and from Dora Marsden.

New Directions Publishing Corporation for permission to quote from the copyrighted works of William Carlos Williams: copyright © 1938 by New Directions Publishing Corporation, copyright © 1982, 1986 by William Eric Williams and Paul H. Williams. Previously unpublished material by William Carlos Williams copyright © 1995 by William Eric Williams and Paul H. Williams, used by permission of New Directions Publishing Corporation, agents.

New Directions Publishing Corporation and Faber & Faber Ltd. for permission to quote from the copyrighted works of Ezra Pound: copyright © 1995 by the Trustees of the Ezra Pound Literary Property Trust, used by permission of New Directions Publishing Corporation, agents.

Dr. Richard Pankhurst for permission to print unpublished letters of Christabel Pankhurst.

Peters Fraser & Dunlop Group Ltd. for permission to print unpublished letters of Rebecca West.

The Poetry/Rare Books Collection, University Libraries, State University of New York at Buffalo, for permission to reproduce an unpublished letter of Harriet Shaw Weaver.

The Society of Authors on behalf of the copyright owner, Mrs. Iris Wise, for permission to print an unpublished letter of James Stephens.

The University of Wisconsin Press for permission to use material from

Bruce Clarke, "Dora Marsden and Ezra Pound: The *New Freewoman* and 'The Serious Artist,'" *Contemporary Literature* 33:1, copyright © 1992 by the Board of Regents of the University of Wisconsin System.

The Yale Collection of American Literature, Beinecke Rare Book and Manuscript Library, Yale University, for permission to print quotations from unpublished letters by Ezra Pound and William Carlos Williams.

Contents

Dora Marsden and Early Modernism

1.

Self Evolution

Some Preliminary Definitions

Dora Marsden's London

Dora Marsden's London was a vigorous and receptive cosmopolitan capital. It subscribed to the *Mercure de France,* attended F. T. Marinetti's Futurist evenings, contributed occasional essays to the *New Age,* and regularly followed the debates in those pages over Nietzsche and Bergson. But it was also well read in Whitman's poetry and Emerson's essays, and it is the pointed Anglo-American complexion of early modernism in London that will be my main concern in this study. Expatriate American poet Ezra Pound established in London from 1908 to 1920 the amplified transatlantic circuit conducting the alternating Anglo-American current of the period. Pound's colorful tenure in London is a handy frame around my primary tableau—the span and significance of the three London journals Dora Marsden created and edited and to which she contributed her most important writings: the *Freewoman,* the *New Freewoman,* and the *Egoist.* As a literary phenomenon, Dora Marsden's London is this text.

In Dora Marsden's London, the movement politics of prewar suffragism and feminism gave way to the personal politics of an individualistic literary practice. Marsden's own intellectual progress took precisely this route and thus offers concrete insights into the development of the early modernist literary sensibility. Although the initial focus of the *Freewoman* was on feminist issues, in the *New Freewoman*—subedited by Rebecca West, then Ezra Pound—Marsden began to blend literary experimentalism with political anarchism. This transformation was confirmed with the arrival of the *Egoist,* subedited by Richard Aldington and Hilda Doolittle, and lastly by T. S. Eliot. Contributors to Dora Marsden's journals included Edward Carpenter, Remy de Gourmont, Huntly Carter, Benjamin Tucker, Dorothy Richardson, Ford Madox Ford, Allen

Upward, Amy Lowell, William Carlos Williams, James Joyce, D. H. Lawrence, Wyndham Lewis, May Sinclair, F. S. Flint, and Marianne Moore. Marsden herself consistently contributed remarkable lead essays and commentaries. But the intimate connections between her writings and subsequent developments in modernist literary production have seldom been properly appreciated.

A virtual anthology of the shifting cast and ideological concerns of early-twentieth-century literary and political culture, Dora Marsden's London had also received the ambivalent gifts of the nineteenth century: anxious and exhausted capitalist empires, intrusive heavy technologies, polarized class and gender conflicts, powerful and tendentious sciences. In the decades before and during the Great War, London's literary and artistic cultures produced as well as absorbed a series of international aesthetic and intellectual movements—cubism, futurism, egoism, imagism, vorticism, expressionism—all with strident manifestos either imitating or parodying those of radical political groups.[1] Modernist ideology in Dora Marsden's London thrived on the polemical confrontation of sociopolitical discourses with aesthetic forms. For instance, early modernist London was a daily witness to the political theater of the Women's Social and Political Union (WSPU). Marsden was herself a product of this street school, the WSPU's militant suffrage campaign.

From a broken lower-middle-class home, but benefiting from the 1870 Education Act and the pupil-teacher and scholarship systems, in 1900 Dora Marsden entered Manchester's Victoria University. She and her classmates—Christabel Pankhurst, Mary Gawthorpe, Theresa Billington-Greig, Rona Robinson, and Emily Wilding Davison—later became prominent actors in the WSPU's militant campaign. Abandoning her teaching career, by the end of 1908 Marsden was a salaried organizer. Between 1909 and 1910, she achieved national notoriety as a fighting suffragette: her picture made the front page of the *Daily Mirror,* she served a month's imprisonment in Holloway Gaol and was released from Manchester after a hunger strike, and her spectacular harassment of Winston Churchill at the Southport Empire from a skylight in the dome went into suffragette legend. But in 1911, she resigned from the WSPU, moved to London, and that November launched the *Freewoman: A Weekly Feminist Review.*

The *Freewoman* was probably the last word in frank public discussion between women and men in the English-speaking world of its day. From November 1911 to October 1912, its defiantly heterogeneous pages established an open circle of cultural debate among feminists, socialists, anarchists, sex radicals, neo-Malthusians (birth-control advocates), "Uranians" (homosexuals), suffragists, spiritualists, money cranks, poets, and aesthetes. This catholic embrace of varied sexualities as well as of marginalized political discourses scandalized the respectable suffragist and feminist communities, not to mention Mrs. Humphry Ward.[2] Ultimately a distributor's boycott brought the *Freewoman's* run to an end. In the *Freewoman*, Dora Marsden's sensibility was fired by her militant experiences, but that orientation represented only the earliest stage in a prolonged and complex intellectual development. In critical response to the organizational tactics as well as the parliamentary goals of the WSPU, Marsden began to write out a theoretical program for a libertarian feminism.[3] With the *New Freewoman* Marsden's explicit focus shifted from radical feminism to individualist anarchism and literary experimentalism, and her cultural criticisms developed into a systematic philosophy of egoism.[4]

Between 1911 and 1914, Dora Marsden had final say on all editorial work, and her writings appeared anonymously; after Harriet Shaw Weaver took over as main editor of the *Egoist,* Marsden usually signed her regular contributions. In either event, literary historians have been somewhat slow to address the pervasive interconnections between Marsden's discourses and the other modernisms being wrought in the numbers of her journals. For instance, her *Freewoman* leaders already traced two doctrinal shifts—transitions from feminist to anarchist and from socialist to individualist idioms—directly connected to her support in the *New Freewoman* for literary innovation within a philosophical practice of "egoistic investigation."[5] As her initial audience of maverick suffragists, "minority" feminists (see Tickner, *Spectacle of Women*, 320), and assorted sex radicals dwindled, a new grouping gathered, this one centered on artistic forms of self-assertion as well as on the conviction that aesthetic creation can be an agency of cultural reform or political revolt. During the short run of the *New Freewoman,* while West and Pound were bringing forward memorable literary material, Marsden was turning her attention to the exposition of an anarchistic aesthetics. After the *Egoist* established itself as a mouthpiece for the Anglo-American literary avant-garde and as an interested observer of other artistic trends, Marsden pursued egoistic investigations of images and concepts. The structural and formulary texture of her *Science of Signs,* developed in the *Egoist* from 1916 to 1919, participated in modernism's overall rupture of realist representationalism.

Nevertheless, the experience of militant political opposition and the logic of feminist rhetoric remained implicit even in her philosophical egoism and continued to determine many of Marsden's intellectual moves and discursive strategies. Providing vehicles for the early critical and creative writings of major modernists, setting a rhetorical example in her own writings, her literary operations infused some of the polemical definition of political militancy into early modernist discourse. Dora Marsden was something of a devil's advocate, an inscrutable smiling sibyl, a philosophical prankster and editorial provocateur interested not in fostering affective solidarity but in promoting analytical individuation. She was also a committed essayist and a visionary ideologue who began editing in order to publish herself. Ironist and oracle, part Swift and part Blake, she invigorated the *Freewoman* by arranging for the collision of warring partisans—for instance, feminists and misogynists, socialists and individualists, sex radicals and sex conservatives. Her leaders and commentaries also reveal her anarchistic spiritualism, her prophetic vocation. Marsden's semiobscurity is undeserved but not surprising: she was a difficult and demanding person with an increasingly uncommon and difficult message.

Dora Marsden's lack of recognition may be traced to several causes. The *Freewoman,* in which Marsden worked through her first major intellectual transitions, has always been difficult to consult. After its demise, her subsequent career was a series of further breaks with further communities. Marsden remained a militant and combative personality, an outspoken individualist who courted strong opponents. In addition, her intellectual changes, from a postsuffragist feminism to a postfeminist anarchism, have often not been held in favor. With the lapse of the *Egoist* at the end of 1919, the already reclusive Marsden devoted herself to esoteric philosophical projects and fell out of sight. The first imagist history—Glenn Hughes's *Imagism and the Imagists*—written on the basis of testimonies biased against Marsden's editorial hand at the *Egoist*, began a tradition of misinformation that has gone mostly unchallenged for more than half a century.[6] Marsden's contributions were thus obscured as the New Critical canon of high modernism was being constructed and disseminated. Despite the advent of second-wave feminism and the recuperation of many female modernist reputations, an informed recognition of Marsden's activities has lagged behind even those of her contemporaries who were strictly editors rather than writers: Harriet Monroe of *Poetry* and Margaret Anderson of the *Little Review*. For all that, during the second decade of the twentieth century, what Dora Marsden accomplished had an appreciable effect on Anglo-American literary modernism.

Early Modernism

I distinguish early modernism from the later strain, consolidated in 1923 with T. S. Eliot's publication of *The Waste Land* and founding of the *Criterion*, by applying Michael Levenson's division of literary modernism into two historical phases: "modernism was individualist before it was anti-individualist, anti-traditional before it was traditional, inclined to anarchism before it was inclined to authoritarianism" (*Genealogy of Modernism*, 79). Levenson's initial phase of individualism, experimentalism, and anarchism nicely summarizes the early modernism developed in Dora Marsden's London. At its outset in the first two decades of the twentieth century, early modernism manifested its antitraditionalism as an obligatory iconoclasm, the literary corollary of the political mood running throughout western culture. Marjorie Perloff has identified the first crest of early modernism with the *avant-guerre* period from 1910 to 1914, a "period of artistic rupture—the rupture of established genres and verse forms as well as of the integrity of the medium."[7] The traditions and genres early modernism departed from may be briefly enumerated.

(1) It followed symbolism in further effecting a rupture with the aims and devices of naturalism.
(2) It published its refusal to accept any further debts under the mimetic contracts of realism.
(3) It attacked the gradualist reformism of bourgeois liberalism.

In terms of the scientific connections I will explore throughout this study, we can say that after Zola, naturalism was explicitly an empiricist and deterministic literary scientism modeled on mid-nineteenth-century observational methods in biology and clinical medicine, whereas the symbolist line into modernism was implicitly an immaterial and energic scientism patterned after the force fields and energy transformations of late-nineteenth-century electromagnetic and atomic physics.[8] Transcendentalist and spiritualist trends in early modernism attempted to recover the theologized or energy-infused cosmos apparently revalidated by innovations such as wireless transmission and radioactivity. The modernist literary avant-garde seconded concurrent moves in scientific thought, in that the very objects of scientific investigation, especially in physics and chemistry, increasingly departed from the classical ideal of empirical verification. Whereas nineteenth-century realism emphasized the detached description of discrete items, energic and atomic realism demanded the intentional construction of interpretive patterns and formulae: Ezra Pound's famous "rose in the steel dust" captures the scientistic metaphoricity of imagist and vorticist modernism.[9] As modernist literature followed other arts into abstraction, it came increasingly to resemble a professional form of technical cipher, to model its "seriousness" on the hard languages of mathematized sciences.

Early modernism criticized liberalism from both wings of the political spectrum: in England from 1908 to 1914, "the radical Right and the radical Left were united in their detestation of capitalism and indecisive Liberal compromise."[10] Early modernism is thus a complex extremism exhibiting the general problematics of political anarchism, a discourse that will enable us to draw some important discriminations among early modernism's various counter-Marxist stances.[11] According to Levenson, in Edwardian London "liberalism decomposed into egoism" (*Genealogy of Modernism*, 68), which he characterizes strictly as a reactionary antihumanism. But Levenson identifies early modernism too squarely with its proto-hegemonic wing, that is, Pound and T. E. Hulme. In fact, Dora Marsden's individualism presents a libertarian anarchism absolved from binding claims of the left or the right in its absolute negation of corporate or collective bodies such as parliaments and political parties. In other words, as opposed to Pound, Wyndham Lewis, Eliot, and other writers who went on to embrace the hierarchical statism of late modernism, Marsden's stance remained "early modernist." And, if it is proper to align D. H. Lawrence and William Carlos Williams with early rather than late modernism, it is important to factor their own political careers into anarchist rather than statist or totalitarian models.

The distinction of modernisms into early and late formations helps resolve some of the paradoxes Astradur Eysteinsson cites in the attempt to conceptualize the movement as a whole.

> While modernism is often accused of being a *cult of form,* it is also (not infrequently by the same critics, such as Lukács) attacked for *formlessness* and for distorted and anarchic representation of society, disintegration of outer reality, and disorderly manipulation of language. It is at this point that the whole notion of modernism moving the communicative act of reading "outside of history" shows itself to be a contradiction of terms. . . . We need to ask ourselves how the concept of autonomy, so crucial to many theories of modernism, can possibly coexist with the equally prominent view of modernism as a historically explosive paradigm. This dichotomy, hardly recognized by most critics, is characteristic for the divergent approaches to modernism as, on the one hand, a *cultural force,* and on the other as an *aesthetic project.*[12]

On the one hand, modernist emphases on formalism, ahistoricism, and aesthetic autonomy clearly outline a later configuration, which is also the main object of Lukács's critique of modernist ideology.[13] On the other hand, the contrasting epithets of formless disorder, anarchic distortion, and historical explosiveness sharply outline an early configuration, in vehicles directly culled from the iconography of anarchism. For Marxist criticism in general, the animus toward literary modernism is bound up with the parallel animus toward political anarchism. Perhaps the cutting edge of these problematics is the complex issue of autonomy, which can also be bifurcated into early and late modalities.

In its literal sense as "self-rule," autonomy is a libertarian construction. What happens midway through the course of Anglo-American modernism is that the earlier emphasis on personal autonomy—individualist anarchism, sexual libertarianism—collides with the doctrine of impersonalism that we typically associate with T. S. Eliot. It is wonderfully ironic that "Tradition and the Individual Talent," the ur-manifesto of hegemonic modernism, was first published in the last two numbers of the *Egoist,* alongside Dora Marsden's egoistic apocalypse, her concluding chapters to the *Science of Signs.*[14] The effect of Eliot's doctrine, however, was to reify and displace early modernism's egoism or existential autonomy as the aesthetic autonomy ostensibly possessed by the autotelic text. Hegemonic modernism's founding gesture was to dispossess the individual talent in favor of tradition and its canonical textual apparatuses. Eliot's cultural conservatism traduced the aesthetic anarchism against which it defined itself: the formal autonomy of the text becomes a travesty of the individualism in which early modernism's radicalism was nurtured. For instance, William Carlos Williams's acute consciousness of Eliot's departure from early-modernist attitudes accounts for the depth of his dismay over his compatriot's London successes.[15]

On a final front, we will trace in early modernism a certain maintenance of radical social traditions: at its inception it was still flush with the ambiguous progressivisms of nineteenth-century vitalism and evolutionism. In this regard, the defining doctrinal rupture marks not the emergence of modernism per se but the later transition into its hegemonic form. One of the first indications of the coming complexion of late modernism was Hulme's course of reaction against his earlier Bergsonism, a forerunner of similar movements toward statism and classicism by Pound, Lewis, and Eliot.[16] Relative to this later modernism, Lawrence and Williams retained in varying degrees their investments in early modernist vitalism and thus remained virtually oriented more toward the doctrinal orbit of Dora Marsden than of T. S. Eliot. The critical reception of Lawrence and Williams flourished only with the lapse of late-modernist doctrines. In the 1960s, when Anglo-American literary culture began to react strongly against Eliotian and New Critical institutions, postmodernism represented a certain recovery of early modernism's revolutionary origins and anarchistic emphases.

The Gender of Individualism

Dora Marsden's suffragette experiences left her disenchanted both with British parliamentary democracy and with the militant suffrage movement aimed at gaining women a franchise in it. In the aftermath of her lapse from movement politics, Marsden ranged liberally over nineteenth- and early-twentieth-century discourse. Appropriating elements from Max Stirner, Herbert Spencer, Friedrich Nietzsche, Havelock Ellis, Henri Bergson, and Edward Carpenter, she set forth an unprecedented egoistic strain of femino-anarchism. By referring to the field of these discourses, we can reassess the cultural politics of individualist discourses in Dora Marsden's London and reevaluate some literary avatars of early modernism who had lines of material connection to Marsden's journals.

Like most things valorized in patriarchal culture, historically the gender of individualism has been masculine. But Marsden's individualism quickly led her to posit an androgynous rather than strictly feminine or heterosexual ideal. One can read that gesture either as a seminal feminizing of anarchism or as an abandonment of feminism. A perennial feminist criticism of Marsden has been that her antisocialism undermines the gender solidarity necessary to advance a feminist politics. But, in fact, has the long demand for socialist/feminist solidarity even now yielded the desired advances? Judith Butler has confronted this issue in terms that could make a reopening for Dora Marsden within a feminism pursuing a wider conceptual coalition: "The insistence in advance on coalitional 'unity' as a goal assumes that solidarity, whatever its price, is a prerequisite for political action. But what sort of politics demands that kind of advance purchase on unity? Perhaps a coalition needs to acknowledge its contradictions and take action with its contradictions intact."[17] In the meantime, Dora Marsden's political career is an important early-twentieth-century example of a radical feminist's refusal to subscribe to an "exclusionary" identity politics.[18]

Rachel Blau DuPlessis has turned some ideological irony on Marsden's complicity in the transformation of the *New Freewoman* into the *Egoist*.[19] Her charges are implicitly related to the larger materialist and deconstructive arguments about the construction of gender and the contextuality of the psyche that Butler examines in *Gender Trouble*. DuPlessis criticizes a long editorial in the last *New Freewoman* in which Marsden presented her decision to rename the journal not as mere acquiescence to the demanding "men of letters" who had supposedly put her up to it but as the signature of her own consummation of a political passage beyond the performative exigencies of gender.

How wonderful to be able to editorialize that the debates on gender were over, that women "can be as 'free' now as they have the power to be," that the assertion of freewoman status no longer need happen, that indeed, such assertions were divisive, backward looking, a form of protectionism, and were not modern. For the assertion of Self in Singularity that the new title claimed was a myth of—let us speak in shorthand—false consciousness. It did not ask how "ego" was socially formed, in what conjunctures. (Du-Plessis, *Pink Guitar*, 45)

Marsden's shifting attitudes responded to the volatile milieu of *avant-guerre* and wartime culture in radical London: accordingly, those attitudes were more or less evenly divided between the constructive and the defensive, the visionary and the reactionary. Marsden's femino-anarchism grasped much of the abusive fiction at play in turn-of-the-century scientistic discourses of sexual types— their status as regressive political strategies, their power to interpellate their hosts into collective structures. That understanding determined the rhetorical levels on which her own discourses operated. The *Freewoman* was set forth specifically to challenge and dissolve misogynist stereotypes. Admittedly, however, Marsden's philosophical individualism was blind to many things we have now learned to see. Her egoistic semantics break down at the threshold of the grammatical structurality of the psyche. In spite of anyone's deliberate acts of doctrinal and rhetorical hygiene, ideological structures persist as invidious terms in a gendered unconscious. Defining the ego as both ontologically primary and existentially fluid, Marsden's system could never acknowledge the extent to which the ego is a secondary effect, the contingent precipitate of a fixating identification, some introjected ego-ideal. Her vitalistic reification of the ego as the life force sublimated into self-consciousness prohibited a deeper grasp of the modalities of the unconscious. From her first feminisms to her later egoisms, Dora Marsden remained a phenomenological idealist.

In a critical environment presided over by doctrines of a decentered self coordinated with variously gendered discursive solidarities, Marsden's grandiose individualism is something of a sitting duck. It is perhaps ironic that her elaborate self-defensiveness now leaves her exposed on all sides to casual ideological attack. The heretical stances as well as the difficulties of Marsden's discourses have often tempted her critics into impoverished accounts that foreclose the possibility of an adequate analysis. As Charles Altieri has said about vulgar ideologism in general, "before we allow ourselves such distanced analytical stances for reading *against* texts, we must learn to read *through* them by coming to appreciate the specific imaginative experiences they offer when taken as deliberate authorial constructs. Without that labor of provisional identification, the suspicious or deconstructive critic is simply not dealing with a sufficiently rich version of the object."[20]

An insurrectionary humor darkly graces the rigors of Marsden's writings. We do well to recall her remarks in the *Egoist* satirizing the worship of words: "Only by laughter—that gurgle of impishness: by the incorrigibly untutored self-assertiveness of the uninoculated have men saved their souls, half alive, from the complete domination of words. Laughter and the spirit of mockery apart, and we should have been flat on our faces before them lost in submission and adoration. Instinctively the human animal has taken on the habit of laughter as a means of defence and set on the Ridiculous to dog the Sublime" ("I Am," 2). To redress the long critical record of misrepresentation, inadequate examination, and summary dismissal and to further the collaborative effort of establishing a sufficiently rich version of her work, in this study I usually take the ostensible role of Dora Marsden's advocate. As devil's advocate for a devil's advocate, I let the lines of my own critique emerge indirectly, by arranging significant discursive juxtapositions, or by teasing out moments of historical or doctrinal irony.

When we return to the final number of the *New Freewoman* and review in detail the issues raised by Marsden's valediction to the persona of the free-woman, I argue that her editorial there, like her work in general, is not the naive transcript of a mistaken conviction but rather a "deliberate authorial construct" the significance of which has yet to be properly appreciated. For the moment, I note that critics Gillian Hanscombe and Virginia L. Smyers have found some room for Marsden's labors within the camp of feminist literary modernism. Between her individualistic views and contemporary feminism's theories of self-possession, "the difference lies in the context for such a view. Dora's was a spiritual one . . . whereas feminists now who pursue autonomy owe their position to a political analysis in which phenomena like prostitution and rape are given global causes (and remedies) beyond the resources of any individual to manipulate."[21] Hanscombe and Smyers present Marsden's shaping of the *New Freewoman* and the *Egoist* into individualist reviews in productive terms: "individualist analysis . . . of the kind Dora Marsden offers fits amicably alongside the anti-conventional poems of H.D. and Amy Lowell, for example, since they, too—in tone, mood and image—disclaim to represent or to speak with familiarity to a known congregation as do the feminist poets of our own time" (172).

The fact remains that Marsden's relations to Anglo-American feminism are "troubled." But what about the light Marsden might throw on her male collaborators? "Individualist analysis" is also an exceedingly appropriate context for the consideration of "male modernism." I propose to seize upon the residually femino-anarchist quotient of Marsden's individualism and turn it directly upon the given, largely male modernism as she discovered it on her doorstep. To proceed in this direction we must dispute some common premises of Anglo-American literary history. One example is J. Hillis Miller's justly influential specification of a male modernist canon in *Poets of Reality,* which deflects the glaring egoistic component of the Anglo-American modernist scene into the benighted Edwardian backwaters, for instance, when it translates the virile individualist aesthetic of William Carlos Williams into his ostensible idiom of objectivism or priority on "things" at the expense of an ego's "ideas." Through the abstruse channels of the *New Freewoman* and the *Egoist,* while she also gave significant sustenance to Rebecca West, Harriet Shaw Weaver, H.D., Amy Lowell, and May Sinclair, Dora Marsden was a fugitive midwife to the miraculous birth of a literary tradition out of the "individual talents" of Pound, Joyce, Eliot, Lawrence, and Williams.

In an early prose passage of *Spring and All,* Williams's obscure phrase "Dora Marsden's philosophic algebra" documents his attention to her writings.[22] Williams's notice first sent me in search of that algebra, and now that I have examined it I will try to draw some diagrams for other sojourners in Dora Marsden's London. There is a fascinatingly complex consistency to her discursive project. Even the earliest numbers of the *Freewoman* purvey the spiritual idiom of a radical ego-idealism. Her assertion of the "spiritual separateness" or absolute individual autonomy of women informed her trenchant material analyses of basic feminist topics such as sexuality, marriage, prostitution, education, and economic employment.[23] Held at the proper analytical angle, Marsden's articulated egoism reveals a wide corridor of cultural history. My main concern in the following study is to show how the unfolding logic of Dora Marsden's writings illuminates the conceptual interiors of early Anglo-American modernism and throws new light on its transition from early to late formations.

"Individualist, Egoist, Anarchist"

The arc of Marsden's development provides a blueprint for reconstructing the timetables as well as the energy circuits of early Anglo-American modernism. Marsden's discursive trajectory is not just significantly parallel to the ideological careers of major literary modernists, it is often years in advance of them. Echoed in the shifting titles of and changing contributors to her journals, Marsden's metamorphoses were as rapid as they were complex. Her transformations may be traced from a residually social-democratic rallying around a shared and sharable gender conception—the prophetic call to a body of freewomen—to the androgynous anarchism of the egoist, an individualistic formula usually appearing in the singular. What drove these changes? What were the sources of these discursive reconceptions? Why, like so many major modernists, would Marsden have considered as progressive, intellectual movements that often showed themselves in the fullness or decay of their development to be reactionary?

To determine the full equation of Marsden's early modernist arc, however, we need to establish at least provisionally the discursive axes on which to plot it. The rest of this chapter recovers some of the cultural environment within which early modernism was incubated and out of which it then moved. First, I plot the connections among three Anglo-American cultural studies published between 1908 and 1913. The intellectual networks and the structures of opinion to which Dora Marsden's London resonated and from which its individualisms developed may be read in the discursive idioms of Floyd Dell's *Women as World Builders*, James Huneker's *Egoists*, and Vernon Lee's *Gospels of Anarchy*. These more ephemeral documents then send us to Edward Carpenter's 1889 essay "Civilisation: Its Cause and Cure" and Walt Whitman's 1870 essay *Democratic Vistas* to establish a crucial relay within late-nineteenth-century Anglo-American literature. Finally, that literary/political circuit divulges the mythopoetic field of evolutionary vitalism, a scientistic idiom that saturated the progressive politics as well as the creative writing of the time. Evangelical evolutionism thrived in the women's suffrage movement within which Marsden's radicalism found its first notoriety. Eventually Dora Marsden reinscribed the political ideology of evolutionary vitalism with her anarchistic egoism, and in this form her individualism entered into commerce with the aesthetic ideologies of early modernist London.

Women as World Builders

In 1913, twenty-five-year-old Chicago journalist Floyd Dell published *Women as World Builders,* assembling a roster of American and British women distinguished for their social activism or artistic creativity—Charlotte Perkins Gilman, Jane Addams, Emmeline Pankhurst, Olive Schreiner, Isadora Duncan, Beatrice Webb, Emma Goldman, Margaret Dreier Robins, Ellen Key, and Dora Marsden: "it is with woman as producer that we are concerned in a study of feminism, rather than with woman as lover. . . . The woman who sets her love above everything else I would gently dismiss from our present consideration as belonging to the courtesan type."[24] That gentle dismissal betrayed a certain patronizing air on Dell's part, compounded by the popular journalistic recourse to social typecasting.²⁵ Nevertheless, Dell participated in some of the rhetorics of rebellion we will trace through Huneker and Lee. His book also offers an edifying example of the conditions necessary for some early-twentieth-century male progressives to embrace the feminist movement.

As his banishment of the courtesan or erotic rebel indicated, Dell was particularly concerned at the outset to establish himself as a hardheaded critic free from either sexual or sentimental motives and advancing not an indiscriminate but a selective appreciation: "these following papers . . . are devoid of the spirit of Romance. I mean that attitude toward woman which accepts her sex as a miraculous justification of her existence, the belief that being a woman is a virtue in itself, apart from the possession of other qualities" (17). He acknowledged his awareness that "the voice of modern science" has deemed women to be congenitally and comprehensively inferior to men, but he has "hearkened even more eagerly to the voice of sociology, which tells me of woman's wonderful possibilities. It is with these possibilities that this book is, in the main, concerned" (18).

For Dell, the world modern feminism was building had barely progressed past some preliminary ground clearing. Its present activity was often more concerned with the demolition of decaying structures than with the construction of new ones: "I think that with the advent of women into a larger life our jerry-built virtues will have to go, to make room for mansions and gardens fit to be inhabited by the human soul" (88). But why should man abet that activity when it disrupts, perhaps destroys, the world he has seized and built on his own? Dell put his own masculinism up front, so to speak, presumably to ward off a hasty rejection by male readers, by suggesting a line of self-interest that could reconcile the enlightened male to insurrectionary feminism, but perhaps also to fend off the threat of female power.²⁶ It is hard to say whether Dell's masculinist audacity was quite in earnest, but in any event, his literal remarks are sufficiently forthright to be worth quoting at length:

> The fact is, as has been bitterly recited by the rebellious leaders of their sex, that women have always been what man wanted them to be—have changed to suit his changing ideals. The fact is, furthermore, that the woman's movement of today is but another example of that readiness of women to adapt themselves to a masculine demand.
>
> Men are tired of subservient women. . . . If only for self-protection, they desired to find in woman a comrade and an equal. In reality they desired it because it promised to be more fun.
>
> So that we have as the motive behind the rebellion of women an

obscure rebellion of men. Why, then, have men appeared hostile to the woman's rebellion? Because what men desire are real individuals who have achieved their own freedom. It will not do to pluck freedom like a flower and give it to the lady with a polite bow. She must fight for it. (19–20)

Insofar as Dell was speaking to women, might he have been borrowing a page from Dora Marsden's handbook of provocation, delivering an ironic taunt intended to fan the flame of women's fighting spirit? It is difficult to take seriously Dell's suggestion that male hostility to feminism has been just a guise assumed like a drill sergeant's wrath merely to motivate the troops. On the face of it, this blithe arrogance performed a classic hegemonic co-optation: it preserved male self-possession and priority in the face of female insurrection while offering male magnanimity as the true drive behind a nascent feminism that must thereby be taken as oblivious to its deepest motives. In any event, this passage blurts out a significant if generally unstated component of modern male-liberal tolerance of feminism: it is expected that freer women will offer livelier companionship, will hold up with greater spirit their ends of the conversation and the household, and, when day is done, will be more fun in bed. That the next morning she may be competing with Floyd for the same job does not seem to come to mind. Dell's introduction ended with an egotistic assertion of his own magisterial role.

It is, then, as a phase of the great human renaissance inaugurated by men that the woman's movement deserves to be considered. And what more fitting than that a man should sit in judgment upon the contemporary aspects of that movement, weighing out approval or disapproval! Such criticism is not a masculine impertinence but a masculine right, a right properly pertaining to those who are responsible for the movement, and whose demands it must ultimately fulfill. (20–21)

Having positioned the feminist movement for a proper male examination, Dell proceeded to laud his canon of world builders in mostly celebrative if generally superficial tones. Mixing fluid imageries of the aquatic and the electrical, Dell averred how Charlotte Gilman's writings rebel "against those artificial channels which break up the strong, pure stream of woman's energy into a thousand little stagnant canals, covered with spiritual pond-scum" (27). The contrast between the implacable British suffragist Emmeline Pankhurst and her less strident American counterpart Jane Addams drew from Dell the observation that women actually do have fighting instincts, and thus, "we have in militancy rather than in conciliation, in action rather than in wisdom, the keynote of woman in politics" (40). In line with suffragist visions from the trenches of the prewar campaigns, Dell predicted that the female franchise would thoroughly reconstruct the lumbering processes of Anglo-American democracies.

The chapter on Olive Schreiner and Isadora Duncan is Dell's best, setting up an agile contrast between the labor of the hand and the play of the foot. Dell got some significant assistance by quoting at length from Duncan's own writings on the spirit of her choreography, and his meditations on Duncan's Whit-manesque lyricism introduce us to the popular discourse of evolutionism. Here again Dell found an opportunity to place male effort behind the female struggle: "The woman's movement is a product of the evolutionary science of the nine-teenth century. . . . It is modern science which, by giving us a new view of the body, its functions, its needs, its claim upon the world, has laid the basis for a suc-cessful feminist movement. When the true history of this movement is written it will contain more about Herbert Spencer and Walt Whitman, perhaps, than about Victoria Woodhull and Tennessee Claflin," two leaders of the American "free-love" movement of the 1870s (44–45).

The "evolutionary science" of the Whitmanian body, denuded of hierarchy and shame, and the Spencerian body, achieving ever greater "fitness" through its developmental differentiations, has allowed the woman = body allegory of West-ern patriarchy to be reread as a positive rather than negative equation. Through Isadora Duncan, Dell echoes the evolutionary optimism bound up with the sex-ual liberalism of a figure like Havelock Ellis.[27] In the prewar decades, when utopian schemes of racial improvement were often advanced by liberal thinkers, eugenics was still capable of socialist/progressive and feminist appreciation.

> "It is not only a question of true art," writes Miss Duncan, "it is a question of race, of the development of the female sex to beauty and health, of the return to the original strength and the natural movements of woman's body. It is a question of the development of perfect mothers and the birth of healthy and beautiful children." Here we have an inspiriting expression of the idea which through the poems of Walt Whitman and the writings of various moderns, has renovated the modern soul and made us see, with-out any obscene blurring by Puritan spectacles, the goodness of the whole body. This is as much a part of the woman's movement as the demand for a vote (or, rather, it is more central and essential a part); and only by real-izing this is it possible to understand that movement. (Dell, 48–49)

Insofar as the figuring of woman as the fallen and erring body has been a source of patriarchal control, Whitmanian doctrines of the divinity of the body and other poetic revaluations of sexuality can promote the release of women from traditional moralisms. However, by such revisions the power of the trope woman = body is not finally disturbed: its essentialist premises remain intact and ready to be turned to the right by reactionary social engineers. In any event, in 1913, Isadora Duncan's aestheticized feminism lifted Floyd Dell to a high pitch of approbation.[28]

Women as World Builders was originally to close with the chapter on Ellen Key, whose pleas for premarital cohabitation in *Love and Marriage* actually indicated the conservative impulses behind female radicalism. According to Dell, "women have a surer instinct than men for the preservation of the truest human values, but . . . their very acts of conservation will seem to the timid minds among us like the shattering of all virtues, the debacle of civilization, the Götterdämmerung!" (89). However, and this is what endows most of the historical value it possesses to Dell's book, as it was going into production Dora Marsden's fame flared up with the notoriety of the *Freewoman*, and Dell felt compelled to add a Marsden chapter to his initial lineup. From this we can recover and measure an appreciable enthusiasm in the American response to Dora Marsden and reception of her first discursive productions.

"This is by way of a postscript," Dell wrote. "Dora Marsden is a new figure in the feminist movement. Just how she evolved is rather hard to say" (90). Sitting in Chicago, he attempted without much success to decipher that evolution from a sampling of her *Freewoman* leaders, which offer little specific information about Marsden's prior careers as headmistress and suffragette organizer. What Dell could vouch for was the following.

> The Freewoman was a weekly. It lived several months and then suspended publication, and now all the women I know are poring over the back numbers while waiting for it to start again as a fortnightly. It was a remarkable paper. For one thing, it threw open its columns to such a discussion of sex that dear Mrs. Humphry Ward wrote a shocked letter to The Times about it. . . . For once sex was on a plane with other subjects, a fact making tremendously for sanity. In this Miss Marsden not only achieved a creditable journalistic feat, but performed a valuable public service. (92)

Marsden and her supporters were able to revive the *Freewoman* as the *New Freewoman*, partly through a One Thousand Club formed to generate start-up

Dora Marsden in 1912. Photo by G. C. Beresford.

capital with prepublication subscriptions, with branches in New York and Chicago. Dell's description of columns thrown open accurately reflected the status of the *Freewoman* as a discussion forum attracting quite a few of the crusaders of Anglo-American cultural radicalism. The paper's sexual libertarianism gave it visibility, but Dell's lengthy excerpts from Dora Marsden's earliest leaders show that her own emphasis was on spiritual liberation: "In the first issue was an editorial on 'Bondwomen,' from which it would appear that perhaps even such advanced persons as you, my dear lady, are still far from free. . . . This was only the beginning of such a campaign of radical propaganda as feminism never knew before. Miss Marsden went on to attack all the things which bind women and keep them unfree. . . . This is frankly a gospel for a minority" (93–98).

Dell was sufficiently acquainted with the dialect of individualist anarchism to place Marsden's feminist radicalism accordingly: "She called upon women to be individuals, and sought to demolish in their minds any lingering desire for Authority" (99).[29] After quoting further from Marsden's leaders, Dell briefly rebutted some of her notions, but then caught himself short and reflected on his response as Marsden's reader, a structure of response that still holds good, I imagine, for most readers.

> There you have it! Inevitably one argues with Dora Marsden. That is her value. She provokes thought. And she welcomes it. She wants everybody to think—not to think her thoughts necessarily, nor the right thoughts always, but that which they can and must. She is a propagandist, it is true. But she does not create a silence, and call it conversion.
>
> She stimulates her readers to cast out the devils that inhabit their souls— fear, prejudice, sensitiveness. She helps them to build up their lives on a basis of will—the exercise, not the suppression, of will. She indurates them to the world. She liberates them to life. She is the Max Stirner of feminism. (103)[30]

In Dora Marsden, Floyd Dell seemed to have found a full incarnation of the feminist warrior he had posited in his introduction, not one who would graciously accept the flower of freedom offered from a liberal man's chivalrous hand, but an egoist who seized her own and was armed to defend it. The new concluding paragraph of *Women as World Builders* warmly expressed his enthusiasm for Marsden's brand of feminism.

> Freedom! That is the first word and the last with Dora Marsden. She makes women understand for the first time what freedom means. She makes them want to be free. She nerves them to the effort of emancipation. She sows in a fertile soil the dragon's teeth which shall spring up as a band of capable females, knowing what they want and taking it, asking no leave from anybody, doing things and enjoying life—Freewomen! (104)

In the light of Dell's approbation, does Marsden fall under his masculinist dispensation as well, not as an unwitting but as a willing tool of man's desire? I would rather say that Marsden eludes Dell's defensive appropriation while drawing to her discourse an ambivalent admission of male desire for female liberation.

Egoists: A Book of Supermen

In Dora Marsden's London, "the ego" referred not to the psychological legacy of Sigmund Freud but to the philosophical legacy of Kant and Hegel, "the Superman" not to a cartoon superhero but to the arrogance of *der Übermensch*, the visionary trope coined by Friedrich Nietzsche. In 1909, the versatile American art critic James Gibbons Huneker published *Egoists: A Book of Supermen*, a collection of literary sketches on subjects ranging from Stendhal to Ibsen.[31] *Egoists* chronicles the currency of an egoistic idiom in the literary discussion of symbolists and decadents and places that idiom in the particular philosophical and aesthetic contexts from which Dora Marsden's London further developed and critiqued it. In 1909, Huneker could expect his chosen audience to regard his title as witty, just as at the end of 1913 Marsden could expect a modest audience to respond positively to the ironic cachet of the *Egoist* as an appropriate renaming of the *New Freewoman*. Huneker's cultural journalism both exploited and dissected the rhetoric of post-Nietzschean egoism, purveying while deflating it.[32] This attitude is amusingly confirmed when Huneker commented on Théophile Gautier's story of Baudelaire, "how the young Charles, an incorrigible dandy, came to visit Hôtel Pimodan about 1844. In this Hôtel Pimodan a dilettante, Ferdinand Boissard, held high revel. His fantastically decorated apartments were frequented by the painters, poets, sculptors, romancers, of the day—that is, carefully selected ones such as Liszt, George Sand, Mérimée, and others whose verve or genius gave them the privilege of saying Open Sesame! to this cave of forty Supermen" (82–83). Out of the decadent excesses of the egoistic pose, however, Huneker hoped to distill an essential individualism and celebrate it as a cultural tonic.

When as yet a graduate student, the future literary editor of the *Egoist* from 1917 to 1919, T. S. Eliot, favorably reviewed Huneker's study.[33] Ian Bell has remarked how "extraordinary" it is that Eliot's voluble champion and a literary editor of the *New Freewoman*, Ezra Pound, never had a "substantial comment to make about Huneker, since the battles he fought in America were virtual replicas of Pound's campaigns in London" (*Critic as Scientist*, 52). Huneker outlined an anarchist aesthetics later to be echoed in certain of Pound's pronouncements on syndicalism, but the anarchism of either was not so much in earnest as it was a rhetoric conveying to their coterie elitisms the gloss of a radical politics.[34] However, this same criticism cannot be directly leveled at Dora Marsden, whose egoism developed out of her concrete participation in the radical nexus of British suffragism, feminism, and political anarchism. We will want to define the fine lines of these discriminations as we catalog the varieties of modernist individualisms.

The forthright elitism of Huneker's book is captured by monotonous repetitions of the term *aristocrat*. Stendhal is credited with an iconoclastic and unpopular mixture of heretical and advanced views: "Stendhal disliked America; to him all things democratic were abhorrent; an individualist and aristocrat like Ibsen, he would not recognize the doctrine of equality. . . . Yet this same gallant was among the few in the early years of the nineteenth century to declare for the enfranchisement, physical and spiritual, of woman. He was a *féministe*" (*Egoists*, 18, 30). For Huneker, Henri Beyle adumbrates the reactionary/progressive or libertarian/anarchist complex in egoistic individualism. Feminism must come forward as a radical anarchism, a cry for individual rather than institutional power, before an egoist can applaud it. Huneker set these latter terms into explicit apposition while discussing the aestheticism of Charles Baudelaire: "Individualist, egoist, anarchist, his only thought was of letters" (98).

The last chapter of *Egoists* rang the keynote for the whole collection by returning to the "prophet" of modern egoism, Max Stirner—"Nietzsche is the poet of the doctrine, Stirner its prophet" (352)—crediting the Nietzsche vogue and the anarchist James Henry Mackay's 1898 biography, *Max Stirner: Sein Leben und sein Werk*, for reviving the fame and fortunes of Stirner's *Der Einzige und sein Eigentum*. Although Stirner's text was written in the 1840s, its major impact was delayed by more than half a century, when like a revenant it emerged to stalk the cultural pathways opened up by Nietzsche's Zarathustra. Thanks to the 1907 translation sponsored and executed by American anarchists Benjamin Tucker and Steven T. Byington, both later to become prominent contributors to the *New Freewoman,* in England and America *The Ego and His Own* became a touchstone for the intellectually rebellious among those coming of age in the first two decades of the twentieth century.[35]

The animus of *The Ego and His Own* toward revolutionary socialism enabled Huneker to assert a clear distinction between "communistic anarchy" from Marx to Bakunin and the individualist insurrections of Stirner and Nietzsche: Stirner was "without a touch of the melodrama of communistic anarchy, with its black flags, its propaganda by force, its idolatry of assassinations, bomb-throwing, killing of fat, harmless policemen, and its sentimental gabble about Fraternity" (355). Since the suffragist and feminist movements of the later nineteenth century were commonly identified with socialist agitation, Stirner's stripping of political issues down to the absolute Self was a handy way to dissolve solidarities of sex and gender: "Where does Woman come into this scheme?" Huneker asks of Stirner's egoism, and replies: "There is no Woman, only a human Ego. Humanity is a convenient fiction to harry the individualist. So, society, family are the clamps that compress the soul of woman. If woman is to be free she must first be an individual, an Ego" (361). Like her contemporary, Emma Goldman, Dora Marsden clearly responded to this chapter of Stirner's gospel and adapted it to her femino-anarchism.

But Marsden's male collaborators generally shared in Huneker's aestheticist appropriation of the doctrine of egoism, the immediate concern of which was not the emancipation and development but the preservation of the ego and its own—hence the slant of Huneker's egoism toward a defensive/possessive masculinism. Huneker jauntily remarked, "Egoism as a religion is hardly a new thing. It began with the first sentient male human. It has since preserved the species, discovered the 'inferiority' of women, made civilisation, and founded the fine arts" (211–12). If Huneker's anarchism is doctrinally suspect, clearly he was in earnest about the immoralism of the arts as a bulwark against the hypermoralism of "sentimental humanitarians" and socialists of all descriptions. Huneker's egoists mostly profess contempt for political democracy, one contemporary cipher for opposition to the political emancipation of the female. He briefly glossed Nietzsche's misogynist aphorisms on the way to remarking, "The aristocratic individualism of Nietzsche came at a happy moment when the stage was bare yet encumbered with the débris of socialistic theories left over from the storm that first swept all Europe in 1848. It was necessary that the pendulum should swing in another direction" (257). And, although Henrik Ibsen's females were often seized as feminist heroines—as, for instance, by Cicily Fairfield, the protégé of Dora Marsden's who took from Ibsen's *Rosmersholm* the pseudonym "Rebecca West" in order to write for the *Freewoman* without scandalizing her family—Huneker quaintly averred that "the 'emancipated' Ibsen woman is the sensible woman, the womanly woman, bearing a not remote resemblance to the old-fashioned woman, who calmly accepts her share of the burdens and responsibilities of life, single or wedded, though she insists on her rights as a human being" (332).

Huneker triangulated Ibsen's cultural politics by the coordinates of Stirner and Nietzsche: "To be candid, Ibsen's belief in the rights of the individual is rather naïve and antiquated, belonging as it does to the tempestuous period of '48. Max Stirner was far in advance of the playwright in his political and menacing egoism; while Nietzsche, who loathed democracy, makes Ibsen's aristocracy timid by comparison" (321). But, although the German thinkers were more bracingly radical than the Norwegian playwright, Ibsen still struck Huneker as the truest forerunner of the century at hand.

Bad as is mankind, Ibsen, who was ever in advance of his contemporaries, believed in its possibility for betterment. Here the optimist speaks. Brand's spiritual pride is his downfall; nevertheless, Ibsen, an aristocratic thinker, believes that of pride one cannot have too much. He recognized the selfish and hollow foundation of all "humanitarian" movements. He is a sign-post for the twentieth century when the aristocratic of spirit must enter into combat with the herd instinct of a depressing socialism. (348)

Gospels of Anarchy

In 1908, Vernon Lee (the pseudonym of the prolific expatriate British writer Violet Paget) published in London a work of cultural criticism entitled *Gospels of Anarchy*.[36] This study rounded up for interrogation many of the same egoistic suspects—Emerson, Stirner, Nietzsche, Ibsen, and Maurice Barrès—soon to be gathered in Huneker's *Egoists*. It is interesting to compare Huneker's libertarian appreciations with Lee's peculiar brand of liberal tolerance in the midst of strong doctrinal misgivings. Lee's book gives further evidence of the wide dissemination of the egoistic idiom in début-de-siècle cultural discussion and usefully sets forward a secular rebuttal from a broadly bourgeois-democratic perspective. Lee dedicates *Gospels of Anarchy* to H. G. Wells, and her idiom of argument echoes his rationalist progressivism. "Now," Lee expostulates in the introductory chapter,

> the evolution by which our *ego* has become less incompatible with its neighbours has taken place, largely, by the mechanism of ideals and duties, of attaching to certain acts an odium sufficient to counterbalance their attraction, till it has become more and more difficult to enjoy oneself thoroughly at other folks' cost. And this Ibsenites are apt to forget. . . . The oversight of Ibsenian anarchists (whatever Ibsen's individual views on the subject) is that of imagining that duties, ideals, laws can be judged by examining their action in the individual case; for their use, their evolutional *raison d'être*, is only for the general run. (20–22)

The note of Spencerian progressivism is sounded by Lee's sociological turns on the concept of evolution, modulated toward Wells's liberalism by the reasoning that as biological evolution has led to ever more "differentiated," thus "higher," beings, so too the evolution of human society is toward ever finer ethical behaviors. But, since that development is secured only at the level of the mass or species, the egoistic self-assertion of an "Ibsenite anarchist" can represent at best a cautionary stance, a symptom of social immaturity, at worst a destructive friction, a pocket of futile resistance to the course of evolution.

> The champions of the *Will of the Ego*, whether represented by bluff Bernard Shaw or by ambiguous Maurice Barrès, start from the supposition that because the individual is a concrete existence, while the species is obviously an abstraction, the will of the individual can alone be a reality, and the will of the species must be a figment. They completely forget that there is not one concrete individual, but an infinite number of concrete individuals, and that what governs the world is, therefore, the roughly averaged will of all these individuals. (22)

As a liberal meliorist of her day, Vernon Lee conceives of the social majority, or *demos,* under the type of the species: by the mechanism of democratic averaging she arrives at the vital ideal of human society as an evolutionary whole. Lee articulates the secular/positivist wing of Edwardian evolutionism, as opposed to the mystic/vitalist orientation of many left-anarchist progressives. For instance, while sharing many of her meliorist convictions, Edward Carpenter would never blaspheme "life" by recourse to mechanistic metaphors such as Lee's.

> Violence over body and over mind; violence against the will of others; violence against fact: these represent the friction in the imperfect machinery of life; and progress is but the substitution of human mechanism more and more delicate and solid, through which the movement is ever greater, the friction ever less.
>
> Meanwhile, do we possess a human mechanism as good as it might be? . . . Egoistic decadents like Maurice Barrès, the whole heterogeneous crusade of doubt and rebellion, are doing good work in showing that we have not. . . . (Lee, *Gospels,* 26)

"The whole heterogeneous crusade of doubt and rebellion" is a wonderfully capacious phrase for the Western milieu of political insurrection in the decades before the Great War. In the years before and during World War I, Dora Marsden's London was also part of that profound crusade. In the aftermath of the Great War and the Russian revolution, the "gospel of anarchy" to which Lee's crusaders had marched was effectively demolished, in its flower if not in its roots. In particular, political anarchism as a revolutionary rival to state communism more or less withered away, to be cut down entirely by the Spanish Civil War. More broadly, many progressive and insurrectionist rationales of the prewar period were largely co-opted by postwar reactionary movements, just as the moral idiom and street tactics of the American civil-rights movement have been hijacked and radicalized by the anti-abortion and animal-rights campaigns of our own day. For instance, the imperious Nietzschean Superman along with the more wistful vitalisms informing the utopian schemes of Edward Carpenter and the existential epiphanies of Henri Bergson lapsed drastically into dogmas of punitive eugenics and went on to die captive to the blood-and-soil organicism of Nazi ideology.

These unhappy ironies, while outside the concerns of this study, still throw their shadows over the discussion. They are dramatic ironies of history: as we view the characters of western modernism, we are aware of a catastrophic future about which they must remain ignorant. It is in fact a nice problem just what causal relations may exist between anarchist discourses of individualism and egoism and statist discourses of bourgeois capitalism, fascism, and totalitarian communism. For instance, in *Egoists*, Huneker mentioned in passing that Max Stirner's economic notions concerning property rights "sound suspiciously like those of our 'captains of industry'" (369).[37] However, some of the force of that likeness may hinge on the bourgeois equivocation between the individual and the corporate agent, on a statist misreading of political anarchism's intrinsic anti-corporationism.

Vernon Lee's explicit critique of Stirner's doctrines—"the darkest, if not the deepest, pit of anarchical thought" (29)—is not political but psychological.

> We stand in need of a new science of will, thought, and emotion; or, rather, of the practical application of such a science of the soul as recent years have already given us. It would put us equally above the new-fangled theories of freeing the *ego* by abolishing ideals and habits, and above the old-fashioned notions of thwarting the *ego* in the name of morality. For it would show that the *ego* is not the separate momentary impulse, but the organic hierarchy of united and graduated impulses. (31–32)

The political note returns to this discourse, however, in Lee's choice of "organic hierarchy" as a metaphor for psychological structure. Her insistence on hierarchical distinctions among psychological functions contrasts with the anarchistic ego. In the vitalist configurations of Carpenter, Bergson, Marsden, or Lawrence, the "integral self" sustains or induces a potentially monomaniacal sense of synthesis, reducing the multiplicity of psychical energies to a single stream, a unitary wellhead. As such the dialect of vitalist egoism represents a rhetoric of defense against self-contradiction or inner turmoil. Egoists have been notable for the single-mindedness of their inspirations.

Lee's next discursive turn evokes one of the major literary inspirations for both individualistic and communistic anarchy, the poetry of Walt Whitman. The British expatriate Lee defines the limits of her "organic hierarchical" liberalism against the American poet's indiscriminate, polymorphous socialism.

> After the psychology of anarchy comes its metaphysics, or, I would almost say, its theology. . . . It has its treatises of highest metaphysical subtlety; and its little popular catechisms, quite full of explicit absurdities. Such a catechism as this was made up by the late J. A. Symonds out of the opinions, or what he took to be the opinions, of Walt Whitman. It is the declaration of the equal rights and equal dignity of all the parts of man's nature. . . . The democratic view, as it is called, of Whitman, as expounded by Symonds, consists in asserting that all things are equally divine. (33–34)[38]

For Western premodernism, Walt Whitman was a supreme avatar of visionary unity, a comprehensive purveyor of synthetic reconciliations. What Whitman immediately abetted for Symonds and Carpenter was a practical reconciliation between Victorian morality and male homosexuality; for socialists, between capital and labor; for feminists, between male and female roles and opportunities; for sexualists, spiritualists, and others in search of a secular theology, between body and soul, evolutionary nature and divine purpose.[39] As Lee's mordant comments indicated, Whitman's "gospel of anarchy" was made to serve the ideals of sexual egalitarians, civil libertarians, pantheistic vitalists, revolutionaries and evolutionaries of all descriptions.[40] Lee's superb rebuttal to the heterogeneous crusaders for equality's Whitmanesque arguments was simply that all this radical insubordination is "unscientific."

> Science teaches us that all life, and especially the life we human beings call *progress*, is not a mere affirmation . . . but a selection and rejection, the perpetual assertion of fitness against unfitness, a constant making of inequality. . . . There is no place for democracy *à la* Whitman in the soul; its law is co-ordination, subordination, hierarchy. . . . The later Darwinism is training us to perceive that in the process of evolution there is, alongside of the selection of the fittest, the rendering even unfitter of the initially unfit, degenerative tendencies as well as tendencies to adapt. (35–37)

What *is* "scientific" to Lee's mind is "the later Darwinism," the stern bourgeois amalgam of Spencer's social and Huxley's economic Darwinism with the hysterical eugenic alarmism disseminated by Max Nordau's *Degeneration*, the topic of chapter 3 of *Gospels of Anarchy*. Lee did not adopt Nordau's particular conclusions concerning the unmitigated degeneracy of fin de siècle art and thought—Richard Wagner and Huneker's many egoists included—but she would adapt his organicist premises to her calls for self-discipline and moral fortitude to counter the ineluctable "deterioration of soul." At the moment, Lee concluded her introductory discussion with a late-Victorian flourish rendering "instinctive" the powers of moral discrimination needed to forestall social degeneration: "it is our human instincts which decide, as they have determined, everything. And among the ideas they have set on foot they decide for good against evil, for order against chaos" (38). For Lee, in the last recourse "science" yields to the "nature" it has supposedly revealed. In fine circular fashion, Vernon Lee grounds her bourgeois humanism on its own reflection in the form of a scientific ideology.

Idealism and Scientism

Vitalism, Evolution, and Thermodynamics

Georges Canguilhem's concept of scientific ideology describes complex discursive mutations in the cultural field.[41] In his *Ideology and Rationality*, Canguilhem notes that "ideology is an epistemological concept with a polemical function" (29), but by stipulating a *scientific* ideology and thereby wrenching the concept out of its standard provenance, he tries to depolemicize the term while retaining its epistemological force. According to Canguilhem, scientific ideology is constituted by the retroactive recognition of an extension of science beyond the proper domain. Scientific ideology enters history by its exclusion from science and its slide toward social dissemination. The opening for literary critical interest in the concept of scientific ideology occurs directly at this point of extension, this threshold of metaphorization. For the deviation of scientific statements into social formations also traces the structure of discursive metaphors in cultural action. Scientific discourses cannot be cordoned off from the ideologizing appropriations that have always occurred at this threshold of metaphorization. That which falls away from the merit of science retains some of the glamor of science as it enters into its social formations.

Modernist appropriations of vitalism, evolution, and thermodynamics can be read along Canguilhem's lines as further extensions of the cultural projections by which the developments of science blur over into ideology as a matter of course. Moreover, the emergence and career of Anglo-American literary modernism can be defined and inflected by reference to a particular shift in scientific ideologies. From the late-Victorian mystic humanism of Edward Carpenter to the radical discourses of Dora Marsden's London, thermodynamic vocabularies of social energetics mingle with and eventually supplant the idioms of evolutionary vitalism. Marsden and other early modernists apply this discursive amalgam of scientific and social ideologies to the political critique by which they cast off a libertarian socialism in favor of an individualism of pure self-evolution.

Canguilhem is interested in those points at which certain discourses are ushered into and out of the discourse of science per se.[42] Scientific ideology's historiographical function is to provide a discursive category for disverified knowledge. By this definition Canguilhem preserves the positivity of science as a body of doctrine perpetually open to critical correction and reformulation. Depending on prior science for its initial formation, in its inception a scientific ideology shares science's relative autonomy from social ideology in the standard Marxist sense of inauthentic or inverted content. Scientific ideologies begin in good intellectual faith, as it were, and are identified as ideology only by disverification, the moment at which they cease to be science and become history: "A scientific ideology comes to an end when the place that it occupied in the encyclopedia of knowledge is taken over by a discipline that operationally demonstrates the validity of its claim to scientific status, its 'norms of scientificity.' At that point a certain form of nonscience is excluded from the domain of science" (32).

In "What Is a Scientific Ideology?" Canguilhem dwells at greatest length on the evolutionism of Herbert Spencer, which initially conforms to the definition of scientific ideology in that, in Canguilhem's apt image, it "*squints* at an already instituted science whose prestige it recognizes and whose style it seeks to imitate" (*Ideology and Rationality*, 38). However, Spencer's evolutionism passes quickly from scientific to social ideology.

> Spencer's work . . . used von Baer's and, later, Darwin's biology to lend scientific support to his views concerning social engineering in nineteenth-century English industrial society, in particular, his advocacy of free enterprise, political individualism, and competition. From the law of differentiation he deduced that the individual must be supported against the state. . . .
>
> The laws of mechanics, embryology, and evolution cannot validly be extended beyond the domain proper to each of these sciences. To what end are specific theoretical conclusions severed from their premises and

applied out of context to human experience in general? To a practical end. Evolutionist ideology was used to justify industrial society as against traditional society on the one hand and the demands of workers on the other. It was in part antitheological, in part antisocialist. Thus evolutionist ideology was an ideology in the Marxist sense: a representation of nature or society whose truth lay not in what it said but in what it hid. (36–37)

Although Canguilhem's initial concern was to set scientific ideology apart from social ideology, in this instance the two modes collapse into each other. His methodology does not expunge the equivocal status of the term *ideology*. In this seamless transition from scientific to social ideology, the discourse of evolutionism was a scientific ideology as long as it remained "theoretical." Once it declared a sociological praxis—once it got politics—it devolved into social ideology.[43] Canguilhem's equivocation actually demonstrates that social ideology is the inevitable residue of science, that science is itself, in the final instance, an ideological practice.

For instance, vitalism has powerfully inflected the literary sensibility of the last two centuries, and these cultural effects were empowered by the residual prestige vitalism enjoyed from its discursive apprenticeship in the scientific academy. The transition of vitalism from science, to a scientific ideology, to a social ideology shows this complex historical dynamic in action. As it issued into its social formation, vitalist ideology still operated as a metonymy of the science from which it was in the process of being excluded. The doctrine of vitalism states that in the world at large the forces that move matter about and the forces that produce and maintain living beings are completely different. As a scientific hypothesis, vitalism derived from an eighteenth-century reaction against the dominance of Newtonian mechanics, but for that very reason its vocabulary was inscribed within Newtonian paradigms. If matter in motion alone could not account for the emergence, functioning, reproduction, variation, and beauty of living beings, then a further, imponderable, perhaps immaterial, power—a "life force," or *Lebenskraft*, modeled after Newton's gravitational force—must be responsible. Departing from the Newtonian mechanics of *force*, nineteenth-century physics would develop the modern paradigm of *energy* as a physical category as fundamental as matter: "the central doctrine of scientific materialism—the unity of matter and motion in energy—succeeded in erasing the distinction between them."[44] The milieu of vitalism's countermechanistic origin left its signature in the way that, after the mid-nineteenth century, vitalistic theories retained in the life "force" the anachronistic idiom of their inception.

The history of vitalism, then, followed the precise path Canguilhem lays out for a scientific ideology, as

> a discourse that parallels the development of a science and that, under the pressure of pragmatic needs, makes statements that go beyond what has actually been proved by research. In relation to science itself it is both presumptuous and misplaced. Presumptuous because it believes that the end has been reached when research in fact stands at the beginning. Misplaced because when the achievements of science actually do come, they are not in the areas where the ideology thought they would be, nor are they achieved in the manner predicted by the ideology. (57–58)

In the present context, this means that modern biology did not find an authentic life force as opposed to vitalism's ideological prediction. Rather, molecular genetics established that heredity and metabolism operate not by means of forces or energies but due to the biochemical implementing of informational programs coded into macromolecules. Increasingly severed from institutions of scientific research, vitalism was reconnected with romantic idealisms and loosely reorganized into a social ideology operating alongside other biologistic schemas such as Spencer's evolutionism. When we turn to the writings of Edward Carpenter, we will see that, relative to Spencer's social Darwinism, social vitalism was more often a progressive oppositional stance: Carpenter's evolutionism was overtly prosocialist. But, insofar as vitalism intertwined with mainstream evolutionism, it was also implicated in the hegemonic ideological implications of Anglo-American bourgeois scientism. In distinct but related ways, both vitalism and evolutionism lent themselves to modes of individualism: social vitalism favored an anarchistic, social Darwinism a bourgeois form of individualism.

Before pursuing these matters, we need to review the history of science a bit further. Due to the easy congruence between vitalism's ungraspable "life force" and any number of theistic first causes, it is important to keep in mind vitalism's original scientific credentials, its earlier development in biomedical explanatory models set forth within orthodox scientific communities and philosophical academies. Until a genetics capable of expounding the structure and function of DNA emerged, it seemed to many that life "forces" would never be entirely opened to analytical comprehension. Vitalistic theories remained plausible well into the twentieth century. Even with the broad acceptance of Darwinian theory at the ecological level of speciation, "a general theory of living systems" did not exist "in scientific knowledge prior to molecular biology. Until then the 'secret of life' could be viewed as essentially inaccessible."[45]

Vitalism occupied the epistemological gap in life science that began to close definitively only with the emergence in molecular genetics of a theory that finally clarified the mechanisms that sorted and ordered material elements into living organisms, that produced the invariant replication of species, and that enabled the retention of evolutionary variations as they randomly arose. The doctrine of the life force began with the reasonable idea that the new chemistry of its day could fill the gap in biological knowledge: "the belief in the existence of some vital substance, force, or principle arose from the attempt to explain living organisms by means of chemistry."[46] The hypothesis of a life force appealed to many as a necessary supplement to material forces within the context of a chemical explanation of biology. So vitalism emerged as a scientific alternative to mechanistic reductionism, drawing its initial sustenance from early modern chemistry at a time when chemistry rather than physics was the main field in which the phenomena of electricity and magnetism were being investigated.

In the earlier part of the nineteenth century, the mysterious force thought most likely to provide the clue to vital phenomena was the power of electricity, with its ability to induce lifelike twitches in dead limbs. Vitalist and organicist investments in models based on electricity led to the extension of its observable modalities to the phenomena of life and mind. The most striking and hardy example of this was the early-nineteenth-century adaptation of electrical *polarity* to both natural and phenomenological systems. In *The Age of Science*, David Knight has expounded the connections between chemistry, electricity, and the German *Naturphilosophie*.

> The concern with a life force was not confined to Germany, but had many supporters in Britain; but in Germany it went with that dynamical emphasis in science which had the authority of Leibniz, Goethe and Kant. Romantic successors of Kant, especially F. W. J. Schelling, worked out a philosophy of nature, *Naturphilosophie*, which was based upon the notion of polar forces. . . . Chemistry with its elective affinities was really a science of forces rather than of matter. And in chemical reactions the clash of opposites resulted not in annihilation but in synthesis: oxygen and hydrogen came together and formed water, themselves ceasing to exist as separate entities. The crude model of the dialectic of Hegel and Marx began in the chemistry of about 1800. . . . Schelling postulated a world in which the various polar opposites that we see are all expressions of one underlying

force. What were about 1800 generally supposed to be weightless fluids—heat, light, electricity, and magnetism—were all seen as effects of this universal force. And just at this period came the first interconversions of forces which gave an empirical justification to Schelling's views. (56–57)[47]

Once adapted to an electrical model, the unitary life force bifurcated into positive and negative forces, which were then variously coordinated with the particular phenomena receiving an electro-vital explication. For the early modernists, such electrical dynamism would remain crucial to their investments in physico-vitalist models. Once the electrical model is granted, one can locate its vital polarities within an individual organism, as between mind and body, or among separate organisms, as between discrete classes of persons, or both at once. This unconstrained mobility of the electro-vital polarity model was especially evident and problematic when combined with the inescapably moralized discourses of sexual and gender differences. Already in the ideas of the German romantic physiologists, the valence of electro-vitalism was masculinist, in that the male or masculinity was characteristically assigned to the positive pole, the female or femininity to the negative. One significant premodernist heir of this misogynist paradigm will be the influential Viennese author of *Geschlecht und Charakter*, Otto Weininger.

From this perspective it is worth noting the synchronicity of Hegel's *Phenomenology of Mind*, the redoubtable fortress of dynamic idealism first published in 1807, and Lamarck's *Zoological Philosophy,* considered by many as the foremost pre-Darwinian scientific statement of evolutionary principles, published in 1809. Lamarck's physiological "escalator" is at least loosely reminiscent of the ineluctable spiraling progress of Hegel's phenomenological dialectic. In Channell's words, "First, Lamarck believed that an 'inner life force' drove an organism toward some higher level of perfection. . . . Through the 'inner force' and the 'inheritance of acquired characteristics,' Lamarck was able to transform the static great chain of being into an escalator on which organisms continually emerged from inorganic material and evolved toward some 'perfect organization'" (*Vital Machine*, 62). Similarly, the mechanisms of Lamarckian inheritance—evolutionary mutations and developments due to an interplay of inner desire and outer contingency—recall the transformative preservation of dialectical moments in Hegel's schema of Aufhebung.

If Schelling married the life force to electricity, and Hegel the development of *Geist* to the chemical synthesis of opposites, then Lamarck may be said to have wedded the conceptual motor of vitalism to the progressive dynamic of biological evolution. In Lamarck, the life force not only combines with material motions to produce and sustain living things, but it also drives living forms onward to diversity and increasing complexity as the working out of a teleology of gradual perfection. As with vitalism, Lamarck's system—especially its hereditary device, the inheritance of experientially acquired characteristics—occupied a crucial epistemological gap in the science of genetics. It was as a supposedly viable scientific alternative to the antiteleological notion of random selection in Darwin's system that Lamarck's theories retained their appeal to scientistic antimechanist ideologists such as Edward Carpenter.

Edward Carpenter's Evolutionary Sunshine

Few radical propagandists had a more pervasive influence on the discursive milieu of Dora Marsden's London than did Edward Carpenter.[48] To spread out his many writings is to set up an oriental bazaar of nineteenth-century progressive idioms. Carpenter's political affiliations ran the gamut of socialisms from communist to anarchist manifestations, with the emphasis finally falling toward the latter. His anarcho-vitalist adaptation of the Marxist critique of capitalism was heavily accented with Victorian strains of scientism and spiritualism. Ultimately Carpenter developed a complex form of mystic humanism, some strands of which would be woven into, others plucked out of, the doctrinal fabric of early modernism. Carpenter's texts present an array of doctrines germane to an investigation of modernist individualism: an organicist or vitalistic adaptation of evolutionary theories, a radical sexual liberationism, and a sanguine form of spiritual anarchism. Moreover, for the British audience of the late-nineteenth and early-twentieth centuries, Carpenter was an indispensable purveyor of Walt Whitman's gospel, an inspired transmitter of the American poet's prophecies into the idioms of cultural modernism.

A long essay of the 1880s, "Civilisation: Its Cause and Cure," provides a detailed overview of Carpenter's cultural philosophy and indicates as well the structure of motives behind his quest for an anarchist millennium.[49] The epigraph—from section 39 of Whitman's *Song of Myself*: "The friendly and flowing savage, who is he? Is he waiting for civilisation, or is he past it, and mastering it?" (1)—intimates the temporal dialectic of robust past, suffering present, and recuperated future that Carpenter adapts to his house call at the sickbed of Western society. Carpenter's organicist and therapeutic premises may be divulged by schematizing his essay on the model of a medical examination. First, the symptomatology: civilization's chronic patterns of cultural pathology are visible in the social disunities of class strife, sex war, abuses of state power, and the moralistic oppression of nonconformist behaviors. Next, the interpretation of the symptomatology, or diagnosis: the manifest disease of civilization has resulted from a latent spiritual germ—the Fall of man out of unity and into the state of sin or separatist self-consciousness. But, in fact, that virus was unavoidable; moreover, it is serving an evolutionary purpose. Thus, the prognosis: if humanity can survive the current crises of civilization, the fever will break and all will be well. For this phase of racial experience will have developed spiritual antibodies against future recurrences. So civilization is more or less the measles of the human race, ultimately beneficial in a youthful and vigorous patient, more worrisome the older the victim becomes. Humanity must slough off civilization before it can arrive at its cosmic majority.

Carpenter's reasoning underlines an important motive for the broad modernist fascination with the "primitive." Far from a crude or childish sketch of developments modernity brings to proud fulfillment, "the friendly and flowing savage" of Whitmanian anthropology offers a needful glimpse of the sort of healthy unity forgone by the guilty divisions of modern life: "however necessary for man's ultimate evolution may be the temporary development of this consciousness of Sin, we cannot help seeing that the condition of the mind in which it is absent is the most distinctively *healthy*" (10). For Carpenter, then, pagan and Judeo-Christian myths of the Fall preserve narrative reminiscences of the prehistorical lapse out of savage health into the disease of civilization. Carpenter's proffered cure of egalitarian anarchism derives from a liberal amalgam of the cultural diagnostics of Proudhon, Marx, and Bachofen: the patriarchal institution of private property "destroyed the ancient system of society . . . destroyed the ancient system of mother-right and inheritance through the female line, and turned the woman into the property of the man . . . and to rivet these authorities it created the State and the policeman" (4–5).

Archaic cultures preserve clues to modern spiritual health. Thus, Carpenter rehearsed mythopoetic views positing a "divine and universal Man" as inner light and guide, a "central radiation" (13, 14). Resubscribing to this heliocentric trope, Carpenter affirmed that "the condition of health in the mind is loyalty to the divine Man within it" (14). This "divine Man" from whom civilization has temporarily fallen away defines Carpenter's brand of mystic humanism. As an eternal, inexhaustible source at the wellhead of human being, this inner sun underwrites his teleological notion of human evolution as the progressive exfoliation, or "unfoldment," of a preinscribed perfection: "in the theory of Evolution we see the place of . . . animals, as fore-runners or off-shoots of special faculties in Man. . . . The Man . . . is the central life ruling and radiating among all organs . . . a central power . . . which thus works towards and creates the distinctive unity of each organism" (15–17).

Thus begins a sun motif running throughout the essay, beckoning back to Walt Whitman's and forward to D. H. Lawrence's writings.[50] Carpenter's solar analogs partake of the Apolline identification of the sun with medical powers and present a heliocentric cosmos that, while postclassical in imagery, seems only marginally modern. Although Carpenter's cosmological tropes were clearly influenced by Whitman's orbic rhetoric, he seemed to see no further than the local or Copernican system: "The solar rays illumine the outer world and give to it its unity and entirety; so in the inner world of each individual possibly there is another Sun, which illumines and gives unity to the man, and whose warmth and light would permeate his system" (18). In contrast, by 1855, Whitman's verse had cognized the greater Milky Way and its noncentrality within a universe of galaxies: "I open my scuttle at night and see the far-sprinkled systems. . . . My sun has his sun, and round him obediently wheels" (*Leaves of Grass*, Cowley ed., 79).

The mid-nineteenth century entertained the theory of a "plurality of worlds" created by a series of separate geneses, each world then setting off on a progressive evolution toward sentient creatures. Like Lamarck's zoological progressivism, this theory followed the teleological line in pre-Darwinian schemas of natural evolution. The "plurality of worlds" theory offered as evidence the spiral nebulae, which were taken to be solar systems in the process of consolidation. Robert Chambers, the anonymous author of the 1844 *Vestiges of the Natural History of Creation*, "believed the Sun to be a typical star, and that it had been formed along with the planets from whirling nebulous matter. Life had then appeared on Earth, and had gradually ascended through reptiles and mammals to man. The same process would occur elsewhere. . . . [Some rational inhabitants] might have got ahead of us, just as in time we could expect a higher species than us to emerge on Earth" (Knight, *Age of Science*, 80). However, by 1850, the nebular hypothesis was exploded, when "Lord Rosse's big (72-inch) telescope in Ireland resolved many nebulae into clusters of stars rather than suns and planets in the making" (81). Nevertheless, this episode indicates how readily nineteenth-century speculators would amplify their evolutionary theories into universal cosmologies. Edward Carpenter's own speculative teleology moved within this milieu.

Although Carpenter's scientific resources are worthy of consideration, they are always under discursive pressures from spiritual or mythopoetic determinations. What will be crucial for the discourses of early modernism is the way that Carpenter used this sun symbolism to adapt a romantic vitalism to Victorian evolutionism. That is, the sun as a "central radiation" is a trope for the universal or divine man as a "central life," which conducted the "central power" by which every individual organism maintained its living organization. The sum of these tautological transfers was the identification of the inner sun with a Lamarckian life force, for Carpenter a power possessing an integral perpetuity above and beyond the life span of any living being: "In this view, Death is simply the loosening and termination of the action of this power. . . . It [the life force] may . . . pass on to other spheres appointed" (17).[51] Vitalism of this sort intimately informs Dora Marsden's egoistic schemes and D. H. Lawrence's self-liberationist notions. What Carpenter posited at the level of the "race," however, they will place at the source of the separate individuated self.

Carpenter's rendition of the life force is parallel with but not identical to the theological soul. In Carpenter's vitalism, scientific ideology produces a scientistic animism, a late-Victorian revalidation of the Neoplatonic world-soul through the concepts of evolution and thermodynamics. A passage from a later work confirms that the discourse of thermodynamics also informs Carpenter's cultural meditations. In *The Art of Creation*, he returns to the topic we have now reached in our progress through "Civilisation: Its Cause and Cure"—the present status of humanity: "The distinction of Subject and Object is fundamental to our minds (as at present constituted)."[52] This parenthetical phrase is a direct quote from the exposition given by William Thomson, Lord Kelvin, of the consequences of the rule of entropy, or "dissipation," as stated by the second law of thermodynamics: in a closed system the sum of energy, while remaining constant, must become increasingly disorganized and thus unavailable for work. In 1852 Thomson laid out three related propositions.

1. There is at present in the material world a universal tendency to the dissipation of mechanical energy.
2. Any *restoration* of mechanical energy, without more than an equivalent of dissipation, is impossible in inanimate material processes, and is probably never effected by means of organized matter, either endowed with vegetable life or subjected to the will of an animated creature.
3. Within a finite period of time past, the earth must have been, and within a finite period of time to come the earth must again be, unfit for the habitation of man *as at present constituted,* unless operations have been, or are to be performed, which are impossible under the laws to which the known operations going on at present in the material world are subject.[53] (my italics)

By quoting this signal passage from nineteenth-century physics, Carpenter inscribed his discussions of given humanity with a complex of social anxieties over the future of the human race—its potential for evolutionary progress or regressive degeneration—and over the apparent mortality of the universe within which, thanks to science, it now found itself. Is the lapse of humanity with the heat death of the universe, Carpenter worried, a foregone conclusion? This specter of entropy added an appreciable sense of urgency to the evolutionary demands of Carpenter and other vitalists: if it is to reverse or outlive the coming heat death, humanity *must* rise above its present constitution. And yet, in "Civilisation: Its Cause and Cure," the outcome of human civilization informs Carpenter that in its current state of "unfoldment . . . man, instead of going forward any longer in the same line as before, to all appearance *falls*" (22) and tumbles into the disunity epitomized by the epistemological split between subject and object. But that lapse may be recuperated with the teleological consideration that man's fall is preordained and necessary, "in order then, at this point in his Evolution, to advance any farther" (25).

Carpenter reads the Fall into civilization as the lapse of instinctual wholeness into a disciplinary culture of outer supplements, by flanking the moral/affective register of self-consciousness and sin with two material analogs of separative force, the cultural technologies of writing and government.

> The invention of writing marks perhaps better than anything else could do the period when Man becomes *self-conscious*—when he records his own doings and thoughts, and so commences History proper; and the growth of private property marks the period when he begins to sunder himself from his fellows, when therefore the conception of sin (or separation) first enters in. . . . And then arises the institution of Government . . . the evidence in social life that man has lost his inner and central control, and therefore must resort to an outward one. (29, 31)

In all this, humanity "as at present constituted" represents the dialectical negation of the "divine Man" that has conducted the course of evolution to this point. The human soul "has in fact to face the frightful struggle of self-consciousness, or the disentanglement of the true self from the fleeting and perishable self" (24). Carpenter couches this argument in political terms by positing socialism as the mass reunion to result from the sum of individual processes of spiritual disentanglement: "For the true Self of man consists in his organic relation with the whole body of his fellows. . . . The mass-Man must rule in each unit-man, else the unit-man will drop off and die" (28). Carpenter founded his mystic anarchism on the conviction that humanity is essentially one substance in the "divine Man" to which we will return by the overcoming, the transcendental cancellation, of civilization.

"The true Democracy has yet to come" (33), Carpenter prophesies in the wake of Whitman's *Democratic Vistas*: "For no outward government can be anything but a make-shift—a temporary hard chrysalis-sheath to hold the grub together while the new life is forming inside. . . . When the true life of society comes all its forms will be fluid and spontaneous and voluntary" (34). The ecstatic peroration of "Civilisation: Its Cause and Cure" is profuse with metamorphic imagery in which humanity's higher development is figured with biological images of embryological development as well as with Neoplatonic soul-lore concerning the trials and triumphs of the psyche. Mystic anarchism in Edward Carpenter is quite emphatically a scientistic reconfiguration of Platonic ideals, complete with echoes of the *Phaedrus*, Plato's allegory of the allotted fall and erotic resurrection of the human soul. Carpenter foresees an infinite resolution of all human limitations: "the impossibilities will yield very easily when the time comes; and the anatomical difficulty as to how and where the wings are to grow will vanish when they are felt sprouting!" (35). There is also an allegory of gay and lesbian liberation here, for Carpenter is recalling the gorgeous metaphors of the *Phaedrus*, where Socrates couches homoerotic desire as the energy of philosophical illumination.[54]

The inner sun radiating Edward Carpenter's evolutionary sunshine is ultimately the Platonic sun, allegory of the Good, awaiting those who escape from the cave by throwing off the frayed rags of an unenlightened civilization: "the process of evolution or exfoliation itself is nothing but a continual unclothing by Nature" (36). Naked in the sun, humanity will flower above and beyond its present entropic constitution, for "the consequent instreaming of energy into his system will carry him to perfections of health and radiance of being at present unsuspected. . . . Thus the Sun in the physical world is the allegory of the true self. The worshipper must adore the Sun, he must saturate himself with sunlight, and take the physical Sun into himself" (36, 44–45). But within this spiritually therapeutic radiance are also shadows of the anxieties evoked by the thermodynamic scenario of universal entropy—the literal death of the sun. Carpenter elaborated his heliotropic vision of everlasting vitality in defense against just such a nightmare of cosmic annihilation.

Edward Carpenter envisions an escape from the atomic self through the evolutionary liberation of humanity's inner communality, its essential unity in the idea of man. Dora Marsden's London will struggle to shelter and cultivate the atomic self, at the expense of the wider community if necessary, but for much the same reasons as Carpenter—in order to rescue, if not the race, at least themselves from the lapse of the life force. It is significant that at this juncture Carpenter framed that universal problematic in terms of the cosmic isolation of the individual ego, the separate self. Thus, the final passages of the "Civilisation" essay divulge the inexorable ego at play in Carpenter's quest.

> To the early man the notion of his having a separate individuality could only with difficulty occur; hence he troubled himself not with the suicidal questionings concerning the whence and whither which now vex the modern mind. For what causes these questions to be asked is simply the wretched feeling of isolation, actual or prospective, which man necessarily has when he contemplates himself as a separate atom in this immense universe—the gulf which lies below seemingly ready to swallow him, and the anxiety to find some mode of escape. (46)

Carpenter's anxiety articulated the uncanny double not of "civilization" per se but of the bourgeois individualism and social fragmentation of imperial Victorian capitalism. He envisioned the millennium of communistic anarchism exactly as the necessary remedy for the present human "state": cure may be had "in these two movements—towards a complex human Communism and towards individual freedom and Savagery" (49). The escape Carpenter desires, however, is as much a defense as a denial of the separate self, because the freedom and the vital renovation of the individual appear to him to be the sole "mode of escape" from thermodynamic entropy, the only way to reverse the dissipation of civilization.

Walt Whitman's Ideal Democracy

Edward Carpenter borrowed his two progressive movements from the dialectic of aggregation and individualism developed in Walt Whitman's *Democratic Vistas:* "we see steadily pressing ahead and strengthening itself, even in the midst of immense tendencies toward aggregation, this image of completeness in separatism, of individual personal dignity, of a single person, either male or female, characterized in the main, not from extrinsic acquirements or position, but in the pride of himself or herself alone."[55] From the perspective of Dora Marsden's London, one crucial synthesis purveyed by Walt Whitman's long discussion of American political philosophy was its bardic assertion of the interdependence of politics and literature, its affirmation of the collective power of an articulated vision. Whitman's America was to be an exemplary unfolding of unlimited possibilities for artistic as well as social accomplishment.

At the beginning of *Democratic Vistas*, Whitman gathered some cosmic imagery around this anticipation of America's cultural fulfillment.

> I suggest, therefore, the possibility, should some two or three really origi-
> nal American poets, (perhaps artists or lecturers,) arise, mounting the hori-
> zon like planets, stars of the first magnitude, that, from their eminence,
> fusing contributions, races, far localities, &c., together, they would give
> more compaction and more moral identity, (the quality to-day most
> needed,) to these States, than all its Constitutions. (368)

Later in the essay, he returned to a series of cosmological metaphors, figures derived from the astronomical discoveries of the 1850s and 1860s and from the interpretation of those discoveries within a schema of universal progress or evo-lution.[56] Whitman admits that the difference between the present state of American literature and the fulfillment projected by his *Democratic Vistas*

> is, in some sort, no less a difference than lies between that long-continued
> nebular state and vagueness of the astronomical worlds, compared with the
> subsequent state, the definitely-form'd worlds themselves, duly com-
> pacted, clustering in systems, hung up there, chandeliers of the universe,
> beholding and mutually lit by each other's lights. . . . A boundless field to
> fill! A new creation, with needed orbic works launch'd forth, to revolve in
> free and lawful circuits—to move, self-poised, through the ether, and shine
> like heaven's own suns! With such, and nothing less, we suggest that New
> World literature, fit to rise upon, cohere, and signalize in time, these
> States. (404–5)

Whitman's prophetic suggestion merges his separate calls for the American development of vivid personalities and of proudly indigenous literary works. Such orbs must eventually shoot forth, following in due course the previous world-historical phenomena of the birth and sudden illuminations of great writ-ers and their works, from the ancients "to such as German Kant and Hegel, where they, though near us, leaping over the ages, sit again, impassive, imper-turbable, like the Egyptian gods. Of these, and the like of these, is it too much, indeed, to return to our favorite figure, and view them as orbs and systems of orbs, moving in free paths in the spaces of that other heaven, the kosmic intel-lect, the soul?" (407). Whitman's favorite figure is drawn, of course, from stock Western mythopoetical imagery for the divine and its agents. As with Edward Carpenter's Platonic sun, however, Whitman's orbic rhetoric defines a "kos-mic" or transcendental humanism participating in philosophical as well as sci-

entific secularizations of theological systems, partaking of modern reason's daemonic usurpation of the elements of faith. With superbly daemonic ambivalence, Whitman's cosmic tropes for the poet integrate the powers of the individual and the American electorate: "I demand races of orbic bards, with
unconditional uncompromising sway. Come forth, sweet democratic despots of
the west!" (407).

Whitman's synthesis, however, was itself indebted to an immediate trans-
fusion not of Platonic but of German idealism. In "Whitman's 'Convertible
Terms,'" Kathryne V. Lindberg documents his investment in the later nineteenth-century intellectual charisma of the philosopher Hegel.[57] That investment, part of his self-promotional campaign on behalf of his own poems, is
most fully manifest in the text of *Democratic Vistas*. Although Whitman could
avail himself only of second- and third-hand anthologies of Hegel's writings,
that lightness of direct textual contact facilitated his creative misreadings of the
German philosopher. Lindberg asserts that Whitman flattened out the full play
of Hegel's dialectical method by neutralizing the power of the negative
moment.[58] Thus, Whitman could adapt Hegel's dialectical sequences to an
affirmative historical myth: America's coming cultural preeminence would
result from a glorious synthesis of its complex diversities. Lindberg traces the
"convertibility" of Whitman's major terms, that is, the interminable tropic slid-
ing among the terms *America, democracy,* and *self* by which Whitman manufactures the "vistas" of his desire.

Throughout *Democratic Vistas,* with serpentine syntax Whitman labori-
ously knits together the democratic synthesis of the antitheses of self-interest
and national interest by turning Hegel's own supreme trope, the absolute Idea.

> For, I say, the true nationality of the States, the genuine union, when we
> come to a mortal crisis, is, and is to be, after all, neither the written law,
> nor, (as is generally supposed,) either self-interest, or common pecuniary
> or material objects—but the fervid and tremendous IDEA, melting every-
> thing else with resistless heat, and solving all lesser and definite distinctions
> in vast, indefinite, spiritual, emotional power. (368)

For Whitman, the Idea of American democracy is the power driving the
"immense tendencies toward aggregation" (374) abroad in the nation. However, Lindberg directs our attention to Whitman's appropriation of the
Hegelian IDEA in its other ideological moment, as a structural technology of
American selfhood: "If the true nationality is an idea of nationalism, a sense of
belonging as an individual to the Idea of America, Whitman is dealing, not

merely in abstractions, but quite deliberately in ideology . . . in a specific American ideology of the individual" (259).[59]

According to Lindberg, Whitman's idealistic method encounters its greatest difficulty in the "near antinomies" of "democracy" and "individual." But Lindberg's notion of the individual as the "enemy" of democracy, as the antagonist rather than the antithesis of the state, melodramatizes the Whitmanian self by reading his dynamic, if not utterly dialectical, mutualism as mutually exclusive. In one of the more limpid passages of his text, Whitman acknowledges that his "personalism" depends entirely on the enduring coherence of the political aggregate.

> We shall, it is true, quickly and continually find the origin-idea of the singleness of man, individualism, asserting itself, and cropping forth, even from the opposite ideas. But the mass, or lump character, for imperative reasons, is to be ever carefully weigh'd, borne in mind, and provided for. Only from it, and from its proper regulation and potency, comes the other, comes the chance of individualism. The two are contradictory, but our task is to reconcile them. (373)

Democratic Vistas pursues that reconciliation not merely through syntheses of the contradictions between self and state but more substantially and juridically by balancing their competing claims, by repeatedly shifting the discourse back and forth between them. The essay heaves itself in long slow waves against the ideas of the aggregate state and the isolate self, but it never breaks upon one without a powerful undertow toward the other. So, for instance, at one point Whitman builds toward the following provisional climax: "the last, best dependence is to be upon humanity itself, and its own inherent, normal, full-grown qualities, without any superstitious support whatever. This idea of perfect individualism it is indeed that deepest tinges and gives character to the idea of the aggregate. For it is mainly or altogether to serve independent separatism that we favor a strong generalization, consolidation" (374). But the essay reacts against the idea of individualism almost immediately and reconfirms its "contradictory" commitment to statist ideals that would eventually be adapted to the concrete political programs of socialisms on both sides of the Atlantic: "Not that half only, individualism, which isolates. There is another half, which is adhesiveness or love, that fuses, ties and aggregates, making the races comrades, and fraternizing all. . . . The liberalist of to-day has this advantage over antique or medieval times, that his doctrine seeks not only to individualize but to universalize. The great word Solidarity has arisen" (381–82).

Whitman sustains a dynamic opposition between the idea of the state and that of a self, which, no matter how extended, defends its own definition. The negative dialectical moment within *Democratic Vistas*—that moment Lindberg sees as lacking—has been preserved precisely in its proper Hegelian place, in the positive negation that is the ego, the subject itself.

> This is the portentous power of the negative; it is the energy of thought, of pure ego. Death, as we may call that unreality, is the most terrible thing, and to keep and hold fast what is dead demands the greatest force of all. Beauty, powerless and helpless, hates understanding, because the latter exacts from it what it cannot perform. But the life of mind is not one that shuns death, and keeps clear of destruction; it endures death and in death maintains its being. It only wins to its truth when it finds itself utterly torn asunder. It is this mighty power, not by being a positive which turns away from the negative . . . on the contrary, mind is this power only by looking the negative in the face, and dwelling with it. This dwelling beside it is the magic power that converts the negative into being. That power is just what we spoke of above as subject. . . .[60]

In this passage we confront not the crypto-theological Hegel inverted by dialectical materialism but the proto-anarchistic Hegel who grasped the fluid dynamism of critical understanding and the explosiveness of *Geist* ("pure ego"). Here Hegel comes as close as he ever does to inscribing the dynamical sublime within his own system: Whitman's American sublime in *Democratic Vistas* corresponds directly to this intimation of the power of mind. Lindberg's characterization of Whitman's personalism as "a rather literal-minded humanism in which the individual is the primary ontological and ethical category" (253) trivializes a discourse that possesses more Hegelian grit than she will acknowledge. But her critique is illuminating because it forecasts what will in fact be the anarchistic and egoistic adaptations of Whitman's contradictory complexities in a number of early modernist individualisms.

The most serious problematics abroad in *Democratic Vistas* concern exactly the propensity for the state, when it conceals totalitarianism within libertarian rhetorics of individualism, to become a "monstrous self." To the extent that Whitman's triumphal state offers a vista not of democracy but of fascism, his discourse has departed from or suppressed the anarchism embedded in its individualist component. But to predicate a fascist social organization as the actual fulfillment of Whitman's cultural discourse is to skew his program as much toward its aggregative as its individualist premises. The notion of a "fascist individual" is a powerful ideological premise in the service of Lindberg's Althusserian critique. But to be precise, because fascism is a corporatism or statism, that locution is not an apposition but an oxymoron by which Lindberg flattens out a whole field of differences, canceling out any notion of a nonabusive or even progressive individualism. Lindberg manufactures a conceptual convertibility of her own, the bald conversion of individualism into fascism.

The question put to our topic by structural Marxism's critique of capitalist ideology is whether there is any form of individualism that does not reproduce and reinforce some repressive personal or political regime. At the least, I will argue that Dora Marsden's individualism can be granted significant doctrinal preferability to the aristocratic masculinism of, say, James Huneker's *Egoists*. In fact, Marsden's philosophical egoism develops toward a linguistically mediated and relativized version in her *Science of Signs*. At the moment, Lindberg's strained postmodernist filtering of Walt Whitman's political modernity clarifies a distinction we will take forward to early Anglo-American modernism—that between "humanistic" and "egoistic" individualisms. It is a difference and a development thrown into strong relief by the contrasting national backgrounds of the United States and the United Kingdom. On the one hand, British disciples of Whitman had little use for the specific nationalism funding Whitman's discourse: Carpenter took Whitman's "America" as a universal or transnational political ideal, Marsden's anarchistic individualism expressed an antipathy to the state in any form, while D. H. Lawrence read Whitman's aggregations and mergers as existential rather than political gambits. But, on the other hand, descending in a direct line from the individualist component of *Democratic Vistas,* Carpenter's mystic anarchism was still a humanistic individualism predicated on some form of socialism or democratic statism. For Carpenter, the rational humanism championed by scientific progress united with the mysticism inherent in the vitalistic prophecy of spiritual progress toward a higher or superhuman type.

"Exfoliation"

Like "Civilisation: Its Cause and Cure," Edward Carpenter's essay "Exfoliation: Lamarck *versus* Darwin," bound in the same volume, also proceeded under the signature of Walt Whitman: "Creation's incessant unrest, exfoliation."[61] Immediately underscoring the epistemological impasse confronted by the life sciences of the 1880s—"The simplest thing, or event, baffles us at the last" (129)—"Exfoliation" expresses a social-vitalist agnosticism that would perhaps prefer the secret of life to remain unrevealed, at least to fallen eyes. Carpenter does envision a surpassing of that rational impasse; however, it will be achieved not through experimentation but, as we saw in "Civilisation," by the further unfolding of cosmic evolution beyond humanity "as at present constituted." With regard to the daily miracles that baffle us, "the solution, the intelligent solution and understanding of them *is* in us; only it involves a higher order of consciousness. . . . I say these higher orders of consciousness are in us waiting for their evolution; and, until they evolve, we are powerless really to understand anything of the world around us" ("Exfoliation," 129–30). "Exfoliation" represents the "egoistic" side of Carpenter's mystic socialism: it may be read as propaganda for expending personal existential efforts to evolve toward a higher order of consciousness. As such, this essay maps out much of Dora Marsden's early struggles to embody her own ideal of the freewoman as a higher evolutionary type. "Exfoliation" also helps to explain the conceptual ease with which Marsden and other early modernists could cast off Carpenter's erotic socialist anarchism.

The crucial move for Carpenter is to internalize and so subjectivize the processes of evolution. By the reflex of that intention, his sublime ideological discourse flagrantly reads cultural structures back into nature: "For since each man is a part of nature, and in that sense a part also of the evolution-process, his own subjective experience ought at least to throw some light on the conditions under which evolution takes place" ("Exfoliation," 130). Carpenter pointedly focuses on the actual epistemological bafflement represented by Darwinian theory's inability to posit precise intrinsic mechanisms for the variation of species, for the production of genetic modifications in the first place, antecedent to their "selection" through successful competition, and for the retention of those modifications once they show themselves. In the face of these real mysteries, Carpenter posited a phenomenology of desire as the inner expression of the life force. His idiom of desire—"this inner force producing modification in man and animals" (132)—represents a subjectivist amplification of Lamarck's more mundane attention to *besoin*, the impulsion of instinctual need: "Desire, or inward change, comes first, action follows, and organisation or outward structure is the result" (133).[62] The benefit of this reorientation of Lamarckian evolutionism is that it offers to explain the facts of a progressive heredity on the model of humanity's progressive acquisition and maintenance of cultural accomplishments.

> Lamarck gives the instance—among others—of a gasteropod; how the need or desire of touching bodies in front of it as it crawled along would result in the formation of tentacles. . . . Such modification as this is very

different from the "survival of the fittest" of the Darwinian evolution-theory. We may fairly suppose that both kinds of modification take place; but the latter is a sort of easy success won by an external accident of birth—a success of the kind that would readily be lost again; while the former is the uphill fight of a nature that has grown inwardly and wins expression for itself in spite of external obstacles—an expression which therefore is likely to be permanent. (135–36)

How does such evolution lock in its developments? According to Carpenter, through the same sort of hardy intentional persistence by which persons master the arts and skills they desire and so make their cultural abilities second nature. As cycled through his mystic humanism, Carpenter's evolutionary vision is not focused on the primacy of biological nature but refracted through the conviction of a higher consciousness. The result is that nature becomes a "second nature" adapted to Carpenter's vitalist ideological ideals. In support of the notion that evolution results not merely from survival of the fittest but also and more importantly from the inner urging of a teleological desire, Carpenter offers the following analogy from the realm of personal survival: "is it not thus to-day, when a man has to meet danger, that the ideal which he has within him determines *how* he shall meet that danger, and others like it, and so ultimately determines the whole attitude and carriage of his body?" (136). Ironically, Carpenter's idealism is appropriate enough at the level of human behavior: persons are indeed ideological creatures whose behaviors are profoundly constructed according to cultural scripts. But, as mystic humanist, Carpenter extrapolates from the form of man's desire for the ideal to the cosmos as a whole, whose essential desire must have always been to unfold *us*. And, if that is the case, then our profoundest desire and organic task must be to give nature its way and to continue unfolding: "When at last the perfect Man appears, the key to all nature is found, every creature falls into its place and finds its Interpreter, and the purpose of creation is at last made manifest" (142).

Thus, Carpenter defines the sublime evolutionary perspective that will inform Dora Marsden's London and underwrite those forms of extreme spiritual individualism in which the evolutionistic ends of superhuman development justify in the long run particular means that in the short run may appear either antisocial or antisocialist. This vitalistic version of a higher or cosmic morality, running parallel to Nietzsche's more atheistical invocations of the Übermensch and demystifications of traditional morality, clearly appealed to cultural radicals whose activisms brought them into conflict with given social and ethical codes. In this light, Carpenter's own private and public struggles to express and celebrate his homosexuality significantly inflected his apotheosis of desire and informed his anticipation of the modernist trend toward an overthrowing of rather than building upon given historical forms.

> When a man feels in himself the upheaval of a new moral fact he sees plainly enough that that fact cannot come into the actual world all at once—not without first a destruction of the existing order of society—such a destruction as makes him feel satanic; then an intellectual revolution; and lastly only, a new order embodying the new impulse. . . . It might be said that the work of each age is not to build *on* the past, but to rise *out* of the past and throw it off. (144)

In the next chapter we will encounter Dora Marsden, battle scarred from her previous enlistment in the militant women's suffrage movement but already embarked on a new radical campaign, affirming in the pages of the *Freewoman* that "we are compelled by the progression of thought to recognise the disorder of living according to the law, the immorality of being moral, and the monstrousness of the social code. . . . We are conscious that we are concerned with the dissolution of one social order which is giving way to another."[63] The Whitmanian scientism relayed through Edward Carpenter's lyrical vitalism, progressive evolutionism, and social energetics will leave a considerable impress upon early Anglo-American modernism. With the aid of these scientific ideological configurations we will be able to plot with some precision the political and literary individualisms of Dora Marsden's London.

2

The *Freewoman:* Dora Marsden's Methods

Leaving the WSPU

One of the classical tenets of political anarchism is direct individual action. The literal violence of some anarchistic terrorism in the late nineteenth century prefigured certain symbolic acts of modernist violence, say, the pages of Wyndham Lewis's *Blast.*[1] Another modernist whose tactics owed something to the residual milieu of anarchist agitation was F. T. Marinetti. His early futurist publicity stunts—as in "the proclamation *Against Past-Loving Venice (Contro Venezia passatista),* printed on leaflets, eight hundred thousand of which were dropped from the top of the clock tower in Venice on 8 July 1910" (Perloff, *Futurist Moment,* 103)—were a kind of parodic homage to the revolutionary propagandizing abroad in Europe and America before the Great War.[2] During her career with the Women's Social and Political Union, Dora Marsden manifested a similarly theatrical genius for spectacular antagonism. Eventually her problems with the WSPU stemmed from its attempt to mold an inspired provocateur into a disciplined organizer, to turn an anarchist into a bureaucrat.[3]

The British women's suffrage movement reached its zenith in the years before the Great War in the colorful but immediately unavailing militant campaign of the WSPU. In the *Egoist* of June 15, 1914, Marsden reminisced about her doctrinal odyssey up to that point: "Long years ago—five perhaps—there existed in Manchester a colony of suffragettes, real ones, faithful of the faithful, who sped to do Mrs. Pankhurst's will before she had well breathed it forth. And at the very kernel of the community was a tiny group which in its intimate moments and as an unholy joke called itself the S.O.S. They were Sick of Suffrage."[4] Marsden was, of course, the kernel of this incipient insurrection, and she would carry her penchant for "unholy jokes" into her editorial career.

Still, it is worth recalling what it meant to be a real suffragette in 1909.[5] The women's suffrage movement in Britain had been dragging on for half a century when the WSPU's initiation of militant tactics in 1906 reinvigorated the issue. In 1908, a women's suffrage bill cleared Parliament but was stonewalled by Liberal Prime Minister Herbert Asquith. Public attempts to petition Parliament became increasingly rowdy. In 1910, the promise of a Conciliation Bill raised expectations and eased tensions for most of the year, but on November 11 Asquith substituted for it a manhood suffrage bill. One week later, on "Black Friday," two women died by police violence and two hundred were arrested. In 1909, militant tactics were still primarily symbolic and nonviolent—deputations to petition Parliament and vocal disruptions of meetings—but even those demonstrations could lead to arrest and imprisonment. Hunger strikes were soon countered by forcible feedings. Although window smashing began as early as 1909, the WSPU's campaign was especially violent from 1911 to 1914, a period when the suffragettes set fires, defaced works of art, and, in the case of Emily Wilding Davison, martyred themselves.[6]

In June 1908, a WSPU rally at Manchester's Heaton Park drew 150,000 persons: "many had come to see and hear Christabel and Emmeline Pankhurst and perhaps Mary Gawthorpe and the WSPU's Treasurer Emmeline Pethick-Lawrence too, but a new name also addressed them—Dora Marsden" (Garner, *Brave and Beautiful*, 29). Raeburn spots Dora Marsden in the Manchester Free Trade Hall on March 24, 1909: "volunteers for the deputation came forward at the meeting and among the women were three graduates: Dora Marsden and Rona Robinson of Manchester University, and Emily Wilding Davison, an Oxford graduate" (*Militant Suffragettes*, 93). In October 1909, Mrs. Emmeline Pethick-Lawrence, the treasurer of the WSPU, wrote the following letter to the organizer for the Southport district, Dora Marsden.

> My dear dear brave and beautiful Spirit,
>
> I have not words to express what I feel about your wonderful courage & heroism. When I think of all that your frail body has gone through, when I think of your face as I saw it in prison, my head is full of reverence for the human spirit, & full of grief for the law of suffering.
>
> A great force is being generated in this movement. We shall send out stronger and stronger thoughts, thoughts that will change the course of the world's life. Dear, in spite of all, we are more to be envied than any people living.
>
> My love to you Dora Marsden, sweetest, gentlest & bravest of Suffragettes.[7]

Pethick-Lawrence was lauding Marsden's role in a recent action.

Commemorative scroll presented to Marsden by the Women's Social and Political Union in 1909

Extraordinary scenes were witnessed at Manchester on Monday, when three University women—Miss Mary Gawthorpe, Miss Dora Marsden, B.A., and Miss Rona Robinson, M.Sc.—were violently arrested while conversing outside the Victoria University Buildings. Wearing their university robes, they attended the meeting of the Victoria University, over which Lord Morley, the Chancellor, presided, and before Lord Morley could take his seat they questioned him with regard to the imprisoned women at Birmingham. One of the three added that she also had been imprisoned in the cause of women's enfranchisement. All three women were ejected, and conducted by the police to Cavendish Street Police Station.[8]

A little over a year later, Marsden resigned from the WSPU.[9] However, despite her resignation she did not entirely leave: rather, she retained and adapted the evangelical rhetoric and millennial expectations of the WSPU to her own campaign of spiritual anarchism. Pethick-Lawrence's "A great force is being generated. . . . We shall send out stronger and stronger thoughts, thoughts that will change the course of the world's life," will become in Marsden's *Freewoman* dialect: "We feel we can produce new evidence of creative force, which, when allowed its course, will encompass developments sufficiently great to constitute a higher development in the evolution of the human race and of human achievement."[10] In a similar fashion, a feminist radicalism informed her political discourse even when she began to philosophize explicitly about anarchism and egoism.

Marsden's heroism as a fighting suffragette, as well as her particular flair for direct action, was reconfirmed two months after the Victoria University protest, on December 3, 1909, when Marsden and two others waylaid Winston Churchill at the Southport Empire theater. However, this affair seems to have marked the beginning of the end of her suffragette career. A few days before Churchill's campaign stop, the WSPU had ordered Marsden to refrain from serious civil disobedience: "We cannot afford at the present moment to make many protests which result in arrests. . . . I assure you that you are not serving the best interests of the Union in exposing yourself to more imprisonment. It is far better that there should be no arrests than that there should be these sacrifices of organizers. . . . You must rest assured that we at the centre can judge these matters in their due relationship and importance one with the other."[11] Needless to say, Dora Marsden did not drop her plans. The evening before Churchill's tightly guarded appearance, she and her partners hid themselves inside the theater, then used ropes to climb onto the roof in the middle of the night, abandoning their supplies in the effort, and held out against hunger, cold, and rain for fifteen hours.

Calling down from the roof to the podium in the midst of Churchill's speech, Marsden became a transcendental admonishing figure, a true suffragette "angel," a "brave spirit" floating perilously over a political mass.[12] This exploit is a prime example of Marsden's incipient anarchism as sheer reckless political abandon, a metaphor for her peculiar and imperious intellectual perspective in general. Marsden's audacious stunt became famous enough to be retailed in a contemporary novel, *Suffragette Sally*, in the following dialogue between a female Liberal (an "anti") and a male suffragette sympathizer.

> "What do you think," Mrs. Merton went on, addressing Robbie, "of women concealing themselves on a roof, in order to interrupt a meeting? I was in the house when they were discovered; and what do you think they did? Giggled."
> "Some women will giggle at any occupation."
> "Do you call sitting on a roof an occupation?"
> "Temporary," said Robbie.[13]

However, no giggling was reported at the actual event. The WSPU paper, *Votes for Women*, cited the account in the *Manchester Courier*.

> Mr. Churchill alone looked ill at ease. Once he turned his head sharply round, and several times his gaze nervously sought the wings. He had been speaking for ten minutes or so, and was just getting into his stride, when in a most dramatic manner the complacency of the stewards was turned to dismay and the confidence of the audience was shattered.
> Floating down into the hall in a slight pause in the speech came a faint feminine voice. The words were but partially distinguished, but the effect was electrical. Like one man the audience rose to its feet. For a few seconds the position of the intruder could not be determined. There was a momentary stillness, and then a roar proclaimed that the quarry had been sighted. Round the hall close to the ceiling are a number of ventilators. In one of these apertures, as in a frame, a slight girlish figure could be seen leaning into the hall and evidently addressing some remarks to the platform. At the table on the platform stood Mr. Churchill with his hand raised, vainly endeavouring to make himself heard.[14]

Dora Marsden's career in political journalism began as a participatory correspondent for the WSPU newspaper.[15] Her own account of her capture at the Southport Empire, reported in the same issue of *Votes for Women*, represents one of her earliest published texts.

Miss Marsden writes:—It was quite evident they did not know how to reach us, and pandemonium reigned. Mr. Churchill sat down, frowned, looked up, smiled, got up again, then sat down and folded his arms. Mrs. Churchill looked delighted and waved her hand. When this had been going on about ten minutes, during which I had been trying to make my voice heard, Mr. Churchill got up again, and by means of gesticulations got something like an appearance of calm. We looked down and nodded our thanks to him, and began again. When we stretched farther through the window so that the audience could see us, they broke into applause with clapping and cheering.

It was fully fifteen minutes, one of the reporters told me, before anyone reached us. They evidently did not know the way by which we had arrived the night before, and they had climbed up the roof, broken a window, and clambered in. A dirty hand was thrust over my mouth, and a struggle began. Finally I was dropped over a ledge, pushed through the broken window, and we began to roll down the steep sloping roof-side. Two stewards, crawling up from the other side, shouted out to the two men who had hold of me, "Stop that, you fools; you will all fall over the edge." The man who was pulling my right arm screamed hysterically, "I don't care what happens; we'll manage them." They managed so well that we balanced ourselves skillfully on the water-trough. At the police station an inspector said to me, "You ought to be grateful to me. If I hadn't caught your foot you would have gone to glory."[16]

In some way, Dora Marsden never entirely came down off that roof. A part of her would always remain aloof from the mass and enamored of elevated, commanding prospects. In one issue of the *Freewoman*, Marsden's lead article celebrated "the Over-and-Above,—Joy,—the Thrill . . . the peculiar and single possession which makes life worth living. It is this which makes toil worth while; its flashed vision repays long days of weariness, labour, pain. Its possibility is the lodestar of life."[17] As editor of the *Freewoman*, the *New Freewoman*, and the *Egoist*, Marsden successfully positioned herself to survey and manipulate a significant journalistic and literary field. After she stepped aside from editing in 1914 to work out her systematic philosophies, she eventually took extended refuge in Seldom Seen, a spartan stone cottage on a high ridge in the Lake District overlooking the Ullswater. In the end, Dora Marsden took anarchistic individualism as far as it could go.

Carried out in tacit defiance of their restraining order, Dora Marsden's death-defying bravado at the Southport Empire seems to have alerted the

WSPU that their organizer was a bit of a loose cannon. Pethick-Lawrence's praise for Marsden's exploit was also tempered by the practical repercussion of lawyer's fees.[18] Marsden's having engaged counsel could be seen perhaps as adhering to Pethick-Lawrence's request to avoid imprisonment, if not arrest. In any event, the next day Pethick-Lawrence wrote a longer letter attempting to contain and channel Marsden's energies and place them on "a thoroughly satisfactory basis," ending with a lengthy admonition that again turned on the need for "thrift." But this thrift was not monetary but organic, the conservation of her vital as well as her financial resources. The notion of economizing one's life force is part of the dialect of evolutionary vitalism: "I know that you are so upborne by spirit and enthusiasm that you do not feel the immediate results of over work. Nevertheless you are spending your capital instead of living as you should do on the interest of that capital. . . . I know that this is one of those matters which it is hardest to impress upon ardent spirits. . . . I do most earnestly urge you to be more thrifty in this matter and to resolutely set aside a portion of your week for rest and recreation."[19]

It has proven impossible to assess what physical damages Dora Marsden's suffragette zeal may have done her. It is unclear whether she endured the forcible feedings meted out to and breaking the health of many imprisoned militants, but it seems unlikely.[20] Whether Dora Marsden was ever raped through the nose with a feeding hose I don't know: clearly she came close enough. With the exception of one indirect occasion to which I will turn in the next chapter, to my knowledge Marsden herself never divulged her prison experiences. But, in 1914, still reminiscing about her lapsed commitment to a militant movement that by then had thrown itself foursquare behind the British war effort, she wrote: "If ever a generation were fed on seeming good food which refused to go down it is this female one which has had the 'principle of the suffrage' thrust upon it as an urgent issue."[21] Whatever the case, she was chronically unwell for the rest of her life, tormented by headaches and decades later by paranoid episodes. Dora Marsden's accomplishments over the next twenty years were secured in the face of acute ill health; her early withdrawal from public affairs was also due in part to her chronic distress.

Marsden hoped to return to active militancy in 1910, but, even though the period was relatively quiet in anticipation of a Conciliation Bill, Christabel Pankhurst was unwilling to spare her officers: "In reply to your letter, although a militant demonstration is being arranged, organisers will not be taking part in it. There are many members of the Union ready for action and organisers are needed at their posts."[22] Meanwhile, Marsden's flair for the outrageous led to growing antagonism. Later that year, one of Marsden's flamboyant fund-raising

schemes was also vetoed: "I have consulted others, and we adhere to the decision that a political shooting gallery is not desirable and must not be undertaken."[23] Relations between Marsden and the WSPU worsened throughout the
autumn of 1910. At the same time, prospects for the first Conciliation Bill collapsed completely, leading on November 18 to "Black Friday." In *Suffragette
Sally,* a historically accurate description of that debacle forms the apocalyptic
climax of the novel:

> For hours the battle lasted, not limited to any one place, but fought,
> simultaneously in many places; in Parliament Street, in Downing Street, in
> Parliament Square. Deputation after deputation came up from Clement's
> Inn, and was broken up and dispersed; and here was a wild turmoil of
> struggling men and women; and there a woman lay upon the ground; and
> there again were women hurled by the police into the crowd, and back
> from the crowd against the line of police. Women doctors were there in
> the thick of the tumult, well-known writers, hospital nurses. Women who
> had been told they must not have the vote because they could not fight,
> showed they could fight that day; there was nothing to be done but fight,
> since all around was warfare; since well-dressed men and youths amused
> themselves by striking women; since a man appealed to for help, turned on
> the girl who appealed to him and hit her again and again.
>   And all this because a man in power refused to receive twelve women
> who had none. (302–3)

A month later matters between Marsden and the WSPU came to a head
once again over her plans for a benefit exhibition. This time Pethick-Lawrence
minced no words.

> Since you have taken the hall without referring the matter to us for our
> serious consideration you have placed us in a very serious position of pub-
> lically repudiating your action if we did not go on with it. It is not the first
> time that you have acted on your own authority. . . . Every estimate must
> be submitted to Headquarters. No arrangement must be made without our
> consent. If we find that you are transgressing this rule we shall be obliged
> to send some one else to take your place in Southport to assume charge of
> the Exhibition arrangements.[24]

A corrected typescript, presumably a draft of her reply, remains in Dora Marsden's papers.

I will say briefly what I am driven to saying. You have sent to me, an educated, talented, and thoughtful woman, a lecture couched in tones which the meekest standards of self-respect could only consider intolerable.

The lecture finds its motif in baseless charges, proved to be untrue, unapologized for, and now erected into a reputation.

You say I encroach upon the authority of the Committee. Never at any time have I done so. . . .

In no case has there been retraction or expression of regret. The situation is inexplicable to me. It would be catastrophic to a thousand ideals to believe that leaders of this movement, built up as it has been by the passion of us all, could live in an atmosphere of suspicion respecting the good faith of any of its organisers.[25]

A month later the catastrophe was complete. Dora Marsden resigned, declining two months' severance pay. Her brief liaison with the Women's Freedom League (WFL) was over by the end of April, as recorded in a shocked note from the WFL's treasurer, Constance Tite: "No true Freedom Leaguer would ever spend 2/6 on lunch. . . . I cannot help being extremely astonished at your methods."[26] Marsden had hoped to sell the WFL on the idea of publishing a feminist paper, but by this time her plans for establishing the *Freewoman: A Weekly Feminist Review* on an independent basis were well advanced. The treasurer of the WFL would not be the last person taken aback by Dora Marsden's methods.

"Vivid New Life-Manifestations"

July 30, 1912
confidential

Dear Miss Marsden. I had not time yesterday to write what has long been on the tip of my pen to say to you about the Freewoman, but the impulse is strong enough to make me do so now—& to trust that you may not regard it as a sort of impertinence, but rather (if you can) as a kind of co-operation. For I do feel very great sympathy and unity with the main purpose of the Freewoman as indicated in its chief editorials.

But I am continually being alienated by what seems to me to be the contradiction—the hostile atmosphere—of its later pages (not its "correspondence"). Perhaps you do not feel as I do, that such a paper may and should breathe out through all its pages that atmosphere (or emanation of one constant purpose) which we associate with an active personality—? Even if you do you may well find the practical difficulties almost insuperable. But I rather understand that you judge it good to publish (without *immediate* editorial comment) what is from your point of view the plea of the devil's advocate.[27]

"Bondwomen"

Les Garner's *A Brave and Beautiful Spirit* provides further information about Dora Marsden's suffragist and feminist glory days. In his earlier study, *Stepping Stones to Women's Liberty*, Garner noted how an exclusive focus on the WSPU has often distorted the story of the British women's suffrage campaign. By 1911, when an embittered Marsden became persona non grata in official suffragette history, the feminist movement contained a number of former WSPU members who, like Marsden, were driven out for showing too much independence. The *Freewoman* devoted a number of editorials to critiques of the Union, and the WSPU did not appreciate the feedback.[28] But Garner's biography turns into a sad, protracted saga of personal degeneration, as Marsden all but expended her vital gift in that brief but fabulous flowering from 1908 to 1912 when she went from spectacular celebrity as a fighting suffragette to the courageous production of the *Freewoman*. Regretfully, "Dora retreated into her own individualistic philosophy"; her analyses of power and society "degenerated into an extreme yet woolly individualism that . . . was full of contradiction and assertion, relying totally on intangibles like 'will,' 'intuition' and the 'Soul of Man'" (84, 85). Once Marsden thrust herself away from the socialist feminist nexus, decades of decline set in, until the attempted suicide in 1935 that ended her intellectual career.

It is undoubtedly the case that in the *Freewoman* Dora Marsden's feminism turned toward an anarchist critique of such intangibles as freedom, equality, and the state; that for the span of the transitional *New Freewoman* literary creation ousted political action as a prime interest; and that her *Egoist* writings replaced explicit feminist rhetoric with systematic philosophy. Whether her feminism lapsed entirely when she turned the gender-marked *New Freewoman* into the blandly genderless *Egoist* is an open debate, and the question is complicated by what may be considered the resurgence of a spiritual feminism in the full-blown matriarchal mythology of her late works, beginning with *The Definition of the Godhead*.[29] And if, in the end, Marsden carried her unique campaign beyond reasonable limits, she did so as a writer. Dora Marsden was not only a real suffragette, she was a real writer, wholly committed to the harvest of her own light. Despite my own disagreements with her, I retain a strong respect for such consummate self-determination.

Dora Marsden deserves not only to be properly criticized but also to be properly appreciated for the cultural effects she accomplished in the face of formidable resistance. Her writings still need to be integrated accurately with the larger account of modernist history. As we have already indicated, it would be a mistake to place Marsden in the same file with Tory literati or other modernist or masculinist reactionaries.[30] If her femino-anarchism has the appearance of a right-wing discourse, that is due in part to historical distortion in the aftermath of the Spanish Civil War.[31] Right-wing rhetoricians of bourgeois democracies have often colonized anarchist discourse to apply a spurious radical gloss to statist policies and motives. One utility of Dora Marsden for our own political moment is that her writings express a radical libertarianism inflected from a feminist viewpoint and completely untainted by corporatist, racist, or jingoist complicities.

Readers of Dora Marsden need to avoid unduly constricted models of cultural history. They also need to appreciate Marsden's career as a writer rather than as a political activist, to conceive, for instance, that the *Freewoman* was a free textual creation, the first in a series of unprecedented cultural achievements, never a vehicle solely dedicated to specific topical movements. Moreover, Marsden's writings never retreated from the expression of principles intrinsic to her militancy from the beginning. Without the "woolly individualist" who went on from the *Freewoman* to turn the *New Freewoman* into the *Egoist*, without Marsden's utter creative and existential investments in the cultivation of her successive personae, there would have been no radical feminist, no fighting suffragette, and no *Freewoman* to celebrate. Marsden's wayward career is an epitome of the strained relations between sociopolitical community and serious literary commitment in the modernist era.

Dora Marsden's intellectual development was fluid, but her editorial methods, although not always transparent, remained more or less the same throughout her doctrinal changes. By reading the *Freewoman* sequentially and as a unified text, those methods can be reconstructed, and Marsden's movement toward a systematic philosophy of radical individualism can be traced from its inception. Although it enabled a significant multiplicity of radical discourses to interact, the *Freewoman* was ultimately the product not of a collective but of an individual editorial will. By further reviewing and criticizing her lead articles and topical commentaries for the *Freewoman* and some of what her contributors and correspondents wrote in response, I will treat Marsden as a discursive artist in her own right, a modernist writer/editor shaping a complex textual field and responding to a complex audience.

One basic pattern of Marsden's editorial method was firmly established in the first two issues of the *Freewoman:* an extreme, provocative declaration on a given issue, generating some surprise, some shock and resistance, followed by reflection, redefinition, and dialectical development of the issue, at the price of alienating portions of the audience. Marsden was not a single-minded polemicist but rather a mobile controversialist. Within this oppositional framework, Marsden divided her own writing into two contiguous and complementary modes: the affirmative, aggressive, and unified leader, followed by the reflective and multiform "Notes of the Week."[32] Any given contribution of Marsden's to the *Freewoman* is taken somewhat out of context if isolated from the wider frame of its intended repercussions. A crucial example is the way in which the brash extremity of Dora Marsden's first leader for the *Freewoman*, "Bondwomen," is mitigated by recognizing its role within the newly created paper as an opening salvo, a startling invitation to intellectual controversy, and also by binding it with the "Notes of the Week," following immediately, and the "Commentary on Bondwomen," published the next week.[33]

"Bondwomen," defining by negation the individual freewoman, drives immediately to an outrageously categorical assertion concerning female servility: "Bondwomen are distinguished from Freewomen by a spiritual distinction. Bondwomen are the women who are not separate spiritual entities—who are not individuals. They are complements merely" (1). Marsden goes on to describe typical masculinist sentiments: "For man, woman has become a kind of human poultice, or, more poetically, the illusion softening reality" (2). The first part of "Bondwomen" attempts to explicate the affective logic of antifeminism.

> The opponents of the Freewomen are not actuated by spleen or by stupidity, but by dread. This dread is founded upon ages of experience with a being who, however well loved, has been known to be an inferior, and who has accepted all the conditions of inferiors. Women, women's intelligence, and women's judgments have always been regarded with more or less secret contempt. This contempt rests upon quite honest and sound instinct, so honest indeed that it must provide all the charm of an unaccustomed sensation for fine gentlemen like the Curzons and Cromers and Asquiths to feel anything quite so instinctive and primitive. . . . It is for would-be Freewomen to realise that for them this contempt is the healthiest thing in the world, and that those who express it honestly feel it. (1)

Marsden's psychological reading of the state of the British sex war suggests that cultural progress has been made by militant feminism's success in getting fine gentlemen to express publicly their previously unspoken prejudices, thus enabling their exposure to critical correction. Provoking articulation will remain a crucial rationale for Marsden's editorial methods generally. However, in "Bondwomen" Marsden's social diagnosis remains inscribed within peculiarly British terms of class antagonism, not those of capital and labor but of "master and servant." Servile self-sacrifice has always enthralled women, and "this, after all, is what speaks far more eloquently than a tome of argument to the ordinary man. . . . He therefore quite naturally argues that she has acted like a second because she felt herself a second" (2). As in the opening remarks of "Bondwomen" previously cited, at first Marsden treats the categories of master and servant as essential spiritual types, and on that basis the essay moves to a merciless climax.

It is quite beside the point to say women were "crushed" down. If they were not "down" in themselves—i.e., weaker in mind—no equal force could have crushed them "down." There can be no over-reaching *in the long run* with mind. In the long run, mind plays on its own merits. It can neither receive nor give quarter. Those who are "down" are inferior. When change takes place in the thing itself—i.e., when it becomes equal or superior—by the nature of its own being it rises. . . . At the present time, when man's adventurous and experimental mind has made much of her "usefulness" useless, woman finds herself cut off from her importantly useful sphere, equipped with the mind of a servant, and with the reputation of one. . . . It is this effort to find her place among the masters which is behind the feminist movement. (2)

Yet at this juncture Marsden doubled back from such spiritual absolutism and, returning to the phenomena of bondwomen, suggested a material contingency for women's servile station: "it can only be accounted for upon an understanding of the stupefying influence of security with irresponsibility. And this is what 'protection' always means for the 'protected'" (2). It is thus morally imperative to refuse the prostitution of marriage and to enter the free markets of economic and creative production. Freewomen must throw off the material shackles of conjugal and parental subjections, as well as "learn that freedom is born in the individual soul, and that no outer force can either give it or take it way" (2). The ultimate recompense for enduring the agonizing labor of female self-liberation is to deliver within oneself the new issues of a creative and vital evolution: "it is the truth, and men and women both must learn it, that while to be a human poultice is to have great utility, it does not offer the conditions under which vivid new life-manifestations are likely to show themselves" (2). Marsden's radical vitalism here implicitly refutes the "lean kind," that is, the existentially stingy, like Mrs. Pethick-Lawrence with her kindly but patronizing counsels of "thrift." For Marsden, the life force expended in militant resistance will be recovered from the deep wells of inner exfoliation.

These anarchistic swings from one political wing to another recur in Marsden's discourse and render it a rather daunting text. Was this debut manifesto simply incoherent, or was it a calculated bit of ideological counterpoint, in short, a complex editorial provocation? I have found it more rewarding to credit Marsden's text with a variable fund of irony playing over a radicalism in deadly earnest. Marsden's provocations were indeed intentional: as she went on to affirm, the *Freewoman* was not intended for a passive audience, nor did she ever contend that her ideas composed a popular program. Eliminating thereby a need for intellectual condescension, and thus much of her potential audience, she immediately placed the *Freewoman* on what we can recognize as a "modernist" plane of iconoclastic innovation.

The "Notes of the Week" following "Bondwomen" continued to develop the manifesto of the *Freewoman*.

> For the first time, feminists themselves make the attempt to reflect the feminist movement in the mirror of thought. That this can be done argues at once the strength of the movement, and the conscious knowledge of that strength. If at times to some the reflected images which appear in *The Freewoman* appear harsh and unfair, we would ask those to whom they so appear to show the tolerance and patience which we believe is the fair due of those who put into their work an utter sincerity and everything that is truest in their thought and experience. (3)

In Britain and America, at the end of 1911, Dora Marsden located a community of readers sufficiently responsive to her conception of the issues to be willing to wrestle with it. She justified her use of devil's advocacy in the following manner.

> We believe in the Freewoman, that is, we believe in the spiritual separateness of woman. Because we are convinced of the sureness of her position we are strong enough to welcome criticism from those who are opposed to her conception. For this reason the case for the Freewoman

can be put, placing the fullest emphasis on everything which militates against her. . . . For this reason, in a leading article which appears in this week's issue, on Bondwomen, the anti-feminists are met on their strongest ground—which is prejudice, born of specific experience. . . . We hold that prejudice is to be regarded as subconscious reason, and that it is our business to bring out the reason latent in prejudice. Only then can we judge of its soundness and otherwise. So when in Bondwomen (in somewhat sweeping fashion, because of the necessities of space) we grant anti-feminists what is therein granted, we believe we are getting not only to the root of their opposition, but to the root of the prejudice. (3)

Here still applied to women as a whole, it is clear that Dora Marsden's premium on "spiritual separateness" was no later aberration. It was positioned from the beginning at the center of this rather Nietzschean conception of feminism. In the constructive argument of "Bondwomen," the figure of the freewoman was already envisioned as an individualistic and hermetic type, a reclusive female artist/philosopher: "Nothing but one thing—the sense of quality, the sense that a woman has gifts, the sense that she is a superior, a master—can give her the strength to slip the comfort and protection and be content to seize the 'love' in passing, to suffer the long strain of effort, and to bear the agony of producing creative work" (2).

The Ideology of Types

What Marsden grasped as the "subconscious reason" within prejudice, we now approach as structures of ideology. Tickner notes how the caricatures of feminist and suffragist "types" in the British illustrated press had pictorial ancestors going back to medieval images of the four humors (*Spectacle of Women*, 308). Popular discourses of female typology and their putative rationales are inscribed in a long tradition of patriarchal notions about the connections between sexual physiology and personal character. Determining psychological characters upon sexual differences has also been a standard process of modern scientific ideological typification. Sexological systems emerged in the later nineteenth century in response to the early gains of modern feminism and generally for the purpose of anchoring patriarchal gender moralizations. Once the scientist significance of sexual difference was stabilized, ideological characters could be securely fixed within or affixed onto gendered bodies and coordinated with sociopolitical policy, for instance, legislative attitudes toward female suffrage.

Otto Weininger's *Sex and Character,* which we will consider at greater length later in this chapter, displays some of the spurious premises behind scientific ideological justifications for early modern misogyny.[34] Published in Germany in 1903 and translated into English in 1906, Weininger's characterology was an immediate pan-European success with appreciable repercussions in many literatures.[35] In the first part, Weininger set out the biological theories from which he would extend his sexological arguments.

> Naegli, de Vries, Oskar Hertwig and others have propounded the important theory, and supported it by weighty arguments, that every cell in a multi-cellular organism possesses a combination of the characters of its species and race, but that these characters are, as it were, specially condensed in the sex cells. . . . The investigators to whom I have just referred . . . conceive of the existence of an "Idioplasm," which is the bearer of the specific characters, and which exists in all the cells of a multi-cellular animal, quite apart from the purposes of reproduction. In a similar fashion I have been led to the conception of an "Arrhenoplasm" (male plasm) and a "Thelyplasm" (female plasm) as the two modes in which the idioplasm of every bisexual organism may appear, and which are to be considered . . . as ideal conditions between which the actual conditions always lie. . . . If, instead of writing "masculinity" and "femininity" at length, we choose signs to express these, and without any malicious intention choose the positive sign (+) for M and the negative (–) for W, then our proposition may be expressed as follows: The sexuality of the different cells of the same organism differs not only in absolute quantity but is to be expressed by a different sign. (16–17)

These theories concerning the existence of a character-bearing "plasm" crudely anticipated the present understanding of genetic materials. But it was the sexual polarization of the "Idioplasm" that gave Weininger's system the ideological spin that registered in Dora Marsden's London. Probably with Weininger's system in mind, Marsden explicitly criticized schemas of gender polarity: "a great deal of pseudo-scientific nonsense has been uttered upon this question of 'positive' and 'negative.' It has been held to be a biological difference inhering in the different genders of the human male and female, the embodiment of some great mysterious underlying law."[36] Transfusing human genetics with a romantic electro-polarity model, Weininger bifurcated a biological theory into a sexological ideology. We might say that he converted the theory of a monistic "Idioplasm" into two gendered "Ideoplasms."

Weininger's vicarious and tendentious participation in this scientific groping toward modern genetics illustrates how culturally precarious biological speculation had become at the turn of the twentieth century, with the vogue for eugenics devoted to shoring up the racial germ plasm and with evolutionary theory affirming the nonessentiality of species but unable to locate the micro-mechanisms of genetic mutation and transmission. Into these conceptual gaps Weininger plunged with his ideologized plasms. Beyond Weininger's particular sexology, however, the social discourse of sexual types disseminated gender essentialism for a Darwinian culture. Between the static, divinely ordained species of pre-Darwinian creationism and the mobile but random dynamism of evolutionary development, the elaboration of "types and characters" formed a compromise, reinscribing the fluid and unpredictable as a succession of fixed states. Western culture's accommodation of old stereotypes to new evolutionary paradigms was desultory at best. Bourgeois demands for serviceable ideological counters were much stronger than progressivist countertrends toward fluid indetermination. If the dissolution of previously fixed types was countenanced at all, often it was with a view not of progressive evolution but of its obverse, the degeneration of the achieved type into some decadent atavism of its primitive precursor. The essentialist assumption of sexological typecasting is that character typologies—for instance, those yielded by gendered plasms—are "natural": their alteration can only be a deformation of nature, God's proxy in a scientistic culture. Precise knowledge of the type thus authorizes some definitive cultural judgment upon and punitive treatment of the deviation.

The type of the freewoman—Dora Marsden's projected ideal of genius as a superhuman female, a feminist retort to Nietzsche's Übermensch as egoistic superman—is perhaps her greatest single creation. It is fundamentally a prophetic gesture in the form of a political trope. In elaborating it, Marsden's early *Freewoman* writings exercised some visionary typecasting reminiscent of Whitman's efforts in *Democratic Vistas* to forge new American models of radiant personality: "Of course, in these States, for both man and woman, we must entirely recast the types of highest personality," according to "the all-varied, all-permitting, all-free theorem of individuality" (401–3). To jump forward a bit, in the *New Freewoman* Marsden's individualist logic will determine a reaction against the discourse of types in general, including creative gender types like the freewoman. The genderlessness of the *Egoist* will result in part from Marsden's later resolve to defy the determination of types altogether.

In the meantime, the leader of the *Freewoman*'s second number, "Commentary on Bondwomen," avidly took up a "sheaf of questions and objections," focusing eventually on the concept of individual genius as an evolutionary power.

The cult of the Suffragist would say, "Are women not weak? Are women not crushed down? Are women not in need of protection? Therefore, give them the means wherewith they may be protected." Those of the cult of the Freewoman, however, while granting this in part, would go on to say, "In spite of our position, we feel within us the stirrings of new powers and of growing strength. If we can secure scope, opportunity, and responsibility, we feel we can make realisable to the world a new revelation of spiritual consciousness. We feel we can produce new evidence of creative force, which, when allowed its course, will encompass developments sufficiently great to constitute a higher development in the evolution of the human race and of human achievement." (21–22)

Marsden was clearly sincere about placing feminist issues in spiritual terms, that is, about removing those issues entirely from a biological plane that had been effectively co-opted by the social Darwinists and the medical misogynists.[37] As noted in the previous chapter, before the Great War many radical social movements moved in similar spiritual folds of Whitmanian afflatus, Nietzschean exhortation, and Bergsonian flux. A related strain of this spiritual dialect occurs in Gertrude Colmore's novel *Suffragette Sally,* wherein a confirmed suffragette reveals to a disillusioned and frustrated Liberal suffragist the WSPU's vision of the larger significance of the militant campaign: "I mean that evolution has its own methods, and those who work them out are evolution's instruments. Individually the women who are working in all their different ways to bring about the next phase in the development of humanity are working, each one according to the behests of her conscience, her character, her circumstances" (164).

An evangelical evolutionism like that informing the prose of *Suffragette Sally* also persisted in Dora Marsden's development beyond suffragism. Marsden injected the tenor of suffragette militancy into the discourse of modernism because her own thought remained closely tied to the dialects of evolutionist spiritualism that colored the rhetoric of the WSPU. Suffragists had been obliged to counter antisuffragist and misogynist abuses of evolutionary theory "with evolutionary arguments of their own to the effect that modern womanhood was neither mutant nor perverse"; Marsden's exposition of the freewoman as a new evolutionary type was a maverick variant of this counterideological project: "The WSPU and its allies developed the representation of the allegorical and 'militant' woman, which countered the image of the hysteric as victim and deviant with the image of an active (and phallic) if unearthly agent of moral, social and political reform" (Tickner, *Spectacle of Women,* 205). As an evolutionary type, a trope at play in the social text of an ideological contest, Marsden's postsuffragist freewoman appears to have been a composite of the "militant" and the "modern" woman as developed in suffragist iconography.

Some contributors recognized the prophetic function of the freewoman as a "prototype" of higher being, related to the larger field of progressive evolutionary radicalism and commensurate with Whitman's new man and woman, the Nietzschean Superman, Carpenter's uncanny "intermediate sexual types," and so forth. For instance, one contributor dilated on the Übermensch: "Nietzsche's elaboration of Max Stirner's Superman has his place in the scheme of things, but he is not *final*. . . . A new type cannot be predicted, for the prophet is himself the prototype. Whatever is realised already has existence, and needs only to be expressed. Therefore the Superman, having been extensively preached, is the type of the present—passing."[38] "Militancy in Women," an article later in the same number, debated some of Marsden's ideas about the meaning of freedom but still participated in the construction of the figure of the freewoman: "Is this freedom desired in order that Woman may develop herself to the highest? And why does she wish to do this? If the answer implies that it is that she may *give* more to the world, then it is well. And this developed ideal woman, what is she like? We see her figure in the dim distance, but it is not yet clearly defined. . . . Is the future freewoman militant, then?"[39]

Marsden's feminist elitism turns on a certain prophetic afflatus and needs to be measured against the demands she made on that elite (which is to say, herself), nothing less than the burden of carrying the human species to a higher plane of existence. This wild idealism had as yet its paradigm in Edward Carpenter's exfoliating socialism. However, whereas Carpenter urged pacifistic and meditative self-adjustments, Dora Marsden's dedicated feminist doctrine urged arduous effort: "the doctrine of feminism is one so hard on women that, at the outset, we can only appeal to those who have already shown signs of individuality and strength" ("Commentary on Bondwomen," 21). The course of human evolution aside, it does not seem that Marsden understated the hardships feminism has encountered trying to dismantle patriarchy and reshape the sociopolitical order. In addition, Marsden's point at the moment was that the opposition to nineteenth-century feminism had compelled twentieth-century feminism to reach a more searching analysis of the social structure. That such a seemingly simple and just request as the demand for a parliamentary vote had languished for so many decades argued for an implicit masculinist recognition that even that modest concession to women would speed the unraveling of society as at present constituted. "Whereas in the early days," Marsden wrote in her first installment of "The New Morality," as in all great movements at their inception, we were wont to say, "Is it not a small thing, no revolution, merely belated justice, that we ask?" . . . Yet within a few years we are compelled by the progression of thought to recognise the disorder of living according to the law, the immorality of being moral, and the monstrousness of the social code. We are compelled to recognise that we are not asking a small thing, but a big thing. . . . Another eight million women seeking paid labour in the land! That is not a small thing! Nor is it a small thing to be in opposition to the moral code under which one lives. . . . We therefore seek to formulate no morality for superwomen. We are seeking a morality which shall be able to point the way out of the social trap we find we are in. We are conscious that we are concerned with the dissolution of one social order which is giving way to another. (61–62)

At this point Marsden's sublime evolutionary perspective lines up with post-structuralist feminism's critiques of patriarchal ideology.[40] In her own way Marsden saw that ideological systems are structural totalities within which local dissonance quickly resonates throughout the whole, that piecemeal liberal solutions fall short of the radical restructuring implied by the successful consummation of a feminist revolution.

Anarchism and Literature

Marsden's struggles with the WSPU's structure of command showed her peculiar anarchism taking form. Once she got the *Freewoman* going, the first man and the second person other than Marsden to have a lead article in its pages was Selwyn Weston, a writer for the communist anarchist monthly the *Herald of Revolt*.[41] Weston figured in several of Rebecca West's letters to Marsden: "You wonderful person, you not only write those wonderful front-pagers, but you inspire other people to write wonderfully. . . . Every one behaves beautifully at the Freewoman Discussion Circle—it's like being in Church—except Miss Robinson, Mr. Weston, and myself. Barbara Low has spoken very seriously to me about it."[42] A fairly regular contributor, Weston brought to the *Freewoman* a discursive dialect akin to Floyd Dell's in *Women as World Builders,* an amalgamated progressivism that sheds some light on Marsden's further doctrinal changes. Although Weston was not an original thinker, he could turn phrases nicely enough, and his writings accurately record the evolutionism and aesthetic anarchism current in the literary talk of the time. Names Weston liked to drop were Novalis, Whitman, Pater, Maeterlinck, and Ibsen. In Weston's articles, literary criticism was the vehicle for larger meditations on nature, politics, and personality.

The fifth number of the *Freewoman* carried Weston's first and only lead article, "A Gospel of Goodwill," a pleasantly facetious meditation on the "Christmas spirit" of universal altruism.[43] The first text for this secular sermon was George Meredith's novel *The Egoist*. This is the exact point at which the individualist anarchist discourse of egoism entered the pages of the *Freewoman*, in the words of a man on a freewoman's platform, and in the form of literary criticism: "In the Prelude to 'The Egoist,' Meredith has mentioned an endless great book, 'the biggest book on earth; that might indeed be called the Book of Earth; whose title is the Book of Egoism'"; Weston's criticism of Meredith's novel was basically that the seemingly self-effacing protagonist, Vernon Whitford, who eventually outwits the explicit egoist of the title, Sir Willoughby Patterne, is "no less an egoist than Willoughby" (81).

Weston lined up the notion of goodwill in vaguely Schopenhauerian terms of life, will, and desire. What is the possibility of free will, let alone goodwill, Weston asked, when "there is a rhythmic unity of purpose in Nature compelling and directing human thought and action, whose influence on persons is neither good nor ill, but necessary and non-moral"? (81) Citing bits of Whitman and Strindberg, Weston moved to the following evolutionistic conclusions: "we cannot see that Nature's purpose controls our every choice, working out through our very egoism the design whereof we are no more than a very minute portion" (82). The true egoist is not egotistic, then, but in fact fulfills nature's inscrutable evolutionary purpose, selflessly enacting nature's progressive will. As Whitman averred in *Democratic Vistas*, evolutionary progress is the law of the cosmos: "Law is the unshakable order of the universe forever; and the law over all, and law of laws, is the law of successions; that of the superior law, in time, gradually supplanting and overwhelming the inferior one" (381).

Besides egoistic ethics, another interest Weston shared with Marsden at the time was sexual emancipation. The *Freewoman* did its part to prepare the Anglo-American literary public for modernism's forthcoming sexual explicitness. According to Rebecca West, its "greatest service" to the nation was "its unblushingness. . . . The 'Freewoman' mentioned sex loudly and clearly and repeatedly, and in the worst possible taste" ("The Freewoman," 649). Lisa Tickner notes that the *Freewoman* "became the principal outlet for minority feminist debates on women's personal freedom and sexual autonomy" (*Spectacle of Women*, 320):

There was no agreement on the nature and rights of female sexuality in the Edwardian period, but suffragists were chiefly successful in pushing to the margins of their campaign a dissident tradition that argued for "free unions" and women's right to equal sexual expression with men. Male sexual radicals like Havelock Ellis and Edward Carpenter, and advocates of birth control and free unions including Annie Besant, Stella Browne and the libertarian Dora Marsden, offered a challenge to the social purity position which continued to dominate the Edwardian women's movement. . . . This challenge . . . represented in some respects the most "modern" position on female sexuality. (223)

Sheila Jeffreys has described the controversy in the *Freewoman*'s correspondence columns over the relative merits of spinsterhood and celibacy as against sexual activity in and out of marriage.[44] Apparently Jeffreys assumes that because Marsden gave a platform to critics of spinsterhood, she agreed with them. Such assumptions are clearly unwarranted, but it is often the case that doctrinaire readers have difficulty appreciating how authentically libertarian Marsden's editorial attitude was. Unfortunately, Tickner picks up Jeffreys' one-sided view of the *Freewoman*. Although its sexual openness was but one thread in its composite texture, Tickner treats it as though it were the sole point of interest. Her further depiction of this "feminist minority" considering sex as important as suffrage and so failing to adhere to the majoritarian "purity stance" is incorrect with regard to Marsden's attitudes and presents a distorted picture of the *Freewoman*'s content.

> But this challenge, which represented in some respects the most "modern" position on female sexuality, was seriously weakened by the fact that its definitions of sexual activity were drawn from heterosexual male models, that it joined a misogynist tradition in discrediting the spinster's life as one of "sterility and a slow atrophy of bodily and mental power," that it overlooked the material conditions which made "free unions" impractical for most women, and most of all that it lost the cutting edge which the purity stance gave to women's critiques of male sexuality and the double standard. (*Spectacle of Women,* 223)

For one thing, Marsden was herself single by choice. In her own writings the spinster is not vicious but a victim, and she railed against traditional marriage on numerous occasions.[45] The prejudice in question issued from a few contributions by F. Stella Browne, an insignificant part of the *Freewoman* except insofar as its readers numbered women who later figured in socialist history (see Rowbotham, *New World*). For another, the "free union" concept within the *Free-*

woman was largely due to a few articles by the anarchist sex libertarian Guy Aldred.

Perhaps we should attend to Marsden's own pronouncements on sexual issues such as asceticism, sensuality, and passion. In "The New Morality—II," she wrote: "Women, as we have said, are the social ascetics. They have become ascetic through their long exercising of restraint. They have restrained themselves in order to remain 'pure.' They have remained 'pure' because men like them 'pure.' . . . Many women are coming to realise their own psychology, and are abandoning their long mistrust of life, with its impulses and pleasures. They are beginning to realise that capacity for sense-experience is the sap of life."[46] These counterpuritanical considerations led directly to the matter of "passion and sex-passion" as distinct from "the base counterfeit of passion . . . sensuality, lust, the tippling with sensation, the snacking at sex" (102). True passion is concentrated and protracted, intensifying the senses, raising them to the level of creative vision: "it disintegrates the outer *husk* of semblance"; "sex-love" is meaningful to the extent that sexual passions create visionary experiences: "Sexual passion . . . will have to be for us the holy ground, for walking whereon we make due preparation. . . . Sex-love is, or ought to be, the most highly wrought experience that the conscious universe has yet produced" (102).[47]

In the *Freewoman,* Dora Marsden explicitly connected sexual emancipation, evolutionary progress, and libertarian politics, along lines similar to Emma Goldman's concurrent anarcho-feminist campaign. In his discussion of Goldman in *Women as World Builders,* Floyd Dell commented:

> So little is known, and so much absurd nonsense is believed, about the Anarchists. . . . Secret organizations of Anarchists plotting a violent overthrow of the government do not exist. . . . Anarchists do not believe in violence of any kind, or in any exercise of force. . . . Since 1887 the Anarchists have lost influence among [American] workingmen until they are today negligible—unless one credits them with Syndicalism—as a factor in the labor movement. The Anarchists have, in fact, left the industrial field more and more and have entered into other kinds of propaganda. They have especially "gone in for kissing games." (57–59)[48]

In the eighth number of the *Freewoman,* Selwyn Weston presented an anarchistic conception of socialism in language prefiguring Dora Marsden's doctrinal evolution to and through sexual anarchism. Critiquing Francis Grierson— a theosophist who would himself contribute a leader and other items in the late days of the *Freewoman* and early days of the *New Freewoman*—concerning Grier-

son's notion of an "aristocracy of intellect" as well as "Nietzsche's elaboration
of Max Stirner's Superman," Weston commented:

> Socialism, or (as we have said) that element in the world-scheme which
> leads to the ultimate welfare of humankind, is anarchic in nature. . . .
> Regarded as the ultimate human aim, an aristocracy of intellect cannot
> hope to realise individual freedom. Since an aristocracy, of whatever kind,
> cannot embrace all mankind, it must needs conflict with the liberty of
> *some.* Beyond the *ego* of Superman there is always an *ego;* behind the thinly
> shrouded *alter* of the State an *ego* is scarcely concealed. But through the
> avowed *ego* of anarchy an *alter* may be glimpsed. It is through the conscious
> lapse into egoism which leads to the slopes of Superman that Socialism
> strives to gain the heights of final freedom.[49]

Weston's egoistic anarchism was to be the basis for the formation of individuals
capable of a libertarian socialism. It would take an "avowed" or "conscious"
egoism's "lapse" from the culture of self-sacrifice to produce a true overcoming
or transcendence of the tyrannical, hierarchical State. Marsden quickly joined
these issues in her leaders, but she had begun to question Weston's equation of
anarchism with socialism. These issues remind us that in the radical politics of
the time, anarchism generally was not seen as a right-wing libertarianism but as
a revolutionary socialism, the left-wing alternative to communism.[50] Marsden
started to desynonymize them in commenting on a recent newspaper column
by the bishop of Exeter, who had stated, "The Anarchist refuses to be governed
at all[, t]he Socialist aspires to be governed too much." Marsden responded:
"Because this is true, there are men and women of intellectual clarity who
refuse to call themselves Socialists, not, indeed, because they regard the appropriation of the profits of labour to the benefit of those who produce them as
robbery—indeed, not to do so they consider robbery—but because they dread
the tyranny of this socialised civic rule. . . . Anarchy is the fit condition for a
mature community."[51]

For the communist anarchists in league with the *Freewoman,* however,
socialism slid easily into sexualism. In counterpoint to Marsden's political
themes, at the end of the same number Guy Aldred contributed a discussion of
sexuality criticizing respectable suffragism and arguing that the conception of
the freewoman demanded an anarchistic sex morality.

> Women advocate for equality, yet marry men and lose their identity in that
> of the man by taking his name. Why do they not assert the supremacy of

motherhood, insist on the negation of the conception of woman now abroad as an instrument of man's lust, put an end to man's power to send innocent girls and women on the road to prostitution, by daring to form free-love unions, and preserving their own names, without fear or shame?[52]

Presumably it was the production of propaganda promoting sexual liberation that Dell was referring to with his coy phrase "kissing games." If Dell was right, then to a great extent for most of this century the main imperative and effective public face of anarchism has been "free love," the drive to emancipate sexual behaviors from ethical condemnation and oppressive legislation. Twentieth-century Anglo-American literature has had a major stake in instigating as well as chronicling the checkered progress of modern sexual liberation. In this light, the long modernist campaign against literary censorship—in which Dora Marsden, Harriet Shaw Weaver, the *Egoist,* and the Egoist Press played their roles as champions of and outlets for James Joyce's work—may be considered a kind of anarchist front.

However, Dora Marsden left explicit calls for "free-love unions" to Aldred. Her *Freewoman* anarchism was a more subtle response to her clear perception of the post-Nietzschean spiritual predicament. That is, if in fact God is dead, then

the idea believed in, and in behalf of which the purpose is made strong, is to be found in oneself also. The self has to guarantee, therefore, the reality of the idea, the worth of the idea, and the strength of purpose to carry the idea into effect. . . . To freewomen this conception is becoming clearer. It is to face life unafraid, to welcome its emotions, to try their value, to be alive and capable of living intensely; to seek life, and that more abundantly; and, if there is a price to be paid for it, to be ready with the toll. ("The New Morality—V," 162)

For Marsden the self is not referable, is not to be referred to any idea, emphatically not to statist ideas. Rather, for *their* worth ideas are to be referred to selves and their several purposes. As in Weston's phrase, "the prophet is himself the prototype." Marsden's remarks also replay the organicist economics that had been invoked by Mrs. Pethick-Lawrence in her futile admonitions over Marsden's exhaustive militant enthusiasms, a bottom-line accounting of the expenditure of life force: the "toll" exchanged in return for abundant vital intensity is the element of self-sacrifice in Marsden's egoism.

Marsden's individualism is an early modernist form of philosophical idealism. It is overwritten by an evolutionary vitalism that organicizes and reinscribes
the ego-ideal as the "living," or preideational, self. Vitalism and anarchism both
postulate a unitary, metaphysical life force, Weston's "rhythmic unity of purpose," which drives individuals into differentiated selfhood and then unifies
those atoms relative to a common telos, for instance, Whitman's visionary
"democracy." In an article entitled "Anarchy in Art," Weston expounded some
more connections between modernism and anarchism. Although he did not
single out literature, he included it in a comprehensive view of modern art as
practical rebellion.

> Whatever may be the particular aspects of art to-day, it cannot be doubted
> that there is a general trend towards revolt. And whatever may be urged in
> favour of the theory, that art has no aim but to express the artist's individ-
> ual view of life, we claim that this very fact, if such it be, further establishes
> that the spirit of revolt is one the world over, regardless of the forms its
> expression may assume; that the anarch of art is own brother to the social
> or political rebel, and that their aim is one.[53]

Alongside the main diet of sociopolitical discussion, the *Freewoman* published lyric poetry, numerous literary and dramatic reviews, and assorted articles
devoted to aesthetic theory. By such degrees, the *Freewoman* prognosticated the
New Freewoman and the *Egoist* as primary forums for literature and criticism
while remaining essentially and implicitly political in fundamental premise. To
borrow from Selwyn Weston's phrases, Dora Marsden's individualism comprehended the "anarch of art" and the "political rebel" as it enacted a "conscious
lapse into egoism" in pursuit of an anarchistic millennium. In the *Freewoman* of
March 28, 1912, Marsden seized on the type of the artist-hero as an ideal image
for the uplifting of freewomen.

> The souls which can search out reality, look it in the face, take it into their
> being, bring it forth in a material medium, and show it to other men in a
> form which men can understand, are the forerunners of that new creation
> of beings who shall inhabit this earth, not as men, but as super-men,
> embodied not in matter but in spirit. And this is the conception which
> forces the belief that women are down, down, down in the scale of being.
> This is the belief which encourages us to wean them from their content-
> ment with the perpetuation always and all-time of the merely physical; this
> explains what we mean when we say life demands from them not merely

reproduction but achievement; that in the kingdom of the mind creation cannot be vicarious; why we preach individuality, not as a possible alternative to something else, but as a primal soul-necessity.[54]

Like the freewoman, the egoist would be a poetic invention, a complex trope that is most productively considered as the sign of a further recondite provocation. Such a transition into a heretical postfeminism, and specifically into a postsexual anarchism, would at least be in line with Marsden's own sense of the development of her "identity" or persona. On the first page of the second volume of the *Freewoman*, now subtitled *A Weekly Humanist Review,* Dora Marsden asserted a creed that many modernist writers were able to live with.

> *Where is life going?* All basic questions of conduct turn on the answer to that question. *We* think life is setting unmistakably in one direction. Give life chance enough, and it tends to show itself for what it is. It tends to assume individual form in the soul. This characterised, form-impregnated life with articulated differentiation is personality. A personality is no ordinary achievement. It is the biggest thing in creation. This differentiation appears to us to be cut out of the life-force itself, and unless obvious *soul-*deterioration sets in, it is not possible for this differentiated life to fall back into the undifferentiated whole. . . . The individual has no final guide, save the inner voice, and if he is deaf to that, he travels without chart or compass. That is the reason why freedom is demanded so constantly—that we may follow the voice. It is why we believe in free institutions, and why in the last resort we recognise there is no law save the law of our own being, why we are anarchists, in short.[55]

The Freewoman Discussion Circle

Sept 24 1912
Dear "Freewoman"

I have pleasure in enclosing 2 subscriptions & I have urged all my friends to *subscribe* as well as enjoy.

I think you ought to go to press earlier in the week. You certainly ought to be out in time to let the "Freewoman" circle have the new issue—it would mean a regular source of income every fortnight (I suppose the circle will meet every week if you become a propagandist paper)?

I greatly resented the removal of your subtitle a "Feminist" paper—and as I understand that Miss Marsden isn't perfectly contented with her new

THE
FREEWOMAN
A WEEKLY FEMINIST REVIEW

No. 26. Vol. I.　　　THURSDAY, MAY 16, 1912　　　THREEPENCE

[Registered at G.P.O. as a Newspaper.]　　　　　　　　　　*Editor:*
DORA MARSDEN, B.A.

CONTENTS

INTERPRETATIONS OF SEX.

III.

WE stated in a preceding article that the begetting of children was not the purpose of sexual love-passion. Only a misdirected scientific sense and a certain sense of shame have led us to put up this false line of explanation. Children are the product of the same kind of impulse as that which has led animal and plant to reproduce their kind. It is impossible to have a passion for the procreation of offspring. Perhaps the reason we cannot regard child-begetting as a passion lies in the fact that parents cannot *create* a child, and passion necessitates creation. They merely afford it an opportunity of appearing. They appear to have little influence upon the determination of the child's characteristics, its nature, or its endowment; and true morality—essential rightness—forbids even experimentation in such matters. The most we can lay claim to in the begetting of children is a strong speculative interest. We are amused, perhaps, to wonder what kind of offspring we should produce; what a certain kind of "crossing" would effect, and so on. But this is not passion. An interest is not a passion—a fact we must not lose sight of. A hobby is an occupation—something which fills the time. It is an affair of the intellect and fancy at most. If we consider the emotions of a person in love, we find that the idea of begetting children through the beloved is a jarring element; an element to which one concedes acquiescence after a struggle to keep the two elements apart. Strong-minded, sensible people, particularly moderns, take a sort of pride in asserting that, did we only know more accurately what we were about,

we should understand that to look "love" into another's eyes is essentially to look "babies." This is just what it "essentially" is not. Only when love has been baffled, not by attainment, but by the failure to appear of new peaks of attainment, does love fall back upon a culmination in the physical. What man or woman would exchange a fascinating courtship for the steady comforts and kindnesses of married life? How many have felt infinite regret when a relationship which has been pure joy has reached the stage when one or other has declared that it has gone as far as it can in the ideal direction—that the time has come to *do* something? Doubtless, the common-sense majority would support the one which felt that things had gone far enough in an ideal way, would support the one who asks for a sign—a reward. Ye gods! What a reward! A reward which strikes down a cup of water from the lips of a thirsty man. But the majority would not be right, except to this extent, *i.e.*, that caste is a real thing: that classes should not mix: that lover should find lover on his own level—which brings us to a consideration which will clear up many difficulties: the consideration of class. The inverted scale of value which holds good in social class conventions, whereby the parasite is ludicrously considered as of higher class than the producer, has made us fear to speak of class; or, if we speak of it, only to imply that the "lower" classes are better than the "upper." We cannot, however, safely or for long do without appeals to "class." For class implies standard, and absence of class implies absence of standard. What holds good in regard to class in the social world at the present time is that the standards are wrong, and the consequent class grades obviously ridiculous; but rather

The Freewoman *of May 16, 1912*

subtitle may I suggest your discarding it altogether Why not *"The Free-woman"*—why add to it?

You will certainly do the paper incurable injury if you call it Egoist or Individualist or Anarchist[56]

While Marsden's individualism was flowering, many of her readers preferred to socialize, and the community around the *Freewoman* coalesced briefly into the Freewoman Discussion Circle, another momentary creation Dora Marsden's tropes set into motion, a minor whorl in the fluid dynamics of radical London in 1912–13. Three months into the *Freewoman*'s run, at the end of an editorial appeal for readers to subscribe and enlist new subscribers, a second appeal on "'Freewoman' Clubs" appeared.

It has been pointed out to us by friendly critics that *The Freewoman* contains each week matter so highly debatable, and of such serious human import, that it is difficult to digest all that it contains, and to find one's bearings, in view of the many articles which express opposing points of view. It has been suggested, therefore, that *Freewoman* clubs, or informal gatherings of men and women, should be started for discussions, of which the weekly *Freewoman* would form the basis. Of this suggestion, coming from several readers, we highly approve, and pass it on to other readers for their consideration. (244)

As it turned out, the Freewoman Discussion Circle not only materialized, it also provided an organized support group that would outlast the lapse of the *Freewoman* proper in October 1912. Without the Freewoman Discussion Circle, the *New Freewoman* and the *Egoist* may never have existed. Specifically, Harriet Shaw Weaver was drawn into the Discussion Circle, and ultimately it was her financial support and organizational assistance that enabled Marsden to float the *New Freewoman* and kept the *Egoist* going as long as it did (Lidderdale and Nicholson, *Dear Miss Weaver*, 48-107). In addition, the Discussion Circle was an example of spontaneous, gregarious sociality, an anarchistic collectivity in counterpoint to Marsden's growing egoism and increasing reclusiveness, and so it offers a microcosm of the readership gathered by the *Freewoman* and eventually more or less abandoned by the *Egoist*.

Two of the "friendly critics" Marsden mentioned may have been Barbara Low and Guy Aldred. Low, who would later become a practicing analyst and author and translator of psychoanalytic works, had written Marsden early in February 1912: "I wish some of us *could* start something Co-operative. If only to show it can be. I am immensely interested in such a movement. How would it be to get all those who would join in such a scheme, to send in their names to the Paper? I believe we could do it in a Set of Flats, quite humbly and cheaply, without any great Funds & Buildings. What do you think?"[57] Five days later, Guy Aldred made the following communication.

> I have been thinking how best we could push the *Freewoman;* and I suggest the following plan. Its success largely depends on the extent of your London Circulation. Whenever the yiddish Anarchist paper, *The Worker's Friend*, wishes to raise funds it takes *The South Place Institute* for a weeknight lecture for £2/2/-; & it generally clears about £3 to £4 profit besides getting its propaganda known. I would deliver *free* a benefit lecture for you at this Hall, on, say a Friday night, if you made arrangements to take this hall. My lecture could be: "The Necessity for Sex Radicalism." . . . Among Anarchists, Freethinkers, & Socialists my name will "draw."[58]

The next week's *Freewoman* repeated the notice concerning "Freewoman clubs" and a week later published a letter with the same title signed B. L.: "It is absolutely impossible to digest properly such large topics as are treated in the paper, and I fear both writers and readers are in great danger of falling into superficial and vague generalities, without ever properly thrashing out any one subject" (291). Early in March, Marsden reported that "The Freewoman Clubs are started. They have sprung up almost spontaneously & I have already arranged for an Honorary Secretaryship."[59] The *Freewoman* for March 28 announced the formation of a discussion circle with a call for an organizational meeting on April 18; Barbara Low was named as secretary.

Clearly Marsden could have presided over the Discussion Circle and cultivated a certain body of disciples had she had any interest in doing so. Her anarchistic faith in self-organization was evident at the end of April when Marsden wrote her publisher, Charles Granville, who seems to have been miffed at not receiving an invitation to attend the circle: "I did not want any who were officially connected with the Freewoman to be much in evidence at the preliminary meeting as I want the clubs to run themselves. . . . It was therefore to my great amazement that instead of the twelve or 15 people we expected, abundant people crowded into a room to hold half that number, all intensely interested to accept responsibility in regard to the clubs. It was much to be regretted you were not there. You would have seen how impromptu the proceedings were (Alas! my speech!!)."[60] Marsden may have been lamenting a speech entitled

"The Evolutionary Meaning of the Freewoman," delivered at an early meeting, if not the first meeting, of the group. In any event, she devoted the "Topics of the Week" for May 26 to "Freewomen and Evolution," a lively rejoinder to the responses generated by this talk.[61]

Speaking in the third person, Marsden confessed that "there was a lack of definition in the address given by the Editor of *The Freewoman* . . . and to this fact doubtless is due the lack of agreement which led to such fiery argument" (503). I will draw out some of this discussion, because it presents germs of Marsden's own development toward the linguistic discourse of the *Egoist* and also because many readers today will have similar problems with Marsden's "spiritualism." Her meditation on the "fiery argument" at the Discussion Circle began with a reflection on existential temporality, the rapidity of intuitive intellect relative to the fixity of verbal signs: "The failure of language to advance parallel with the new differentiations of thought presents a problem of increasing dimensions and difficulty. . . . Indeed, for those of us who became involved in the multiplicity of meanings of the words 'spiritual' and 'material,' in a recent *Freewoman* discussion, we suggest the gradual compiling of a 'Select Glossary'" (503). In these remarks Marsden charted the course of her own development toward the projects of her "Lingual Psychology" and *Science of Signs* as pursued throughout the last four years of the *Egoist*. The linguistic mode of Marsden's individualism—the key to her egoistic semantics—is precisely this demand for *definition* in the midst of a progressive flux.

Marsden recounts that after her talk to the circle an "unsatisfied listener" had written to her.

> I feel so keenly that you did not answer my question—"What do you mean by spiritual?" I now ask you again if you will kindly enlighten me. . . .
>
> In your most interesting address, I understood you to say that the next development of man would be towards the man-woman, and the woman-man; that this will not, or may not, be achieved physically; that to achieve this end the procreation of the race is not necessary; although we may not see the non-sex man with mortal eye, we may see "it" in the spirit. We shall see "it" with the spiritual eye.
>
> Now, we ought to know what you mean by spiritual. Your answer was that the spiritual force was the life force—was that which made you start *The Freewoman,* the spirit that made man do and dare; the fire of life within us.
>
> Now, I beg, dear Madam, respectfully to say that that is no answer. (503)

Marsden's response to this request and her attempt at further definition constitute a remarkable tour de force in evolutionary vitalism from the perspective of
a feminist libertarian.

> The Man-Woman idea had nothing essentially to do with sex. We used it
> rather to show what elements women are bringing to the world's work,
> and what they were likely to acquire in a man-equipped world. Women
> do not come giftless. They bring the subtle, intuitive faculties which are
> virtually life-feelers, tentacles which push up into new conceptions of life
> without necessarily being conscious of the fact. . . . Life has no law, save
> that of its own being. It is not to be interpreted in accordance with laws of
> matter, a fact of which women are more aware than men, thanks to the
> freedom from the over-great struggle with the world of matter—of dead
> resistance—from which they have induced men to relieve them. What
> men will more and more learn from women is the Way of Life; what
> women are seeking in the haunts of men is a brain of their own. Knowing
> and Feeling join hands when women acquire the mentality of men, and
> when men understand, give a place to, and foster in themselves the intu-
> itive faculties of women. It is a combination of forces such as we recognise
> in creative geniuses already; such are, indeed, the firstfruits of the man-
> woman mentality. (503)

Marsden's bisexual or "intermediate" evolutionary ideal probably owed its most
immediate debt to Edward Carpenter, who had speculated in *The Art of Creation*
that "the *recovery* of the organic consciousness, the realisation of the *transparency*
of the body and the splendour of its intuitions, is not an impossible feat. . . . In
the West, the modern upgrowth of Woman and her influence will ere long
make possible a Humanity which shall harmonise even in each individual the
masculine and feminine elements" (109).[62] At the moment, the evolutionary
ideal of an intermediate sexual type helps explain Marsden's decision with the
second volume of the *Freewoman* to redefine her project by altering the subtitle
from *A Weekly Feminist Review* to *A Weekly Humanist Review*. This "humanism"
was in no way akin to our common notions of either classical or liberal humanism: for Marsden it meant strictly a "postfeminism." The humanist freewoman
would be the man-woman or woman-man who had evolved beyond the separatist dualities of patriarchal engendering. It should be remembered that Carpenter and Marsden formulated these androgynous ideals against the backdrop
of Victorian and Edwardian scientific and medical establishments, which held

that such gender indeterminacy was neither evolutionary nor progressive but ruinously degenerate.[63]

In a later paragraph of "Freewomen and Evolution," Marsden allegorized her vitalistic terms. Freedom, she declared, "is the Scout of Life. It is the outrider which goes before the king. It is the daring, deathless Child of the king. . . . Freedom is the first herald of the oncoming Pageant of Creation" (504). However, in this particular mythic scenario, Life—which had been identified previously with the feminine/intuitive "Way"—was now personified as male. Perhaps Marsden's archetypal gender switching was a purposeful enacting of the bisexual ideal of the man-woman: "Let us follow the pageant. Life in his chariot follows Freedom, and close after Life runs Knowledge, the faithful servant . . . [who] has so many things to tell of, behind, that he would rest awhile to tell them. But Freedom is rushing ahead, and Life is imperious" (504). Feeling runs ahead of knowledge, which lags behind life, but feeling and knowledge meet in and administer to life, which is also a definition of spirit.

> "Spirit" . . . meant not merely that more extended and less differentiated life-force which is found in every budding leaf and breathing animal. We meant rather that self-conscious spirit of man which lives and knows itself to be alive . . . the spirit which can turn round on itself and say, "I am I,—the living Being, and I know that I live."
>
> The Spirit is life-force made *self-conscious,* and it is self-consciousness which separates the human spirit from the sub-human life. Self-consciousness is the eye of the soul. . . . But the wonder of the "I am I" is passing. We have become familiarised with our own greatness as the crown of creation, and we are groping with the life tentacles, outward, to find the new sense of the soul. "I am I" is receding only to give place to "*What* am I?" When the struggling spirit has burst through this bond we shall no longer be men, we shall be supermen. We shall have moved to the "next stage on." (504)

So Marsden defined the vital/evolutionary prophecy of the freewoman. She must be free to teach as well as to learn those vital/spiritual qualities that when added to other human qualities already mastered can produce the further, bi- or postsexual stage of superhuman being. In the vocabulary of visionary allegory, Marsden reconfigures the superhuman or daemonic female—the freewoman—as the daemonic androgyne—the egoist.

At this stage in her mercurial career, then, Marsden expounded her femino-anarchistic egoism as a philosophy of androgyny, "one of the most ancient concepts of Western civilization, that of the original, harmonious, sexually integrated constitution of the person before being divided into the artificial, externalized opposites of male and female. The ideal of the androgyne expresses humanity's yearning to return to that primal state of perfect interior balance."[64] Later-twentieth-century Anglo-American feminism has severely criticized the androgynous ideal, especially as it dilutes or disrupts female gender solidarity for political purposes.[65] But early-twentieth-century literary modernism, particularly female modernism, was heavily invested in the exploration of bisexuality: "Women writers of the 1920s and 1930s deliberately transposed the male sexual metaphors into a feminist language. . . . Gender conventions lay at the heart of the confining traditions they, as modernists, fought against. Androgyny was their ideal."[66] Smith-Rosenberg's sketch of modernist androgyny is exactly that foreshadowed in 1912 by Dora Marsden's political evolution: female modernists like Virginia Woolf and Djuna Barnes were androgynous individualists who alienated themselves from socially effective forms of feminist solidarity. The literature of androgyny is more egoistic than socialistic.

Despite Marsden's recondite doctrinal provocations, as the frequent publication of Barbara Low's minutes attested, the Freewoman Discussion Circle was well established and flourishing without Marsden's personal involvement. In the June 27, 1912, number, a program was published detailing the circle's forthcoming activities (115).

July 3. Sex Oppression and the Way Out	*Mr. Guy Aldred*
July 17. Some Problems in Eugenics	*Mrs. Havelock Ellis*
July 31. The Problem of Celibacy	*Mrs. Gallichan*
Sept. 4. Neo-Malthusianism	*Dr. Drysdale*
Sept. 18. Prostitution	———
Oct. 2. The Abolition of Domestic Drudgery	*Mrs. Melvin and Miss Rona Robinson, M.Sc.*
Oct. 16. The Reform of the Divorce Laws	*Mr. E. S. P. Haynes*

After the demise of the *Freewoman*, Marsden moved to Ainsdale, Southport, a coastal town north of Liverpool, and communicated by letter with its active remnant, the Discussion Circle. The nineteen-year-old Rebecca West had published many accomplished pieces in the *Freewoman*.[67] An avid member of the circle, she wrote Marsden some fine letters describing these meetings:

The Discussion Circle is quaint. That dandy of cranks, D'Auvergne, is always jumping up demanding that we should all be kind to illegitimate children, as if we all made a habit of seeking out illegitimate infants and insulting them. And there is the funniest person, a Swede called Hugo Dick, who plays a continual card game: he produces tickets for demonstrations of cosmogonous rhythmic dancing and presses them into your hand, dealing them all round the Circle. Stella Browne sends me horoscopes occasionally. I am to "form a union with an American" and "not wear Chinese curios." So the path of life is clear before me.[68]

Ultimately, the Freewoman Discussion Circle enabled the seed of Marsden's next developments to winter over the collapse of the *Freewoman*. It gathered together two crucial players in the recovery of Marsden's journalistic career, Rebecca West and Harriet Shaw Weaver. And, during its own brief existence, it also confirmed the original inspiration of the *Freewoman*'s creator, that an open forum of free debate between women and men would bring forth some unaccountable issue of "vivid new life-manifestations."

The Otto Weininger Provocation

In the "New Woman as Androgyne" chapter of *Disorderly Conduct*, Carroll Smith-Rosenberg discusses the manipulation of female types by various patriarchal cultural institutions. To begin with, by the 1870s, the type of the "new woman" was well established as a social category for the Victorian generation of college-educated career women such as Jane Addams and Lillian Wald. However,

with the 1890s male physicians and social critics initiated a new wave of attacks upon the respectability and legitimacy of the New Woman. . . . [They] shifted the definition of female deviance from the New Woman's rejection of motherhood to their rejection of men. From being "unnaturally" barren, the autonomous woman, outside of heterosexual marriage, emerged as "unnaturally" sexual. Adopting the novel "scientific" categories of the European sexologists, British and American physicians and scientists insisted that unmarried career women and political activists constituted an "intermediate sex." They violated normal gender categories. They fused the female and the male. (265)

The sexological intermediate type was then deployed to define the new woman as an androgyne, a cultural inscription of hypothetical bisexuality variously

THE
FREEWOMAN
A WEEKLY HUMANIST REVIEW

No. 36. VOL. II.   THURSDAY, JULY 25, 1912   THREEPENCE

[Registered at G.P.O.]
[As a Newspaper.]

Editor:
DORA MARSDEN, B.A.

CONTENTS

THE POOR AND THE RICH.

THE machinations of the Rich against the Poor are malicious, ubiquitous, unending. They conspire against them with a zest which could only be born of a lack of any sense of kinship. The Poor can no longer step outside their hovels in safety. The agents of the Rich are watching them, ready to pounce on them and hale them off to some "certified" detention-house. If their tongues loll, if their heads wag, if they are shaky at the knees, if they get drunk, if they have not the business capacity for getting something for nothing, or if any of their ancestors for a few generations back have been guilty of such-like misdemeanours, the agent of the Rich will seize them, and with little more ado, chain them up for life. And these villainies, which have long been hatching in the minds of the Rich, are to be placed under the ægis of the law. Law, of course, has one purpose, which is to make the Poor powerless in the hands of the Rich, and it is not therefore a matter for surprise that the damnably wicked Feeble-Minded Bill has passed its second reading in the House of Commons with only a handful of members in opposition. The law is definitely against the Poor; and it is now up to the Poor to smash the law. The retort of the Poor against the Rich Men's law is lynch-law. The Poor will be compelled to make their own law, avenge their own honour, and administer their own justice. When they do, it is to be hoped they will accord but short shriving to the authors of this Bill. Happily, they are known. In a report which was published a short time ago, these evil-doers in their own haunts met together and boasted of their evil deeds. The Eugenics Education Society is a danger to the community.

Lost alike to a sense of justice, prudence, and shame, they boast, in their annual report, of being the authors of this rascally conspiracy against the poor.

"The year 1911-12 is likely to stand out as one of the most important in the history of the Eugenics Education Society. Its record of work accomplished affords abundant proof of the value of the educational campaign carried on by the society during the last four years in creation of a sound eugenic public opinion. The fact that the first International Eugenics Congress should be held in London with what appears to be every promise of success is a striking testimony to the interest taken in this subject. The aims which it exists to further have already won acceptance in the sphere of practical politics. Indeed, one of the most gratifying features in connection with the Congress is the membership of official delegates representing Government departments. And the attitude of the press generally towards the recent Feeble-Minded Control Bill indicates that the people of the nation are not behind their legislators in being alive to the necessity of determined eugenic action. Apart from the Congress three items in the year's work call for particular mention: (1) On December 5th, 1911, a non-party meeting, arranged by Mr. Walter Rea, M.P., was held to consider the Feeble-Minded Control Bill, prepared by a Joint Committee of the National Association for the Care of the Feeble-Minded and this society. Later a letter was sent to all members of Parliament. Grateful mention also should be made of the energetic way in which members of this society canvassed their members, in order to obtain support for the Bill, with the happy result that Mr. Gresham Stewart drew eleventh place in the ballot for private members' Bills, and presented the Feeble-Minded Control Bill to the House of Commons. It was read a condemned as pathological or celebrated as revolutionary depending on the sexual orientation of those receiving these medical discourses as the latest scientific word. Sexologists such as Krafft-Ebing and Havelock Ellis proceeded to delineate androgynetic subtypes: Krafft-Ebing "divided lesbianism into four categories or degrees of homosexual deviance" (Smith-Rosenberg, *Disorderly Conduct*, 270), while Ellis distinguished between congenital "inverts" and non-congenital "homosexuals" whose sexual inclinations resulted from their innate bias being triggered by the contagious proximity of an invert.

The discussion of Otto Weininger in the *Freewoman* began within a side debate carried on between Harry J. Birnstingl, who came forward as a spokesperson for "intermediate sexual types," and Charles J. Whitby, M.D., an invited respondent who debated Birnstingl regarding homosexuality but was otherwise generally supportive of women's emancipation. First, Birnstingl contributed an article entitled "'Uranians,'" drawing on Edward Carpenter's *Intermediate Sex* in order to make his case for the tolerance and appreciation of "Urning men and women": "Nature, that much-abused female, who has been adopted by the Philistines to be the synonym of rank conservatism, abhors rules and regulations with as much intensity as she hates the proverbial vacuum. She casts her goods recklessly amongst us mortals. Consequently we have in our midst a class of people who hover, as it were, midway between the sexes, and their position in society is as yet undefined."[69] Birnstingl's "Nature" is a rebellious power: here is the (r)evolutionary view of the political progressive countering the classical conservative view of a "Nature" in organic but not in formal flux. The general point of the argument is that, since homosexuality is a "natural" variation, it is neither pathological nor immoral. Birnstingl's specific application was to the "Woman's Freedom movement," whose opponents "draw attention to the numbers of women in the ranks of the agitators who are celibates and childless, and who seem insensible to the passion of love, thus, they declare, leaving unfilled the greatest mission in life. It apparently has never occurred to them that numbers of these women find their ultimate destiny, as it were, amongst members of their own sex" (128). As Carpenter did, Birnstingl celebrated this phenomenon as an affirmation of progressive modernity: "It is splendid that these women, who hitherto have been unaware of their purpose . . . should suddenly find their destiny in thus working together for the freedom of their sex. It is one of the most wonderful things of the twentieth century" (128).

Two weeks later, in a contribution entitled "Tertium Quid," Dr. Whitby began by praising the *Freewoman* for letting "the light of day into these dark and dusty corners. . . . The difficulty seems to be that homosexuality is one of those subjects which those who are competent to discuss would prefer to leave alone. This factor of competency I possess; as to any others—well, at all events, I am a medical man! So that I do not feel justified in declining an editorial invitation to deal, from the medical standpoint, with the subject of Mr. Birnstingl's essay."[70] Clearly it was Dora Marsden who arranged for Whitby's response, and I imagine that she intended to relish the sparks that would fly between these various male sympathizers with the *Freewoman*, between the gay earnestness of Birnstingl and the magnificent medical and heterosexual arrogance of Dr. Whitby.[71] Drawing on the technical vocabulary of Krafft-Ebing's sexology, Whitby proceeded to inform Birnstingl that "Genius is androgynous, but it is never homosexual. A man of genius may be feminine, but he must *not* be effeminate" (168). Whitby did not directly address the matter of lesbianism as an aspect or outcome of women's emancipation. He discounted the hereditary or congenital as well as the spiritual factor in favor of environmental explanations for the emergence of homosexuality in either sex: "marriage is to thousands of educated men and women an economic impossibility. . . . The passional and affective part of their natures, thus denied its natural outlet, seeks alternative satisfaction. Homosexual alliances are to be regarded as the euthanasia of love" (168).

Birnstingl's reply took issue with Whitby's ideas but also thanked him for his willingness to air the subject of homosexuality in public discussion: "These people Dr. Whitby strongly disapproves of, and I do not; but he approves of the mutual adoption of certain qualities. Therefore Dr. Whitby and myself only differ in a matter of degree."[72] A week later Whitby responded: "No, Mr. Birnstingl, the difference between us is not a difference of degree. It is either fundamental or nothing—I am not quite sure which."[73] Birnstingl had upped the ante by implying a certain healthy continuity between the "intermediate" and the "pure" sexual types—between himself and Whitby. So Whitby started throwing down his high cards: he steered the issue to a point from which he could vent an anxiety over the idea of a merging or exchange of gender indications: "once let a man overstep the line which divides femininity"—which is an organic "endowment"—"from the least suspicion of effeminacy"—which is an affectation or "aping"—"and he will incur the aversion, yes, and the downright contempt of his fellow-men. It is no idiosyncrasy of taste on my part which makes me feel and write thus: it is the ineradicable instinct which warns us to shun the conditions that make for decadence and disease" ("Matter of Taste," 216).

In this context, Whitby then cited Otto Weininger's theories of sex affinity, which he assumed were so well known as to need no attribution to their source, *Sex and Character*.

I shall not easily admit that a human being may be anatomically male and physiologically or psychologically female. . . . Nor does Weininger's theory of sex-affinity, rightly understood, support such a contention. If we take the sexual formula of a true hermaphrodite as 50M + 50F, and that of an extremely feminine male as 51M + 49F, it is obvious that the nearest affinity of the latter will be a *woman* with the formula 51F + 49M. . . . But Weininger's theory, after all, needs confirmation; and, assuming its adequacy, does not help us much, seeing that we are miles removed from the position of being able to form a quantitative estimate of the sexual make-up of a given individual. Moreover, it is to be remembered that Weininger was very far from regarding the sex-differentiation as a *mere* matter of degree. (216)

Whitby's halfhearted recourse to Weininger's theories of gender notwithstanding, his argument came down to a thermodynamic turn with a stern eugenic flourish. In the matter of homosexuality, "taste" must defer to "ineradicable instincts": "There can be no question but that we are at present engaged in a new revision of our traditional tastes. . . . I hope that we shall stop short of disregarding those deep-seated instincts which warn us from the sloping edge of the abyss of vital dissipation and racial ruin" (216).

The discussion of Weininger within the pages of the *Freewoman* emerged as the product and the sign of a male anxiety over the cultural consequences of sexual unconventionality or extreme lapses from patriarchal arrangements. Weininger's theories were closely connected to the punitive eugenics of Nordau and Lombroso, the regressivist obverse inscribed beneath evolutionary progressivism, inhabiting Vernon Lee's subscription to "the later Darwinism." That these anxieties regularly rose to the rhetorical violence of Whitby's apocalyptic tones indicates as well the social violence bound up with Whitby's prejudices. Birnstingl's final retort to Whitby wisely ignored the degenerationist fantasies while considering "that it is to be deeply deplored that those people who discuss this subject from an unsympathetic standpoint dwell with such tedious and unnecessary persistency upon the physical side of the question," as in Whitby's irrelevant asides on the theatrics of effeminacy.[74] But Birnstingl did indicate that Weininger's gender formulas could be turned to support either side of the debate: "Now with regard to the Weininger theory of sexual attraction—a theory, by the way, in which I have not over much faith, for I do not believe that these things can be decided mathematically. . . . The amount of feminine plasm in a man (thelyplasm) is not limited to half the total amount of sex in that man. It is by no means inconceivable that a man should be composed 30M + 70F (taking 100 as our total), in which case his complement would be a man or a

woman 70M + 30F" ("Human Minority," 235).[75] But both men brought
Weininger to bear on the question of homosexuality without mentioning that
the main thrust of *Sex and Character* was to expound the philosophical bases of
a rational misogyny.

The two topics are separable because Weininger divided *Sex and Character*
into two parts: the preliminary, ostensibly scientific and medical discussion of
intermediate sexual types to which Birnstingl and Whitby were referring, and
the main, philosophical discussion of pure, or "absolute," masculine and feminine types. In the first part, Weininger advocated tolerance: "Sexual inverts
must be brought to sexual inverts, from homo-sexualists to Sapphists, each in
their grades. Knowledge of such a solution should lead to repeal of the ridiculous laws of England, Germany and Austria" (51). But this was an incidental
point. The structure of Weininger's ideal sexual polarities automatically generated an "intermediate realm" wherein intermingled the pure extremes—the
male and female "plasms." Thus, the ostensible, or "natural," bisexuality of any
organism and the gender-algebra of individual formulas were simply stations on
the way to his primary arguments in the second part over the moral negativity
of the feminine type, which demanded an intolerance of feminist politics: "the
idea of making an emancipation party, of aiming at a social revolution, must be
abandoned. Away with the whole 'women's movement,' with its unnaturalness
and artificiality and its fundamental errors" (71).

In the *Freewoman* of April 4, 1912, Dora Marsden addressed Weininger
directly for the first time.[76] Perhaps she was responding to the Birnstingl-
Whitby debate as well as to the eminent physician Sir Almroth Wright's letter
to the London *Times* about "militant hysteria," which Marsden reprinted in its
entirety in the same issue (392–93).[77] Again playing the role of devil's advocate
for antifeminism she had promulgated in the first "Notes of the Week," Marsden deployed Weininger as a kind of sarcastic taunt to Wright and other establishment exponents of indigenous scientistic misogyny, a challenge to British
antifeminists to achieve the supposed logical clarity of the Germans.

> With a Queen on the throne, with the clinging Victorians hanging about
> them, the air thick with romanticism, . . . with Tennyson solving feminism
> according to "The Princess," how could Englishmen find the face to tell
> the small handful of women fighting for the higher education of their sex
> what they thought was their true station in the scheme of things? How
> could they tell the delicate, lovely, drooping women that they were
> lunatics twelve times a year, as was amiably suggested some time ago in the
> House of Commons and as Sir Almroth Wright with praiseworthy

courage puts it to-day? Unlike the German, for instance, the Englishman
missed his opportunity of confessing his soul. The German, in Schopen-
hauer, Nietzsche and Weininger, is prepared beforehand for any uprising
of German women, coming as it does more than a generation behind ours.
Has any one in England dared to speak such views as Weininger here
bespeaks, far as we have gone towards being submerged in the rising sea of
feminism? (381)

Marsden cited several passages from *Sex and Character*'s chapter 12, "The Nature
of Woman and Her Significance in the Universe": "the abstract male is the
image of God, the absolute something; the female and the female element in the
male, is the symbol of nothing." She then concluded, "What Englishman has
the courage and clarity to speak his inmost thoughts like that?" (382).

Marsden must have considered such drastic irony to be a fit rejoinder to
the medical misogyny of Dr. Wright. Moreover, in what I am calling the Otto
Weininger provocation, we see Marsden's counterironic premium on straight
talk, her revolutionary desire to blast through polite reserve and reveal through
bare utterance the full extent of the sexual antipathies at large in Western culture. Here again, Marsden has transferred to the discursive arena of the *Freewoman* components of militant political strategy, provocations intended to
expose the true face of the patriarchal state, to induce the establishment to show
its heavy hand, and to remind the feminist rebel not to harbor unrealistically
low estimates of the resistance she faces. Marsden saw clearly enough that
Wright and Weininger's articulate misogyny had its use as a gauge of the underlying virulence of masculinist reaction. For Marsden at the moment,
Weininger's antifeminism was a potent if bitter tonic, a Nietzschean *pharmakon*
intended to counteract the sentimentalisms that anesthetize the radical will, if
the radical feminist could be induced to swallow it.

Perhaps it was to that end that Marsden arranged for the concluding chapter of *Sex and Character* to be published in two installments in the *Freewoman* for
April 25 and May 2, 1912.[78] Marsden prefaced the first installment with this
note: "As there is no serious anti-feminist in England, and as it has been pointed
out to us an extract which we recently quoted from Weininger was calculated
to give only the apparent absurdities of his theory, we are glad to be able to
reprint the last chapter of this work—the one which best renders the idealism
underlying Weininger's philosophy" (452). At the end of the second installment
was this brief notice: "We hope to give a criticism of Weininger's work very
shortly" (473). The "idealism underlying Weininger's philosophy" was its celebration of the cosmic separateness of the immortal personality. Weininger's ide-

alism is also an atavism of Neoplatonism and quite explicitly an adaptation of Kantian moral categories to the polar electrical models developed in Schelling's Naturphilosophie and more largely in romantic and vitalist medical speculation. The manifest trick of Weininger's sexual idealism was to construct the conceptual "types" of the male and female as absolutely polar and exclusive categories, to elevate the male type as cosmic positivity—"form"—and abase the female type as cosmic negativity—"matter"—to give lip service to the recognition that neither the "absolute male" nor the "absolute female" has any actual existence, and then to strap his sexual anthropology onto the rack of his moral absolutisms.[79] Thus, Weininger could indulge in misogynistic generalizations about the given world of given women while maintaining that he was simply distilling the conceptual type of the "female element" from the mass of concrete female "tendencies": "I shall hope to be acquitted of false generalisations if it be remembered that what I have been saying relates to the female element, and is true in the same proportion that women possess that element" (*Sex and Character*, 215).

In the meantime, at one end of the gender spectrum, Dr. Whitby rose to the occasion.

> If one could speak of the "traditions" of a journal which numbers its existence in weeks, one would say that the publication of a chapter of Weininger's great and terrible masterpiece in *The Freewoman* was worthy of them. It was a characteristic display of intellectual courage and good faith, upon which my heartiest congratulations to all concerned. Women have to face the fact that a man of genius thought so meanly of them; and I am glad to find that they face it in so absolutely the right spirit. . . . I agree that a false philosophy of sex is more complimentary to women than the wishwash of sentiment and condescension that usurps its place in this country.[80]

Whitby grasped some of Marsden's editorial motivations accurately enough, and he concluded his evaluation of Weininger with a vitalist flourish of his own: Weininger's "root-error is the presumption of the logician who thinks to restrain the life-impulse within the cast-iron trammels of categorical imperatives and such-like formal monstrosities."[81] At the other end of the spectrum was a letter, signed "True Womanhood," printed in the correspondence column of the *Freewoman* of May 30.

> Madam,—I am at a loss to understand your object in giving scope in your pages to the monstrous theories—misnamed "philosophy"—of Weininger regarding women. It is a shame that such revolting and degrad-

ing views should ever find space anywhere in print, but that they should be quoted, and without condemnation, in an avowedly feminist journal, seems incredible. . . . I repeat—I cannot understand your procedure. What possible good is to be accomplished by giving place (and space) to error, unrebuked? . . . Let us rise up and assert the pride and power of our womanhood—a spiritual power destined to lead men out of darkness into light.[82]

"True Womanhood" mistook the devil's advocate for the devil, but it was clearly a sore issue. Not only were Marsden's ironic devices difficult for the broader mass of an earnest readership to grasp, but it may be suspected that her ironic distance was itself in danger of collapsing. Another, unpublished letter, from "A.H." to Marsden, raised a similar issue in more sophisticated terms: "I *do* hope there is no more of the W.S.P.U. this week. After all cannot you regard it as the forcing house of feminism? You have *been* through it & others are now *going* through it. Moreover men hang together (*don't* they my word!) & so let us learn from them. . . . They love to see us at each other's throats. They feel their cherished empire will last all the longer for it."[83] "A.H." and "True Woman-hood" both made futile pleas for doctrinal solidarity, for Marsden's pulling together with the feminist ranks in the insurrection against patriarchy's "cher-ished empire." But Marsden's "procedure" already depended exactly on the refusals to solidify, to rest theoretically on any one manifesto, to cling to any one collectivity—including the suffragist and feminist communities as consti-tuted in England in 1912. Pursuing a politics of self-empowerment through the existential spontaneity of an anarchistic egoism, "individuality" had already become her idée fixe.

When Marsden finally provided her promised critique of Weininger, she remarked how the positive scientific claims of his misogyny collapsed into the nominal fictiveness of his ideal constructions, his elements and types: "'Female-ness,' as Weininger defined it, is the Thing to be Destroyed. It is the Great Denial—the thing to be overcome. But this 'femaleness' has no special kinship with the females of the human species."[84] In addition, I think Marsden would have been especially sensitive to the following caveat Weininger issued toward the end of *Sex and Character*, in which he admitted that, in terms of the cate-gorical deductive logic at play in his arguments, one proven exception exploded the universality of his major premises: "It is clear," Weininger wrote, eerily anticipating his suicide by pistol at the age of twenty-three, "that if only one single female creature were really asexual, or could be shown to have a real rela-tionship to the idea of personal moral worth, everything that I have said about

woman, its general value as psychically characteristic of the sex, would be irre-
trievably demolished, and the whole position which this book has taken up
would be shattered at one blow" (261). The universal typifications of
Weininger's characterology functioned exactly to produce spurious essences, to
imprint stereotypical masculinist prejudices onto the "Idioplasm" of the "race."
Perhaps Dora Marsden took it upon herself to be the exception that demolished
Weininger's rules.[85] But to demolish them, in some degree she would have to
subscribe herself to them.

Placated it would seem by Weininger's ostensible tolerance for intermediate types and drawn to his praise of individual genius and the immortal soul, the
devil's advocate found a way to redeem the devil. Marsden's "Sex and Character" leader declared: "the powers of his genius hacked through the amorphous
mass of human contradictions until they rang out clear upon the one great
human affirmation, Personality" (61). Although Marsden recognized that
Weininger's gender marking of "male" and "female" elements was entirely spurious, Weininger had affixed that superficial sexual polarity to an ontological
polarity the vitalist premises of which Marsden emphatically endorsed.

> Weininger, the poet, heard, and might have given to humanity a mighty
> gospel of deliverance. Unhappily, this youth, who saw so penetratingly the
> literally damned nature of all prostitution, was lured away by the popular
> acceptation of the word prostitute. He gave up to sex what was meant for
> mankind. In the world, he saw, there were two tendencies, the Down, the
> Up; the Death, the Life; the Moral, the Immoral; the Bound, the Free; the
> Pro-Personality-Tendency and the Anti-Personality-Tendency; and to all
> this dualism of principles, to all these unlimited sets of opposites, he postu-
> lated human analogues in Man and Woman, Male and Female—his M.
> and F. Let the Pro-Personality-Tendency be called male, says Weininger
> in effect, and let the Anti-Personality-Tendency be called female, and, this
> granted, he proceeds to pour forth his diatribe against women. (61)

In effect, Marsden deconstructed Weininger's binary gender physics only to
reinvest in his electro-vital metaphysics of ego-idealism. The masculinism
engrained in the Western metaphysical tradition rises vigorously to the surface
of Weininger's scientistic discourse, not as a sexist aberration but as a flat declaration of phallocentric prejudice raised into a cosmic scheme. Marsden's reckless attempt to turn her apparatus of provocation against his sexism ended up
further precipitating her own withdrawal from the discourse of gender altogether. As far as Marsden was now concerned, "the status of men and women
defined by personality has nothing to do with sex" (63).

In the fall of 1912, when a distributor's boycott had precipitated the near collapse of the *Freewoman,* the long-suffering Mary Gawthorpe sent Marsden a letter marked "Between us," offering a strong critique of the journal and some detailed advice about its possible reform.

> I gather from the paper, and from a message received from a friend whose financial aid I had been seeking on behalf of the paper, that prospects are not exactly rosy. . . . But I ask permission to say a few very personal things about you and your paper. . . . The first six months work was written out of the fullness of *heart* and brain together. Within recent times you have been working on your brains and flogging them into the bargain. . . . In some way or other you *must* be relieved of the housework of the weekly rush. You must be relieved of it because otherwise the real D.M. will never come to her own. The real D.M. is a poet and the sooner you realize this aspect of yourself the better.[86]

Mary Gawthorpe would now play a pivotal early role in moving Marsden toward the literary orbit of the *New Freewoman.* When the *Freewoman* was being planned in 1911, Marsden had relied heavily on Gawthorpe's connections with A. R. Orage and the *New Age.*[87] Despite her appearing for a time on the masthead as coeditor, Gawthorpe had been too ill from severe manhandlings endured during WSPU demonstrations to take up any major responsibilities for the *Freewoman,* but she continued to promote the enterprise behind the scenes. Now she advanced the idea of a less topical approach, perhaps not entirely out of disinterested motives, for she had had to take some abuse from her suffragette colleagues for her association with the *Freewoman*'s vehement critiques of the WSPU. In this letter she began to sketch out the shape of the *New Freewoman.*

> If I had the means and you were not averse from the proposals I would make *The Freewoman* a fighting weapon for a pure disinterested individualism on such lines as these:—
>
> 1. I would enlist Mr. Carter as co-editor and give his organising powers scope subject to your agreement.
> 2. I would ask Mr. Norman e.g. to do a weekly review of the week's politics.
> 3. I would ask Mr. [———?], Mr. Upward, Dr. Whitby, and Miss West to give their best regular thinking to the paper.
> 4. I would make it unnecessary for D.M. to do more for the weekly rush than the valuable philosophic commentaries on her reader's positions where they reflected upon Current Events.

5. Her best work being the fruit of leisure I would accept as it
   grew—a middle-page feature of permanent value!

C. H. Norman had been a regular contributor to the _Freewoman_ on political and economic issues. Huntly Carter and Allen Upward were _New Age_ connections of varying degrees of prominence. Carter's drama reviews began
appearing in the late days of the _Freewoman_ and became a regular feature in the
New Freewoman and, to a lesser degree, in the _Egoist._ A symbolist aesthete
unsympathetic to the futurists, and later to the imagists, he was given to soggy
effusions over "art and the soul," but philosophically he was not out of line with
Marsden's sibylline side. Upward—belletrist, popular novelist, a kind of anthro-
pological journalist and jack of all disciplines, with special interests in Confucius
and comparative mythology—had significant publications to his credit.[88]
Through Gawthorpe, the _New Freewoman_ would establish a relationship with
Upward and publish his material, in all probability an incentive for Ezra Pound
to initiate and maintain his own involvement with the journal.

Gawthorpe had declared earlier in the letter:

> If I could have my way I would surround you with a great ocean of quiet-
> ness (note: not stagnation) and I would provide you with means for leisure
> (note: not laziness). In such an atmosphere the steady quiet crystallization
> of the ideas of your fertile brain should take place. You should have time
> to qualify as a medical woman not for purposes of practice; but that you
> might, _with authority,_ meet the medical materialists in one or two mighty
> _world_-battles on woman's (and man's behalf). You should give the _reply_
> (not merely criticism) to Weininger for example in a book as big as his
> own. You should meet united current medical criticism and in addition
> illuminate the darkness of present medical sense (and nonsense). In other
> words you should _see_ for us and as a see-r you should break a thousand
> erroneous values for every one that _your present methods_ but harden in resis-
> tance ten thousandfold!

Mary Gawthorpe neatly outlined the drawbacks of Dora Marsden's _Freewoman_
strategies of provocation: the fluidity of the provocateur notwithstanding, many
of those provoked will not rise to the intellectual or ironic demands being
made, but will "harden in resistance." And as the Otto Weininger provocation
demonstrated, there is also a certain danger that the devil's advocate will be
seduced by the devil.

We have already noted Marsden's endemic ideological mobility. Well before the Weininger provocation, the terms of her individualist developments were explicitly in place. Is Marsden's literary and philosophical drift only a belated reversion, by way of Weininger's misogyny and Stirner's egoism, to an aestheticized masculinism? Is the trajectory of the *Freewoman* toward the *Egoist* merely an antifeminist apostasy? The matter cannot be reduced simply to these terms, but neither can it be extricated completely from them. My reader may place the emphases where she likes. In partial defense of Marsden's intentions, if not her methods, I would situate them as a kind of postsuffragist project, a discursive negotiation over the terms and categories of radical action and debate. Marsden was perhaps unique in her time for her concerted and deliberate conceptual attempt, in arguing these terms, to propose not just redefinitions but new terms, foremost of which was the freewoman. Given the sociological milieu in which she began to formulate her discourse, it is not surprising that few could fully appreciate the "poetic" nature of her project. What Mary Gawthorpe may not have intended, but what Marsden seems to have grasped, is that the "poetic" side of the "real D.M." was also the egoist, the sibyl of personality within whose journalistic folds so many future luminaries of Anglo-American modernist literature would soon gather.

3

The *New Freewoman:* Abandoning the Phrases

"The Moving Impulse"

Early Modernist History: Some Revisions

By the summer of 1913, at the age of thirty-one, Dora Marsden had already graduated from the University of Manchester, abandoned a career as a head schoolmistress, gone to prison for acts of civil disobedience committed in the cause of suffragism, been thrown out of the WSPU for insubordination, brought an unprecedented radical weekly journal into existence, and systematically articulated in her lead articles throughout the *Freewoman* a "gospel" of self-empowerment. With the manifold aid of Harriet Shaw Weaver, she had successfully revived the feminist weekly as an individualist biweekly. Nevertheless, it has often been assumed that when Ezra Pound began to work with the *New Freewoman* that summer he encountered no significant intellectual resistance and simply commandeered Marsden's journalistic operation to make propaganda for imagism. Such misimpressions have unduly obscured the extent of Dora Marsden's role in modernist literary history.

Mary Gawthorpe's letter of September 29, 1912, proclaiming that "the real D.M. is a poet," must have made a serious impression on its recipient. It is likely that Marsden was already hoping to cultivate further the literary aspect of the journal when, early in 1913, Rebecca West set forth her own ideas to Marsden about the content of the yet-to-be resuscitated *New Freewoman:* "I have been looking over old copies of The Freewoman, and I notice there was no literary side to it at all. Visiak and my still small voice were the only notes of dissent in a storm of purely moral and intellectual enthusiasm."[1] West was exaggerating somewhat, since the *Freewoman* had contained a considerable amount of literary and dramatic criticism, not the least of which was her own. She meant specifically that with the exception of a smattering of unmemorable lyrics, there had been no creative literary side to the journal. Her letter continued:

> A literary side would be a bribe to the more frivolous minded in London, and I don't see why a movement towards freedom of expression in literature should not be associated with and inspired by your gospel. . . . If The [New] Freewoman is really coming out on March 27th we've none too much time. Don't you think the best thing would be to issue some kind of statement about the *literary* side of the paper and send it out to writers (not necessarily famous or even well-known) accompanied by a personal note. It is so vague just to ask people to write for The Freewoman.

So the young Rebecca helped to lay down a welcome mat for the not-so-frivolous upstart Pound and wound up personally brokering his working relationship with Marsden, although West later regretted having done so. As if on cue, Pound appeared on the scene complete with impressive credentials: sizable publications, good connections, a bit of a coterie with an articulated manifesto, and a money man in the wings. West's introduction to Pound "was made, early in the summer of 1913, at one of Violet Hunt's literary parties in her house on Campden Hill" (Lidderdale and Nicholson, *Dear Miss Weaver*, 66). West then bid Pound write to Marsden, or perhaps Marsden write to Pound, about the possibility of his delivering literary material to the *New Freewoman*.

West's own memoir concerning Pound's arrival on the scene is not wholly reliable. She recalled that after the lapse of the *Freewoman* late in 1912 "Dora Marsden and her flock were homeless for a time. Then odd people turned up and financed it, and it was reissued as 'The Egoist,' of which paper I was literary editor. That did not last long. My position seemed to me impossible. The routine of the office was not impeccable. There was an *arrivist* American poet who intended to oust me, and his works and those of his friends continually appeared in the paper without having passed me" ("The Freewoman," 649).[2] In fact, West was the first literary editor not of the *Egoist* but of the *New Freewoman*. Pound was the second. And, if the work Pound forwarded appeared without having passed by West, that does not mean that it had not passed by Dora Marsden. Rather, as editor-in-chief, Marsden simply allowed Pound to assume West's functions. West at this moment was increasingly distracted by her affair with H. G. Wells. When a few months later Marsden took on Pound's protégé Richard Aldington as subeditor, West was understandably furious: "Richard Aldington, isn't it? That set has a sweet intention of buying us when our money runs low, getting rid of *me* and then of *you*."[3] She was not far wrong, but as matters turned out Marsden was not to be dislodged.

The canonical masculinist misreading of Pound's relation to Marsden's projects was first set forth by Glenn Hughes in *Imagism and the Imagists*. He wrote that when the phallic "eye of the imagists" espied the *New Freewoman*, "the shrewd Mr. Pound convinced the two philosophical feminists that what they needed for their publication was an up-to-date literary department. Forthwith an agreement was reached under the terms of which the literary group was to do as it liked with the whole paper, except for the leading article, which was always to be written by Miss Marsden. . . . What she wrote had not the slightest connection with the other contents of the paper" (31–32).[4] At the most, these statements retroactively fulfilled a certain aggressive desire on the imagists' part. What Hughes's informants were papering over may be partly recovered in a letter H.D. sent to Amy Lowell, detailing the imminent Special Imagist Number of the *Egoist* for May 1, 1915: "R[ichard] has done his best for that blooming old Egoist—though I know how disappointed you & Fletcher will be to see Miss M[arsden] on the first page. I assure you we both fought hard enough—But Miss Weaver runs the paper for Dora Marsden—swears by her—and R. is after all only subeditor!" (quoted in Hanscombe and Smyers, *Writing for Their Lives*, 175).[5] Hughes's account has contaminated most later attempts to adjudicate the responsibility for the transformation of the *New Freewoman* into the *Egoist*.

It is often thought that in this instance, to the lasting benefit of modern letters, Pound simply steamrollered the frail, reclusive, and cranky Marsden into submission. Timothy Rogers's compound misstatement is a typical example of a commentator unwilling to look beyond Pound's or Aldington's condescension and read what is printed in the *New Freewoman*: "typical of [Pound's] achievements was the persuasion of Dora Marsden . . . to change the title of her paper to 'The Egoist,' and transform it from a periodical devoted to woman's suffrage and woman's place in society to one which was to give most of its space to the support of Imagist poets."[6] Even critics unburdened with Hughes's biases and familiar with Marsden's political background and intellectual tenacity have tended to underestimate her editorial will and doctrinal resolve. A recent feminist misreading of the Marsden/Pound relation is quite similar to the canonical version just mentioned but with heroes and villains reversed: to the unfortunate but predictable setback of women's discourse, an exhausted and ailing Marsden was snookered by a shameless proto-totalitarian who proceeded "to organize, to claim, and finally to control the *New Freewoman*" (Barash, "Dora Marsden's Feminism," 49).

These hardy misconceptions about Marsden's responsibilities and the credit owed to her for the shape and content of her journals have also derived sustenance from the accounts given in *Dear Miss Weaver*, Lidderdale and Nicholson's fine biography of Marsden's (and later Joyce's) patron and Marsden's editorial collaborator. Although it is true that in later years Marsden "cut herself off from the give and take of discussion, and isolation [made] communication difficult" (72), and that Weaver took over the daily editorial affairs of the *Egoist* in the summer of 1914, before that time and throughout the period of the *New Freewoman*, Marsden controlled and supervised the enterprise. In particular, Lidderdale and Nicholson overstate the extent of Dora Marsden's withdrawal from editorial work during the summer and fall of 1913, when Marsden and Pound were actively corresponding. Marsden's editorial correspondence with Weaver throughout the period of the *New Freewoman* and the *Egoist*, deposited by Weaver at the British Library, shows clearly that Marsden continued to be actively engaged with the journal's daily affairs well after she appointed Weaver to handle the office and freed herself from the topical round in favor of systematic philosophical writing.

The transition in Marsden's interests from political feminism to philosophical and creative individualism was already operative in the *Freewoman*. We will see that an explicit "egoistic" current also ran consistently from the first to the last issue of the *New Freewoman*, that no manipulations on Pound's part were needed to bring about its growing literary orientation, and that it was never devoted to advancing women's suffrage and was not, strictly speaking, a feminist periodical but rather an anarchist one. Pound's presence was certainly significant, but it ratified and lifted to new heights a shift already in the works. We will put the matter to rest once and for all at the end of this chapter.

The Manifesto of the *New Freewoman*

The discourse of gender types was a definitive feature of the *Freewoman:* the epistolary debate between Dr. Whitby and Mr. Birnstingl over the "Uranian" type was one of many examples. The figure of the freewoman itself was a composite of the "modern woman" and the "militant woman," two "countertypes" culled from the arsenal of suffragist retort. "Suffragettes refused hysteria"—refused to identify with the stereotype of the "hysterical" woman—"and produced the counter-type of the allegorical warrior-maiden" (Tickner, *Spectacle of Women*, 172). The freewoman is an extreme form of countertype to the "bondwoman," the "typical" female enslaved to patriarchal determinations and bereft of legal and spiritual personhood. However, over the course of the *Freewoman*, Marsden began to relinquish the discourse of types altogether. It seems likely that her wrangle with Weininger's sexual typology helped to impel the reorientation of her conceptual terms. The ultimate demise of the figure of the freewoman was to an important extent a rhetorical as well as a doctrinal decision; that is, its doctrinal element rested on a new level of self-consciousness over her rhetorical practice. The arrival of the figure of the egoist signaled Marsden's attempt to produce not simply a countertype but an antitype, a type to end all types. As Marsden would aver in Stirnerian idiom, "types are spookish."[7] Nominal rather than substantial entities, ghost stories for grown-ups, types have textual powers to frighten and mislead. We will capture these transitions in the discourse of the *New Freewoman*.

Playing on Edward Carpenter's sexology, we might say that Marsden negotiated her personal evolution from millennial feminism to the philosophical panoptics of the *Egoist* through the intermediate type of the *New Freewoman*. It combined and amplified two lines of interest already prominent in later numbers of the *Freewoman*: anarchism and aesthetics. There is a swift diminishing of the two most prominent topics in the early numbers: feminism and spiritualism. By removal from gender polarity, the evolutionary feminism at the heart of Marsden's earlier *Freewoman* leaders modulated into a more Bergsonian form of anarchism: a celebration of vitalistic flux in the absence of a definitive telos, an affirmation of pure existential velocity without the drag of a predetermined or collective destination.[8] Correspondingly, and in tandem with the development of imagism and Pound's modernism generally, the *New Freewoman* downplays overt spirituality: the anarchistic and literary discussions show a renewed effort to weigh evolutionary idealism against the material conditions of cultural production. Passing through such changes, leaders like "The Heart of the Question" refocused on the material economics of self-determination.[9] In place of the spiritual self-creation Marsden developed in the *Freewoman* was an increased emphasis on discourse and literature as concrete vehicles of individual expression and development.

Marsden's leader for the first *New Freewoman* was a diatribe against self-sacrificial and submissive approaches to political causes. Under the aegis of the nineteenth-century anarchist precursor Pierre Proudhon, she attacked bourgeois property laws that fix the flux of possessions in favor of the wealthy, advising the dispossessed that boldly seizing property will benefit them more than meekly asking others for justice.[10] In the "Views and Comments" that followed, Marsden's meditation on the tyranny of collective causes modulated significantly to a discussion of rhetoric, the hypnotic but morbid power of militant sloganeering: "Mrs. Pankhurst may die and great is the Cause. What Cause? The Cause of the empty concept—the fount of all insincerity: the Cause

of the Symbol—the Nothing worked upon by the Dithyramb."[11] Marsden's
stark nominalism traced the primary tendency of her own current intellectual
flux: from the critique of manifest collective movements such as feminism and
millennial spiritualism to the skeptical, anarcho-philosophical analysis of their
latent psycholinguistic foundations.

The first number of the *New Freewoman* is a good example of the way that
many of Marsden's important writings emerge not in her oracular or program-
matic leaders but in the more reflective, conversational polemics that usually
followed. In her "Views and Comments" for that number, Marsden's immediate personal interest in the strategic rhetoric of political causes was the distinction between two current spectacles—on the one hand, Mrs. Pankhurst's
hunger strike, and on the other hand the fate of Marsden's erstwhile militant
colleague Emily Wilding Davison, who had just succeeded in martyring herself
for the cause of women's suffrage by running onto the racetrack at Derby, waving a WSPU banner before the king's horse and getting trampled to death.[12] In
Marsden's analysis, Davison's suicidal delirium of self-sacrifice had fed itself on
the poison of cause-rhetoric. In psycholinguistic terms, what Marsden isolated
was the ego-troping function of the *Todestrieb,* the death drive that can take
possession of those who literalize in their persons the abstract ideals of causes.

> Strong natures, who act out their beliefs in their own person . . . occa-
> sionally are fascinated by the jargon, with consequences disastrous in the
> highest degree to themselves. Miss Davison, for instance, was in the pres-
> ence of something innocuous to most of her companions, but very deadly
> in relation to herself when she lent ear to the pleadings of the great Cause
> "Freedom." Her soul strong for action, sucked in the poison. . . . It was
> inevitable, that, short of abandoning the "Cause" some such tragedy
> should gather round her. A fatalism must inevitably attach to those who
> cannot abandon the phrases of their yesterdays: who must spend more on
> them because they have already spent much. (4)

The edge of these remarks is Marsden's implicit recognition that she herself had
not been a mere token but an impetuous "strong nature." Had she been unable
to relinquish the "phrases of her yesterdays," she, too, would likely have come
to some "disastrous consequence." For instance, four years earlier she could
have slipped from the roof at the Southport Empire and gone to a glorious mar-
tyrdom of her own.

As in Marsden's case, Davison had also come into conflict with the WSPU
leadership: "if we remember rightly, the last occasion upon which we saw her,

more than a year ago, she was under warning of dismissal from her 'post with a pittance' (twenty shillings weekly if we remember aright) upon her next attempt to 'militate' upon her own account, a dismissal which we believe actually had effect later" (4). Davison's final, self-imposed militation was not coordinated with or subordinate to a directive from the main office at Clement's Inn. Rather, it was a pure piece of direct political action, a self-assertive or "egoistic" gesture of total defiance. Davison was "ready with the toll" for her supreme moment of self-immolation. And it is on these grounds that Marsden eulogized her last choice: "Chance betrays so many occasions, for her as for all who attempt to fill in a spectacle, and her experience had had its bitternesses. Here, luck crowned her courage: she has been permitted to secure what we know she cared to have: the well-done of those whose work she chose to do. And we are profoundly glad. A daring deed, a perfect spectacle, and the cost all hers. It might have been otherwise—life and recriminations" (5). Fatally poisoned with self-sacrificial rhetoric, Davison nevertheless wanted to die in a certain way and had the courage and strength to seize her desire.

At the end of these "Views and Comments," Marsden stated the point about Davison's implicit egoism in its general formulation. In what may be taken as the new manifesto of the *New Freewoman,* Marsden announces the nullity of typological conceptions.

> Accurately speaking, there *is* no "Woman Movement." "Woman" is doing nothing—she has, indeed, no existence. A very limited number of individual women are emphasising the fact that the first thing to be taken into account with regard to them is that they *are* individuals. . . . The centre of the Universe lies in the desire of the individual, and the Universe for the individual has no meaning apart from their individual satisfactions, a means to an end. The few individual women before mentioned maintain that their only fitting description is that of Individual: Ends-in-themselves. They are Egoists. (5)

The Movement Movement

Life is flux; it must move or die. Fixity is morbid. One type may be substituted for another, but any type is essentially fixed. Therefore, types are morbid. Such is the categorical logic of Marsden's new phase of thought. In "The Lean Kind," the *New Freewoman*'s new rhetoric of dynamic flux emerges immediately in its economic variant, the flux of private property by which one grasps the virtual swindle, the institutionalized criminality of bourgeois legality. Marsden notes how entrepreneurial buccaneers, because they already own the state, have no great compunction about placing themselves above its laws. The robber baron is implicitly opposed to the true anarchist, who, disdaining such complicity, must venture outside or beneath the state, whereas the capitalist enjoys "chance and adventure in the flux . . . *above* the state" (my emphasis). Marsden's remarks find a nice contemporary application in the United States' savings-and-loan debacle of the 1980s.

> Theft is the time-honoured, success-crowned means to property. . . . A constant state of *flux* (Oh, Cause of Honesty!) flux of property, from hands which yield into hands which seize! . . . Property once seized, the seizers set about to make flux static. . . . Henceforth, the lean, the law-abiding, the honest, are the pillars of the STATE, while the possessors of it are left well-established, free to pursue chance and adventure in the flux which has never ceased to flow in the secret order above the state. ("The Lean Kind," 1–2)

But for the most part, *flux* in the *New Freewoman* is applied not to economic but to existential and discursive considerations. Marsden reformulates her abiding vitalistic commitment as the celebration of an interminable current of existential transformation. This vitalism is no longer of the collective teleological variety impelling some vast evolutionary or feminist millennium. Rather, the goal of life in any individual manifestation, in any *ego,* is to fend off fixating forces and maintain itself in pure onward motion. Marsden's eulogy for Emily Davison implied that doctrinal and rhetorical fixations can be literally as well as morally lethal. The *New Freewoman* was "abandoning the phrases" of the *Freewoman*'s yesterdays to forestall decay and keep apace with "Life."

The *New Freewoman* celebrated individuality as vital movement by removing itself from all collective movements. In her leader for the second number, Marsden asserted the insufficiency of mere intellect, whose "acquaintance with the static *outward*" does not avail for authentic apprehension of "the vital *inward.*"[13] The intellect too readily comes to a halt in the contemplation of the symbols by which it would comprehend life's enigmatic motions: "The historic record of human life on earth, is the tale of this bewilderment of Intellect faced with the phenomenon of life. . . . Life which reveals itself to the intellect only when it moves, in its moments of change, is an enigma. . . . Thus is the Symbol begotten: the Symbol which is not even an approximation to anything in life, but is the tracery of an arrangement among dead things which accidentally life in its passage through, has left" ("Intellect and Culture," 22). It is in this conceptual context that Marsden inaugurates her *New Freewoman* phase of aesthetic discussion. Dividing the field between a sham art vitiated by a one-sided intellectualism and a genuine art that coordinates the intellect with the primary motions of the soul, Marsden applies a dynamic vitalism as the cutting edge of this aesthetic discrimination.

> Intellect is far commoner than strength of being—Soul, to wit. Hence its presumption. Only when personality is strong is Rationalism put into its proper human relationship and only then do we get the creator of true art, the Light-bringer. The artist-in-ordinary, the creator of the marsh-lights which glimmer in human culture, is the worker in Intellect rather than in Soul, such a one who has never hovered over the deeps of personality—sighted his own vision of the moving impulse first-hand . . . the living moving soul-impulse. . . . Art, the record of the Soul moving consciously in Light. (22–23)

Several months later, still defending the *New Freewoman*'s unwillingness to nominate its "Cause" against a contingent of disgruntled correspondents who would have preferred some more stable terms on her part, Marsden again affirmed its dedication to nominalistic negativity as coordinated with the creative ideal of discursive mobility: despite appearances to the contrary, "this journal is not run in the interests of sport. We expect from it a return of definite advantages, of which not the least are life-data expressed in terms of the mobile. By being critical of the static, we at least create a void which in itself will force the production of a more accurate substitute."[14]

Chief among dead and static things is, of course, the characterological type, understood now as a reified trope that travesties the literal individuality of living things. First, in reply to the rhetoric of a monolithic feminism, there is the nullity of gender types: "Woman-as-type is reproduction-in-all-its-stages personified, that is, a simple reality messed up into a fiction. It is as nearly related to the first Amoeba as to any particular woman. . . . The gender of the self we have yet to learn" ("Views and Comments," July 1, 1913, 24). Next, in reply to eugenic arguments of all stripes, there is the nonentity of racial types: "The Race is the concept formed by adding one individual to another, carrying on the process to boredom, slurring the finish, and dabbing on a label. . . . The 'Race' is empty when that which it opposes is taken from it. It is *Nothing* apart from the individual. The word should be abolished and a periphrasis put in its place" (24). And eventually, having come this far, Marsden criticizes the interest previously displayed in the *Freewoman* over the "intermediate type" as an evolutionary ideal: "there appears unwisdom in the attempt to make out a new sex-'type' in what is called the Uranian—a term of more than ambiguous content, as defined by those who use it. As we are concerned to break down the conception of types into individuals, we cannot be expected to look too friendlily upon an attempt to create another of doubtful accuracy" ("Views and Comments," October 15, 1913, 166).

The full text in the midst of which these pronouncements occurred shows that Marsden's commentaries were almost always responses to contributors' and correspondents' written responses to her. For instance, the discussion of "art and the soul" in "Intellect and Culture" replied directly to Huntly Carter's "The Golden Age" in the previous *New Freewoman;* her remarks on race anticipated an article in the same number, Winnifred W. Leisenring's "A Race of Individuals," which aired a theosophical rebuttal to Marsden's egoism. This wild dialogism underscores the singular editorial authenticity of Marsden's journals as cultural documents. Nor was she averse to publishing and addressing the sentiments of the many readers who experienced dismay over her movement beyond all movements. This was a particularly touchy issue when it came to the disappointment of those *Freewoman* loyalists and Thousand Club subscribers who felt with some justification that they had invested in the *New Freewoman* under false pretenses. Marsden acknowledged that "the 'emotional push' which landed *The New Freewoman* on its feet came from a tiny group of American women."[15] However,

> our disappointed American friends . . . imagined that *The New Freewoman* was "to stand for something." Whereas it stands for nothing: it is the flexible frame waiting to be filled with the expression of the constantly shifting tale of the contributors' emotions. . . . With an expression so mobile that what was said yesterday flows under the check of what we feel to-day, it behoves us to pick phrases even gingerly. There is no urge so compelling towards consistency of expression as the refusal to recognise any claims to hold consistently to any past expression. It is the "protected" consistency which plays havoc with consistency. Hence the "quibbling with terms" and the absence of those old "clear notes, ringing like blows from Thor's hammer." ("Views and Comments," November 15, 1913, 204)

"Consistency" to a discursive identity in vital flux must produce a verbal residue of "inconsistency" in the written record left behind as life moves on. In this insight Marsden's text leaps toward a poststructuralist sense of the textual constructedness of any identity-in-writing. It is as if Marsden presided more than once over her own doctrinal funeral, refusing to mourn for the "death of the author" whose life she refused to protect because its death must be the toll paid for the constant renovation of the discourse.

Ezra Pound, Serious Artist

"I suppose I'm individualist"

There is common agreement on and much truth to the idea that Ezra Pound used Dora Marsden's journals as much as possible for his own particular ends and greatly transformed the journals in the process. It can now be admitted that Marsden had her own ends and that she used Pound and his connections as well to further them. The private correspondence and printed give-and-take between Marsden and Pound over his well-known essay of 1913, "The Serious Artist," also show that Marsden was Pound's equal in intellectual will.[16] Their tangle over "The Serious Artist" will clarify why he may have wanted to distort or gloss over the actual lines of editorial authority. The fact remains that Pound's proprietorial attitude toward the *New Freewoman* and the *Egoist*—as recorded in numerous letters to William Carlos Williams, Margaret Anderson, Amy Lowell, and others—was simply an egotism. His complicity in the name change to the *Egoist* was in fact a happy coincidence between his ambitions and the complex development of Marsden's thought. Whatever his own aspirations and epistolary misrepresentations to others, Pound neither wrested editorial control from Marsden nor conferred it upon anyone else: for instance, when his interests turned elsewhere, he did not simply bequeath the *Egoist* to Aldington. Rather, Marsden accepted Pound's suggestion of Aldington as a replacement for the virtually departed Rebecca West. Yet chroniclers of modernism as astute as Marjorie Perloff still pass on spurious attributions like "Richard Aldington's *The Egoist*" (*Futurist Moment*, 264). By examining Pound's letters to Marsden and reading Marsden's corresponding contributions to the *New Freewoman*, we can develop a more balanced account of their relations and, accordingly, a more precise appreciation of Dora Marsden's particular talents and accomplishments in immediate conjunction with the exposition and launching of literary modernism.

Ezra Pound's letters in the Dora Marsden Collection start in the summer of 1913, as the *New Freewoman* was beginning publication, and end in the spring of 1914, once the *Egoist* was well launched. Marsden was handling the editorial matters out of Ainsdale, Southport. Although Pound's postcards usually bear a postmark with a legible date, his letters are almost all undated. In the following discussion I have constructed a plausible chronology. In the passages quoted I have regularized the spacing between words and occasionally altered the punctuation. In what I take to be the first of Pound's letters to Marsden, he began by laying out to her his schemes and terms.

> Miss West . . . wrote requesting contribution and I made the following offer. (The only offer I can make unless I am to be paid) A. That I fill a page per number, for, say, six months tho' I might be quite willing to go on after that. As follows.
>
> 1st. of each month. Verse, selected by me. Including my own stuff and other work which I should be able, probably, to pay for and thus to spare the authors the disgrace of printing creative stuff without being paid.
>
> 15th. of each month. Prose article. Critique presumably of current books, especially poetry. Here, and possibly in France.
>
> Miss West accepted this suggestion. I also offered to try to get for you a translation of Remy DeGourmont's *Chevaux de Diomedes*. And have succeeded in doing so (I said I thought sufficiently well of *The Freewoman* to be willing to give it my verse free, which I would not do for any other periodical.)
>
> . . . I've got to do the selecting. I've a fairly complete program already. It is not so much that I "won't" as that I "can not" work on any other terms. I have certain standards and the work printed would have to come up to them. As collector for two of the best paying U.S. magazines I see a good deal of the best work, and of the work showing promise. Even with the anonymous donor we would be able to pay only £2 or £3 for the page so we should have to print for the most part work "of promise." But I happen to know of some interesting men who are not yet known and it is upon them that I count. I gather that I am not wholly divergent from the editorial policy, in that I dont want the sort of nondescript verse that could just as well appear in the Pall Mall or in "Poetry and Drama" etc.[17]

In a second letter, Pound supplied further information about his convergence with what he took to be the *New Freewoman*'s editorial policies. It is uncertain whether Pound had confirmed for himself Marsden's lack of editorial dogmatism by reading the July 1 number.

> Dear friends and readers, *The New Freewoman* has *no* Cause. The nearest approach to a Cause it desires to attain, is to destroy Causes, and for the

doing of this it finds its reward and incentive in its own satisfaction. *The New Freewoman* is not for the advancement of Woman, but for the empowerment of individuals—men and women. . . . Something like the foregoing is what the editorials will have to say: but for the rest of the paper, only a general sympathy with our "attitude" will be sought. Having no Cause we have no sacred ground, and no individual interpretations of life will be debarred beforehand. In the clash of opinion we shall expect to find our values. (Marsden, "Views and Comments," July 1, 1913, 25).

Pound's second letter contains a droll, rather recalcitrant protest over any question about his suitability for a journal subtitled *An Individualist Review.* And he appears somewhat exasperated at Marsden's particular emphases, for she seems to have ignored Pound's literary minutiae, as expounded in the previous letter, in favor of sounding out his "philosophical credentials."

The seven minutes at my instant disposal is hardly enough to define my philosophical credentials adequately.

I suppose I'm individualist, I suppose I believe in the arts as the most effective propaganda for a sort of individual liberty that can be developed without public inconvenience.

I suppose Ibsen and Henry James have does [sic] their bit for the general boosting of individual liberty—the less crude varieties.

I don't suppose a literary page will queer the editorial columns.

Miss West has inspected the data of our particular sect, and has not been alarmed unduly. I am probably amenable to reason. (?????,!??). . . .

About the poetry. You don't say anything about it, I hope you understand my position re/ what goes into the paper. I don't want to "boss" but if I am to make the page efficient, I must follow my own scheme. I can't work it if "diluted" with chance stuff of a different sort.[18]

Garner follows Lidderdale and Nicholson in taking Pound's impression of Marsden's silence or unconcern about his poetic program to indicate her lack of interest in the literary affairs of the journal. However, with a supreme controversialist like Marsden one can interpret neither silence nor severe criticism as grounds for disinterest. I think it much more likely that she was entirely satisfied with Pound's literary ideas and editorial schemes: he had come forward with Rebecca West's stamp of approval, and as a reader of the *New Age,* Marsden may well have been familiar with his work. In her second *New Freewoman* leader she had already declared that the "creation of Art is the supreme effort of Soul and Intellect" ("Intellect and Culture," 23). Thus, she dwelt instead on the matter of ascertaining precisely the nature of his politics.

Marsden's emphasis on discursive definition is already evident in this letter, as it would be several months later in the opening paragraph of "The Serious Artist," where Pound wrote, "we are asked to define the relation of the arts to economics." The epistolary record behind "The Serious Artist" prompts one to speculate about the nature and extent of the defensiveness with which Pound responded to Dora Marsden's earnest and ironic intellectual challenges. Pound's mock uncertainties in the letter last cited—"I suppose I'm individualist"—seem curious indeed. Perhaps he was nonplused by having intellectual demands placed upon him by an assertive and confident woman, a woman altogether more radical and cerebral than himself. In any event, in less than a year he would be participating in all manner of propagandizing for ideas like "individualism," at least the "less crude varieties" expounded by the vorticist vanguard. We must assume that Pound gave his blessings to Wyndham Lewis's manifestoes: "*Blast* . . . will not appeal to any particular class, but to the fundamental and popular instincts in every class and description of people, TO THE INDIVIDUAL. . . . *Blast* is created for this timeless, fundamental Artist that exists in everybody. . . . Popular art does not mean the art of the poor people, as it is usually supposed to. It means the art of the individuals. . . . *Blast* presents an art of Individuals."[19] Pound himself repeats these sentiments later that year: "The vorticist movement is a movement of individuals, for individuals, for the protection of individuality."[20] Although Pound seems to have been incapable of directly acknowledging her, the individualistic doctrines and to some extent the rationale for the aesthetic provocations of the vorticists had often been anticipated and articulated in the writings of Dora Marsden. She was simply more thoroughgoing in her individualist practice, eschewing group movements altogether, whereas Pound's commanding instincts led him to leaven his individualism with an active elitism, something on the model of Stirner's paradoxical Union of Egoists or Allen Upward's Order of the Seraphim, a "trades-union of poets."[21]

In the summer of 1913, Marsden was wasting no time getting some work out of her second literary editor. "Behold," Pound begins another undated letter, "I have been very good: I have done these dam'd reviews. . . . You or R.W. or whoever it is, hasn't put my verses in the Aug. 1st number. They are to be the first installment of my dept. And the enclosed 'In Metre' the second."[22] In fact, a version of "The Contemporania of Ezra Pound," recycled from a prior appearance in *Poetry* for April 1913, including "The Garden" and "In a Station of the Metro," appeared in the August 15 number along with the first two chapters of de Gourmont's *Horses of Diomedes*.[23] "In Metre," which reviewed books of poetry by D. H. Lawrence, Walter de la Mare, and Robert Frost, appeared in the September 1 number.[24] Incorporating Pound's contributions kept up Marsden's end of the editorial bargain implied by Pound's setting forth to generate material. And in writing to Marsden at least, Pound was careful to refer to his "department" of the journal; for instance, "As soon as it [is] definitely ascertained that I am the Literchure Dept. you can send me some sub-scription blanks and I will try to impound a few (a very few) friends, acquain-tances and relatives, here and transpontus."[25] In other correspondence, for instance, with the "transpontus" William Carlos Williams, he would allow this distinction between his "dept." and the journal as a whole to lapse. At the moment he was still negotiating with Marsden over the exact parameters of his involvement. Still, his letters show him proceeding energetically, rounding up the translation of *The Horses of Diomedes,* arranging for someone to clip the French literary press, and leaning on Ford Madox Hueffer for a contribution, two installments of "The Poet's Eye."

"The Serious Artist"

The composition of "The Serious Artist" is a further indication of Pound's immediate good faith in adhering to the informal contract he had negotiated with Marsden. Two sections of "The Serious Artist" appeared in the *New Free-woman* of October 15, 1913, and two more in the next two issues. Part of the interest in this early prose piece is that Pound is discovered here in the midst of a major intellectual transition. Despite its choppiness and uncharacteristically tentative tone, the essay was deemed worthy by T. S. Eliot of reprinting in his edition of Pound's *Literary Essays.*[26] It represents a relatively appealing early attempt to come to terms with some fundamental aesthetic and critical issues, and it has long been granted serious critical consideration.[27] In later years, Pound himself would refer rather grandiosely to passages of "The Serious Artist" as examples of the "ideogrammic method" (*ABC of Reading,* 96–97).

Following William Wees and Donald Davie, Levenson has drawn out a political subtext of "The Serious Artist" that helps relate Pound's development to Marsden's discourse. He sees the essay as a kind of valediction, a departing expression of humanist sentiment from a writer about to blast off from social decorum and take up a militantly elitist artistic resistance against democratic vulgarities.

As late as the autumn of 1913, in "The Serious Artist," Pound had dis-played a certain restraint in his apology for art. . . . [There his] attitudes find a place within the humanist tradition, and Pound himself connects the essay to Sidney's *Defence of Poesy*. He conceives of art as fundamental and consequential, and he willingly acknowledges the social obligation of any such serious endeavour. But over the next several months, Pound's attitudes suffered dramatic change. . . . [By February 1914, he] comes to a position as anti-democratic and as anti-humanitarian as that of Stirner, Nietzsche or Upward. The social justification for art, as found in "The Serious Artist," has disappeared. (*Genealogy of Modernism*, 74–76)

Although one can question whether Levenson's political readings are sufficiently subtle, clearly his "genealogical" datings are accurate. Robinson also considers the period from "The Serious Artist" to "The New Sculpture"— October 1913 to February 1914—as a time of fundamental transition, although for Robinson the change is not in Pound's basic ideas but in the rhetorical strategies by which they are expressed (*Symbol to Vortex*, 193). Nevertheless, it does not seem to have been appreciated that in this "conversion" from a residual humanism to the militant antagonisms of vorticism, implicitly, and perhaps somewhat deliberately, Pound was following Dora Marsden's lead.[28] Or, at least, he was following her leaders, the many articles that led off the *Freewoman* and the *New Freewoman,* which had already traced a progress or progressive reaction against democratic socialism—suffragist feminism—and toward the anarchistic individualism of "Stirner, Nietzsche and Upward."[29]

It is interesting to set all this against the quite forgotten fact that the essay came into existence due to Dora Marsden's specific instigations. A letter to Marsden written around September 1913 indicates that Pound had begun "The Serious Artist" in response to her request and that he entertained a fairly accurate judgment concerning it: "I have spent the major part of this very fine day writing you a very dull, very rambling and very sensible article. You can use it whenever you like. . . . I probably shall pour forth another article on 'Emotion & Poesy.'"[30] "Emotion and Poesy" in fact became the heading of the third section of "The Serious Artist." The following letter, the body of which I quote in its entirety, appears to have covered the manuscript of that installment: "'He babbled of green fields.' Here's the second 'bab.' I become more convinced than ever that good prose can only be about things about which one is wholly indifferent. Then one can stop to make nice phrases and be amusing. However, 'you done it.' You axed me questions. And I'm not through yet."[31]

In fact, "The Serious Artist" was the first leader other than one of Dora Marsden's to begin an issue of the *New Freewoman*, and it began thus: "It is curious that one should be asked to rewrite Sidney's 'Defence of Poesy' in the year of grace 1913. . . . We are asked if the arts are moral. We are asked to define the relation of the arts to economics, we are asked what position the arts are to hold in the ideal republic. . . . I take no great pleasure in writing prose about æsthetic. . . . Nevertheless I have been questioned earnestly and by a person certainly of good will" (161). The lead position of the article and the drift of the questioning are suggestive, and Pound's correspondence with Marsden shows conclusively that Dora Marsden was the unnamed questioner behind "The Serious Artist." It should also be noted that the emphasis of Marsden's questioning is not sociological or political but philosophical and semantic—it is on *definition*. If Marsden did inquire specifically after an "ideal republic," it would have been I think not "earnestly" but with an irony that Pound may have missed. By the fall of 1913, Marsden had carried her own anarchistic manifestoes to the point that to her the phrase "ideal republic" would read as a joke, or as the thing to be destroyed, not pursued. In any event, in partial return for her taking him on as literary editor of the *New Freewoman* and in a typically provocative editorial gesture, Marsden put Pound up to the task of defining his artistic credo.

Thus Noel Stock's account of this event, reworking the lines of Hughes's version, is equally misleading: "With Dora Marsden and Harriet Shaw Weaver attending to the feminist and philosophical contents of the *New Freewoman* Pound was left free to run the literary section more or less as he liked. He took the opportunity to insert into its pages two essays of his in which he attempted to put some of his ideas in order. The first was 'The Serious Artist.'"[32] Pound did not "insert" the essay into the journal; Marsden quite consciously pulled it in. By the same token, MacKendrick's remark that the publication of "The Serious Artist" was "a considerable coup for the *New Freewoman*" (*"New Freewoman,"* 186) is unintentionally ludicrous but is another typical product of Pound's prestige overshadowing Marsden's activities. Bringing Pound into the journal's fold in the first place may well have been a coup of sorts, but the opening paragraph of "The Serious Artist" already indicated that Pound did not initiate the piece on his own and magnanimously offer it up, or vigorously insert it in, but that it owed its existence to Marsden's promptings.

Literary histories that cite Nietzsche, Yeats, Remy de Gourmont, T. E. Hulme, or Allen Upward as primary formative influences on Pound's early politics will have to be revised to make some room for the influence of Dora Marsden. What *did* Pound have in mind when he took up Marsden's call to define the relation of his aesthetics to society, and what might he have discovered in the process of clarifying his own positions? Was his "humanist" stance in "The Serious Artist" itself entirely in earnest or was it ultimately a defensive attempt to avoid confronting the intellectual precedence of Marsden's postfeminist, exhumanist anarchism? For instance, although Pound used a number of analogies between art and science to wrap the seriousness of art and the artist in the mantle of scientific positivity, there was some noticeable discursive squirming on his part as he tried to negotiate between a sweeping humanism and an ego-istic insistence on the uniqueness of the individual. Pound modeled the serious artist on the figure of the scientist as a universal humanist type, yet his typifications kept collapsing against the definitive atypicality of the individual artist: "The serious artist is scientific in that he presents the image of his desire, of his hate, of his indifference, as precisely that, as precisely the image of his own desire, hate or indifference" (162, 163). Pound's scientism, so crucial for the rhetorical edge of his modernist campaigns, emerged here as polemical allegory for the imputation of impersonal universality to the personal and idiosyncratic: it was a complex mantle thrown over his residual mysticism. As a number of critics have noted, in the public authority of science Pound sought revalidation for the significance of his most private epiphanies.[33]

In the "Views and Comments" section of the October 15 issue, in implicit response to the dialect and matter of "The Serious Artist," Marsden set out some of her own attitudes on art and the artist.[34] Here is the precise beginning of her aesthetic manifesto, Marsden's single most important doctrinal achieve-ment during this phase of her writing. What Pound was gathering under the notion of "seriousness," Marsden interpreted in terms of strength of soul, as she vigorously adapted an electro-vitalist idiom to her aesthetic discussion.

> The first thing of which we have any knowledge—the only thing of which we have first-hand knowledge—is the life within ourselves. We call it our soul, meaning thereby an individuated entity thrown out free by the stream of living energy. The soul is not a thought, and has nothing to do with thought. It is a "thing" as electricity running along a wire is a thing. . . .

Marsden's view here could be triangulated between Nietzsche's long aphorism in *On the Genealogy of Morals* deconstructing the idea of the subject—"just as the popular mind separates the lightning from its flash and takes the latter for an *action*, for the operation of a subject called lightning, so popular morality also separates strength from expression of strength"—and William Carlos Williams's hardy aphorism "No ideas but in things."[35] Marsden's soul is the prophecy of a moving individuality: the artist of the future will trace its motions.

> It is this thing, a soul, which it is the province of art as distinct from sci-ence, to make chart of. . . . Art is the scientific spirit applied to soul, observing, collating, noting. . . . The creative artist is one in whom life

beats strongly; whose emotions, instead of being so feeble that he is capable of mistaking them for something else, are so strong and defined that
they secure their right description. Most men feel very little to which they
are capable of supplying articulate expression, and most poets are like most
men. The major artists are major *men,* and their "works" are a conse-
quence. (165–66)

Dora Marsden's commentaries on "The Serious Artist" are equal to their subject, if not altogether more cogent, unified, and incisive. Are Pound's considerable lapses of memory concerning this particular episode a defensive amnesia
due to his latent awareness of having been upstaged?

Or is that amnesia due to his having borrowed from Marsden's formulations to pursue his own? In the "Emotion and Poesy" section of "The Serious
Artist," Pound remarked that "we might come to believe that the thing that
matters in art is a sort of energy, something more or less like electricity or radioactivity, a force transfusing, welding, and unifying" (194). Aesthetic electro-
vitalism of this sort was available in Marsden's commentary on his previous
installment, wherein Pound had also passingly seconded such a conception: "If
an artist falsifies his report as to the nature of man, as to his own nature, as to the
nature . . . of god, if god exist, of the life force, of the nature of good and evil,
if good and evil exist . . . then that artist lies" (162). It would seem significant
that Pound presented the "life force" without the qualifications reserved for
either "god" or "good and evil." However, in this oblique elaboration of a scientistic aesthetic based on a vitalist ethics, the fact that Pound was still purveying more image than substance was lost neither on Marsden nor himself. His
tropes played out, Pound eventually took shelter in the ostensible ineffability
and unfathomability of the life force at the back of artistic expression, for which
recourse he took an apologetic turn not just in his letters to Marsden but also in
the body of the article: "As all the words that one would use in writing about
these things are the vague words of daily speech, it is nearly impossible to write
with scientific preciseness about 'prose and verse'. . . . On like account if you
ask a good painter to tell you what he is trying to do to a canvas he will very
probably wave his hands helplessly and murmur that 'He—eh—eh—he can't
talk about it'" (194).[36]

In the next number of the *New Freewoman,* containing the "Emotion and
Poesy" installment of "The Serious Artist," Dora Marsden returned to the lead
position with an explicit response to "The Serious Artist." Having lured him
within range of her barbs, Marsden was unwilling to let Pound off the hook,
and the comedy of this little-noticed discursive encounter remains undiminished.

Published the 1st and 15th of each month.

THE NEW
FREEWOMAN

AN INDIVIDUALIST REVIEW.

No. 10   Vol. I.   SATURDAY, NOVEMBER 1st, 1913.   SIXPENCE.

Editor:
DORA MARSDEN, B.A.

CONTENTS.

THE ART OF THE FUTURE.

THERE is, about artists when asked to define their business, a coyness which would be exquisitely ludicrous if it were evinced by chemists or mathematicians, by carpenters or brick-layers. This coyness, and the vague waving of hands to give the expression of helplessness, in-a-sort, in the grip of some high force, which if not divine, is at least too much above the common level to be comprehended by the Philistine, or common-sense man—these are quite sufficient to place art as we now know it, in its sub-conscious period. There is nothing to be gained by calling out against artists : their lack of comprehension as to what they are about, is a matter for regret rather than reprehension. They are in the position the alchemists and astrologers were, before alchemy became chemistry, and astrology astronomy. Nothing deterred by the caveat against the intruding of "outsiders'" opinions into their territory, we make bold to define the sphere of Art, as the complement of Science. If science is the knowledge gained by applying to non-vital phenomena, the method of accurate description as opposed to that of imaginative interpretation, art is the product of the same method applied to vital (and mainly humanly vital) phenomena.

The knowledge massed by science is stupendous in bulk relatively to that amassed by art, which boasts only the unco-ordinated work of geniuses, few and far between. Science has made its advance chiefly in the last three hundred years, because during this period it has trusted to the results of unprejudiced observation of the "thing." Before, as now in art, save for one or two outstanding geniuses, it had guessed about things, and its guesses made a pile of useless words and ideas, unproved and incapable of proof. The energy of the greatest as well as the least of investi-gators was wasted in spinning these futile guesses. But the experiment, i.e., the essaying what could be done to a thing and what could be done with it, put an end to all that. Experiment broke the dominion of the guess—the imaginative interpretation. The idea broke upon the perception of the fact. Thought was bridled by knowledge of the "thing"; thought's utmost reach attained only to a "suggestion"; the hypothesis holding tentative existence only until the experiment should dissolve it into error or fact. The experimental method brought the scientific free-thought period to an end. Observation of the subject put verbal notions out of court. With art on the other hand, matters have but reached at their ultimate limit the "interest" of the verbal treatment, the imaginative interpretation. And this only with the few. Most artists are content to pass on the conventional tradition with a few personal variations. It is only the few who have entered upon the free-thought period, where all the variety of unbridled fancy is spread out before them to be seized upon. These are attached to no reality. They are indeed as unaware as the conventional that there exists a reality by faithfulness to which their works will be judged. They are the half-charlatans where the conventional are the dullards. The unconscious charlatanry of art has invaded every sphere of culture : it is indeed the substance of existing culture. In philosophy, theology and theosophy, in ethics, psychology, and sociology, throughout the whole length and breadth of literature, there spreads the record of the charlatan artists ; of those who pretend they follow the motions of the soul, but who follow merely the idea ; of those who speak with the certainty of knowledge concerning that of which they have made a bold guess.

There is, about artists when asked to define their business, a coyness
which would be exquisitely ludicrous if it were evinced by chemists or
mathematicians, by carpenters or brick-layers. This coyness, and the vague
waving of hands to give the expression of helplessness, in-a-sort, in the
grip of some high force, which if not divine, is at least too much above the
common level to be comprehended by the Philistine, or common-sense
man—these are quite sufficient to place art as we now know it, in its sub-
conscious period. There is nothing to be gained by calling out against
artists: their lack of comprehension as to what they are about, is a matter
for regret rather than reprehension. They are in the position the alchemists
and astrologers were, before alchemy became chemistry, and astrology
astronomy.[37]

Marsden is clearly continuing in a mode of editorial provocation familiar
to any reader who had followed her from the days of the *Freewoman*. Just as
there she consistently and relentlessly challenged a feminist audience to rise
above mental cliché and doctrinal equivocation, here she launched the same
treatment at her new audience of would-be revolutionaries, anarchists, and
artists. One would-be poetic revolutionary in Marsden's audience was William
Carlos Williams, whose responses to Marsden are useful for gauging the various
effects of her provocations. In a letter to Williams dated December 19, 1913,
Pound wrote concerning the *New Freewoman,* soon to be the *Egoist:* "You must
subscribe as the paper is poor, i.e. weak financially. The *Mercure de France* has
taken to quoting us, however. It is the best way to keep in touch. . . . If you
haven't had that paper, send for back numbers since Aug. 15th."[38] The August
15 number of the *New Freewoman* marked Pound's emergence in its pages as a
contributor and as literary editor. I think it fairly certain that Williams took
Pound's advice and thus had long had "The Serious Artist" and Marsden's
rejoinders in hand.

In 1917, Marsden's philosophical discourses spurred Williams to submit to
the editor of the *Egoist* the following gender critique of Marsden's "Lingual
Psychology": "from the start there is evidence of an exuberant and arrogant
power. . . . For the first time, here is philosophy from the female standpoint:
militant female psychology. . . . For me, however, the edge of all Miss Marsden
says lies in a covert attack on the 'creative artist.' For this reason, and being profoundly impressed with the great practical importance of her work, I will take
delight in striking back."[39] Marsden's writings had largely forsaken the explicit
discussion of aesthetic matters by then, so Williams could very well have been
referring in part to these episodes of Marsden's sparring with Ezra Pound,

occurring just when Williams began following the *New Freewoman* and in which
she set up her notions of creative authenticity against "the unconscious charlatanry of art" and "the charlatan artists . . . who pretend they follow the motions
of the soul, but who follow merely the idea" ("Art of the Future," 181). As we
will note when we return to the topic of his relation to Marsden's writings,
Williams at least was sufficiently detached to take Marsden's "attacks" in the
right spirit, as constructive critiques and deflations of pretension.

In the meantime, "The Art of the Future" set forth an articulate vitalist
schema for the interrelation of scientific and artistic effort: "we make bold to
define the sphere of Art, as the complement of Science. If science is the knowledge gained by applying to non-vital phenomena, the method of accurate
description as opposed to that of imaginative interpretation, art is the product of
the same method applied to vital (and mainly humanly vital) phenomena"
(181). Mike Weaver has noted how Marsden's several reflections on literature in
the *New Freewoman* appeared "almost contemporaneously with the appearance
of the Imagist manifestoes in *Poetry*" (*William Carlos Williams*, 27). Presumably
this simultaneity was the product of Pound's immediate discursive proximity
and contributions to the *New Freewoman* and of Marsden's actual attention to
the various pronouncements of her second literary editor. Clearly she was participating in the idiom of imagism, "the method of accurate description." However, another of Pound's letters to Marsden captured not his pleasure at having
inspired Marsden's dialogical collaboration but his displeasure over the satire she
was also directing toward his residual aesthetic occultism. In hindsight, his
protests of "complete indifference" appear ironic if not disingenuous.

> My statement that the series of articles was begun in answer to a ques-
> tion—I did not specify that it was an editorial question—concords with
> my position that an artist should not gass about art. He should create. If he
> is asked questions there is no harm in his replying.
>
> [As for arguing. I very plainly wont. I consider it, for the most part, use-
> less.][40] Again, you must credit me with a complete indifference to printing
> and publishing prose. Certain things I am forced to, by necessity to do. I
> have never been edited and I dare say I am now "too sot in my ways" to
> understand advice. . . .
>
> I dare say I am, in the articles, a long time getting to what you take to
> be the point ????? . . .
>
> P.S. I differ from Upward, in that I don't in the least mind your assail-
> ing me from the editorial columns. You can print any sort of refutation or
> disagreement you like.[41]

Pound's postscript trails off in a long series of quibbles and *aperçus* concerning the ineffability of artistic creation. The postscript notwithstanding, one imagines that Pound did not especially enjoy being assailed in such a way that located him upon a level field with an articulate and rigorous female. These behind-the-scenes confrontations place his willingness to forgo the "literchure dept." in favor of Richard Aldington, as well as his several unsuccessful attempts to wrest the *Egoist* away from Marsden and Weaver, in a new light. Nevertheless, he never abandoned the *Egoist* as an outlet, publishing more than forty signed and numerous pseudonymous and unsigned items there over the next six years, and, most famously, arranging for the serialization there of Joyce's *A Portrait of the Artist as a Young Man.*

This particular "coup" represents perhaps the finest flowering of the "serious artist" motif within the pages of Dora Marsden's journals, the character of Stephen Dedalus being a definitive specimen of the type. In 1955, Harriet Shaw Weaver wrote to correct some comments of New York publisher Ben Huebsch, reminding him that it had not been herself but Dora Marsden "to whom Mr. Pound had sent the typescript of the first 3 chapters of the *Portrait* and who had accepted it for serialising in *The Egoist*" (Garner, *Brave and Beautiful,* 141). Once more, in this matter as well, it had been forgotten that Ezra Pound, James Joyce, and literary modernism at large owed an appreciable portion of their opportunities to Dora Marsden's individualism.

Evolution and Entropy

Passion and Duration

FOURTH INTERNATIONAL SUMMER SCHOOL
To promote unity in Religion, Philosophy and Science, and its
expression in all branches of Social Service.

Oakley House
Bloomsbury Street
London, W.C.
14th June, 1912.

Dear Miss Marsden,

We have received a reply from you through Miss Dunsmuir to Mr. Dunlop's letter in regard to lecturing at the Summer School, and note that you will lecture for us on the evening of Thursday 15th August, on the subject "Evolution and Freewomen". I am therefore putting you on the programme for this and hope that nothing will prevent your coming.

I hope that your recent vacation has been of benefit to you.

Very sincerely yours,

THE FOURTH INTERNATIONAL SUMMER SCHOOL

W. W. Leisenring

Secretary.[42]

In the *New Freewoman,* what became of Dora Marsden's evolutionary spirituality, that element of the *Freewoman* so insistent at her most grandiose moments? The record is sketchy here, and my commentary must be largely speculative. I believe that Marsden's postsuffragist career was launched by a specific visionary experience, a moment of "cosmic consciousness" that she would intimate in the *Freewoman* as the "flashed vision" of the "Over-and-Above in Life" (201). So far as I have discovered, Marsden left only one record of this event, and that one was oblique at best. Clearly she would continue to be committed to other forms of metaphysics: her spiritualism did not simply dissipate. But in its development from millennial feminism to nominalist anarchism, it did suffer a fall of sorts. There was also a falling out with the theosophists who were greatly supportive of the *Freewoman* and whose Bloomsbury Street premises Marsden's London office shared with Winnifred Leisenring and other local disciples of Madame Blavatsky. Embedded in the *New Freewoman* is a certain record of the progress of this further disillusionment with organized humanistic spiritualism. At the level of resonant discursive figures, Marsden's angelic metaphors of superhuman altitude in the *Freewoman* give way in the *New Freewoman* to a subterranean, even subaqueous, imagery of isolated survivalism. A phase of defensive armoring appears to follow after a phase of extreme psychic dilation.

Marsden's development in this regard may be measured against that of Walt Whitman, Edward Carpenter's main inspiration and the greatest poetic avatar of the progressive evolutionary vitalism in which Marsden's earliest writings were steeped. In his introduction to the 1855 edition of *Leaves of Grass,* Malcolm Cowley suggested that the poem at its inception resulted from Whitman's visionary experience as recounted in chant 5.

I believe in you my soul . . . the other I am must not abase itself to you,
And you must not be abased to the other. . . .

I mind how we lay in June, such a transparent summer morning;
You settled your head athwart my hips and gently turned over upon me,
And parted the shirt from my bosom-bone, and plunged your tongue to
    my barestript heart,
And reached till you felt my beard, and reached till you held my feet.

Swiftly arose and spread around me the peace and joy and knowledge
    that pass all the art and argument of the earth. . . .

(Leaves of Grass, Cowley ed., 28–29)

Cowley failed to mention that he had cribbed his interpretation from the pages
of Dr. Richard M. Bucke's 1901 volume *Cosmic Consciousness,* and then theologized Dr. Bucke's scientific humanism by translating his secular evolutionary
cosmology by way of Jungian psychology back into traditional models of religious illumination.[43] Reading this passage as spiritual autobiography, Cowley
identified Whitman's ecstasy with the long mystical tradition and then offered
to explain thereby the gradual attenuation of Whitman's poetic gift: "his exhil-
arating pride of discovery began to change into humorless arrogance. . . .
Remaining for a long time in this dangerous phase of self-inflation (or 'dilation,'
as he called it) and regarding himself as a God-inspired prophet, he kept looking about for other new doctrines to prophesy" (xxvii). So Cowley gave a skeptical and literalistic spin to a millennial reading of Whitman widely promulgated
at the turn of the century.

In fact, Bucke's *Cosmic Consciousness* is remarkably free of mystical hokum:
there are no hierarchies of divine powers, extraplanetary excursions, or mind-
numbing invocations. The Canadian alienist simply offered to interpret the history of prophetic experiences from Moses to Whitman as the increasingly frequent irruption of a higher consciousness signifying the gradual elevation of the
human species toward "a new plane of existence" (3). He is strictly interested in
the individual psychology of those who have been cosmically conscious for the
few moments or minutes that testimony commonly allots to the experience: "a
state of moral exaltation, an indescribable feeling of elevation, elation, and joy-
ousness, and a quickening of the moral sense . . . a sense of immortality, a consciousness of eternal life" (3). Personally acquainted with Whitman and Carpenter, Bucke placed the two of them side by side as the most notable recent
exemplars of cosmic illumination (215–53) and synthesized their visionary discourses with his own brand of scientific and linguistic rationalism. In all likelihood his text formed a significant link in the chain that transmitted Whitman's
idealism and Carpenter's vitalism to Dora Marsden's London.

On this matter we have the benefit of a letter from an astrologer Marsden seems to have met at the fifth annual theosophical summer school, which records Marsden's admission of an experience akin to Whitman's "dilation":

> roughly speaking the little chart represents *you* in the center, sitting on your own Mother earth, & listening to the call of the celestial powers or "Gods" all around you. . . . [The planets] are in close conjunction which always *adds forcefulness;* as if the Gods were standing shoulder to shoulder as they called to you. It depends on the stage of evolution how clearly the call is heard by us. . . . One call indicated in your horoscope is the call to enter into what is nowadays called "cosmic consciousness," that tremendous expansion of being which you suggested when you used the phrase that you felt as if the stars were part of *you*.[44]

Dora Marsden's original prophetic afflatus was in direct correspondence with a visionary experience, one that she narrated midway through the run of the *Freewoman*. That she recounted this experience at all is perhaps an indication that its affective power was threatening to wane, for up till then she had closely guarded this information. Dr. Bucke remarks that "while in all forms of insanity self-restraint—inhibition—is greatly reduced, sometimes even abolished, in cosmic consciousness it is enormously increased" (70). The passage I am referring to occurred in a *Freewoman* leader treating the joy of sexuality and politics in their relations to the spiritual evolution of the freewoman and immediately concerned to stipulate a spiritual meaning for the term *passion*.[45] Her diction in the opening of this leader echoed Whitman's evocation of the ineffable world-soul—"Something it swings on more than the earth I swing on" (*Leaves of Grass*, Cowley ed., 84)—and indicated that Marsden herself, or at least her discourse, was still strongly "dilated": "what sex was up to the fringe of the human, passion is to the limits of the super-human. What the lure will be in the super-super-human, human mind totally fails to apprehend. But swinging now midway between human and superhuman, we can have intuitive knowledge of the human as we have biological knowledge of the sub-human" ("Interpretation of Sex—II," 481).

She then told of the experience of "a feminist rebel." Marsden's leaders were always unsigned (by which one can also measure the irony within her egoism, or in Bucke's term, her "inhibition"), and this "rebel" remained unnamed, but clearly Marsden was speaking circumspectly in the third person and passive voice about her own imprisonment and hunger strike in 1909.

A feminist rebel, who vouches for the accuracy of the experience was arrested in connection with circumstances, the leading up to which had involved moral decisions sufficiently serious as to involve the risks of life and death in regard to other persons. These decisions were arrived at alone, and involved individual responsibility. In the consequent trial, this individual responsibility was accepted with a clear consciousness as to what it implied. In prison, passive resistance to prison routine led to collision with officials, which naturally led to rough handling. Food was refused, but actual lack of food had not gone far enough to account in any way for the subsequent mental phenomena, which were as follows: Shut up for the night in the cell, suffering acute physical pain, with the quiet came an extraordinary sense of "spirit" expansion. The sensation of increased size was the first marked, but this was followed by the sensation of unlimited power. There was, too, a conscious sense of lightness of weight, and a distinct "seeing" of the atmosphere in vibration. The whole was suffused with the consciousness of calm, radiant, *abiding* joy. The entire experience *lasted,* how long cannot be stated, but it was extended enough to appear "long." It was extended enough for the mind to be able to move round in it, and get its bearings. How it disappeared is not now clear to memory, but for shorter periods it returned on the following days. It seemed, however, that the violent headaches which the hunger-strike developed were later too acute to allow the experience adequately to fix itself. . . .

It is, therefore, our belief that passion is the first necessity of human life as opposed to the sub-human. It is only in passion (of one kind and another—the various kinds are, doubtless, interchangeable) that the conscious vital forces can get their full opportunity of action, and when opportunity fails them they work mischief by overcharging the physical. A passion represents a directed vital force, and these forces undirected, are as dangerous as live wires would be left lying haphazard. (481–82)[46]

Cultivated as she had been in the suffragist and progressivist milieu of evolutionary vitalism, Marsden originally seized her illuminations and prophetic passions as increments in the mass unfolding of a superhuman consciousness. Yet her moment of highest vision occurred during solitary confinement: I would argue that the discursive imagery of her individualism can be referred to this supreme sublimation of virtual isolation. At least two novels of Marsden's day also treated the visionary experiences of suffragette prisoners in solitary confinement, Gertrude Colmore's *Suffragette Sally*, mentioned above, and May

Sinclair's *Tree of Heaven*.[47] In *Suffragette Sally,* the character Lady Geraldine Hill
(a fictionalization of the historical Lady Constance Lytton) undergoes forcible
feedings, during which period she passes through a dark night of the soul, finally
to be redeemed from her hatred of her tormentors by a vision of Calvary
(270–79). May Sinclair had befriended Pound and H.D. early in the decade, and
later contributed five items over several years to the *Egoist,* so it is quite likely
that she had kept an eye on Dora Marsden. In *The Tree of Heaven,* the character
Dorothy Harrison—conceivably modeled to some extent on Dor(a
M)ar(sde)n—relates the following account of a vision in prison: "I sort of saw
the redeemed of the Lord. They were men, as well as women, Frank. And they
were all free. They were all free because they were redeemed" (221). In both
novels, Dora Marsden throws a fugitive but discernible shadow.

Six months into the *Freewoman,* then, a feminism limited to the physical
side of sexual issues fell far short of Marsden's glimpses of cosmic emancipation.
Her visionary politics seized spiritual passion as self-empowerment. Sexual joy
was one door onto passion, in Marsden's spiritual sense, but it was neither the
source nor the goal of passion's progress. Now, the record of her own sexual life
appears to have been obliterated; neither her published writings, the remnants
of her papers, nor the biographies shed light upon it. Presumably she went
through a phase of lesbian relations on the way to a hermetic celibacy or, perhaps more precisely, an alchemical androgyny. But by all appearances Marsden's
active passions were primarily engaged by polemical rather than erotic struggle.
What can be established is that in the *New Freewoman,* Marsden simply ceased to
purvey the *Freewoman* "gospel" of superhuman evolutionism. For the first few
numbers, vestiges of it remained in the articles of theosophists. For instance, an
article in the first *New Freewoman* (June 15, 1913) related the feminist movement to cosmic cycles and Dora Marsden's writings to the teachings of Madame
Blavatsky and Mary Baker Eddy: "By means of psychic illumination, 'women
will push open the door of the super-world,' to use the words of Miss Dora
Marsden. There must be an actual awakening to the spiritual side of life and
thought before anything great can arise out of the present chaos."[48]

The back page of the same *New Freewoman* number bears a full-page adver-
tisement for the Fifth International Summer School (20). As indicated in the
epigraph to this section, a year earlier Marsden had lectured at the fourth meeting on the same terms as those of the talk she had presented to the Freewoman
Discussion Circle, "Freewomen and Evolution," discussed in the previous
chapter. Listed on the syllabus for the fifth meeting of the summer school was
"The Free Woman (Section IV.) Miss Dora Marsden." It would seem
significant that the title of this lecture lacked the mention of evolution and

broke the type of the freewoman into the singularity of the "free woman" offering the lecture. The summer school's motto had also been modified from the previous year's version, in the direction of aesthetics: "To promote Unity in Religion, Philosophy, Science, *and Art*" (my italics). Throughout the period of the *New Freewoman,* concurrently with Ezra Pound's own overt relinquishing of Neoplatonic and mystical tropes, Marsden would rechannel her "passion" away from an overtly spiritual philosophy and toward the ostensibly more concrete spheres of science and art.

I have been able to recover two items concerning Marsden's second and last appearance at the theosophist retreat at the Peebles Hotel-Hydro in Peebles, Scotland, between July 19 and August 2, 1913. The first is a note Harriet Shaw Weaver sent to Marsden's companion and editorial assistant: "I am glad to hear Miss Marsden demolished most of the arguments of the Theosophists . . . and that the stock of the N.F.W. was sold out in consequence!"[49] The second is a letter from Marsden to Weaver, written a month later, in which Marsden discussed her plans to sound out Ezra Pound and Allen Upward. Concerning Upward, she explained: "I am terrified he will turn out a sentimentalist. 'High Priestess' sounds very suspicious. It would be intolerable to have someone of the *exalté* type, living on our doorstep, with a business connection with the paper! I simply couldn't stand it. Moreover no good comes of these unreal alliances. Look at these 'Path' people—all antagonistic where, before I spoke at Peebles, they were indifferent. They made no effort to understand the 'Freewoman' doctrine is just the rooting out of 'Theosophia.'"[50] The " 'Path' people" were persons connected to the theosophical journal *The Path,* to whose displeasure, it seems, Marsden's individualism now demanded a renunciation of theosophy's humanistic mission.

In the *New Freewoman,* Marsden's hard-edged nominalism operated alongside an aesthetic vitalism that was now absolved from the exaltation of a collective evolutionary teleology. Nevertheless, her last aesthetic leader indicates that in some way she was still seeking clues to the reconstruction of that *abiding* vision of 1909.[51] Here Marsden returned to the question of the *duration* of passion and offered in passing what appears to be a status report on her current state of overmind. Her plaintive conclusion, that the habitual overcautiousness of the senses restricts the flow of prophetic passion, I take to confess some of the psychosexual consequences of the ideological constrictions within Marsden's narrowing egoism.

> The grievance which most of us have against our sensations is that they are too short to allow emotion to turn round in them. Feeling is but rarely

able to sense the quality of itself in the moment of experience. Consequently we are thrown back upon the secondhand knowledge of memory for confirmation; and memory is faulty because sensation, in addition to being brief, is feeble. This briefness of realisation is the most baffling thing in life: it is that which lies at the root of all excesses and all attempted voluptuousness; the excess is the outcome of a series of efforts to appease to a fuller satisfaction sensation tantalisingly incomplete. Repetition attempts to do what only duration could achieve; its effect is to make even repetition impossible. The sensation of the beautiful is the one case where realisation is long-drawn out. It is voluptuousness in excelsis, unfretted by repetitions because satisfying in a single time-length. It is pleasure caught on the wing; brought to a pause to be enjoyed. It is a moment in which realisation is fixed; then grows; sublimates; then fades, and the flux of normal being moves on. But the momentary stay in the flux has been enough to enable one to feel life living, and to hear its unborn sound. ("Beauty and the Senses," 202)

For Dora Marsden to admit bafflement is noteworthy in itself. But, after all, she had to come down sometime, and it is only after one is undilated that the self-righteousness of ecstatic conviction yields to the subsequent processes of recollection and rationalization. Marsden's reorientation in the *New Freewoman* is also clarified, insofar as she turned to literary and aesthetic experience as a source of or substitute for the political rush that had previously carried her out of the WSPU and into the persona of the freewoman.

"Running to Waste"

As noted earlier, in her "Views and Comments" in the second number of the *New Freewoman* (July 1, 1913), Dora Marsden initiated a polemical campaign against the overweening intellect. Much as Kant had done in the *Critique of Judgment,* she positioned art as the ideal mediation, here between vital soul and reflective mind. In this context, Marsden figured the intellect as a "machine," which in a vitalist idiom is always a form of ontological demotion. The machine figure draws with it other facets of mechanism and mechanical operation: as Marsden extended this instance of the mind = machine metaphor, her subordination of intellect to life allegorized what ought to be the subservience of technology to culture as a whole. However,

> our present culture is a thought-culture—sicklied over with the cast of the
> pale concept: it has nothing to do with changing life—nor with what is

essential and true in Intellect. Thought is delusion: thinking is a definite process: set in motion to liberate not *thoughts* but living impulses, not the fixed frameworks of concepts, but self-directed force whose direction will be as unforeseeable as the individual—whose living soul it is—is solitary and unique; sole one of its kind; thinking's effect is to liberate life ready for action, not to bind it up to construct a system. Good thinking would prevent the formation of thoughts, as a good machine minimises waste. (23)

Clustering around the theme of waste in Marsden's *New Freewoman* writings is the scientism derived from the discourse of Victorian thermodynamics, the conservation and dissipation of energy in particular systems. As the idiom of thermodynamics came alongside the vocabulary of vital force in scientistic cultural conversation, waste came to signify the forces of death, disorder, and resistance opposed to the forms and progress of the life force. Ultimately, motions and movements that squander the energy needed to produce them are submitted to the second law of thermodynamics and moralized as entropic. In the scientific ideology of social energetics, the individual was conceived as a "human motor," a closed energy system in which fatigue and ennui are the affective registers of physical entropy.[52] By Marsden's day, for many of those already inclined toward the vitalistic scenario, these (en)tropic transfers resulted in a heightened sense that individual existence was submitted to the cosmic struggle of energy versus entropy.[53] The ego must owe its living integrity to the militant conservation of a life energy preyed upon by the forces of entropic degradation.

Such thermodynamically conceived physiology was technologically applied to industrial and social campaigns for increased efficiency, for instance, Frederick Winslow Taylor's influential doctrine of scientific management. Out of this scientistic milieu, the problem of waste—fatigue, inefficiency, friction, conflict—came forward to early modernism as a cipher of social disharmony. We have had an instance of this idiom already in Vernon Lee's remark that "progress is but the substitution of human mechanism more and more delicate and solid, through which the movement is ever greater, the friction ever less" (*Gospels of Anarchy*, 26). Another significant example of the broad cachet enjoyed by Taylor's system in 1913 may be had in Rebecca West's introduction to Pound's first appearance in the *New Freewoman*, a selection of poems entitled "The Contemporania of Ezra Pound": "there has arisen a little band who desire the poet to be as disciplined and efficient at his job as the stevedore. Just as Taylor and Gilbreth want to introduce scientific management into industry so the *imagistes* want to discover the most puissant way of whirling the scattered star dust of words into a new star of passion."[54] This marvelously mixed comparison tags the long-exploded nebula theory of the 1840s to the thermodynamic

cosmology of the early twentieth century. Nevertheless, West's figures clearly
took their cue from Ezra Pound's own poetic scientisms, as they were soon to
be expressed in "The Serious Artist," and indicate the embeddedness of imagist
doctrines of hardness and "maximum efficiency of expression" (214) in a wide
field of social energetics.[55]

The social energetics inflecting Marsden's current thinking about waste are
registered in the economic notion of expenditure. In a *New Freewoman* leader to
which we will return in the chapter on William Carlos Williams, Marsden set
forth an allegory of Life, personified by an "uncommon youth," who must
undergo fit trials to earn his majority, and Mind, personified as an "aged crone"
who commands the youth to exercise his powers: "thy fires are to be spent."[56]
Marsden's allegory reproduced the cultural agon between mechanical and vital
forces, between Works, or materialistic accomplishments—"Works enough
were there, with matter lent to manipulations multiple"—and "creation's mir-
acle . . . the living force which feels, can leap, and run" ("Tales for the Attentive," 142). Marsden has Mind blame herself for the misuse to which humanity
has put her works, the machines she has given it. When I—Mind asks rhetorically—"construct the engines which make Life in men beat low, what am I but
as the dead resisting force which would press Life deathwards in the scale?"
(142). The question earnestly enjoined by Marsden's vitalist allegory is how the
burning of the Fires—if that expenditure of life force is equivalent to the con-
sumption of a finite energy-producing fuel—can lead to anything but the burning out of the living organism and the life force altogether. What economy of
power is appropriate to the enhancement as well as maintenance of the living
ego?

To begin with, in the same *New Freewoman* number that published
Pound's electromagnetic scientism in "The Serious Artist," Marsden refurbished her own brand of electro-vitalism as an existential ecology of single
organisms. Her figures here envision the isolate ego, or soul, as a kind of spiritual hermit crab, "an individuated entity thrown out free by the stream of living energy . . . a 'thing' as electricity running along a wire is a thing, with movements, consciousness, repulsions, attractions, making excursions and returning
to its shell through the apertures for entry and exit it has made; a thing which
forages, feeds, dissipates or grows, by means we can learn if we keep watch"
("Views and Comments," October 15, 1913, 165–66). Marsden's vital economy
would appear to be a defensive stance toward a predatory arrangement unmitigated by mutual aid or cooperative schemes, much like the social Darwinist
milieu of laissez-faire capitalism and scientific management. The unique ego is
a precarious and vigilant life form "thrown out" into a world of threats and

competitors, in immediate need of effective survival tactics. As Stephen Dedalus will phrase a comparable attitude in the *Egoist* two years later, the renegade artist chooses "silence, exile, and cunning."[57]

Marsden returned to similarly stark figures in "Beauty and the Senses," in which a correspondent's critique of her aesthetics moved her to discriminate among the terms *body, sense,* and *soul.* As Marsden proceeded through these definitions, she continued to rehearse the idiom of electro-vital energetics, a vocabulary that marks a definitive departure from biological vitalism's solicitude for the living body. In this thermodynamic redescription of her idealism, Marsden detached the nucleus of life from the material body and transferred it to its energy source in the soul.

> We would rather say that the "body" was a screen of dead matter specially acted upon by a unit of living energy to serve as a buffer and a neutral zone between the latter and the world (*i.e.,* all things not itself) outside. . . . Dead, the organised life which encouraged the illusion that the body too was organised is gone and has left no address. The remnant left behind at death is all that there existed of "body" in life. . . . So much for the "body," dead matter even in life, from our point of view.
>
> The senses, in our way of using the term, are the thin streams of soul which filter through the screen of matter outward towards the external surface. They are the fringe of soul where feeling, *i.e.,* life, runs thinnest, slender feelers, some too fine to feel more than the dimmest awareness of the shiver of contact; and some broader and stronger. The effect, if not the purpose, of this difference in density and intensity which is indicated in the use of the two terms "soul" and "sense" is to enable a life-unit to ingratiate itself into the phenomenal world with a minimum implication of emotion in experience. The organisation of the senses represents caution embodied in the structure of life. (202)

The Newtonian mechanical dualism between matter and motion, itself a scientized vehicle for the theological dualism between body and spirit, is here refurbished by social thermodynamics as the distinction between the inert material corpus and its moving principle, the energetic soul. Marsden appears to have adapted to this description the social-prophetic moralization of an entropic cosmos coming down from Victorian physics: the God who energizes the world is infinitely conserved but the material world fed from that energy is abandoned to entropic dissipation.[58] The primary tasks facing any ego would then be maintaining and refining its organization through the augmenting and hoarding of its vital resources. In Marsden's vital-energetic register, the implacable demand for thermodynamic efficiency is translated into the existential caution by which the senses defend the soul in order to produce a "minimum implication of emotion."

This is the doctrinal context from which, in her "Views and Comments" for the same number, Marsden reaffirmed the primacy of "the egoistic unit" (November 15, 1913, 203) and proceeded to define her egoism in terms of its defensive reaction against the "Woman Movement," the "Cause" to which it had previously subordinated itself. Marsden's most serious charge against suffragism and mass political movements in general is couched exactly in these ideologized terms of vital-energetic economy. Causes sap the soul by demanding the forfeiting of individual energies. They levy an onerous tax on the life force.

> It was Oscar Wilde who illuminated the arid regions of causes and propaganda with the observation that great movements come to an end with the birth of their founder. . . . Before the "birth" of the "leaders," before the trumpets, banners and catchwords, a phenomenal advance was quietly being made: It was "actual" in individual women. Then arose "leaders" who reduced it to a "cause," a fixed idea, stationaryness and consequent stagnation. The streams of living energy and understanding spreading in every direction, each the expression of the individual's instinctive development, they called "running to *waste*." They proposed at once to dam it up: make a cause of it: the individual must give her energy to the cause. Propaganda started to teach women what they owed to the "Cause": the "duty" of draining their stream of energy into the dam. (203)

What was life to Marsden, to the WSPU was waste, concretely speaking, her private self-motions uncoordinated with the centralized efficiencies of the movement as a whole, her own irrepressible insubordination. As we saw in the last chapter, Mrs. Pethick-Lawrence had patronized Marsden in just such terms: "you are spending your capital instead of living as you should do on the interest of that capital. . . . I do most earnestly urge you to be more thrifty in this matter." Marsden's anarchistic vitalism went Pethick-Lawrence's bourgeois social energetics one better. Her postsuffragist anarchism was commensurate with Carpenter's in considering the state to be inherently corrupt and corrupting. But Marsden also reacted away from Carpenter's vital socialism by extending her critique to all mass movements and corporate institutions: they, too, are like punitive nation-states, operating on graft, tapping off the vitality of their proponents, debilitating rather than empowering the populace. Marsden's anarchism shared with modernist literary experimentalism an antisocialism expressed as a sublime contempt for communal duties.

Changing Names

The *New Freewoman* has long been glanced at through late modernist lenses or filtered through the correspondence and reminiscences of the imagists and so circumscribed to F. S. Flint's or Richard Aldington's poetic agendas. Critics unclear about the origins of the *Egoist,* unaware or unappreciative of the significance of the *Freewoman,* have been especially prone to marginalize Dora Marsden's editorial omnipresence in the *New Freewoman* as a nuisance or an irrelevance. Readers giving a cursory scan to the *New Freewoman* solely in search of either canonical literary modernism or, more recently, a clear indication of mainstream feminism, have had some trouble appreciating the journal's true status, especially as it came to its self-determined close. Thus, it is not surprising that the full resonance of Marsden's remarkable "Views and Comments" in the thirteenth and final number has also not been appreciated. Right at the start, for instance, one could misconstrue the lead sentence—"It is proposed that with our issue of January 1st, 1914, the title of *The New Freewoman* be changed to *The Egoist*"—by taking the unnamed agent of Marsden's typically passive clause "It is proposed" to be someone other than herself, perhaps one of "the undersigned men of letters . . . Allen Upward, Ezra Pound, Huntly Carter, Reginald W. Kauffmann, Richard Aldington."[59] In fact, the proposal proper originated with Marsden, Harriet Shaw Weaver communicated it to Allen Upward, and several months later Pound relayed Upward's response back to Marsden in the formal garb in which it became public.

This is the evidence. Midway through the *New Freewoman*'s run, three months before the public announcement of a name-change decision, Harriet Shaw Weaver sent Marsden a note that began, "I enclose a letter from Mr. Upward. I suppose we shall not have any definite scheme from him just yet. I have told him you are thinking about a change of name. *I* quite like your suggestion of 'The Egoist'. It is a good challenge to sentimentalists."[60] Marsden's papers also preserve a carbon-copy typescript with the full text of the name-change proposal, differing from the version published in Marsden's "Views and Comments" of December 15 in only one particular. Whereas the typescript reads "without regard to the ignorant public," the published version runs as follows.

> We, the undersigned men of letters who are grateful to you for estab-
> lishing an organ in which men and women of intelligence can express
> themselves without regard to the public, venture to suggest to you that the
> present title of the paper causes it to be confounded with organs devoted
> solely to the advocacy of an unimportant reform in an obsolete political
> institution.
>
> We therefore ask with great respect that you should consider the advis-
> ability of adopting another title which will mark the character of your
> paper as an organ of individualists of both sexes, and of the individualist
> principle in every department of life. (244)

In ink on the typescript is one signature, Ezra Pound's. But following the main
text and Pound's signature, the document also contains this postscript: "Mr.
Allen Upward has drafted the following petition to the Editor of the 'New
Freewoman' and forwarded it with a request that before publication it should
be submitted for signature to as many other supporters of the paper as are likely
to concur in the suggestion." Thus came about the cheerful identification with
the epithet "individualist" by which the five men of letters signed their aestheticized version of agreement with Marsden's anarchist premises.

The reader who has followed Marsden's earlier transitions will recognize
the consistency of her doctrinal positions and the impress of her usual methods.
Her ironic self-effacement—framing her decision by way of its relation to a
recent piece of correspondence—was a common editorial procedure. In and of
itself, the act of title changing was a habitual reflex, almost a repetition compulsion, determined by her discursive vitalism. Marsden's titular valediction to an
explicitly feminist practice consummated a conceptual departure that began
well before the demise of the *Freewoman,* and that was clearly in evidence from
the inception of the *New Freewoman.* In Marsden's words on this occasion, the
journal's "present title . . . contrives to suggest what the paper is not, and fails
to give any indication whatsoever as to what it is"; when the present title was
chosen, "there existed considerations strong enough to lead us to its adoption,"
an allusion to the practical matter of maintaining with the *New Freewoman* what
slim public and financial base the old *Freewoman* had possessed. With the dedicated patronage and editorial assistance of Harriet Shaw Weaver, these considerations "no longer exist" ("Views and Comments," December 15, 1913, 244).

However, Upward's politely outrageous letter has become something of a
charged spectacle in recent feminist discussion, in Rachel Blau DuPlessis's presentation, "a symbolic moment" (*Pink Guitar,* 44). Superficial readings have it
that an arrogant vanguard of male modernism is here exposed red-handed over-
running a lone feminist outpost. DuPlessis's subtler reading perceives a doctrin-

ally compromised maverick postfeminist capitulating to masculinist demands. Both readings are cut to larger patterns of literary sex war by which feminist critics have been renarrating the history of Anglo-American modernism. However, in this specific, admittedly recondite, instance, such readings go astray. The entire source of the name-change decision was Marsden, who used the phalanx of Pound's coterie to buttress her own self-will. And, although the *New Freewoman* and the *Egoist* were never overtly feminist journals, under the final control of Marsden and Weaver neither were they ever masculinist ones. For Marsden, well before the blunt emergence of the *Egoist*, the figure of the egoist already represented for her the individualistic untyping of the freewoman. In fact, the new title proclaimed the gender of individualism to be anarchistic androgyny, as Marsden attempted once again discursively to finesse simplistic gender binarisms.

DuPlessis attributes Marsden's further claims—what women "*can* do, it is open for them to do; and judgment as unbiased as ever it is likely to be, is ready to abide by the evidence of their work's quality" (244)—to a "hopefulness" that with hindsight appears "chilling" (*Pink Guitar*, 45). If it *was* hopefulness that moved Marsden to follow the men of letters' lead, then her submissive mistakenness provides the cautionary moral for feminism to draw from this symbolic moment: "women must be suspicious, dubious of declaring that gender asymmetries have ended" (45). However, did Marsden's declaration actually make or imply such a premature conclusion? One could also interpret her statement less as a sanguinary expectation than as a clear-sighted awareness that such cultural biases change exceedingly slowly: for Marsden to claim that such judgment was at the end of 1913 "as unbiased as ever it is likely to be" doesn't necessarily state that it was in fact unbiased. My reading would fall into line with Marsden's stringent efforts throughout the *Freewoman* to confront misogyny head-on and to disabuse feminists of naive overoptimism. If that was the case, then Marsden's attitude was not so much a chilling hopefulness as a cool realism. The basic point would be that one must act on one's own present desires without final regard for others' later judgments.

"Rays of Sensitive Life"

In its shifting of concern from female disempowerment to individual self-empowerment, Marsden's discourse developed directly out of the feminist perspective on servility and defenselessness and then generalized that perspective to all power arrangements. If her egoism was reactionary, it was so first and foremost from the social tyrannies of self-sacrifice that thwart the individual power motive and with it any "vivid new life-manifestation." Raymond Williams's characterization of D. H. Lawrence's self-exile is worth considering in this context: "he has been vulgarized into a romantic rebel, a type of the 'free individual'. . . . It cannot really be sustained. . . . Lawrence's rejection had to be so intense, if he was to get clear at all."[61] Social conscience, Marsden now argued, benefits the state far more than it protects its possessors: "A man who subscribes to a fixed idea is a 'safe' man. The 'idea' can be relied upon to keep him anchored. But one who trusts to himself is an incalculable, unreliable unit which no safe and respectable body of opinion would tolerate" ("Views and Comments," December 15, 1913, 245). Compare this with Lawrence in "Education of the People."

> You can obtain one kind of perfect citizen by suppressing individuality and cultivating the public virtues: which has been the invariable tendency of reform, and of social idealism in modern days. A real individual has a spark of danger in him, a menace to society. Quench this spark and you quench the individuality, you obtain a social unit, not an integral man. . . . On the other hand, by the over-development of the individualistic qualities, you produce a disintegration of all society. . . . You must have a harmony and an inter-relation between the two modes. Because, though man is first and foremost an individual being, yet the very accomplishing of his individuality rests upon his fulfillment in social life.[62]

Here is one example at least of Lawrence's ultimate balance, one he draws from Walt Whitman's *Democratic Vistas,* in the presentation of these issues. It is a balance rarely forthcoming in Marsden's writings. She was simply more radical, due I take it to the greater extremity of the female perspective on power and powerlessness and to her militant defiance of all violations of individual integrity. On the rare occasions when she discusses community she does so in classical anarchistic fashion: "Society itself is not based on any Conception whatsoever, it is based on the inborn predilections and instincts of individuals. When these instincts break through the overlying Verbiage and reveal themselves for what they are the 'Stability of Society' is unaffected. For whatever these instincts are Society is and will be."[63] The anarchist vitalist trusts to the instinctive bias of the life force. The conception of a self-transforming, metamorphic self complements the anarchist vision of a social evolution toward statelessness. In the words of Peter Kropotkin: "No ruling authorities, then. No government of man by man; no crystallization and immobility, but a continual evolution—such as we see in Nature."[64]

The need to justify once and for all "obliterating the 'woman' character from the journal" (244) also gave Marsden the opportunity to interrelate her anarchist politics to her incipient philosophy of language. In the next section of these "Views and Comments" in the last *New Freewoman,* Marsden adumbrated a semiotic perspective on individual participation in collective movements forecasting her major accomplishment in the *Egoist—The Science of Signs,* a critical philosophy examining all conceptual vocabularies for evidences of ideological graft: "The irony of 'standing for' a thing lies in the fact that the first return the thing stood for makes is to bring its advocates kneeling before it. A man will lie down prone before the thing he 'stands for' and serve it, and the one assertion of egoism is, to our minds, that a man shall make it his concern with things to force them to minister to him" (244). Marsden's anarchistic semiotics begin by questioning the unstable semantics of political representation. Anarchism contests the tendency of bourgeois parliamentary states to reify elective delegates, to grant to public "representatives" powers denied to the people represented, or to substitute for authentic representatives duplicitous signifiers beholden to private agendas. Anarchism would eliminate such authority, do away with badges, regalia, uniforms, and other signifiers of collective coercion. Similarly, Marsden reasoned, one who stands for a collective movement assumes the role of an interchangeable token for an absent and imaginary signified—the cause—often literalizing their status as a signifier by attaching themselves to an inscription, say, a picket sign or political placard bearing someone else's name. One's empowerment thereby is dubious, one's demotion from originary or responsible agency an equally likely result. Political rights cannot be effectively conferred: persons without the power to command their own person possess only the systemic obligations of the dispossessed. Essential qualities of human agency cannot be transferred like units of capital from one self to another. Marsden's egoism would have any person signify only their own self-constructed worth.

From 1913 to 1919, Dora Marsden's philosophical egoism elaborated a proto-deconstructive semiotics for the purpose of disassembling liberal humanism. Post-Nietzschean devotee of the "over-and-above," she coolly investigated a bottomless semantic vertigo half a century before our recent deconstructors leaned over the abysses of signification. Perhaps as early as her solitary confinement in 1909, what Marsden saw was the self enclosed in a verbal cell. Rather than decenter the textual self, however, Marsden celebrated the visionary cell, on the condition that she herself could write the text of her own confinement. Following out her vital light she issued ever further into existential differentiation.

In the penultimate section of the *New Freewoman*'s last "Views and Comments," Marsden attacked the ideals that promote the sacrifice of the self on the altar of humanity—"Humanity, the sacred 'Unity of the All,' has in some mysterious fashion acquired a worth which the reputation of its compounding units does nothing at all to explain" (245). In Marsden's concluding section, she combined the critique of mystic humanism with a powerful evocation of her own egoistic phenomenology. The great virtue of Marsden's entire passage is its remarkable revelation of the discursive and aesthetic parameters of early modernism—iconoclasm, subjectivity, and exploration.

> If we could get into the habit of describing a man as he feels himself instead of in the terms of the physical image under which he presents himself to sight, we should break through this deadening concept of unity. If we described him—as an artist would—that is, as he feels himself, we should say an intense flaming heart of sensitiveness in a sheath of material substance, in and out of which it can send piercing fingers, keen tongues of itself as foragers into an external world. . . .

Marsden's sublime iconoclasm participates in the aesthetics of antirepresentationalism at large in early modernism. She would break apart not only the panoply of deadening ideals but also the habitual apparatuses of social perception in the name of life's infinite individuation into fiery points of vivid apperception. *Flame* is an insistent figure inflecting the notion of continuous vital flux with the notion of expended energy: in the next chapter we will examine Lawrence's vital/energetic fire imagery in his *Study of Thomas Hardy*. Marsden's developmental sequences provide an index of modernism's overall cultural shift from an evolutionary to a thermodynamic vitalism and thus from the forgiving contours of biology to the rather merciless formulas of physics. We have already noted Marsden's current demotion of the body to its nonvital materiality and promotion of the senses as the outrunners and guardians of the ego or vital soul. Bodily figures remain, however, in ambiguously eroticized fingers and tongues, akin to the eerie "feelers" mentioned in "Beauty and the Senses," by which the inner life both insulates itself from and insinuates itself into the outer world. Continuing to unfold the positive consequences of allowing "feeling" to break up the "physical image," Marsden went on:

> We should say that a man was confined with his bodily sheath no more than the rays of an arc lamp are confined by the transparent globe; that unlike the rays of a lamp which, once shed, dissipate with degenerating potency, the rays of sensitive life return to their source with increased power; we should say that this is the inner meaning of "building up" an

organism: that it is the withdrawal of the living threads, heavy with gathered impressions, back within itself that distinguishes life from energy: distinguishes that which is being built up into the egoistic unit from that which is running down towards disintegration; that experience is the food of life: that the senses of sight, sound, and scent, sympathy and understanding, and a vague growing awareness too immature to be given a name, stretching out into the world pass outside the limits of the body to ransack the universe—for experience. . . .

The current economy of Marsden's cosmic egoism envisions this vitalistic ego precisely in its ability to escape from the dismal entropic fate of nonvital energy. What "distinguishes life from energy" is the former's higher powers of self-organization and self-maintenance. But the Marsdenian ego must seek its own survival; it must earn its transcendence of entropy exactly by immersing itself into the field of experience where it can exchange its lower energies for "increased power" and so "build itself up." It must send its feelers abroad.

With a million tentacles they invade the world of appearance; pierce, scour, scan, scoop up with a mighty arm the panorama of the world: but they return an army laden with spoil always to their own. They have lost nothing of their individualised uniqueness in their excursions. They have scooped impressions from that with which they have had contact all they were capable of assimilating: but they have in no way merged their identity in what they have fed on: rather they have intensified it: made the distinctness from all that was not of itself more definite. Nor does experience—which is awareness—absorb or diminish the thing it grows on. Each retains its integrity. . . .

What level of ironic deployment should be granted to such drastically predatory/colonial imagery? The imperial ego sends forth its armed invaders to despoil the realm of the other, they return to the self uncontaminated and reinvigorated, yet the other is thereby "undiminished." Is this a sheer ideological mystification of the historical reality of colonial imperialism? Or does it trope and critique that history by imagining the other not along racist lines of exploitative bourgeois objectification, but as itself a self? "The thing" the ego "grows on" maintains itself and extracts its own benefits from existential commerce. This is perhaps Marsden's spiritual/libertarian version of "free trade": the finest intercourse occurs only between agents equally self-possessed and, thus, equally distinct and individuated.

Marsden's course of discourse in the *New Freewoman* concludes in these "Views and Comments," and does so, ironically enough, by reining in the absoluteness of the ego. To resist entropic disintegration the ego must at least confront and forage upon the field of the other, it must expend itself in order to maintain its capital. So Marsden explodes the mystic ego along with its corollary notion as advocated by Buddhistic Whitmanians like Edward Carpenter— the factitious solidarity of the theological or humanistic "All."

> Contrary to the testimony of the hymn which tells us "We are not divided, all one body we, One in hope and doctrine, one in charitee," we *are* divided, and division grows increasingly with our growth. Because an individual is not confined within the cover of his skin, he is not therefore limitless; because he can make excursions beyond the limits of his body he is not therefore "merged" in the "All" and the "All" in him; because the self gleans among that which is not itself it does not thereby become part and parcel with it—democratic opinion and the devastating blight of an Oriental philosophy, now everywhere spreading, notwithstanding. (245)

The "democratic opinion" receiving this attack is a system such as Edward Carpenter's mystic democracy; the "Oriental philosophy" refers to the purveyors of Madame Blavatsky's woozy theosophy. In Marsden's view at this stage, for all its manifest sun worship, Carpenter's system appears to capitulate to entropy. Social-energetic productivity on the thermodynamic model demands the maintenance of (heat) differentials, which Marsden's system moralizes as maximum egoistic differentiation. More bourgeois forms of possessive individualism operated the same scientistic paradigm to uphold given class distinctions. Universal social equality appeared to envision only an amorphous equilibrium tending in the end not to the continuous productive flux of higher life but to devolution and ultimate immobility (the thermodynamic "heat death"). In *The Art of Creation*, Carpenter had remarked that "to regard the world as simply an arena of separate warring beings and personalities is impossible, because (as all Science, Philosophy, and Experience convince us) there is inevitably a vast unity underlying all. . . . In that thought there is liberation, in that thought there is rest" (34). By contrast, Marsden's consistently militant system was now deliberately antagonistic to such pacifist quietism. The fight for individual freedom must be waged without respite to maintain vital pressure against material and social entropy. This was the prime motive Marsden shared with other purveyors of monumental modernism, to pursue "the individualist principle in every department of life."

4.

Rooms in the *Egoist* Hotel

Egoism and Imagism

Richard Aldington

The criticism of literary modernism tends to establish invidious factions by replicating the personal interrelations and polemical contentions of its main figures. Once the critic can divide the field into low versus high, progressive versus reactionary, male versus female, or Anglo-American versus continental, one is set to moralize it accordingly. Certainly the present study's differentiations between early and late modernisms display that same propensity. Be that as it may, one master of the invidious within the *Egoist* group was Richard Aldington: Hughes's skewed version of editorial affairs at the *Egoist* was based in fair measure on Aldington's testimonies.

Yet at first, it seems, Aldington seized his subeditorial opportunity with gusto and was encouraged to provide a light touch.

> Dear Miss Marsden,
>
> I went down to Oakley House this morning and heard from the clerk that you are ill. I hope that it is nothing serious? The incapacity or rather, to avoid ambiguity, the indisposition of the editor of the N. F. is a blow to civilisation!
>
> I propose that on Jan 1st and after we have two sandwichmen to advertise and sell the Egoist. We should print two bills. One containing in large letters the strange device: "THE EGOIST, AN INDIVIDUALIST REVIEW, PRICE 6d." The other with the same device in smaller letters and a list of the contents. . . . I suppose I had better interview them, because I shall know if they're drunk and be able to kick them if they're impertinent. . . .

137

Am sending you along some poems by Flint. I have a narrative poem by Robert Frost for the number after. I have a chap in Germany who is doing us some articles on German literature. I will be as funny as I can.[1]

But early in 1917 his sponsor at the *New Freewoman/Egoist*, Ezra Pound, expressed some disappointment to Margaret Anderson, the editor of the *Little Review*. In the midst of negotiating his editorial arrangements with Anderson, much as he had done a few years earlier with Marsden and the *New Freewoman*, Pound explained: "The young stuff here that hasn't a home, would be an occasional poem from Rodker or Iris Barry. The rest are clustered to the Egoist. I got Aldington that job some years ago. He hasn't done quite as well as I expected, BUT he was very young."[2]

The only other letter from Aldington in the Dora Marsden papers—also, like the previous facetious one about the sandwichmen, written on *New Freewoman* stationery—is an undated and serious note that seems to record an encounter with Marsden's peremptory editorial methods. The imagist group was not in fact doing "as it liked with the whole paper" (Hughes, *Imagism*, 31).

> Dear Miss Marsden,
>
> Our experience of the last few days should prove to us that it is easier to write a bad play than to correct a bad review of it. I have no objection to any of your emendations, except to that marked with blue pencil. I object on the ground that the "participle construction" takes off from the force of what is said, & is not English but Latin. All schoolmasters &c use that kind of writing, but does one *speak* like that? I ask humbly. You will see I have not altered the sentence, but left it to your conscience![3]

Pound had also felt the lash of Marsden's emendations, and his eventual disenchantment with his subeditorial post and deferral to the even younger Aldington may well have been spurred by her high-handed altering of his copy. An undated letter from Pound to Marsden's assistant, Grace Jardine, perhaps written during the period of the publication of "The Serious Artist," reads: "Yes, I should very much object to removing the paragraphs you mention. . . . Also I prefer my own phraseology. Not even the Quarterly has ventured to interfere with it."[4] Aldington himself later indicated just how bruised were the subeditorial egos at large in the offices of the *Egoist*. On June 6, 1916, he wrote to Amy Lowell: "Hilda is taking over [for me at] the Egoist. I seem to be a little 'out' with Miss Weaver just now. Whether it is due to Ezra or to Miss Marsden I can't say, but there it is. . . . Miss Marsden seems to have a great 'down' on you—anyhow she is a beastly woman, I dislike her very much" (cited in Hanscombe and Smyers, *Writing for Their Lives*, 176).

James Stephens

Until 1914, when Harriet Shaw Weaver provided a permanent subvention, Dora Marsden's journals were usually on the brink of financial collapse. Nevertheless, she had remained uncompromising both in her own polemical development and in the catholicity of the contributions she accepted. Rather than solidify a public base by repeating a single line or perspective on a given set of affairs, she cultivated her own intellectual development and so shifted her discursive focus faster than any mass audience could have followed. In the *Freewoman* she alienated most of the suffragists and many of the spiritualists and mainstream feminists. As Marsden ratcheted up her radical individualism further in the *New Freewoman,* all those former audiences diminished. Political anarchism and literary discussion began to dominate the body of the paper. Marsden's pre-*Egoist* egoism proclaimed precisely the freedom to abandon past positions, to embrace new roles and terms. To fend off doctrinal and spiritual fixity, Marsden practiced and promoted a consistent inconstancy, a procedure she not-so-subtly underlined by following her emphatic "Views and Comments" in the December 15 *New Freewoman* with an extract from Henri Bergson's *Creative Evolution.*[5] She promised as much for the policy of the incipient *Egoist:* "We prefer to say we 'stand' for nothing since the 'selves,' to whose power and satisfaction this effort administers, are too changeful for anything which 'stands' to keep up with; their satisfactions must move forward. . . . Any work therefore bearing the marks of first-hand vision, and the ring of honest and economical expression will, if it interests us (it is necessary always to allow for a wide streak of personal preference) have a chance of finding its way herein" ("Views and Comments," December 15, 1913, 245).

However, despite such manifestoes, to many in Marsden's audience, from its outset the *Egoist* appeared to be largely in the grip of Pound's coterie, an impression enshrined in official imagist lore and persisting in most literary histories. On this precise score, Marsden's papers contain a substantial letter dated January 7, 1914, signed "J. Stephens."[6] James Stephens, poet, novelist, spiritualist, was a minor figure in the Irish literary revival. Two months prior to writing the letter to Marsden, he had been the 1913 recipient of the Polignac Prize of £100 awarded by the Royal Society of Literature. Stephens wrote Marsden the following telling critique of the premier number of the *Egoist,* for under Aldington's nervous influence, soon to be curbed by Marsden and Weaver's editorial rearrangement, it was an especially chummy production.

> I have been looking through the first number of the Egoist. Its appearance after reading the manifesto in the last number of the N.F.W., I have anticipated with much curiosity. The manifesto led me to hope that you had gathered round you a vital group of men bent on doing intimate, real sort of work, able to put up a strong fight against reaction and to go deep into the heart of things. But alas, there is ve[r]y little in the paper before me to sustain my hope. There is a superficial and ephemeral air about the paper. Most persons appear to know the gang who are running it. Aldington, Hueffer, Pound, and others—none of whom really matter. They are at their old game. It is getting a stale affair this business of writing each other up, Hueffer-Pound, Pound-Hueffer, Pound-Aldington, Aldington-Pound, Aldington-Hunt (Hueffer's mistress), Aldington-Wyndham Lewis (the man with a toy trumpet). Is the game going to be kept up? Will Violet return the compliment? Will she write up Aldington or Flint or some other member of the Pound-Hueffer group? . . .

Stephens's impression that Pound's "gang" was now in charge of the *Egoist* had been reinforced by a series of circumstances. First, there had been Pound's vigorous literary editorship of the *New Freewoman* and his leader "The Serious Artist." In addition, with "Beauty and the Senses," Marsden had concluded her own series of aesthetic meditations by the eleventh of the *New Freewoman's* thirteen numbers: a readiness to shift discursive gears may well have driven her effort to reestablish the journal on a broader footing. As we have seen, she continued to write significant "Views and Comments" columns in the last two numbers, but what Stephens saw was that the leaders had gone to Pound's allies F. S. Flint and Allen Upward. Marsden returned to the lead in the first number of the *Egoist* with "Liberty, Law, and Democracy," a political diatribe blasting libertarians for sentimentalism, an opening salvo in her current campaign to define the egoism of the *Egoist* against the anarchism of the American Stirnerians Benjamin Tucker and Steven T. Byington. However, about half of the first *Egoist* was given over to Wyndham Lewis's "The Cubist Room," assorted Aldington reviews, de Gourmont's ongoing *Horses of Diomedes,* and the poems of Flint. Stephens's letter went on to explain his disdain for this clique and to take Marsden to task for countenancing it.

It would not matter if these persons got fundamental truths out of the job. But they are simply out for a lark and have nothing whatever to do with the real aim of your paper. They have nothing to do with egoism or the great issues it implies. It would not matter if they had individuality. I defy anyone to say that they have. Where is Wyndham Lewis' individuality? He is simply trying to do what Picasso *does* do because he Picasso has the individuality to do it. There are only two writers in the Egoist who possess strong and assertive individualities, and they at each end of the paper. Between them are the literary persons who talk about expressing their age without feeling it, quite forgetful of the fact that the men and women who do express their age are those who dig their experience, not out of literature, but out of themselves. You yourself would be doing this were you not so bent on rowing with your contributors on matters that are not of the slightest importance.

"The Serious Artist" did not seem to have convinced James Stephens that the aesthetic manifestoes and productions of the Pound-Hueffer group were truly in earnest. His sense that they were essentially "out for a lark" seems to be corroborated by Aldington's initial letter to Marsden.

Huntly Carter

The two writers "at each end of the paper" James Stephens did appreciate were, so to speak, the serious egoists, Marsden at the front and Huntly Carter at the end. Carter had earlier been invited to participate in Dora Marsden's journals as a result of Mary Gawthorpe's enthusiastic recommendation.

Even you, heroic worker that you are, cannot meet all the claims of an all-round situation. Cannot you take on Huntly Carter (*It is perhaps unnecessary to add that this present idea comes *not* from H.C.) as your co-editor while you have the chance? I know from a long way back that his heart's wish has lain in the direction of Editorship and your paper *could do* with his special gifts. I am sure he would be a great asset to you. Together you could *quadruple* present efforts. He would relieve you of the heaviest formalities of editorship and *be glad* to do it. He has a typewriter which he uses himself. He is a magnificent worker, also an all round student. From what I know of his methods of work they are much like your own. In short he would make a fine ally in the organising of your side. He would need an equal salary to your own but that would be no more than yours and mine together, as first thought of. As co-editor he would be able to make special use of his position in running a *series* of such valuable symposia as were printed in the *New Age*. Well think of it. (I merely suggest. The individual who is really free has no personal ends to serve one way or the other. Accept or reject que vous voulez!)[7]

From the last days of the *Freewoman,* Carter had been a regular but presumably unsalaried contributor of literary and dramatic reviews to Marsden's journals. Stephens seemed to think that Carter's position was threatened by what appeared to be the ascendancy of the Pound-Hueffer group. From Stephens's favor of Carter we can infer the generational literary skirmish at play here—which Pound dramatized several years later in *Hugh Selwyn Mauberley*—between the aesthetes of the 1890s and the modernists of the 1910s. Stephens and Carter exercised the residual sensibility of the earlier Yeats and the Anglo-Irish symbolists, a discourse more directly related to the aesthetic egoism of Huneker's *Egoists* than to the modernist egoism Marsden was still developing. In this clash of factions the explicit transcendentalism of the fin de siècle confronted the modernists' scientized retooling of the visionary mode.

What Stephens did not recognize was that Marsden was content to "row" with the Pound-Hueffer group because she was already reconstructing her own transcendentalism on a modernist model.[8] The egoism of the *Egoist* was still in process. Thus, the imagist and vorticist assertions Marsden let run through the *New Freewoman* and the *Egoist* clashed head-on with the aesthetic egoism maintained by Huntly Carter. For Stephens and Carter the "great issues" egoism stood for concerned the existential premium on unique personal witness in esoteric experience, the uncompromising individualism demanded by radical spiritualism as well as by artistic commitment. Stephens's letter of January 7, 1914, proceeded to fill Marsden in on the personal circumstances of her faithful contributor.

> I happen to know that he has been digging things out of himself for quite a long time in face of insuperable difficulties. I heard quite by accident when I was in Paris, where Carter's name is mentioned a great deal, that he is lying physically crippled and quite destitute, in some lonely place or other, and that for many months past he has refused to write for any paper but yours. He has peculiar notions about selling his soul and I am told he takes the greatest precautions to prevent his present rotten position and circumstances becoming known.

Carter's devotion to the *Egoist* may have had something to do with his strained relations to the *New Age*. On this score we possess a letter in the *Egoist* files dated early November, 1914, explaining that "Mr. Carter wrote some weeks ago from Golder's Green but said he didn't want the world to know as yet that he had returned to London; later on he let out that he didn't want to [see?] the New Age people at present. I think I have succeeded in offending him now, by saying he can't have an article in the next issue, nor a note re the censorship of his last article which he says 'left it incomprehensible' (when are they ever anything but incomprehensible?)."[9] A few months earlier it had been the *Egoist*'s turn for the dose of satire administered to current periodicals by C. E. Bechhöfer in the *New Age*. Marsden, Aldington, and Carter were singled out for needling: Marsden for unseemly philosophical pretensions and torturously interminable syntax, Aldington for clubbishness and poetic self-importance, and Carter for metaphysical mumbo-jumbo.

IS

By Huntly Carter

"What is art?" my Carter-hoarse critics ask. Let me try to explain to their feeble intelligences. Art is Soul! Soul is Art! Soul is everything! Soul is pine-apples! Art IS! Pine-apples ARE! I received this revelation eight years ago, when I was tending sheep with my old patron, Professor Munchausen, for a mahatma in the Falkland Islands, some seventeen miles east of Greenwich. He it was who taught me that mass-rhythms and soul-settings and every other wave of beauty have their rise from the spiritual harmonies of a woman's . . .[10]

In fact, the *Egoist* continued to stand by its reclusive contributor. Marsden herself was now living the same sort of spartan or Nietzschean cold-water life. But Weaver had no patience with Carter or his consistently diffuse articles. In a momentary burst of editorial irritation at Marsden's tardiness, Weaver cast herself as Caliban and Marsden as Prospero, and cried out: "Sometimes am I / So short of copy that I am driven to make / A leader out of Carter's trash. Shrug'st thou, Malice?" (cited in Lidderdale and Nicholson, *Dear Miss Weaver*, 94). Around the same time, Weaver confided to Marsden her failure to visit Carter when she had been in his vicinity and also apologized for her little *Tempest* send-up. Harriet knew that Dora's chronic indisposition was usually at fault: "I have been staying with my Hampstead brother . . . in Kent—only two stations from Whitstable. I could easily have dropped in on Mr. Huntly Carter alone with the Cosmos! I do hope you are all right again. My curses were only intended to work when you had been bad—faithless—not when you had been good as last time!"[11]

In any event, Carter carried on for the duration of the *Egoist* and then to my knowledge dropped out of sight. In the aftermath of the *Egoist*'s Special Imagist Number of May 1, 1915, he contributed a quite explicit statement of his credo not to the *Egoist*, where it would have been redundant, but to its feisty, contemporaneous American counterpart, the *Little Review*. Despite her strong personal disagreement, *Little Review* editor and avid imagist partisan Margaret Anderson gave him ample space to air his splendidly cranky opinions. The aesthetic egoist Carter, properly undaunted by the *New Age* spoof, immediately affirmed his primary commitment to the cultivation of his own prophetic capacity: "A few years ago I went to the Falkland Islands to sheep-farm for a bare subsistence. . . . I felt the currents of transcendent energy which I felt in my childhood. . . . I saw something ridding me of solid things and leaving nothing but a fluid universe. . . . Later reflection showed me that I was moved by some ineffable thing which I believe to be poetry."[12] For Carter, then, authentic poetry is an "ineffable thing," the purely oracular revelation of an esoteric experience; the text of a poem is a verbalistic transmutation of this visionary energy; but in the hands of the imagists, either there is nothing to convert—the poet being visionless to begin with—or the poem is too formal and intellectualized to sustain its prophetic origin.

These Bergsonesque considerations brought Carter to the question of the relationship between the *Egoist* and the imagists. In their own ways, the imagists would also make an effort of desynonymization. Neither faction wholly grasped just where Marsden's latest movements were taking her. But, because the imagists were on the winning side of the war for the soul of modernism, it has been their versions of cultural history we have credited. Given the history of misrepresentation we have been detailing, it is useful to recover in Carter's "Poetry versus Imagism" the forlorn, contrary, and momentarily quite cogent account of a vanquished and almost forgotten aesthete.

> I suppose most intelligent persons are inquiring what Imagism and *The Egoist* have to do with each other. . . . Of course, egoism is an entirely individualistic affair. It consists in putting on the armour of self-assertion and defending the special faith and interests of one's own. The power that one seeks to win is that of subjecting material conditions and exacting the utmost spiritual toll from everything. One pays no regard to the opinion of others, and refuses to play the part of a cypher, and at the same time

refuses to play any part with others. To stand alone, and with a light heart to do the necessary bargaining with external influences for the possession of one's own soul—this, it seems to me, is the true ground of egoism. (29)

Carter's egoism shared with Marsden's a deliberate "armouring," an extreme defensive posture by which one gains some insight into the psychological determinations of an egoistic stance. He echoed Marsden's defiance of representativeness: neither would willingly submit themself to a collective signifier and so "play the part of a cypher." But Carter's mystic egoism was finally too hermetic altogether to coincide with Marsden's more supple postspiritualist positions. He noted a most disturbing drift toward coterie and mutuality in the journal: being himself under no misapprehension about the ultimate lines of editorial authority at the *Egoist,* this indictment would implicitly include Marsden and Weaver.

> When men obliterate not their corporeal natures but the spiritual part of themselves, by coming together and acting together, and so juggle the play tricks [*sic*][13] in order that they may gain the applause and reward of their fellows, they are cyphers, not egoists, and deserve to be treated as cyphers. Persons who take this view of egoism have naturally been watching for the appearance in the pages of *The Egoist* of numerous writers with aspirations beyond the group or societal level and not seeing them appear have begun to ask what *The Egoist* "stands for." . . . For some issues it has been affected by a very strong habit of Imagism. Now Imagism is not egoism. I do not think the Imagists themselves are egoists. To me they appear to be socialists by instinct and individualists by profession, just as Mr. Bernard Shaw is an individualist by instinct and a socialist by profession. (29–30)

We have repeatedly seen Marsden maneuvering her own discourse in response to her contributors and her correspondence, evidence that in fact she had an active, if finally secondary, dialogical regard for the opinion of others. In tandem with imagist and modernist emphases on formal structure and rhetorical hygiene, in the *Egoist* Marsden was shifting her discourse once again, away from the unique phenomenology of an oracular vitalism to the structural plane of semantic definition. In 1915, in the series of preliminary philosophical exercises Marsden was performing in advance of the *Science of Signs,* Carter's absolutist egoism would remain only at the level of virtual epistemology, and his Bergsonian disparagement of the verbal medium would be forgone in favor of a meticulous and methodical renovation of collective concepts. Whether or not any particular imagist was paying attention, James Stephens and Huntly Carter could see clearly enough that Dora Marsden had left their aesthetic egoism behind and was now rowing alongside the sculls of the early modernists.

D. H. Lawrence, Individualist

D. H. Lawrence never had any direct relations with Dora Marsden. His contacts were all mediated through Pound, Aldington, or H.D. I cannot say for sure whether he ever read her material, either in or beyond the numbers of the *Egoist* in which his poems and the reviews of his work were published. However, for reasons that will become clear, I presume that he was at least cognizant of Marsden's contributions to the April 1, 1914, and May 1, 1915, numbers. His problem could have been that, as many subsequent readers of the *Egoist* have discovered, without possessing some knowledge of the *New Freewoman's* egoistic transformation of the *Freewoman*, it is difficult to pick up all the parameters of Marsden's methodical serial discourse in the *Egoist,* as she directed it toward the rigors of the *Science of Signs.*

In any event, their sensibilities would seem to be far apart: Lawrence pursued sexual communion, Marsden seemed to pass it by; Marsden worshipped the ego, Lawrence execrated it; Marsden may well have struck Lawrence as one of the pernicious, willful, egoistic female types satirized or demonized throughout his fictions. Nevertheless, in the full development of their respective work, there are many significant parallels and not a few uncanny echoes. Hilary Simpson was the first to indicate the connection: although she declined to mention Marsden by name, she accurately noted that "there are marked similarities between the general tone of the *New Freewoman* and the trend of Lawrence's thought."[14] Lawrence's first political and literary interests and appearances had inhabited surrounding neighborhoods—A. R. Orage's *New Age*, Ford Madox Hueffer's *English Review*, J. M. Murry and Katherine Mansfield's *Rhythm*. And, in fact, Dora Marsden's London is a strong context for situating and evaluating his work. Taken together, the unlikely but contemporaneous bedfellows Marsden and Lawrence interilluminate the full scope of the British contribution to early Anglo-American modernism. Lawrence's assorted enthusiasms and animosities are handy gauges of Marsden's own modernist extremities. Most importantly, through Dora Marsden we can effectively rewire D. H. Lawrence's intellectual connections to his sociocultural milieu.

In large overview, by reference to Dora Marsden's London we can anticipate the precise series of Lawrence's personal and doctrinal stances: an early suffragist and feminist liberalism proceeds to an absolute commitment to artistic experimentalism bound up with heterosexual libertarianism and anarchistic individualism, which then, in a rolling series of defensive responses to sexual anxieties and state harassments, eventually fray into a physiological mysticism, a strident masculinist hierarchical separatism, and a desperate survivalism, which still could not efface his ultimate attraction to an androgynous or asexual solution to his residual homoerotic inclination. In addition, we can take from Dora Marsden's particular movements a precise reading of Lawrence's important scientistic investments, his secular mythopoeses, those shifting attitudes toward matter, energy, and life that saturate his writings and his ongoing construction of values. They both derived initial doctrinal bearings from a feministic appreciation of the evolutionary sexual vitalism of Edward Carpenter.[15] At the broadest level, Lawrence's great sequence from the *Rainbow* through *Women in Love*, including ancillary doctrinal texts like the *Study of Thomas Hardy* and "The Crown," traces an early modernist progression parallel to what we have noted in Dora Marsden's London. In scientistic terms, it is the movement from biology to physics, the progressive evolutionary reconciliations envisioned by Edwardian socialism giving way to futuristic physics and thermodynamic models. The polarities suspended under Whitman's and Carpenter's mystic humanisms rupture into antithetical antagonisms, as between individual and state, male and female, mass and elite, life forces and death forces.[16]

The *Egoist* Group

The *Egoist* group contained two tiers: those who immediately shared responsibility for the journal's content—Dora Marsden, Harriet Shaw Weaver, Ezra Pound, Richard Aldington, H.D., and T. S. Eliot—and those who published repeatedly in it. According to this definition, although he would surely have declined the honor, D. H. Lawrence was a minor but notable part of the *Egoist* group, as he would also be in relation the Georgians and the imagists.[17] From 1914 on, Lawrence also had a lot to say about egoists and egoism, none of it remotely positive. His critiques were aimed at Western culture at large, not at a minuscule if vocal and symptomatic London clique. Nevertheless, there is a specific and appreciable connection between Lawrence's dealings with the *Egoist* group and his significant and sustained polemics against "egoism," a connection that draws Lawrence back toward a doctrinal orbit that his polemics would obscure. In fact, the milieu of the *Egoist* illuminates Lawrence's particular brand of modernist individualism.

Lawrence formed relationships of various sorts with several members of the *Egoist* group. He had maintained more or less cordial relations with Ezra

Pound since 1908.[18] In the summer of 1914, Lawrence and his wife, Frieda, first met Aldington and H.D. at Amy Lowell's famous dinner at the Berkeley Hotel.[19] By that time, he had already had some experience with the *Egoist*. On December 26, 1913, from Lerici, Italy, Lawrence wrote a letter in reply to Ezra Pound, which Pound passed on to Dora Marsden, thus lodging it in Marsden's papers.[20] "Dear Pound," Lawrence wrote: "I don't know what the Polignac award is, but I shall be very glad to have it, when the sun opens flowers of fortune. I don't know . . . what is *The Egoist*. . . . But if *The Egoist* is not likely to get me into trouble by publishing 'Once,' and if I am not likely to get the *Egoist* into trouble by offering them the story, then I don't see why they shouldn't have it, for as much as they can afford" (Lawrence, *Letters*, 131–32). This correspondence took place in the interval between the final *New Freewoman* of December 15, 1913, and the as-yet-unborn *Egoist* of January 1, 1914, about which the Polignac prizewinner James Stephens expressed his displeasure to Marsden. So, Lawrence's sojourn in Italy notwithstanding, there was no way that he could have known about the *Egoist*. However, clearly Lawrence perked up at the idea of competing for the Polignac Prize. Although Pound's promotional efforts in this regard were unavailing, he deserves some credit for having supported Lawrence's *Love Poems and Others*.[21]

Having received Lawrence's permission, Pound submitted "Once" to Dora Marsden. His deference demonstrates once again her maintenance of ultimate editorial authority at the *Egoist*. Pound had already tried unsuccessfully to place "Once" with the *Smart Set*, nor was he successful with the *Egoist*. The editor of the *Smart Set* rejected "Once" out of apprehension over the story's eroticism. However, it is doubtful that Marsden rejected it for the same reason. My suggestion is that she was simply unwilling to pay Lawrence's price. Pound's letter to Marsden covering "Once" must have postdated his receipt of Lawrence's reply, placing it at a time when Pound had already turned over the literary editorial chores at the *Egoist*, at least nominally, to Richard Aldington. Pound wrote to Marsden:

> Can we blow £3 or 4 on this tale of Lawrences.
>
> Of course his rates for modest & decorous tales are far beyond us. (£ 20 etc.).
>
> This tale is not improper—only frankly healthy. It is—well—Wright wrote—"I wish to god we could print it." It is realism—*yes*. Having done Diomedes I see no reason why we should not procede.
>
> It will be known that we have done it.
>
> Of course there's no need my saying that Lawrence would be *some* adjunct to the paper if you can get him interested.[22]

Coming from Pound, never one to mute his critical opinions, this letter is a valuable document illustrating the prominence and respect Lawrence's three novels and one book of poems had gained him by the turn of 1914.[23] In "Lawrence, Pound, and Early Modernism," Litz has called attention to Pound's review of *Love Poems and Others* in the *New Freewoman* of September 1, 1913, which revised an earlier review of the same collection that had appeared in *Poetry* that July. In his first write-up, Pound had opined, "If this book does not receive the Polignac prize a year from this November, there will be due cause for scandal."[24] Pound's second write-up of *Love Poems* was equally emphatic: "Mr. Lawrence's book is the most important book of poems of the season. With the appearance of 'Violets' and 'Whether or Not' the Ma[se]field boom may be declared officially and potentially over."[25] Thus, it is safe to presume that, when Ezra Pound wrote concerning the story "Once," Dora Marsden was well aware of D. H. Lawrence, but due to shaky finances she did not care to "blow £3 or 4" on another, very short work of prose fiction at a time when the serialization of Remy de Gourmont's *Horses of Diomedes* was still running and Joyce's *Portrait of the Artist* was about to begin. I conclude that the *Egoist*'s rejection of Lawrence's "Once" was strictly a practical matter of finances and space.

However, poetry was another matter. As Rebecca West wrote to Marsden early in 1913, "'Rhythm' gets quite fair stuff sometimes and I believe does not pay many of its contributors. . . . Poetry, I believe, is quite easy to beg."[26] Although Pound was unable to get financing from Marsden to place "Once" with the *Egoist*, he was instrumental in arranging for the first of Lawrence's four poetic appearances in that journal, presumably due to the largesse of his own financial backer, John Gould Fletcher.[27] On March 14, 1914, Lawrence wrote from Lerici to Arthur McLeod: "I think there will be some of my poems in a paper called the *Egoist*. I don't know anything about it. Ezra Pound took some verses, and sent me £3..3—. Try to get a copy, will you" (Lawrence, *Letters*, 156). On April 16, Lawrence wrote his friend "Mac" another letter.

> I feel a fearful pig when the newspapers come so regularly. Are you *sure* it isn't an imposition on you. . . . What a beast of a paper is the *Egoist*. I wouldn't have given them those verses had I known. And there were 7 misprints—swine, swine. (162)

Although Lawrence published three more poems on three separate occasions in the *Egoist* over the next three years, he did so presumably at the behest of either Aldington or H.D. and with no great enthusiasm.[28] In this letter to McLeod there are several currents of feeling involved. As expressed later in the letter, worry over Frieda's abandoned husband Professor Weekley's vindictiveness against her may have put Lawrence in a foul mood. The porcine imagery is striking but double-edged, since it begins with self-accusation—"I feel a fearful pig"—before the condemnation of the *Egoist*—"7 misprints—swine, swine." It may be simply that the expletive *swine* expressed Lawrence's justifiable displeasure over the *Egoist*'s editorial sloppiness. Yet this imagery also seems appropriate in the context of a complex reaction against egoism, if that is taken to signify a creed of perverse selfishness. We sometimes speak of selfish pigs, and that was in fact the burden of Lawrence's apology: it may have been selfish of him to trouble McLeod so much. In any event, in the midst of "a pig" and "swine," Lawrence called the April 1 number of the *Egoist* "a beast of a paper."

Granting that Lawrence's verdict here involves more than mere anger over the crop of misprints, to what in particular was he objecting? It seems unlikely that it was Leigh Henry's lead article, an appreciation of Arnold Schönberg expressed in terms many of which Lawrence himself could have written.[29] Could it have been the installment of James Joyce's *Portrait* immediately preceding Lawrence's poems?[30] His later distaste for *Ulysses* is well known. Lawrence's objection to this particular section of *Portrait* may have been that it depicted a schoolroom scene—that episode early in the novel when Father Dolan unjustly cracks young Stephen Dedalus's hands with the pandybat. Did that take Lawrence back to some unpleasant memories of his teaching days in Croyden? Still, the passage was not one to which Lawrence could have maintained serious aesthetic or doctrinal objections unless he took exception to its jaundiced view of Irish Catholicism.

Looking over the other contents of the number, however, I think I see Lawrence's "beast" in the combined contributions of the current mainstays of the *Egoist* group—Marsden, Aldington, and Pound. Marsden offered her usual blend of radical anarchism and sardonic irony. Dilating on a favorite topic—the contemptibility of the bourgeois state—as evidenced at the moment by the current hypocrisies of both the Liberal government and the labor unions, Marsden ended with the following mordant observation: "there is much to be said in favour of a gala-performance of Civil War."[31] Having been away from England for the better part of two years, perhaps Lawrence was unaware just how explosive domestic British politics had become by the spring of 1914, and so he took Marsden's polemic to be out of proportion, rather than commensurate, with its occasion.[32]

In any event, Marsden's disquieting "Views and Comments" were immediately followed by an Aldington exercise in lame irreverence, climaxed by an imaginary dialogue in hell in which Nero informs John Wesley that, "as for

Published the 1st and 15th of each month.

THE EGOIST

AN INDIVIDUALIST REVIEW.

Formerly the NEW FREEWOMAN.

No. 7.　Vol. I.　　WEDNESDAY, APRIL 1st, 1914.　　SIXPENCE.

Assistant (RICHARD ALDINGTON.　　　　　　　　　　*Editor* : DORA MARSDEN, B.A.
Editors : (LEONARD A. COMPTON-RICKETT.

CONTENTS.

LIBERATIONS :

Studies of Individuality in Contemporary Music.

By LEIGH HENRY.

I.

PRELUDE.

MUSIC as all other arts must be evolutionary to justify its existence. There have entered into life many hitherto unrecognised elements consequent upon the changed environment of humanity, and if art is to be of any avail it must be cognisant of these facts : it must be a record of its epoch, not an inert sentimentalism stagnant with out-worn tradition. It is for the musical artist not slavishly to imitate precedent, but to continue the expression of art progressively without wasting energy upon repetition. Virility above all else is the most necessary element, and if at times an overflow of superabundant energy produces work which is seemingly freakish we have yet to be thankful that such productions emanate from a living force of which they are the extravagant manifestations and are not to be numbered among dead things, since death and out-worn vitality breed corruption and decay. Further, in judging work which is termed iconoclastic we must take into consideration the fact that in certain epochs art from various causes is removed from the influences contemporary with it, to the consideration of isolated groups of formalists who concern themselves with theoretical ideas and not with living spirit, and in such surroundings takes on a garb of inhuman formality—the product of over-cultivation, and sentimental affectation—which requires drastic measures to restore it to health. It is easy to follow a beaten path, but it is another matter to cleave a new one, and the mental postures of an era of hollow formalism are of no avail to artists seeking inspiration in living facts. In conse-quence of this continual upheavals are necessary in order to obtain individual expression and reinfuse vitality. It is the eternal war of Dionysos and Apollo. At no period in the annals of Art has this desire to revivify borne greater fruit than at the present time, and in modern music this is particularly evident.

Music has become a force for expressing mental individuality and conceptions as wide as those embraced by literature. Following on this develop-ment a new critical body is necessary, one which will not subordinate music to the trivial and fashion-able conceptions of the public nor to the standard of technical acrobatics required by the theoreticians, but which will examine motives, analyse the force and mental standpoint of the composer and indicate his significance in relation to life and the intellectual individualism surrounding him. As an academic art music has become a refuge for those people lacking everything but the mechanical dexterity obtainable by continual rehearsal. Thus we obtain the deal level of technical standards which, if permitted to dominate music, will result in the destruction of personal expression. It is with the purpose of attacking this false standard, and the critical body subordinate to it, that I write these studies. Art is a servant of individuality, and individuality cannot exist without vitality.

To those who love degeneration be left the embalming of dead phases of intellectualism. The expansive artist seeks life and health even though his aim necessitates the destruction of things about which sentiment has woven a fictitious value.

I. ARNOLD SCHÖNBERG AND THE PROTECTION OF INTROSPECTIVE PSYCHOLOGY.

The appearance of Arnold Schönberg [born Sept. 13th, 1875] in the world of music is an event which apart from its intrinsic significance has been exceed-ingly valuable in another important direction. The general restriction of vision and incapacity for appreciating values which are marks of the average musical critic have within the last few years been repeatedly exposed; but with the advent of Schön-berg the absolute necessity for a new critical faculty has been finally demonstrated. It may be said that the need of a new criticism was also evident with the advent of Wagner. Even were this the case, the finality of such a revolution as was necessary for the appreciation of Wagnerian theories is questionable to-day. Wagnerism, from being a revivifying element, has become a superstition. This is due to

Jesus, whom you have taken to be the founder of your castrated cult of tinkers and apprentices he is over there, lying on cushions and girls' shoulders, drinking iced Falernian and playing vignt-et-un with Phryne, the Marquis de Sade and St. John."[33] Here was clearly something at which the residual Congregationalist in Lawrence could well have taken offense. In the spring of 1914, still on the near side of the *Rainbow* debacle, Lawrence was rather more stiffly Christian than he would become in 1916 and after, when his humanisms had been blasted by war censorship and his metaphysics paganized by John Burnet's *Early Greek Philosophy* (Delany, *Lawrence's Nightmare*, 118–19). And, finally, the back cover of this number of the *Egoist* combined the affectations of both radical militancy and brash irreverence with a full-page announcement for the journal *Blast*. Advertised were "Poems by Ezra Pound," then a "Discussion of Cubism, Futurism, Imagisme and all Vital Forms of Modern Art," and then the following weird proclamations: "Putrifaction of Guffaws Slain by Appearance of BLAST. NO Pornography. NO Old Pulp. END OF THE CHRISTIAN ERA" (140). Lawrence, it seems, was not amused by this tin-pot Nietzscheanism. The ad for *Blast* was perhaps the last straw, drawing from Lawrence the verdict that the *Egoist* was "a b[l]ast of a paper."

Lawrence and Egoism

Lawrence's career of polemical attacks on egoism and egoists dates from these events of 1914. In his correspondence that year, egoism emerges as the particular spiritual malady of the modern soul. For instance, in a letter to John Middleton Murry written on April 3, 1914 (in the midst of his anticipation of the *Egoist* of April 1), Lawrence wrote: "I am rather great on faith just now. I do believe in it. We are so egoistic, that we are ashamed of ourselves out of existence. One ought to have faith in what one ultimately is, then one can bear at last the hosts of unpleasant things which one is en route" (*Letters*, 160–61). Even before receiving that fatefully irreverent number of the *Egoist*, then, Lawrence had predefined egoism as a shameless faithlessness to and abandonment of the ultimate self.

In these attacks on the faithless ego, Lawrence was defending what he termed "another ego," or what Lawrence, like Marsden, often called "the soul." Perhaps Lawrence saw in the *Egoist* of 1914 a convenient target for his oppositional thinking and seized upon the ego as a foil to the ultimate self he was seeking to define as the *Rainbow* and *Women in Love* were under construction. It is suggestive that these lines of thought and phrase came together in Lawrence's single most famous letter, written from the Ligurian coast of Italy to

Edward Garnett on June 5, 1914, about his experimental characterizations in the *Rainbow*. This letter has been judged "the most important" of Lawrence's "several theoretical statements on the nature of his technical innovations" (Herzinger, *Lawrence in His Time*, 132), and it has certainly become a touchstone for Lawrence critics, many of whom, if they must deal with theory at all, prefer to get it straight from Lawrence himself. His epistolary remarks connect directly to the cosmopolitan milieu of the *Egoist, Blast,* and the overall London retort to Marinetti, for Lawrence was meditating at that moment on a futurist manifesto treating free verse and the "perpetual evolution" of the lyric ego: "Il verso libero futurista è il dinamismo della nostra coscienza malleabile, interamente realizzato; *l'io* integrale cantato, dipinto, scolpito indefinitamente nel suo perpetuo divenire aggressivo."[34] "*L'io* integrale" is a futurist version of Lawrence's other ego, as posited in these familiar comments.

> When Marinetti writes: ". . . The heat of a piece of wood or iron is in fact more passionate, for us, than the laughter or tears of a woman"—then I know what he means. . . . You mustn't look in my novel for the old stable ego of the character. There is another ego, according to whose action the individual is unrecognizable, and passes through, as it were, allotropic states which it needs a deeper sense than any we've been used to exercise, to discover are states of the same single radically-unchanged element. (Lawrence, *Letters*, 183)

Lawrence's modernist scientism adapts Marinetti by extending the futurist's own chemical vehicles. Marinetti had lyricized in preference to a stereotypically sentimental female emotionalism an "inhuman alliance of molecules." Lawrence pushed that figure toward the elemental purity of carbon, which swerve allowed him to reconnect as "allotropic states" the psychological and elemental levels. This metaphorical chemistry of character—the "elementality" of the "other ego"—resonates with some of the thermodynamic tropes we will examine later in *Women in Love*. But, in general, the notes rung on the ego in this correspondence reverberate throughout the rest of Lawrence's career, as he runs the moralized, polar, and yet equivocal distinction between the "old stable ego" of fixity and "another ego" of growth and change through numerous permutations. The ultimate doctrinal point of this characteristic train of thought, asserted on the far side of Lawrence's own later swerve into survivalist isolationism, is nicely rehearsed in a late essay: "We may as well admit it: men and women need one another. We may as well, after all our kicking against the pricks, our revolting and our sulking, give in and be graceful about it. We are all individualists: we are all egoists: we all believe intensely in freedom, our own at all events. We all want to be absolute, and sufficient unto ourselves. And it is a great blow to our self-esteem that we simply *need* another human being."[35]

Ego, self, soul: the rhetorical fluctuations of Lawrence's moral currents snap these identity terms back and forth between positive and negative valence. However, these self-implicating, interdependent moral polarities, as Lawrence himself occasionally realized, are fated to oscillate without resolution: there is no ultimate term to arrest their play. More important for critical analysis than merely rehearsing Lawrence's moral psychologies, then, is placing them within the social and ideological contexts from which they emerged. As with Dora Marsden, what needs to be emphasized is not so much their dated participation in outmoded phenomenologies as the ruptures and revisions occurring within these inherited models of selfhood. What we might better trace in Marsden and Lawrence are equivocal early modernist anticipations of, as well as resistances to, the poststructuralist critique of the self or unified subject. However much Lawrence may have desired some final state of absolute authentic being, the texts he authored show that such fulfillment resides only in the incessant rhetorical flux by which it is posited. In his finest fictions, Lawrence allowed his own egoistic anxieties to dissolve into the flux of his text.

Study of Thomas Hardy

Paul Delany has summarized the first part of Lawrence's *Study of Thomas Hardy* as "a rambling argument for individualism in the personal life and anarchism in social life" (*Lawrence's Nightmare*, 31). Michael Bentley has also observed Lawrence's political orientation toward an individualism that verges on anarchism, as in the *Rainbow* and *Women in Love* "pure beings" pursue their "proud individual singleness." Lawrence's individualism began "with his physio-psychological understanding of what the individual 'soul' comprised and of what was necessary to its life. This unit of social analysis was not co-extensive with the notion of 'personality' as conventionally conceived. . . . In itself the idea was not the base for a political position, but it could become one when Lawrence entered the next phase of his life after 1915."[36] Although Bentley seems unaware of Dora Marsden, his treatment of "the quirky individualism which Lawrence had been incubating since 1912–13" (76) synchronizes the convergence between Marsden and Lawrence. Discussing Lawrence's treatment of the suffrage movement in the *Rainbow* in terms borrowed from Sheila Row-botham, Hilary Simpson relates Ursula Brangwen's "individual liberation" to the discourse of the *New Freewoman:* " 'an individual "emancipated" woman is an amusing incongruity, a titillating commodity, easily consumed.' Neverthe-less, it is interesting to note that similar views found expression within the broad church of feminism itself. The *Freewoman*, later the *New Freewoman*, set itself up as the mouthpiece of those women who were not interested in mass movements and who attributed oppression to individual weakness rather than to social causes" (*Lawrence and Feminism*, 23).

Given Lawrence's "quirky individualism," his animosity toward egoism may have been in part a defensive deflection of competing ideas away from his own discursive development. That Lawrence's philosophy often ran in a dis-tinctly parallel course with Dora Marsden's emphases was perhaps an added incentive to set himself quite apart from the *Egoist* group. It must be pointed out that Lawrence's descriptions of egoism had no inherent connection with Dora Marsden's doctrines and cannot properly be taken as a direct critique of her dis-course. On the contrary, in most areas the overlap between their vocabularies and interests is striking. Due to a common vitalist orientation, their early mod-ernist turns—away from progressive evolutionism and toward a counteren-tropic emphasis on the maintenance of individual energies—are remarkably similar. So I will accept Simpson's implicit invitation to read Lawrence's *Study of Thomas Hardy* for its resonance with "the general tone of the *New Free-woman.*" The period of the *New Freewoman*—the summer and fall of 1913—was the time when Marsden was especially concerned to relate her insurrectionary egoism to aesthetic innovation. Lawrence started writing the *Study* in late 1914 and revised it throughout 1915.[37] An editor's suggestion that he produce a mod-est critical casebook accounts for its initial impetus and its title, whereas Lawrence gradually abandoned any thought of its marketability. First published posthumously in *Phoenix,* the *Study* is a long lyrical elaboration of Lawrence's early "metaphysic" occasionally peppered with vigorous readings of Hardy's novels. This first concerted attempt to expound an existential philosophy pro-duced a substantial critical manifesto linking together his aesthetic and ethical convictions.

I will schematize the imagery of Lawrence's *Study* into four cultural regis-ters that accord with the thematics of the *New Freewoman*. The first three regis-ters are "elemental" and may be differentiated by scientific field. There is a pri-mary biological line, a vitalist evolutionism expressed in organic and vegetal imagery epitomized in the *flower,* in particular, the scarlet poppy; a thermody-namic register of physical and chemical images epitomized in tropes of *fire;* and an aqueous line of fluidic and oceanic imagery, symbolized by the *spring,* the *stream,* and the *wave.* The fourth register is psycholinguistic, a territorial marker concerned with ego-boundaries whose emblem is a *flag.* As Lawrence winds his incremental repetitions, these lines intertwine through the *Study* to produce his typically overloaded discursive effects. For instance, the peremptory poppy is a gloriously wasteful flower-flag signifying an existential claim—an act of ecstatic transgression leading to a new frontier of experience—and the scarlet of its petals conveys the fluid fire of the blood, the figurative medium of maximum living energy.

From the beginning of the *Study,* a thermodynamic cosmology overlaps a vitalistic psychology. "Of Poppies and Phoenixes and the Beginning of the Argument" picks up a theme prominent in Marsden's *New Freewoman* aesthetics and implicit in the rhetoric of imagism, the thermodynamic question of dissipation or waste. But here Lawrence identifies waste with the cultural surpluses that fund artistic expression as well as sexual communion: "from the very first man wasted himself begetting children, colouring himself and dancing and howling and sticking feathers in his hair, in scratching pictures on the walls of his cave, and making graven images of his unutterable feelings" (7). Satirizing cautionary moralism, Lawrence purveys the poppy as an ironic figure for this superb creative wastefulness, "the excess which always accompanies reproduction" (9). So Lawrence immediately addressed himself to the burning issue Marsden was also grappling with, the proper form of an existential economy in which entropy, or the squandering of energy, can also be figured as the vital labor of sexual and cultural production. How should one invest one's vital capital? Self-conservatives such as Marsden's "lean kind" counsel preservation, but the *Study* aligns its voice with the existential liberalism of vital expenditure, because "this excess that accompanies reproduction . . . is the thing itself at its maximum of being" (11). Existential liberalism, however, is libertarian rather than communitarian in emphasis. In the *Study,* Lawrence's ethical vitalism already comes forward in an individualist configuration. Evolutionary progress is finally dependent on personal freedom.

In the second chapter, "Still Introductory; About Women's Suffrage, and Laws, and the War, and the Poor, with Some Fancyful Moralising," Lawrence's meditation takes a specifically antistatist or anarchist form. He surveys the complicity of the state in the catastrophe of the Great War but returns the responsibility for that waste of life to every individual too timorous to accept their true duty to waste themselves in the creation of life. Rather than enlist ourselves in the irregular ranks of being, we waste and squander ourselves in orgies of collective destruction. Lawrence's antimilitarist vitalism, while still reminiscent of Edward Carpenter's pacifistic socialist exfoliation, redirects rather than dissolves the militant imperative. That is, quite in line with Marsden's militantly mobile egoism, we must "risk ourselves in a forward venture of life, as we are willing

to risk ourselves in a rush of death" (17). Lawrence identifies now with the gloriously wasteful and self-consuming orgasmic blossom of the flowering poppy:
"there it hangs at the brink of the void, scarlet and radiant for a little while,
imminent on the unknown, a signal, an out-post, an advance guard, a forlorn,
splendid flag. . . . I go to fight for myself. Every step I move forward into being
brings a newer, juster proportion into the world . . . allows me in the end to fly
the flag of myself, at the extreme tip of life" (18–19).

On the model of Whitman's bardic individualism in *Song of Myself,*
Lawrence's flower-flag is the "sign of myself": the creative self as the extremest
leaf unfurled at the tip of human evolution's "leading-shoot" (34), an ecstatic
token of self-renovation by possessing a new region of human consciousness.
Among Lawrence's concurrent poetic writings, which are also engaged in con-
structing life visions to compensate for the horror of the war dead, the obvious
parallel is to "New Heaven and Earth," where the new earth upon which the
lyric voyager plants his flag is quite explicitly "the flank of my wife" (Lawrence,
Complete Poems, 260).[38] However, in the *Study of Thomas Hardy* Lawrence has
not as yet broached the question of how gender fits into his schemas of onward
being.

Taking stock of the scientific ideologies at play in the *Study,* we note a
thermodynamic cosmos yielding to the fundamental vitalist premise of an inexhaustible life force: "a man is a well-head built over a strong, perennial spring
and enclosing it in" (32). The imagined threat of the second law of thermodynamics, the entropy that enforces a progressive deterioration of forms within
the nonvital cosmos of mechanical forces, makes the vitalist appropriation of the
first law declaring the infinite conservation of energy all the more crucial. Early
modernism in Lawrence and Marsden declares its ideological priorities in a
vitalistic dualism of life, the primary flux of the deep spring, and mind, the secondary damming up of the stream to run millstones. The mind taps off its energies from life. Its functions are demoted from the vital/teleological to the
mechanical/instrumental: "this is the final meaning of work: the extension of
human consciousness. The lesser meaning of work is the achieving of self-
preservation" (41).

However, at the moment Lawrence lays greater stress than Marsden on the
lapse of the ego in favor of the "unconsciousness" of prophetic or self-evolutionary experience, at times ringing the note of mystic or Bergsonian ineffability for which Marsden in "The Art of the Future" had already poked some fun
at Ezra Pound. The habit developed perhaps in her career as an editor/com-
mentator with an inexorable weekly deadline, but Marsden always placed the
highest premium on an immediate and momentarily definitive articulation of

the existential flux, even while allowing any given articulation to be rendered obsolete by the next. In a few years Lawrence would converge with Marsden's quest for spontaneously articulate prophecy. In the 1918 text "Poetry of the Present," he will define free verse as the momentaneous cry of the now, a "direct utterance from the instant, whole man": "Tell me of the mystery of the inexhaustible, forever-unfolding creative spark. Tell me of the incarnate disclosure of the flux, mutation in blossom, laughter and decay perfectly open in their transit, nude in their movement before us."[39]

In the *Study of Thomas Hardy,* Lawrence explicitly distinguishes between life and mind in terms directly borrowed from the social discourses of thermodynamics and evolutionism. In the fifth chapter, "Work and the Angel and the Unbegotten Hero," Lawrence's treatment of physical and mental work is already inflected by the science of *Arbeitskraft,* or labor power, when he argues that the acquisition of knowledge is not an end in itself but a means to evolutionary vitality. James Knapp has commented on the paradox that Lawrence's vitalist priorities in the *Study* actually situate his own system within the mechanistic paradigms informing the science of work. By submitting mental knowledge to the laws of material mechanism, "Lawrence consigns knowledge to the realm of the merely instrumental. This instrumentalization of knowledge was essential to the reorganization of work in Europe and America which was taking place during the first two decades of the twentieth century."[40] Knapp perceives in Lawrence's doctrinal configurations vitalism's residual location within the classical mechanistic universe of matter and force.

For Marsden and Lawrence, this recognition is deflected from life to mind: the mind is a machine we have constructed to make life more efficient. In the *New Freewoman* Marsden had remarked that "good thinking would prevent the formation of thoughts, as a good machine minimises waste" ("Intellect and Culture," 23). In the *Study,* Lawrence asserts that "the mind itself is one of life's later developed habits. *To know* is a force, like any other force. Knowledge is only one of the conditions of this force, as combustion is one of the conditions of heat. *To will* is only a manifestation of the same force, as expansion may be a manifestation of heat" (41–42). As an immediate reflex to the thermodynamic turn in these figures, Lawrence jumps to the contiguous discourse of Spencerian evolution, that is, from the relatively random collisions of material molecules to the purposeful strivings of organic forms: "It seems as though one of the conditions of life is, that life shall continually and progressively differentiate itself, almost as though this differentiation were a Purpose . . . as if it were working always to the production of the infinite number of perfect individuals" (42).

Thus, the *Study* comes around once again to the vitalist exposition of an individualist ethic, "almost as though" it were an "elemental" necessity.

Lawrence's charged figures are not even remotely idiosyncratic; rather, they are vivid and reasonable imaginative responses to the social milieu of spilt science within which his ideas were incubated. In the decades before the publication of Darwin's *Origin of Species,* Lamarck and Spencer had insinuated the operation of an evolutionary motive throughout the biological and material cosmos; by emphasizing that the rule of entropy pertains to humanity "as at present constituted," Thomson had seconded the evolutionary note at the very inception of his thermodynamic formulas. What these nineteenth-century scientific discourses sowed into cultural discussion Marsden and Lawrence are reaping as an extreme valorization of the individual, or "egoistic unit," and as a scientifically authoritative mandate for the living ego to clear out the dead wood of instrumental thought and fill itself with nature's "rhythmic urge" toward higher forms. Drawing on scientific models, Lawrence now presents individualism as a process of distillation and purification, a sorting operation leading to ever higher levels of vital organization: "the more that I am driven from admixture, the more I am singled out into utter individuality, the more this intrinsic me rejoices" (42).

Scientistic tropes derived from social vitalism and social energetics have had an astonishing and dismaying range of cultural effects. Early literary modernism represents to some degree the first concerted systemization of their cultural power, a process that splintered once again in the aftermath of World War I. The "exfoliation" of scientistic tropes defines a major texture of modernist lyricism. In particular, we are at a nodal point in Lawrence's entire text, a vortex, if you will, of complex discursive implication informing both the matter and manner of his greatest fictions. These particular early modernist scientisms adhere to the anarchistic adaptation of evolutionism: running counter to collectivist and statist scenarios of the "social organism," they celebrate the existential privatizing of society as the path to personal and social perfection.

The sociability of Lawrence's pure individuality is anarchistic: it is to result from the sensitive discretion developed by closer apperception of vital differences and a consequent relinquishing of mechanistic authoritarian schemes for political conformity. We have already examined in the April 1, 1914, number of the *Egoist*—the same number containing Lawrence's cluster of misprinted poems—Marsden's "Views and Comments" on the current political strife in the United Kingdom, which express a more extreme or insurrectionary version of a similar vitalist anarchism.

We are in sight of the break-up of a Verbal System—not of the loosening of the ties of affection and common-sense as between men and men. Society itself is not based on any Conception whatsoever, it is based on the inborn predilections and instincts of individuals. When these instincts break through the overlying Verbiage and reveal themselves for what they are the "Stability of Society" is unaffected. For whatever these instincts are Society is and will be. (125)

At this point in the *Study of Thomas Hardy,* the resplendent poppy has been apotheosized as the daemonic forerunner of human transcendence, the androgynous angel of perfected individuality. In this Lawrence has followed a doctrinal route Marsden previously traversed. Now Lawrence puts his own fold in the map. In implicit response to the nominal itinerary of explicating Hardy's plots, the topic of gender rolls its tidal wave upon that placid angelic surface. The poppy recurs in its glory of thermodynamic expenditure—"Out from the crest and summit comes the fiery self, the flower, gorgeously" (52)—but the combustion imagery is now submerged in the "waves" of gender, and the practical matters of sexual difference and procreation are folded into Lawrence's sexology of evolutionary self-production: "Always the dual wave. Where does my poppy spill over in red, but there where the two streams have flowed. . . . There, only there where the male seethes against the female, comes the transcendent flame and the filling of seeds" (53). From the communion of the waves in Lawrence's sexual vortex, however, the genders fall back glad and revivified exactly because their supreme moment of timeless unison precipitates them back into individual life more finely sexually distinct. Lawrence's text has begun to read being into gender by polarizing the sexes: "Every impulse that stirs in life, every single impulse, is either male or female, distinct, except the being of the complete flower, of the completed consciousness, which is two in one, fused" (55).

This discourse reflects the growing clash in Lawrence's thinking between the Carpenterian or androgynous ideal of an "intermediate sex" and the Weiningerian emphasis on the secondary, fortuitous confluence of gender plasms and the primary, elemental character of sexual essences. Whereas Dora Marsden's doctrines seem to have occupied an androgynetic position before she discarded gender difference from her explicit consideration, Lawrence's individualism will move rather decisively in the opposite direction, eventually modulating into the defensive masculinism of his later writings. But at the moment, the *Study* captures the fundamental allure for Lawrence of an androgynous solution. Clearly he desires to identify with the complete flower of angelic con-

sciousness and suffers his masculine engendering as a lapse into temporal limitation. This residual orientation throughout Lawrence's career points up the sublime comedy in the ongoing spectacle of D. H. Lawrence being held up as an
avatar of some sort of masculinist renaissance. Yet, when Lawrence loses sight of
his evolutionary angel, he will also present the transcendence or dissolution of
gender as morally unthinkable and the confusion of gender as morally corrup-
tive.

The *Study of Thomas Hardy* reflects a powerful clash between anarchistic
individualism and scientistic genderism. While individualism may be given a
gender, as in anarcho-feminism or masculinist egoism, it need not come forward so marked. Dora Marsden allows us to perform a certain destigmatizing of
individualism and to envision on that basis some recuperation of the androgynous vision, not as a crypto-patriarchal universalism but as a mobile configuration of idiosyncratic desire. When Lawrence first concentrates his discussion on
the free-standing poppy, his tropes produce a singular existential testament that
retains its appeal despite the lyrical garishness. When he begins to thrash the
poppy amid the waves of gender distinction and sexual separatism, his text
breaks apart on the rocks of misplaced substantiation, the gender essentialisms
he borrows from a loosely Weiningerian sexology. While retaining its fascination, midway through the text the *Study* commences to dissipate its initial
charge.

Evolution and Entropy in *Women in Love*

> In some remote corner of the universe, poured out and glittering in innu-
> merable solar systems, there once was a star on which clever animals
> invented knowledge. That was the haughtiest and most mendacious
> minute of "world history"—yet only a minute. After nature had drawn a
> few breaths the star grew cold and the clever animals had to die.[41]

In the latter half of the nineteenth century, vitalist and evolutionist ideologies intertwined with theoretical physics. The Darwinian notion of the
nonessentiality of living species operated alongside Kelvin's premonition of the
ephemerality of the material universe.[42] The rule of thermodynamic entropy—
within closed systems available energy can only become more disordered and
thus increasingly unavailable for human ends—seemed to predict the inevitable
heat death of the cosmos and thus a final dissolution of life's evolutionary
progress, if man remained, in Kelvin's phrase, "as at present constituted." Dire
Victorian prophecies of inevitable or imminent cultural crisis were quite

specific responses to the thermodynamic dispensation as well as to Darwinist ideas of a randomly evolving or devolving creation. One broad response to this sense of crisis was to press evolutionary theory for a solution to the rule of entropy. Lawrence's own discursive and novelistic social prophecies, his particular imaginations of forms of salvation from the dilemmas of cultural debasement, were early modern variations descending in a direct line from prior anxieties that took specific shapes in the cultural reception of Victorian scientific cosmology.[43]

As we have seen, these evolutionist scenarios could operate at either the species or the individual level. In the decades before and during Lawrence's intellectual development, social prophets of various sorts produced visionary outlines for the development of higher creatures to surpass the entropic dilemma, forms of daemonic imagination that eventually flowed with significant effect into Lawrence's doctrinal convictions and fictional treatments. Notions of progressive evolutionism came to be personified in images of superhumanity, for instance, the cosmic persona of Walt Whitman as disseminated by devotees such as Dr. Bucke, Nietzsche's Übermensch, and Dora Marsden's freewoman. Alongside any number of antiprogressivist scenarios of racial degeneration, radical progressivists sought scientific foundations for a belief in the imminent emergence of higher states of individual and social being. The imperative to escape from the rule of entropy tied progressive and reactionary evolutionisms together: they diverged merely in their counterentropic strategies. Edward Carpenter envisioned a spontaneous and uncoerced individual and communal exfoliation beyond the rule of entropy, whereas social Darwinists in the wake of Spencer and Huxley would make themselves fit for survival by defying entropy and hoarding their prerogatives, by maintaining and strengthening defensive differentiations of class, gender, and race.

An early threshold in the philosophical search for a margin of escape from the rule of thermodynamic entropy may be said to have occurred in 1871 with James Clerk Maxwell's *Theory of Heat,* in which he presented to the world a heuristic fiction soon to be known as Maxwell's Demon. Maxwell's Demon and Lawrence's vision of the daemonic individual are cultural cousins: both represent fictive swerves from the big chill of a thermodynamic apocalypse.[44] In his Demon, Maxwell imagined a superhuman but subdivine being that could reverse the rule of entropy by restoring order to random systems. Counteracting the drift toward equilibrium by sorting out swift from sluggish molecules, Maxwell's Demon would reestablish the heat differentials from which work could once again be extracted.

If we conceive a being whose faculties are so sharpened that he can follow every molecule in its course, such a being, whose attributes are still as essentially finite as our own, would be able to do what is at present impossible for us. . . . Let us suppose that [a vessel full of air] is divided into two portions, A and B, by a division in which there is a small hole, and that a being, who can see the individual molecules, opens and closes this hole, so as to allow only the swifter molecules to pass from A to B, and only the slower ones to pass from B to A. He will thus, without expenditure of work, raise the temperature of B and lower that of A, in contradiction to the second law of thermodynamics.[45]

In fact, it was Kelvin who identified Maxwell's imaginary sorting operator as a demon, thus inscribing a Neoplatonic/Christian moral discourse into further deployments of Maxwell's heuristic fiction. If Kelvin was the Moses of Victorian thermodynamics, one might say that Maxwell's Demon is the Christ, a supernatural savior come to abrogate the (second) law by sorting out the molecular quick from the dead. As christened by Kelvin, Maxwell's Demon is an angelic consciousness releasing mankind from the dismal fate of eternal death by entropic annihilation. In *Women in Love,* Birkin, with his "Salvator Mundi touch," will speculate that if the "creative mystery" driving human evolution is to progress beyond its present limitations it will demand the daemonic emergence of postentropic creatures: "Man is a mistake, he must go.— . . . I believe in the proud angels and the demons that are our fore-runners."[46]

Lawrence joined a major segment of early modernist culture in advancing an evolutionary vitalism as a plausible response to the threat of entropy. At its inception as a scientific theory, vitalism established an agonistic dualism between the inanimate and animate realms, between the physical forces decomposing organic syntheses and the metaphysical forces producing and preserving living bodies. As an ever-renewed struggle, however, vitalistic life is inherently militant but ultimately futile: "vital properties . . . become rapidly exhausted. 'Time wears them away,' said Bichat" (Jacob, *Logic of Life,* 91).[47] The theory of vitalism could be factored into the thermodynamic paradigm, in one way, by means of body temperature—the vital heat that runs in cold- and warm-blooded creatures—and also by relating the notion of vital exhaustion to the social-energetic discourse of entropic fatigue. Vitalism as a scientific hypothesis in fact likens the living body to a heat engine, in that the living body is a transformative vessel receiving its (life) force from a finite internal reservoir. In the vitalistic view, an organism "would begin life with a reserve of vital force enabling it to maintain its organization. Death would come with the exhaustion of the reservoir" (Paulson, *Noise*, 44). Thus there is a social ideological need to modulate toward a mystic vitalism in which life is serviced from "a strong, perennial spring" (Lawrence, *Study*, 32) and so is ultimately detached from the frictional machinery of material dissolution.

Lawrence consistently portrays certain human practices as "exhaustive" processes. For instance, as late as 1929, in "Apropos of 'Lady Chatterley's Lover,'" Lawrence offers the physiological advice that "the katabolism of 'nervous' sex-activity may produce for a time a sort of ecstasy and a heightening of consciousness. But this, like the effect of alcohol or drugs, is the result of the decomposition of certain corpuscles in the blood, and is a process of impoverishment. This is one of the many reasons for the failure of energy in modern people; sexual activity, which ought to be refreshing and renewing, becomes exhaustive and debilitating."[48] A closely related theme of vital exhaustion occurs embedded in thermodynamic imagery in the suppressed prologue to *Women in Love*.

> After these nights of superfine ecstasy of beauty, after all was consumed in the silver fire of moonlight, all the soul caught up in the universal chill-blazing bonfire of the moonlit night, there came the morning, and the ash, when his body was grey and consumed, and his soul ill. . . .
>
> How to get away from this process of reduction, how escape this phosphorescent passage into the tomb, which was universal, though unacknowledged, this was the unconscious problem which tortured Birkin day and night. (Lawrence, *Women in Love*, 495–96)

These typical passages intertwine romantic vitalism with Victorian thermodynamics: Lawrence gives Bichat's romantic physiology a late turn while Birkin extrapolates from a notion of individual soul-exhaustion deriving from the vitalist paradigm to a vision of thermodynamic entropy as a universal curse. In fact, vitalism's residual mechanistic framework led directly to the moralized physics of Victorian thermodynamics. The notion of an inevitable exhaustion of a reservoir of vital force, modeled on the mechanics of coal-fired steam engines, was ready to be subsumed into the notion of an inevitably increasing measure of entropy within a cosmic system, producing the degradation of energic differentials that would lead to the icy demise of the cosmos as well as of Gerald Crich. Thus, the anxious vitalist Birkin repeats the question dogging the Victorian critics of the second law: "How to escape?"

The characters and dialects of *Women in Love* articulate significant modernist variations of cultural anxieties that first took shape in the reception of

Victorian science. Maxwell's Demon held out a certain vision of salvation: were it to exist, mankind could be released from the specter of entropy, the dismal fate of annihilation in universal heat death. Birkin's misanthropy and desire for a non- or posthuman world may be seen to express his longing to escape the entropic current sweeping all humanity toward a frigid annihilation. His vision of the "river of dissolution" is exactly the tide of thermodynamic entropy applied specifically to the spirit of a corrupt humanity. If Birkin aspires to an angelic escape from entropy, Gerald personifies the failure to find out and seize that narrow margin. Locked in a lethal sexual struggle, a kind of entropic wrestling match with Gudrun, which he will fail to sort out, Gerald battles psychic entropy but finally capitulates and suffers his own microcosmic heat death when he turns into ice on the slopes of the Alps. The narrator evokes Gerald's role as avatar of the thermodynamic demonic fairly explicitly: "Birkin thought of Gerald. He was one of these strange white wonderful demons from the north, fulfilled in the destructive frost mystery. And was he fated to pass away in this knowledge, this one process of frost-knowledge, death by perfect cold? Was he a messenger, an omen of the universal dissolution into whiteness and snow?" (254)[49]

Although these intimations prove true, at first Gerald sets forth to prove Maxwell's Demon an industrial reality. Directing his human will upon his workers and their machines to produce fuel for the heat engines of his industrial society, applying the latest techniques of scientific management, he achieves unprecedented efficiencies in coal mining.[50] Gerald's managerial brilliance at the coal mines replicates Maxwell's Demon's sorting function, a productive ordering that by creating and manipulating heat differentials wins available energy back from the rule of entropy. But Lawrence inserts Gerald's industrial sorting into the antivital register of destructive mechanism. In the narrator's evaluation, Gerald's mechanical willfulness promotes rather than reduces entropy: "It was the first great step in undoing, the first great phase of chaos, the substitution of the mechanical principle for the organic" (231).

And eventually this demon of energy begins to run down, as if his vital reservoir were being exhausted, "like a machine that is without power" (266). Rabinbach has commented that the

> obsession with fatigue in nineteenth-century thought was not merely a
> sign of the "real" weariness of individuals in industrial society, but of the
> negative aspect of the body conceived as a thermodynamic machine cap-
> able of conserving and deploying energy. The body's fatigue was, as von
> Helmholtz pointed out, a particular instance of entropy. . . . Fatigue thus

emerged at the threshold of the body's economy of energies; with its own internal laws of energy and motion, it was the corporal horizon of a mechanical universe. (*Human Motor*, 48)

To escape his entropic inertia, Gerald stumbles into Gudrun's boudoir, where he strikes her as "an apparition, the young Hermes" (343). Gudrun's mythic intuition of Gerald's demonic status is sound, for Gerald arrives under the aegis of the god of thieves to steal her vital capital, to replenish his own stock of vital force. The thermodynamics of their encounter are starkly underscored as Gudrun's reservoir of vital warmth flows irreversibly into Gerald's heat sink, leaving him momentarily restored and her momentarily destroyed: "he plunged deeper into her enveloping soft warmth, a wonderful creative heat that penetrated his veins and gave him life again. . . . He knew how destroyed he was, like a plant whose tissue is burst from inwards by a frost" (344–45). By the morning, Gerald and Gudrun have swapped thermodynamic status: "There was a certain coldness in her voice. . . . He was warm and full of life and desire" (347). Gerald's quick erotic fix, however, will not forestall his ultimate freeze into allegorical fixity as an emblem of final heat death.

The counterentropic sorting function of Maxwell's Demon is more subtly and more troublingly evoked by Rupert Birkin in his desire for the individualism in communion he terms "star-equilibrium" (319). The chapter title "Man to Man" in fact encodes the particular sorting function—the sorting out of genders—Lawrence had initiated a year or two earlier in the *Study of Thomas Hardy*. With his own thermodynamic and electro-vital flourishes, Birkin thinks how "he wanted something clearer, more open, cooler. . . . He wanted a further conjunction, where man had being and woman had being, two pure beings, each constituting the freedom of the other, balancing each other like two poles of one force, like two angels, or two demons" (199). Birkin now interweaves the vitalist and thermodynamic threads of his thought with an electromagnetic schema of gender polarity, giving "coolness" a positive valence, as of crisp spring mornings, relative to the negative fires of mechanical passion, and then complicates the whole complex with the added twist of a daemonic evocation of superhumanity. Birkin's thoughts represent a further phase of the ideas Lawrence had rehearsed in the *Study of Thomas Hardy* when he factored gender polarity into his antientropic, vitalistic individualism.

However, does this transcendent "star-equilibrium" represent a productive polarity, on the model of the mechanical exchange of heat and cold, or a formula for inertia and inarticulate stillness. For in the vocabulary of thermodynamics "equilibrium" names the state of maximum entropy, when all order has become randomized, all differentials dissolved.[51] In the continuation of this passage, the narrator, deeply merged with Birkin, describes the particular sorting operation Birkin envisions and clarifies its rationale: "the sex is that which remains in us of the mixed, the unresolved. And passion is the further separating of this mixture, that which is manly being taken into the being of the man, that which is womanly passing into the woman, till the two are clear and whole as angels, the admixture of sex in the highest sense surpassed, leaving two single beings, constellated together like two stars. . . . So Birkin meditated whilst he was ill" (201).

Many readers have accepted this gendered cosmology as the final Lawrencean word on the topic of sexual relations. Before we subscribe to such a reading, however, let us remark that this theory offers an essentialistic sexual dialectic distinctly reminiscent of the polar opposition of male and female plasms and the compounding of individual gender from their various mixtures in Otto Weininger's *Sex and Character*. It is difficult today to appreciate the profound cultural authority early modernity granted to such socioscientific ideologies based on dynamical and biological analogies. But we have already seen the parallel lines of Edward Carpenter's and Dora Marsden's scientist adaptations. Marsden, in particular, jettisoned the gender-polarity model while retaining a polar configuration in her description of the ego. Birkin's presentation of millennial gender polarity is ostensibly more egalitarian than Weininger's outright misogyny but no less troubling, nor will Lawrence entirely resist investing in the masculinism inscribed in the sexual-polarity models of romantic vitalism, those residues of the cultural reception of electrical phenomena before the energy concept of the electromagnetic field had been detached from the material paradigms of mechanical and vital forces.[52]

A sexual ideology descending directly from German romantic philosophical medicine is to say the least a dubious reservoir of gender tropes. In the next chapter, when we study William Carlos Williams's "The Great Sex Spiral," a long two-part letter to the editor of the *Egoist* written in 1917, we will encounter a similar schematizing of gender difference on the model of electrical polarization, and in that text Williams makes the Weininger connection explicit. Lawrence's and Williams's texts are both synchronized with the darkest period of the Great War. John Palattella has argued that Williams's increasingly emphatic masculinism of this period is connected specifically to the heightening of gender issues for male noncombatants faced with the gendered spectacle of fighting men at the front and civilian women at home.[53] A comparable anxiety over issues of masculinity is probably a part of Lawrence's concurrent, ostensibly neutral and mutual rehearsals of gender separation.[54] What else might be the motive behind Birkin's theory of sexual separatism? The singling away of sexual admixture is in fact Birkin's supreme strategy for a self-evolutionary differentiation aimed at saving his own soul from entropy, figured as a soul-confusing merger at the individual level and the "flux of corruption" at the collective level.

At this point in the text the thermodynamic, sexual, and evolutionary threads of *Women in Love* are tied together in a massive ideological folding of physical laws and biological theories over questions of human existence and gender difference. Despite the manifest organic motives of Lawrence's vitalism, Birkin tendentiously analogizes the sexual polarity of male and female to thermodynamic or electrical differentials, that is, to the mechanics of physical systems. If thermodynamic difference is necessary to produce usable energy—if there must be polarity to generate an electrical current—then, by analogy, polar sexual differences are needed to maintain any possibility of a "productive exchange." It then follows that bisexuality is entropic, the neutralization of an elemental polarity, whereas sexual purification is the counterentropic amplification of the vital circuit. It is ironic as well as symptomatic of the conflicts embedded in these notions that as Lawrence himself follows Birkin's arc toward Gerald Crich and the sorting of the masculine self into gender homogeneity leads "man to man"—as he reacts away from the closed system of marital and heterosexual intimacy, Lawrence passes through a phase of sublimated homoeroticism in which he will also celebrate Whitmanesque homogenic arrangements in their turn as the true key to evolutionary and social progress. In all this we have an example of rhetorical oscillation and serial displacement parallel to that besetting Lawrence's polemics against the ego.

A final complication in the passage from *Women in Love* under examination is that Lawrence's narrator eventually sorts itself out, so to speak, and reasserts its difference from Birkin and his ideas, when we are told, "So Birkin meditated whilst he was ill." In fact, Birkin's theories do articulate a virulent form of ideological malaise, the hyperdefensive masculinist response to the first major wave of feminist agitation, a powerful eddy off the overall bourgeois hysteria precipitating the Great War in the first place. Nor does the continuation of *Women in Love* necessarily ratify a Weiningerian or sexist solution of gender difference. Granted, as Gerald and Gudrun toboggan down the slippery slopes of erotic chaos on their Alpine vacation, their sexual polarity is short-circuited by the ambiguous Loerke, the lurking and dissolute specter of gender entropy personified.[55] The destructive lovers are gradually neutralized as Gudrun hardens into the phallic blade by which Gerald is spiritually castrated: their catastrophic passion "'blasts your soul's eye,'" Gerald tells Birkin, "'and leaves you sightless'" (439). A blinded demon, Gerald can no longer sort out life from death. But in the further relation of Ursula and Birkin, the narrator equivocates on the "singleness in doubleness" or polar duality theme by evoking residually androgynous or gender-transcendent counterimages of entire unity: "In the new, superfine bliss, a peace superseding knowledge, there was no I and you, there was only the third, unrealised wonder, the wonder of existing not as oneself, but in a consummation of my being and her being in a new One, a new, paradisal unit regained from the duality" (369).[56]

Michael Ragussis has argued that this erotic depolarization is not an entirely desirable existential goal, insofar as the "perfect silence of bliss" (369) it valorizes moves counter to the progressive production of individual utterance.[57] In Ragussis's view, Lawrence's foreword defines the truly creative, antientropic effort in *Women in Love* at the level of the novel's virtual composition: "this struggle for verbal consciousness . . . *the passionate struggle into conscious being*" (*Women in Love*, 486). But perhaps Ragussis's critique of the creative lovers' apocalyptic communal fusion is still a captive of Birkin's romantic polarity paradox. Lawrence's essential dilemma was the difficulty of balancing the egoistic desire for pure singularity against the inexorable relativity of differences constellated by any erotic or social community. The consummate "mystic passion" Ursula and Birkin achieve nicely reworks the "dual wave" scenario of the *Study of Thomas Hardy,* and the notes rung on "consciousness" in the foreword, if also read against the *Study,* link Lawrence's erotic quest back to the androgynous or angelic formula of the "two in one," a formula for ecstatic merger *Women in Love* holds in ambivalent solution with Birkin's homogenic sorting operations. In Garrett Stewart's strong formulation: "We might think of the 'star-equilibrium,' then, as a Lawrencian coinage, an original sexual metaphor, for the mutual relation between separate selves as those selves have more or less traditionally been defined, whereas 'a consummation of my being and her being in a new one' offers the other side of the coin, a time-worn metaphysical conceit bravely reconceived under the pressure of the self's radical (in the chemical sense) redefinition" ("Lawrence, 'Being,'" 241).

One small benefit of our postmodernity is the relatively recent scientific affirmation that thermodynamic entropy does not pose an imminent or elemental threat, that an "escape from entropy" is both impossible and unnecessary. We now think of entropy as the partner of information. Disorder is not entirely random—it can be made to signify—nor is it necessarily destructive—it may herald or provoke higher organizational levels. With infusions of energy into open systems, entropy decreases at specific localities. The statistical methods advanced by thermodynamic science in fact superseded the rigid determinisms of the classical Newtonian mechanics from which the vitalist counterparadigm emerged. However, none of this was obvious in the world Lawrence inhabited along with Dora Marsden's London. If Lawrence often fashions elaborate defenses against "dissolution" and "corruption," it may also be said that on occasion he saw past the ideological chimeras of his culture and seized upon the utility of dynamical chaos, as we now understand the term: at times he grasped both the promise of anarchic creativity and the positive energies to be derived from entropic processes of "waste."

Vitalist ideology was invigorated by the social discourse of entropy while at the same time commencing to lapse as science due to the development of thermodynamic models into modern statistical mechanics. The statistical analysis of thermodynamic entropy initiated by Maxwell set off a chain of events leading to quantum mechanics, information theory, and modern genetics. But a full appreciation of the fundamental nature of information as a conceptual entity on a par with matter and energy would not occur for another century. Until the mid-twentieth century, vitalism's hypothesis of a noumenal life force plausibly occupied a systemic aporia left open by the nonconceptualization of information. Whereas "in modern biology . . . molecular order, this choice between possible structures, is interpreted by the concepts of entropy and information," Jacob reminds us, "in organic chemistry at the beginning of the nineteenth century, a mysterious force had to be invoked to assign atoms to their places" (*Logic of Life*, 97). So to some extent the quarrel of vitalism with mechanistic materialism was prescient, an obscure anticipation of the cybernetic redescription of molecular genetics as an informational system. "The notion of vital force stands proleptically" for information, "the work of sorting and ordering energy and matter that is necessary for life in a universe governed by the second law" (Paulson, *Noise*, 45).

With entropy as refactored in information theory, we come back around to the paradigm of Maxwell's Demon. The crucial shared element is the sorting function, that is, the reproduction of organization. Genetic scripts sort out inanimate atoms and as-sign them "to their places" in organic structures. The notion of thermodynamic entropy as cosmic breakdown has been replaced by the paradigms of information entropy and the self-organization of far-from-equilibrium structures integrated by intercommunications among nested levels of complexity. If in fact entropy bears redescription not as life's opponent but as its partner—an irreversible process carrying the information needed to produce biological sorting—then entropy always was life's oblique, equivocal double.

Lawrence's fugitive sense of the vitality of death processes and his fascination with the flux of corruption intertwined with the flow of creation anticipate the revaluation of entropy achieved several decades after his death.

As Hayles has remarked about recent discussions of Maxwell's famous trope, "the Demon no longer function[s] as a liminal figure mediating between human limitations and inhuman entropy. The dream behind the Demon was realised in another sense, however, for the potent new force of information had entered the arena to combat entropy" (*Chaos Bound*, 46). Ezra Pound's vortex doctrines remind us that early modernism in general is a period when serious writers are reconceiving the substance of their activities according to models of cultural information, the efficiencies of its creation and transmission, and the problems of its suppression, distortion, and loss. In the whole of his writings, Lawrence intimates that the creative utterance and dramatic codification of cultural information—the quest for verbal consciousness that produces written texts—maintain the most enduring pressure against human disorder. Cultural entropy is actually most manifest in corporations' and states' monopolistic or totalitarian efforts to abolish individual differences. If Lawrence himself wavered at the edge of this recognition, that was perhaps a form of daemonic ambivalence—a strife between the evolutionary angel and the thermodynamic demon—inscribed in his particular "*struggle into conscious being.*"

William Carlos Williams, Imagist and Egoist

Near the beginning of *Spring and All*, a 1923 publication blending sharply disjunct lyrics with rambling exhortations on art and the imagination, William Carlos Williams wrote:

> A terrific confusion has taken place. No man knows whither to turn. There is nothing! Emptiness stares us once more in the face. Whither? To what end? Each asks the other. Has life its tail in its mouth or its mouth in its tail? Why are we here? Dora Marsden's philosophic algebra. Everywhere men look into each other's faces and ask the old unanswerable question: Whither? How? What? Why?
>
> At any rate, now at last spring is here![1]

The prose passages of *Spring and All* became generally available only in the *Imaginations* edition of 1971; the passage cited above contains Dora Marsden's one great explicit notice in modernist literature. If Marsden owes Williams this debt, it is also to his credit that he alone has admitted his debt to her. In a playfully oblique or willfully obscure manner, Williams seems to imply that "Dora Marsden's philosophic algebra" offers some answer to life's "old unanswerable question." To construct the sense of this passage, and perhaps a rationale for its teasing opacity, we will investigate the full span of Williams's responses to Dora Marsden's doctrines. Recent documentary and interpretive articles have dealt directly with Williams's relations to the *Egoist* in general and Marsden's writings in particular.[2] These relations are of considerable interest, for Marsden's writings offer a crucial index to the modernist individualism in the midst of which Williams's earlier work was cultivated.

The case for Williams's sustained appreciation of Dora Marsden was first documented by Mike Weaver: "No other poet had evidenced much interest in egoism as a contributory force in the Imagist movement in poetry. In fact the view then, as later, was that egoism was an irrelevance introduced as the name of the Imagist paper by the two 'philosophical feminists,' Harriet Weaver and Dora Marsden; and since they were responsible for its financial existence the poets merely acquiesced."[3] Weaver alludes to the write-off of Dora Marsden carried out by standard imagist historiography, which we have detailed with regard to the roles of Richard Aldington and Williams's London patron, Ezra Pound. For Williams in particular, Weaver continues, "nothing could have been further from the truth. He read Miss Marsden assiduously, and addressed long letters to the paper. He began with her writings on egoism as an alternative to feminism, continued with her nominalist aesthetics, and finally took up her so-called 'Lingual Psychology'" (23). Carl Rapp's work also invites a reexamination of Williams's egoistic affirmations of the war years.[4] Rapp's view of Williams's aesthetics as a late type of romantic idealism is at odds with more common views of Williams's objectivist or even postmodernist poetics, and Rapp is correct to say that a form of idealism has some relevance to Williams's outlook.[5] But we need not go so far afield as Hegel or Emerson to find its primary avatar in Williams's case. By recontextualizing Williams's early writings in their contemporary milieu, we enhance our grasp not only of his text but also of the intellectual culture to which it responded. The modernist egoism Williams participated in was a quite specific response to the violent countercurrents of socialist agitation and imperialist reaction that crested in the vast capitalist tantrum of the Great War. As written out of this milieu of defensive as well as constructive individualism, early Anglo-American modernism was an anarchistic protest against the collective pressures of poetic and historical communities, social movements and mores, corporate mendacity, and imperious warring states.

Ezra Pound's Invitation

In the *New Freewoman* of September 1, 1913, reviewing books of poetry by D. H. Lawrence, Walter de la Mare, and Robert Frost, Ezra Pound published a first installment of "In Metre," about which feature he had written to Dora Marsden a month earlier: "I have done these dam'd reviews, and I hope they're not too beastly dull." On the next page were six poems gathered under the heading "The Newer School," the last of which was Williams's lyric "Postlude."[6] I believe that this was Williams's first appearance in the London press. In the December 1 issue, Pound reviewed Williams's collection *The Tempers*, singling out for praise "the splendid 'Postlude.' . . . At times he seems in danger of drifting into imaginative reason, but the vigour of his illogicalness is nearly always present to save him; and he is for the most part content to present his image, or the bare speech of his protagonist, without border or comment."[7]

Writing to Williams on December 19, 1913, Pound passed off the impression that he was bestowing Aldington not with partial but with total editorial control of the *New Freewoman:* "Richard is now running the *N F* which is now to appear as *The Egoist*. You must subscribe as the paper is poor, i.e. weak financially. The *Mercure de France* has taken to quoting us, however. It is the best way to keep in touch. . . . About your 'La Flor': it is good. . . . I think I shall print 'La Flor' in *The Egoist*. . . . If you haven't had that paper, send for back numbers since Aug. 15th" (Pound, *Letters*, 27–28). As we have seen, the August 15 number of the *New Freewoman* had marked Pound's emergence in its pages as a contributor and literary editor. Certainly Williams took Pound's advice, if only to possess copies of his own appearance and mention. I trace Williams's knowledge of Dora Marsden's writings, then, at least as far back as the August 15, 1913, number. Granting that he secured the back issues in question, what else would Williams have encountered in these pages?

Looking over the *New Freewoman* for August 15, presumably he would have been familiar already with the tenets of "Imagisme," here mediated by Rebecca West, and "The Contemporania of Ezra Pound," alternate forms of both having appeared earlier that year in *Poetry*. If Williams also gave some of his attention to the leader, he would have been introduced to Marsden in fine egoistic fettle, doing battle with the fixed products of ideation, ratiocination, and other obfuscations cultivated by authoritarians, and advocating caustic doses of semantic hygiene, "analysis of the process of naming . . . the work of purging language."[8] Clearly he would have discovered in this discussion an attitude congenial to his own development toward a credo of "No ideas but in things."

> It is strange to find searchers coming here [to the *New Freewoman*] seeking thoughts, followers after truth seeking new lamps for old, right ideas for wrong. It seems fruitless to affirm that our business is to annihilate thought, to shatter the new lamps no less than the old, to dissolve ideas, the "right" as well as the "wrong." "It is a new play of artistry, some new paradox," they reflect, not comprehending that artistry and paradox are left as the defences of power not yet strong enough to comprehend. If a man has the power that comprehends, what uses has he left for paradox? If he sees a thing as it is, why must he needs describe it in terms of that which it is

not? . . . Idea, idea, always the idea. As though the supremacy of the idea
were not the subjection of men, slaves to the idea. Men need no ideas.
They have no use for them (unless indeed they are of the literary breed—
then they live upon them by their power to beguile the simple). (Marsden,
"Thinking and Thought," 81)

Marsden idealizes individual will as a vital/evolutionary source. Her conception
of the creative ego as a center of protean origin explains the animus toward
those literati who simply merchandise "ideas" for weak-willed intellectual con-
sumers. Here then is a plausible example of what Williams would characterize
several years later as Marsden's "attack on the 'creative artist'" ("Great Sex Spiral," 46). If this leader initiated Williams's acquaintance with Marsden's writings, then his response would have been immediately shaped by her penchant
for challenging "ideologists" to press their efforts away from popular appreciation and into the service of individualistic assertion, as would soon be the case
in her sparring with Ezra Pound over "The Serious Artist."[9]

"Tales for the Attentive" and "The Wanderer"

After the publication of "Postlude" in the *New Freewoman*, Williams placed
material—poems, prose pieces, and letters—in the *Egoist* eleven times throughout the decade.[10] But his most significant contribution was his second, the publication on March 16, 1914, of "The Wanderer: A Rococo Study." A crucial
early manifestation of his poetic development, this narrative lyric recounts a
young poet's initiation into "modernity" through the agency of a "marvelous
old queen," who takes the poet on an Endymion-like ride through the air, for
an invisible walk through the back streets of Paterson, and who finally baptizes
him in the "filthy" Passaic. My surmise that Williams was attending to Dora
Marsden's *New Freewoman* leaders from August 15 forward now becomes especially important, for it reinforces the likelihood that "The Wanderer" incorpo-
rates Williams's rewriting of Dora Marsden's leader for October 1, 1913, "Tales
for the Attentive," the allegory of life striving against mind I touched on in the
last chapter while discussing Lawrence's *Study of Thomas Hardy.*

"Tales for the Attentive" appears to be Marsden's sole published effort at a
creative literary production, perhaps in belated response to Mary Gawthorpe's
encouragement.[11] Unlike the more supply sardonic voice of her discursive
commentaries, Marsden's composition here is mostly stiff and arch. Anchored
to a symbolic dramatization of the thesis expressed in leaders like "Thinking and
Thought," the piece argues that "searchers" after "thoughts" must redirect

impersonal universalizing intellect toward egoistic assertions of vitalistic being. The mock-archaic diction of Marsden's "Tale" presages the mythic tones Williams handles quite decently in "The Wanderer," and its basic frame is the sort of Keatsian poet-encounter with a figure of admonishment that Williams would also adapt to his text. But, whereas Williams ultimately has his protagonist kneel down before the "marvelous old queen" to undergo an initiation ritual or secular baptism in "Saint James' Grove," Marsden's "uncommon Youth" is eventually invited to wrestle with and vanquish his superannuated seeress.

> In the mouth of an old quarry sat an aged crone. From before the birth of the first man she had been there. Men came to her to learn how to make tools. . . . Nine layers of furrowed stone hid her face from the light, and a boulder which a glacier had scratched, buried her knees. . . .
>
> To scan her face there came an uncommon Youth: uncommon being he, who for that time, nourished the Fires a far-off sire had brought to Earth from Heaven. Eagerly and often the Youth came and searched her face, but saw no sign; the motionless veils hung unchanged. A last time he came and vainly searched, when, he being angered and unaware, the Fires flashed into his eyes and passed from thence, piercing into the gross texture of the stone shroudings. . . .
>
> "What dost thou seek?" [a voice] asked.
>
> "Thy teaching," he replied. "Why spell thy veils no sign for me?"
>
> "What need of signs have they who know?"
>
> "But I know not."
>
> "Thou hast the Fires."
>
> "I guard them."
>
> "Too well; thy fires are to be spent. . . ."
>
> "Who art thou?"
>
> "I am Mind. . . ." ("Tales for the Attentive," 141)

The crone and the youth hold a long colloquy. Mind explains that she has converted into thought her allotted stock of vital force, and so her time to be overthrown has come: "'I feed on Life's strength, increasing as it grows, yet when it declines, empowered to aid it nothing. In weakness, Life and Mind wither together. I have not power in aught to augment its substance'" (142). What can the youth do? Apply his allotted energies to the liberation of Life: "'Go forth and set free the fires. When all is spent and in thy heart thou knowest thou art a conqueror, return to conquer me'" (142). With that the more ponderous portions of the allegory are over, the youth discovers his powers, and the writing loosens up and takes off, more or less: "The tight cord he had worn round his heart stretched and snapped. The lightning Fires leapt forth. They coursed through his limbs : the tendons stretched : the muscles tightened : a sharp tingling vivified the heavy flesh. . . . Deep baths of air he drew in with his breath" (143). Reaching land's edge the youth exults and enters into the new element: "he plunged far out into the waters. . . . As he rose he saw the black hulls of the ships sailing outwards. . . . Above him, wheeled the strong white wings of the sea-gulls. . . . He awoke and looked up through the blue ether : he knew he could fly. . . . Swift and strongly he mounted, his eyes fronting the sunset. When its last rays had faded he was resting on the snow-covered peak of the mountain" (143). When the youth's Zarathustrian ecstasy subsides, he returns to the quarry. Mind in her terminal glory challenges him to mortal combat. They wrestle through the night.

> The cool air of dawn brought the surge and glow he had known on the mountains. With passion of being, his grip hardened. A wild unseeing movement, and his night-long antagonist was pinioned. He laid his lips on her mouth and withdrew the breath from her. Wraith-like, she dwindled.
> Frailer and sparer, intangible at length, he sucked out the last vapours of her being. Drunk, his eyes closed, his head fell forward. The star dropped upon his hand. His arms were empty. . . .
> He rose to his feet and stood upright, and gazed into the morning sun's splendour. He greeted its beauty and turned towards the cities. (143–44)

I speculate that Williams immediately appreciated the Keatsian tonality of "Tales for the Attentive," recognized how it resonated with his own unsatisfactory juvenilia, and thus was assisted by Marsden's egoistic fantasy in salvaging from his earliest, antiquated poetic efforts one supreme piece of Keatsian verse. "The Wanderer" was also a modestly satisfactory "mirror" to the "modernity" toward which he was developing (l. 18).[12] Williams, Youth-like, accepted an ongoing invitation to wrestle with Marsden's oracular Crone persona. On this occasion, he deflected the strained sublimity of Marsden's delivery by refashioning the crone after his own grandmother.[13] In addition, he adapted Marsden's Youth to his own first-person poet and repositioned the youth's Odyssean plunge into the sea as the climactic baptism of his poet in the Passaic. Several excerpts from "The Wanderer: A Rococo Study," as published in the *Egoist*, provide strong echoes of Marsden's subtext.

> Come! cried my mind and by her might
> That was upon us we flew above the river

Seeking her, grey gulls among the white—
In air speaking as she had willed it—
"I am given, cried I, now I know it!
I know now all my time is forespent!
For me one face is all the world!
For this day I have at last seen her,
In whom age on age is united—
Indifferent, out of sequence, marvelously!"

                                                      (ll. 29–38)

. . . Knower of all fires out of the bodies
Of all men . . .

                                                      (ll. 95–96)

Hot for savagery,
I went sucking the air! Into the city,
Out again, baffled, on to the mountain!
Back into the city! . . .

                                                      (ll. 124–27)

The immediate point to make is how quickly Williams seizes on Marsden's writings as a productive source of creative provocation. Williams's was an intensely absorptive intellect self-consciously positioned on a cultural periphery and hungry for connection to "centers." From Williams's perspective, whether Pound acknowledged the fact or not, Marsden's discourse resided at the center of Pound's London vortex as an integral part of an avant-garde journal representing "the best way to keep in touch." But what accounts for Williams's particular susceptibility to Marsden's aesthetic philosophies? At the cultural level, he could take from Marsden the combination of evolutionary vitalism and aesthetic anarchism strongly valorized in the early modernist milieu.[14] And, at the personal level, his response is an index of his ongoing relations to creative female figures, beginning with his mother, Elena, and falling into line with his literary relations to H.D., Gertrude Stein, Marianne Moore, and, perhaps most significantly, Marcia Nardi, the "Cress" of *Paterson*. There is a long-standing urge in Williams to establish creative agons with strong (if often struggling) females. His relations with Marsden represent an early and entirely typical form of that proceeding and also call forth otherwise recondite aspects of his sexual ambivalence, the psychological subtext for Williams's professed belief in gender polarity, as that will surface in "The Great Sex Spiral," his letters criticizing Marsden's "Lingual Psychology." That ambivalence is importantly expressed in proximity to the *Egoist* several years earlier in Williams's correspondence.

An Epistolary Triangle

Williams met Viola Baxter Jordan, an erstwhile girlfriend and lifelong confidante, through Ezra Pound, who had met her at a dance during his Hamilton College days. Throughout her life the garrulous Baxter Jordan maintained correspondences with Pound, H.D., and Williams, and the copious letters she received from all of them are now housed at Yale University. Patrick Moore's introduction to "Ten Unpublished Letters from William Carlos Williams to Viola Baxter Jordan" provides the information needed to appreciate Viola and the nature of her relation to Williams, but it does not venture full interpretations of the letters' detail. I will provide an interpretive commentary on some Williams's and Pound's early correspondence with Viola Baxter Jordan, with special reference to a particular letter in which Williams clarifies his investment in the discourse of the *Egoist*. Moore's commentary does not mention Mike Weaver, who indicated the potential significance of that letter, remarking tantalizingly, but without divulging Williams's own words, "by July 1914 Williams was able to inform Viola Baxter that he was both an Imagist and an Egoist" (*William Carlos Williams*, 23).[15] I will focus eventually on this letter of June 7, 1914, in which Williams counters what appears to have been Baxter Jordan's distaste for the *Egoist* and possibly for Williams's own poetry therein with a vigorous and imagistic defense of egoism. But I will approach it first through Baxter Jordan's concurrent correspondence with Ezra Pound.

Interfiling Pound's and Williams's letters to Baxter Jordan chronologically during the years 1908–14 is bemusing as well as illuminating. Viola passed Pound information on Williams and Williams information on Pound. Pound veers regularly to the topic of Williams, Williams touches constantly on Pound. In the glow of his initial London successes, Ezra the playful pen pal devilishly amuses Viola by mocking Bill's pretensions to poetry. Pound has no love interest in his correspondent, whereas Williams's letters are driven by an active but unconsummated and ultimately suspended sexual attraction. Williams's letters are both lighter and heavier than Pound's, by breathless turns severe, silly, sanctimonious, and sarcastic. In the process Baxter Jordan's own sensibilities are shadowed by the responses they provoke in her highly verbal correspondents, allowing us to infer more accurately what was at stake in Williams's significant outburst of June 7, 1914.

In a letter to Viola written from 10 Church Walk, London, around July 1909, Pound states: "Bill Wms didn't write me anything. . . . Bill only sends me poesy. 'gentle voice forever piping. etc. I correct & remake as much of it as I can & send it back to him. He is not always soothed by my methods."[16] In another letter from roughly the same period, Pound picks up the same note of mock indignation over Williams's nonforthcoming correspondence: "Bill Wms. does not confide in me his 'affaires de coeur' of his heart I can say nothing. His head is in a shocking condition. . . . I don't know whether he's been dippy & recovered, not. or whether—its the natural state of his mind."[17]

One could fairly inquire concerning the state of Williams's mind, or at least about the nature of his motivations, on the basis of letters he sends to Baxter Jordan in 1911. One letter is sufficiently curious to have merited excerpting in Weaver's *William Carlos Williams:* "You are quite right, Viola, quite right, men are not strong enough to 'bat air' with women. That forever proves to me I am not a man; they, men, disgust me and if I must say it fill me with awe and admiration. I am too much a woman" (22). Does Williams's notion that he is "not a man" mean that, conversely, he himself *is* "strong enough to 'bat air' with women," that is, to enter into their conversations, to participate in "girl talk"? Weaver cites Williams's remarks as conveying an awareness of "the possibilities of inversion" (22), and refers the topic to Williams's familiarity with Otto Weininger's theories of bisexuality expressed in *Sex and Character*. We will return to this larger question later in the context of "The Great Sex Spiral." At the moment, however, we note Williams's seemingly ingenuous admission of at least a sense of his own sexual admixture. Williams's history of sparring with assertive females appears to some extent to be a compulsive process by which he hopes to sort out this sexual confusion by establishing himself as the male half of a gender polarity.

Another letter of Williams's from 1911 would appear to address the same cluster of "anatomical" concerns, but this time with a telling note of "individualism": "Why it is I don't know but all individualists are the same they must live in a mystery of self which is, to them, unsolvable. Therefore to others necessarily unsolvable or they become despondent. Anatomy. I confess it but true."[18] But, if Williams occasionally blurted out to Baxter Jordan such intimate confessions, he could also be close-lipped about other, related topics, forcing Viola to submit to Pound for clarification. For instance, a year and a half after Williams's marriage in December 1912 to Charlotte Herman's sister, Florence, Pound sends Viola the following hilarious intelligence: "WOT !!! you never knew it was Bill's unattainable pinnacle, his bleatin' desire etc. the ungetatable Charlotte, that preferred his bad big brother. . . . No this is too tragic, or something. Bill's never let on as how there was a sandal in his family in law."[19]

Such epistolary high jinks are a certain backdrop to Viola's receipt from Williams that June of a long lecture on art, the intellect, and the growth of the soul. It is perhaps no wonder that Williams would take an unavailing stab at developing Viola's aesthetic sensibility. But her literary tastes were already established and thoroughly conventional: she balked at sexual explicitness in particular and vulgar realism in general. In 1911, Pound had charitably interpreted as irony her earnest displeasure in some of his early *Personae* poems. In anticipation of values expressed two years later in "The Serious Artist," Pound wrote: "I don't know how much you meant of what you said about wanting poets expurgated *etc.* It would be most immoral of me to present Pierre Vidals ravings as a spiritual extacy. What the poems say is simply this. 'Animal passion is very near—in its extreme form, that is—to insanity, or dipsomania.'"[20] We see that, in Pound's slang, to have been "dippy" is to have suffered from erotomania, which seems to have been the young Williams's chronic condition. In any event, Viola's prudery was genuine and ineradicable: "'James Joyce . . . is anathema to me. Anyone who will write about his doings on the toilet daily leaves me cold' (Oct. 21, 1940). Jordan was fond of poems like Stephen Phillips' *Marpessa*, a cloying, melancholy, blank verse work about gods and mortals" (Moore, "Ten Letters," 33).

Since Williams destroyed most of the letters he received from Baxter Jordan, we must reconstruct her side of the correspondence. My theory is that the catalyst for Williams's epistolary lecture of June 7 was his having sent Viola over the course of the spring of 1914 several copies of the *Egoist,* certainly the March 15 issue containing "The Wanderer" and probably other issues surrounding that date, containing pieces by Pound and H.D. as well as leaders by Dora Marsden, to give her the flavor of the *Egoist* milieu. That Viola had not been especially taken by "The Wanderer" might be inferred from an obscure response Williams returned her in a letter that April: "Understanding no word of your letter I cannot answer it except to say: where I am Whitman God damn me."[21] That she was, as D. H. Lawrence had been a month or two before, unimpressed with the rest of the *Egoist* is the basic subtext of the letter in question.

> Have you ever seen a butterfly just after it has emerged from the chrysalis—its wings wet and crumpled? . . . You crumple the crysalis between your fingers and watch those wings grow and grow, and shake and quiver—always unfurling—until the first flight is approached and—begins.
>
> You are slipping and clinging. . . . Trust your wings.
>
> So much for my image since I am and will be an Imagist.
>
> Now then for the husks that are thoughts—if I am not too perfect to use them. . . .[22]

The literary indirectness of this opening, the "imagistic" tack and high irony, indicate that Williams's remarks here are not just off the cuff. Rather, they distill his current poetic attitudes and offer a definitive justification for his investment in the literary and intellectual avant-gardes of the moment. The signature of Pound is obvious in the assertion of adherence to imagism; Marsden's signature may be read in the phrase "the husks that are thoughts," reminiscent of her leader in the August 15 *New Freewoman*, "Thinking and Thought." As grasped by Williams, the confluence of Pound's and Marsden's manifestoes would be that imagism strips from the traditional rhetoric of verse the dead husks of editorializing and intellectualizing displays to reveal the naked body of things. Like Marsden's Youth and Williams's Wanderer, the image in poetic flight leaves the dead shell behind like the butterfly its chrysalis stage. Glimmering through Marsden and Pound we might also detect the writings of Edward Carpenter, for whom the metamorphosis of the butterfly is typical Platonic imagery for the developmental unfolding of the psyche and for whom the display of a proud nudity is sexual/progressivist rhetoric for evolutionary reality. Williams continues:

> You are wrong to overlook the worth of the "Egoist" in a fit of temper against the filthiness you may find there. . . . Hands are to use (So is the Egoist.) for free carrying out of the will (So is the Egoist.) Use them then and learn to keep clean—this is the moral O Vanessa J. Album (a rare butterfly.) . . . You cannot always remain in a chrysalis, you must come out if you are destined to have wings—as you are. What to do then? Be an egoist. Nothing else offers. You must. An egoist is simply a person who owns himself to bestow himself perfectly. And how can you say you own yourself if you are not free to be touched filthily (slapped on the one cheek.) and yet continue your clean purpose. If the annoyance (the filthy articles.) so glut the paper (The Egoist.) that they leave nothing for your pleasure then burn it and never see it again. . . .
>
> I offer you egoism, you refuse it. Very well, I have fought hard for it and it has served me well. Let it rest there.

In this defense of the *Egoist*, clearly Williams is not simply standing up for the merits of imagist poetry, over the length and breadth of which even Viola would have had difficulty locating anything "filthy." It seems more likely that what upset Viola was elsewhere, perhaps in either the last installments of de Gourmont's *Horses of Diomedes* or the initial installments of Joyce's *Portrait of the*

Artist. Or perhaps her distaste was in response to one of Marsden's uniformly blunt commentaries on sexual questions. For instance, Williams may have sent Viola the February 2 number because it featured their mutual friends—noteworthy imagist poems by H.D. ("Hermes of the Ways" and others) and two spoof columns by Pound under the pseudonym Bastien von Helmholtz.[23] That number also contained installments of both de Gourmont's and Joyce's novels, as well as the following vivid reflections on the chastity of women, Marsden's response to Christabel Pankhurst's suffragette broadside against venereal disease and male sexual barbarism, *The Hidden Scourge and How to End It.*

> There are parts of the body more sensitive than other parts, which may be stimulated into sensation by fixing attention on them. The vicious amuse themselves by imagining and thereafter "touching"; the "pure" prolong the excitement by imagining and thereafter refraining. Fundamentally there is nothing to choose between them. . . . The seeking after the "vicious" is a small ineffectual wriggle which life makes to escape the boredom of the "pure," but "vice" cannot throw off its "pure" character. The two are one—related to each other as the obverse and reverse of a coin : the under and over of the same psychological condition : as the prostitute is the twin-trader of the legally-protected "pure" woman. Where there are excise officials there are smugglers. ("Views and Comments," February 2, 1914, 45–46)

Williams's correspondence with Viola over the *Egoist* corresponds as well with major imagery in "The Wanderer." His rhetorical inquiry—"how can you say you own yourself if you are not free to be touched filthily (slapped on the one cheek.) and yet continue your clean purpose"—may be compared with the climax of that poem, when the Wanderer consents to immersion in "The Passaic, that filthy river. / . . . 'Lo, the filth in our hair! our bodies stink!' / . . . I felt the utter depth of its filthiness" (111). The puritanical metaphor equating filth with sex remains part of the broad American landscape: at the beginning of this century, Williams's provocative celebration of bodily lowliness could especially be expected to induce disgust in readers with conventional notions of feminine (and poetic) rectitude and purity. Reciprocally, by reference to this "batting of air" with Viola over the *Egoist*, Williams's pervasive lexicon of filth and cleanliness and his medically inflected concerns over contamination, antisepsis, and prophylaxis take on the coloring of a code vocabulary for the material anxieties of personal sexual conduct—venereal disease and contraception—prior to penicillin and the pill.

Williams's long letter to Viola, then, manifests literary modernism as a form of cultural hygiene. The very point of articulating and publishing sexual concerns is to cleanse the vitalistic realm of individual sexual desires, to wash it clean of the dirt thrown on it by conventional moralism. Thus, for Williams one crucial definition of egoism was strictly as a doctrine advocating the free expression of sexuality as a liberation of the "fires," and one utility of the *Egoist* was its not insignificant role in fostering such expression. In large degree Williams's main point to Viola is to champion the *Egoist* as an organ of sexual libertarianism. In these terms, one could translate "I offer you egoism" not only as an intellectual bestowal but also as an abstruse sexual invitation. Egoism as Williams represents it to Viola Baxter in June, 1914, herself soon to marry Virgil Jordan, was also an imaginative way to stay single, to maintain private rights to self-bestowal, within the strictures of the marriage commitment.

The sexual character of the artist and the appropriate gendering of poetry are some of Williams's perennial interests. His occasional recognition of his own androgyny, however, does not seem to indicate any belief on his part in its preferability. Kerry Driscoll centers her discussion of Williams's strong female affiliations with a claim concerning "his belief in the androgyny of all artists" (*Williams and the Maternal Muse*, 1), as that is said to be directly expressed in a minor lyric, "Transitional."[24] The title may allude to Edward Carpenter's *The Intermediate Sex: A Study of Some Transitional Types of Men and Women*. To make her case, Driscoll cites lines 2–5; but by deleting the first line, "First he said," she turns a dialogical problematic into a monological affirmation reminiscent of Williams's 1911 letter to Viola exclaiming "I am too much a woman."

First he said:
It is the woman in us
That makes us write.
. . . .
I then said:
Dare you make this
Your propaganda?

And he answered:
Am I not I—here?[25]

Read as a dialogue and taking the first-person speaker to represent Williams's own position, this lyric distances the third-person speaker's appeal to the vicarious comprehensiveness of an androgynous sexuality. It does not affirm but questions the possibility as well as the politics of a bisexual identity. I will return to these matters later in discussing "The Great Sex Spiral." For now, "Transitional" may also be taken to indicate Williams's close association of the *New Freewoman/Egoist* with the explicit dialogue of poetry and (bi)sexual character. A related ambivalent dynamic between self-limitation and self-liberation will continue to operate throughout Williams's existential and literary careers. We can see a clear repercussion of it a year later in his personal aesthetic manifesto, "Vortex."

Williams's "Vortex"

In the same letter of December 19, 1913, in which Pound urged Williams to subscribe to the soon-to-be *Egoist*, he also wrote:

> Have just bought two statuettes from *the* coming sculptor, Gaudier-Brzeska. I like him very much. He is the only person with whom I can really be "Altaforte." . . . We are getting our little gang after five years of waiting. You must come over and get the air—if only for a week or so in the spring. . . .
>
> You may get something slogging away by yourself that you would miss in The Vortex—and that we miss. (*Letters*, 27–28)

Pound's terms bluntly outline the dialectic between literary isolation and artistic coterie that would prey on Williams's feelings for decades, as he "slogged away" in stolen moments and relative obscurity. Thus, his craving for "contact" and the "desperation" of his correspondence.[26] All the while Williams was sending feelers out into Chicago, New York, London, and Paris, he maintained a private base of operations in a locality guaranteed not to threaten his immediate preeminence. That Williams was torn between stasis and wanderlust is commonly appreciated. In this instance I believe the discourse of the *Egoist* had a further utility for him: it provided a powerful rationale for cultivating his unique isolation and revaluing it as a source of creative drive. If the egoist is in his or her own place the absolute center of a universe of experience—a point that will come to the fore in Dora Marsden's elaboration of her *Science of Signs*—then anywhere is everywhere, and, as "John Dewey had said (I discovered it quite by chance), 'The local is the only universal, upon that all art builds'" (W. Williams, *Paterson*, vii). One would then read Williams's rhetoric of the local as celebrating not only a differential particularity but also the ultimacy of the individual at any given location and regardless of any particular circumstances.

Such an attitude is clearly the gist of Williams's "Vortex," a private aesthetic manifesto of 1915, handily reconstructed from several variants in Bram Dijkstra's introduction to *A Recognizable Image*. Williams wrote his "Vortex" in response to the appearance in *Blast* of "VORTEX GAUDIER-BRZESKA (Written from the Trenches)," much as "The Wanderer" had issued from the appearance of Marsden's "Tales for the Attentive."[27] It is important to distinguish this second Gaudier-Brzeska "Vortex" from the earlier appearance of "VORTEX. GAUDIER BRZESKA."[28] It is the opening of this first "VORTEX" that Pound would make the leitmotiv of his eulogy in *Gaudier-Brzeska: A Memoir.* "Sculptural feeling is the appreciation of masses in relation. Sculptural ability is the defining of these masses by planes" (155).[29] Gaudier-Brzeska's first "VORTEX" is a breathless world-historical survey of the evolution of sculptural forms; its arrogance is reserved for the final affirmation of the energies concentrated in the extended "Vortex" group.

> And WE the moderns: Epstein, Brancusi, Archipenko, Dunikowski, Modigliani, and myself, through the incessant struggle in the complex city, have likewise to spend much energy.
>
> The knowledge of our civilization embraces the world, we have mastered the elements.
>
> We have been influenced by what we liked most, each according to his own individuality, we have crystallised the sphere into the cube, we have made a combination of all the possible shaped masses—concentrating them to express our abstract thoughts of conscious superiority.
>
> Will and consciousness is our
> VORTEX (158)

The crucial difference between Gaudier-Brzeska's first and second "VORTEX," motivated by the outbreak of the war that wrenched the young sculptor out of his London coterie and into French uniform, is that the magisterial and transcendent "WE" of the first becomes the beleaguered and locally focused "I" of the second.

> I HAVE BEEN FIGHTING FOR TWO MONTHS and I can now gauge the intensity of Life. . . .
>
> THE BURSTING SHELLS, the volleys, wire entanglements, projectors, motors, the chaos of battle DO NOT ALTER IN THE LEAST, the outlines of the hill we are besieging. A company of PARTRIDGES scuttle along before our very trench. . . .

THIS WAR IS A GREAT REMEDY.

IN THE INDIVIDUAL IT KILLS ARROGANCE, SELF-ESTEEM, PRIDE.

IT TAKES AWAY FROM THE MASSES NUMBERS UPON NUMBERS OF UNIMPORTANT UNITS, WHOSE ECONOMIC ACTIVITIES BECOME NOXIOUS AS THE RECENT TRADE CRISES HAVE SHOWN US.

MY VIEWS ON SCULPTURE REMAIN ABSOLUTELY *THE SAME.*

IT IS THE *VORTEX* OF WILL, OF DECISION, THAT BEGINS.

I SHALL DERIVE MY EMOTIONS SOLELY FROM THE *ARRANGEMENT OF SURFACES,* I shall present my emotions by the ARRANGEMENT OF MY SURFACES, THE PLANES AND LINES BY WHICH THEY ARE DEFINED. (33–34)

And it is this "I"—the threatened individual in strident extremis struggling for personal survival in the midst of meaningless masses, attempting to glean aesthetic responses from starkly brutal landscapes—with which Williams would identify in his own manifesto, the "logically rather confused, but characteristically enthusiastic 'Vortex' of 1915" (Dijkstra, "Introduction," 6).

However, Williams's "Vortex" is no more logically confused than any other egoistic pronouncement, whether it be Dora Marsden's or the closely related individualistic provocations of the *Blast* group. Throughout his introduction to *A Recognizable Image*, Dijkstra is in somewhat startled reaction away from the masculinism he ascertains throughout Williams's writings on art in particular and from Williams's individualist stance in general. In *Cubism, Stieglitz, and the Early Poetry of William Carlos Williams*, Dijkstra had sounded no such alarm: then again, literal sociopolitical attitudes are more readily read out of aesthetic manifestoes than from cubistic modernist poems. But ideological commitments deemed regrettable are not thereby confused: they may follow quite validly from the initial premises of the reasoning. Even if the premises are faulty, we still need to account for the power of their appeal and the force of their application within the texture of Williams's thought. In this instance as well, early modernism's doctrinal stances may be illuminated by reference to the milieu and derivation of Dora Marsden's discourse.

In November 1918, Williams misremembers the date of his "Vortex" by two years, aligning it instead with the prewar season of the *New Freewoman:* "I wish that I might set down my 'Vortex' after the fashion of London, 1913, stating how little it means to me whether I live here, there or elsewhere. . . . But the time is past."[30] It was left to archival scholars half a century later to recover the remnants of "VORTEX—WILLIAM CARLOS WILLIAMS,"[31] as it had been composed in the trenches of Rutherford, New Jersey.

> I affirm my existence by accepting other forces to be in juxtaposition to my own either in agreement or disagreement. . . .
>
> Furthermore (by this acceptance) I deny—(affirm my independence from)—the accident of time and place that brought the particular phrases to me, in that, now as always, I express my freedom from necessity and from accident by using whatever I find in my view without effort (to avoid or) to find. Thus I am free to take whatever appearance fits my purpose. . . .
>
> By taking whatever character my environment has presented and turning it to my purpose, I have expressed my independence of it. . . .
>
> I will not make an effort to leave that place for I deny that I am dependent on any place. . . . (Dijkstra, *A Recognizable Image*, 57–58)

Here is another affirmation of that self-bestowing egoism Williams had offered Viola Baxter a year earlier. Williams also confronts what he must already recognize in his compositional methods as a readiness to seize foreign elements and give them the mark of his own local authority.[32] This intellectual acquisitiveness affirms his own possession of a creative "force" in perfect distinction from a larger field of rivaling as well as inspiring and collaborating forces. The egoistic orientation is quite plain: his aesthetic appropriations are justified because he has the strength to carry them off. In addition, the doctrinal idiom of "Vortex" forecasts the vital/energetic rhetoric of "life" and "force" that Williams will pursue and refine in the prose passages of *Spring and All*.

Carl Rapp has seized on Williams's "Vortex" to confirm his interpretation of the climax of "The Wanderer" as an expression of romantic idealism, thereby turning Hillis Miller's reading in *Poets of Reality* inside out. The well-known lines run:

> Then the river began to enter my heart
>
> . . . .
>
> It tortured itself within me
> Until time had been washed finally under,
> And the river had found its level—
> And its last motion ceased
> And I knew all—it became me.

And I knew this for double certain
For there I saw myself, whitely,
Being borne off under the water!

("The Wanderer," 111)

The climax of "The Wanderer" does not represent an overcoming or relinquishing of the ego in favor of a dispersed objective field, Rapp argues, but rather
demonstrates Williams's full inheritance of the problematics of romantic egoism:
like Apollo in Keats's *Hyperion*, "Williams has drawn all things into himself. As
the 'all' enters his mind, it becomes his idea, while he, on the other hand,
becomes the single, transcendent point of unity—the logos, the center, the
coherence. Indeed, on the evidence of this first major poem it might well be
said that, instead of abandoning idealism, Williams actually embraces it" (*Williams
and Idealism*, 18). But, while "idealism" properly names a mental gathering point
or center toward which poetic appropriations converge, Williams does not
occupy and fortify this center in a reactionary mode of static possession. Rather,
he rearticulates his idealism through an anarchist model of vital dissemination.
Nevertheless, Rapp's reading corrects to some extent Hillis Miller's influential
overstatement of the case for Williams's transcendence of romantic subjectivity.
Hillis Miller has Williams emerge from the Wanderer's plunge into the Passaic
on the far side of a late-romantic or decadent nihilism by "abandoning the independence of the ego. Instead of making everything an object for the self, the
mind must efface itself before reality, or plunge into the density of an exterior
world, dispersing itself in a milieu which exceeds it and which it has not made."[33]
Williams's sustained approbation of Dora Marsden's egoism in general, as well
as the text of "Vortex" in particular, makes it clear that in this formative period
he had not abandoned his poetic investment in the ultimacy of the ego.

In this light I would urge several adjustments to previous Williams criticism. First, although "The Wanderer" obviously reflects its author's early poetic
quests, as a mythopoetic text with a fictive persona it cannot be utterly
identified with Williams or his phenomenological experiences. Both Rapp and
Hillis Miller overdraw the autobiographical element, as if Bill Williams had
spent more time haunting the mystic shores of the Passaic than the provocative
pages of literary journals. The case is different with "Vortex," which credo can
be properly taken as Williams's own but with the caveat that he is also putting
distance between himself and the vorticist model he is emulating. Rapp's
romantic idealist reading of "The Wanderer" centers solely on "I knew all—it
became me," while Miller's postmodernist reading pivots on "I saw myself . . .
Being borne off." By the close juxtaposition of these lines, the poem actually

establishes two centers or foci. The climax of the poem circles elliptically in a perpetual movement of self-loss and self-return.

With opposing intentions and evaluations, both Dijkstra and Rapp would reestablish the doctrinal foundation of Williams's career on the blatant idealisms of "Vortex." But "The Wanderer" remains the proper ur-text of Williams's career because it resists a centered perspective by self-doubling, by the multiplication of agencies already implicit in the poet's confrontation with the "marvelous old queen." One then traces those origins around the two centers already incorporated in "The Wanderer," in romantic idiom the poles of the negative and positive sublime, the dialectical simultaneity of a relinquishing and enlarging of the poetic self. "Vortex" then comes forward as an important reminder of Williams's positive or egoistic pole (as in Keats's reading of Wordsworth, the "egotistical sublime"). The modernist egoistic mode is already inscribed in the typical forms of vorticist bombast seconded by Williams's "Vortex" in the first place. As the discourse of the *New Freewoman* demonstrates, with Williams, as with others, the native milieu of early modernist egoism is exactly the crypto-political, doctrinal/defensive mode of the aesthetic manifesto. The most successful medium for Williams's poetic dialectics, especially in an imagistic environment, is precisely the prose/poetry collage—the anarchic compounding of lyric and discursive fragments. *Spring and All* and eventually *Paterson* exploit and synthesize that generic clash, to allow for a full counterpoint of self-assertion and self-abandon.

So we grasp once again the primary importance of a complex phenomenon both Rapp and Hillis Miller leave aside, the early modernist individualism under discussion in this study. Although rightly reconsidering Williams's investment in romantic idealism, Rapp joins Hillis Miller in scanting the virtual discursive and cultural contexts of Williams's early compositions, the Pound/Marsden vortex and the scientized egoism it explicitly purveyed. Whereas Hillis Miller fast-forwards to a later Heideggerian phenomenological model concurrent with, say, the composition of *Paterson*, Rapp recedes to a Hegelian/Emersonian model. What gets lost in these displacements is the specific historical logic of the intellectual movements by which modernist egoism in fact culminates to some degree the traditions of romantic idealism and prepares for the postmodern emphases on linguistic structurality. Dora Marsden's development offers a crucial early model of this modernist transition: following individualist anarchism through to a systematic nominalism, the *Egoist* is led specifically to a *Science of Signs*, that very "Lingual Psychology" to which Williams recorded his responses in two letters to the editor of the *Egoist*, "The Great Sex Spiral." His egoistic or Marsdenian attentions to the poetic sign will

inflect his resolution of the romantic self/world paradox "wherein the phe-
nomenal world is both affirmed and negated" (Rapp, *Williams and Idealism*, 20),
beginning with the parodic apocalypse at the start of *Spring and All* and continuing on to the series of ironic annihilations saturating *Paterson*'s book 3. The
early-modernist interplay between self and sign, manifesto and poem, retains a
fluid ambivalence that eddies between late-romantic egoism and late-modernist
impersonality.

"The Great Sex Spiral"

Eventually Williams was moved to "bat air" with Dora Marsden one on one.[34]
His emphasis on gender difference throughout both installments of "The Great
Sex Spiral" was his own: Dora Marsden's "Lingual Psychology" made no mention of it.[35] Coming after several years of preliminary discussion, this new series
of leaders marked the inception of Marsden's mature philosophy. Beginning in
the *Egoist* of July 1916, and continuing through the ultimate number of
December 1919, as the *Science of Signs*, this discourse initiated a unified program
of linguistic and semantic analyses: "the function of philosophy [is] the censorship of the passports and *bona fides* of all symbols, no matter what their medium
of expression. Philosophy—it is held—is the watchdog, censor, guardian, of the
universal symbolizing activity. . . . The first step—and for that matter the only
one—is that it shall bring its search of the vague and undefined to an end, and
realize the difference between searching for the *unknown* (the undefined) and
searching for the *unfound* (but defined)" ("Lingual Psychology," 97–98). As
Marsden made clear in following installments, her nominalist empiricism was an
adaptation of Berkeleyan idealism: for something to exist it must be present to
and perceived by an ego. Properly defined terms evoke precisely defined
images. The philosopher's task is to purge language of the imposture of apriorism and abstraction: "Such agnosticism has been inevitable ever since philosophy agreed to harbour the conception that it was possible to conceive of a
'Reality' which should be something distinguishable from sense-experience"
(99). Marsden characterizes apriorism as theology for philosophers, a kind of
secularized divine: it maintains a void upon which aesthetic fictions may be
projected, and it allows the "truth" to be made to order.

Attacking aestheticism as a species of apriorism, Marsden included artists
on her critical hit list, identifying philosophers who synthesize a priori claims
rather than discover phenomenological definitions with artists and preachers
who merely purvey aesthetic effects: "The apriorists have indeed grown to conceive of philosophy as of a religion or an art, and to recognize as their own per-

sonal ideal the artist's and preacher's role" (100). These remarks on the artist proceed in a line from Marsden's various digs three years earlier at aesthetical idea-mongers in general and Ezra Pound's recourses to the ineffable in particular. Her critique of aestheticist literature was of a piece with her critical advocacy for a strong version of imagism, but at the moment Williams either downplayed that subtlety in order to argue or was too identified with the artist per se to distinguish between the apriorist and the egoist varieties that Marsden was implicitly proposing.

Williams was more interested in the distinction between "male" and "female" sense experience. According to Williams, to Marsden's credit, "for the first time, here is philosophy from the female standpoint: militant female psychology"; however, that philosophy must remain as one-sidedly female as traditional philosophy has been one-sidedly male: "based on divergent sexual experiences, psychology, the general term, is capable of two very different interpretations: male psychology and female psychology, its basic subdivisions" ("Great Sex Spiral," 46). Williams would divide the philosophic field most profoundly not by epistemological method but by gender difference. His title "The Great Sex Spiral" would seem to refer to this enforcement of separate gender endowments, the spiral being created by an oscillation or dialectical movement between them. Noting Williams's placing of Otto Weininger next to Marsden in the second installment of this text, Palattella has remarked, "this pairing is symptomatic of Williams's attitudes towards sexuality, for Weininger and Marsden could not be more unlikely bedfellows" ("Midst of Hell," 21). However, we know that Marsden had discussed Weininger in the pages of the *Freewoman* at length and even championed his notions of individualism once she had stripped from them his misogynist theses concerning polarized sexual essences. Marsden's critique of Weininger's sexism had accompanied her own lapse from an essentialist feminism: liberal or reactionary, masculinist or feminist, the oppressive abstractions of "typicality" were to be purged from a properly individualist discourse.

Marsden's egoism, then, as a relatively reasonable, properly anarchistic position, can help us to measure and evaluate the wider influence of Weininger's sexism on early modernism. While Williams was hanging back with the gender schematics of Otto Weininger, Marsden was groping toward modern linguistics as distinct from, for instance, statistical methods or symbolic logic.[36] She defended verbal discourse over mathematical coding: if it is to circulate and become broadly usable, the information carried by mathematical functions must be intercepted and interpreted by verbal language. Philosophical language remains the metalanguage of the sciences: thus, the importance of eliminating metaphysics from philosophic language and training it toward sense experience. To her credit, Marsden grasped the outlines of the linguistic constitution of the psychological subject and anticipated some major developments in modern intellectual culture. The basic shortcoming of her system is to discount the communality and thus the relativism of linguistic functions in favor of an absolute egoistic ultimacy, as if any public language could exist whole and entire within any particular ego: "So too while the knowledge conveyed in the symbols of science is limited and relative, that which language conveys can be rendered comprehensive and ultimate" ("Lingual Psychology," 100).

What implicitly draws Marsden back toward the scientistic orbit of Weininger and the early Williams is the residual organicism to which she resorted to defend her conception of "analysis," her term for philosophy's proper function of concretion and demystification. It is not true, Marsden declared, that conceptual analysis is morbid or destructive.

> A faithful observation of the analytic activity makes it plain that only in its surface-stages is its effect a separative one and that what is mistaken for a separative activity is really concentrative, a limitation of the field with a view to an intensifying of the available attention. It represents just that application of the vital forces to images which, failing it, appear settled, static and dead, but under it begin to show those continuous changes of appearance we call development. It is the application of the rich, manuring energy of life and mind in concentrated form. For while its agency is the living energy of mind which impregnates with change and growth everything it touches, its manner of activity (which is its distinction) is mind in concentration. (101–2)

Along with its premonitions of linguistic structuralism, Marsden's "Lingual Psychology" developed a further amalgam of the evolutionary vitalism as yet prevailing in early modernist culture. She attacked apriorist "syntheticism" ("'made' Truth"), as well as Bergsonian intuitionism, insofar as both were woozy "aesthetical" avatars of the vague and undefined. Because the flux of experience itself seems to emerge out of the "unknown and unknowable," Marsden held on to a vitalistic rhetoric of the individual's unique exfoliation of evolutionary change and growth, even in the midst of her desire for structures of definition: "Accordingly, far from *contrasting* [the] action [of intellectual analysis] with the vital attitude toward phenomena, it would be truer to its character to describe it as the supreme fertilizing, vitalizing agency, creating-cause of that particular form of change from the simple to the complex which constitutes growth: just the becoming: the flux: of the anti-analytics" (102).

In Marsden's phenomenology, by "limiting the field" upon which the mind concentrates its living energies, conceptual analysis fructifies the images presented to egoistic experience. With differing but comparable emphases, Marsden and Williams share equivalent mixtures of evolutionist ideology, vitalist organicism, and imagist semantics. Marsden's philosophy sought to apply a more rigorous version of the Bergsonian *élan vital* to questions of semantic analysis, while Williams would adapt the vitalist posture to his gendered notions of artistic procedure. Most importantly, in "Lingual Psychology" Marsden virtually described the egoism embedded in Williams's localist rationales: the "limitation of the field" to the purview of an unlimited ego, which concentrates upon and develops its given images, is the very process that Williams would come to code into his doctrinal commentaries as "the Imagination." The prose of *Spring and All* indicates decisively that he absorbed intact "Dora Marsden's philosophic algebra," that is, the conceptual forms of her vitalist phenomenology.

A letter to Williams from Harriet Shaw Weaver dated February 17, 1917, informed him of her intention to append a brief editorial comment to his first critique of Marsden: "Late though the February *Egoist* is (it will not go out until next week), your letter arrived too late for inclusion in it, but I will put it in the March number. I am appending to it a little note to the effect that your criticism will be more helpful when you make clearer what the distinction is which you draw between male and female psychology: is it anything beyond the fact that the one is written by a man, the other by a woman? Do you care to answer this point for the April number?"[37] Transatlantic mail during the war was unpredictable: in any event, whenever it was written, Williams's reply to this reasonable request for clarification was not published until the August 1917 number. When it appeared it set forth a remarkable statement of Williams's "philosophical credentials." One of Marsden's primary effects on Pound and Williams was to prompt their publication of detailed discursive formulations, to generate their overt disclosure of private philosophical premises. In Williams's case it also led to an explicit if problematic discussion of the gender psychology of Weininger's *Sex and Character*.

As discussed in chapter 2, in the *Freewoman* Dora Marsden's own flirtation with Weininger's ideas had been an act of extreme, probably foolhardy, intellectual provocation. Her excerpting of Weininger's text and heavily qualified advocacy of some portions of his message sent shock waves through many readers. Rejecting the obvious sexism of his types and plasms, she still retained some investment in his discourses of individuality, immortality, and the ontological supremacy of the unique ego of the genius, investments that as Williams shows are readily tilted back into a masculinist apologetics. In any event, Marsden moved on to the more radical, less overtly gendered egoism of Max Stirner, and direct discussion of Weininger lapsed entirely in the *New Freewoman* and almost entirely in the *Egoist*. Not so entirely, however, that Williams did not make a note of it. At the end of his second installment of "The Great Sex Spiral," he comments that Weininger's "most palpable error (as Miss Marsden has herself pointed out) is that in his eagerness to make out a case for man he deliberately perverts and transposes facts" (111). To what passage of Marsden's writings is Williams referring?

After the demise of the *Freewoman*, which paper I presume Williams never saw, to my knowledge Marsden mentioned Weininger explicitly only once, in an early number of the *Egoist*, which number I presume Williams had studied thoroughly. In the midst of a standard nominalist critique of Judeo-Christian moralism, Marsden chided Weininger in a bracketed aside.

> When therefore a correspondent asks in a bewildered way whether or no we believe in "Honesty" and then goes on to ask whether we run up accounts with tradesmen and shirk payment, we get a perfect example of what Weininger would have called the "henid" mind: the confused mind that works on a basis of loose association. [Weininger's description of the "henid" mind is extremely able and well worth attention. It is diverting to note that he used the term to characterise the intelligence of women and yet at the same time one of the principal points which he endeavoured to make against them was that they were incapable of constructing a generalisation!][38]

The likelihood that Williams was alluding to this minute and passing bit of discussion is strengthened by the fact that it addressed the very same topic—the notion of henids—on Williams's mind in the August 1917 letter, for here he moved immediately from the rhetorical gambit of seconding Marsden to his own earnest reversal of the Austrian sexologist: "Man is the vague generalizer, woman the concrete thinker, and not the reverse as he imagined. Man is the indulger in *henids*, and woman the enemy of *henids*" ("Great Sex Spiral," 111). But Williams's repudiation of Weininger was not nearly as trenchant as Marsden's: whereas she succinctly skewered Weininger's logical blunders, Williams merely inverted Weininger's formulation of henids without relinquishing the sexism embedded in characterological generalizations. In this case, Williams was indeed "the vague generalizer." Dijkstra's comments on this passage have been ignored, I presume, largely because they are incontrovertible: "the poet had set up a false disagreement with Weininger, possibly in an attempt to lend credence to his independence as a thinker. In fact, the central argument of both of his pieces on 'The Great Sex Spiral' . . . follows Weininger very closely" ("Introduction," 45).

The point of my trek through these matters has not been to stigmatize Williams one way or another but simply to establish the actual lines of discursive commitment extant in his text. What constructive comments can we now venture? For one, the correlation of Marsden the postfeminist egoist and Weininger the Kantian sexist by way of Williams the aspiring avant-gardist vividly demonstrates the cultural complicity of early modernism with the operative forms of reactionary as well as progressive ideologies. For instance, it will be recalled that Weininger inserted his sexist characterology into broad cultural discussion on the fine edge of a pseudoscientific apology for homosexuality. Thus, for instance, the socialist idealist and gay pioneer Edward Carpenter was willing to champion Weininger's sexual science to the point of taking his epigraph for *The Intermediate Sex* from part 1 of *Sex and Character*. From Marsden's discreet but discernible interest during the period of the *Freewoman* in the concept of the androgynous "man-woman," presumably modeled after Carpenter's intermediate sexual type, it seems that her own earlier attraction to parts of Weininger's message can also be attributed to his plausible rationales for innate bisexual attitudes: "Every human being varies or oscillates between the maleness and the femaleness of his constitution. . . . Like the variations in the magnetism of the earth, these sexual oscillations are either regular or irregular. . . . The homo-sexuality in a woman is the outcome of her masculinity and presupposes a higher degree of development" (Weininger, *Sex and Character*, 54, 66). It seems equally likely that Williams's own investments in Weininger sprang most profoundly from the poet's ambivalence not over feminism but over his own sexuality. The problem is that Weininger also offered Williams strong but spurious rationales for masculinist heterosexism. Weininger's sexual progressiveness with regard to homosexuality was a certain cover for the sexist reaction against female emancipation.

The modernist egoisms of Weininger, Marsden, and Williams were variously invested in the popular ideological discourse of evolutionary vitalism. We have seen how early modernity was saturated in evolutionist and energeticist ideologies cutting across the political spectrum: communist and anarchist radicals such as Marx and Kropotkin as well as conservative apologists for laissez-faire capitalism such as Herbert Spencer typically founded their social sciences on evolutionistic appeals to natural "forces." Weininger's system in particular transmitted a German romantic variant emphasizing the "polarity" of the sexes. By the turn of the twentieth century, scientistic ideas of gender polarity had been filtered through genuine scientific developments such as Darwinian evolution and Maxwell's theory of electromagnetic fields. The cultural proximity of these developments accounts to some extent for the cachet possessed by Weininger's glib formulations, cited above, about the oscillation and variation of the "magnetism" of the sexes, and by Marsden's presentation of egoistic analysis as a "vitalizing agency, creating-cause of that particular form of change from the simple to the complex which constitutes growth" ("Lingual Psychology," 102).

Williams strongly indicated the vitalistic premises of his own reasoning in his second critique of Marsden's "Lingual Psychology": "Life, in the realm of thought as in all other realms of activity, is the first essential, and to maintain life two things are necessary . . . a male and a female element: an engendering force and a definite point of action. . . . As long as there is a vigorous life in the realm of thought it is essential that both poles be firmly established" ("Great Sex Spiral," 110–11). Interestingly, Williams went on to call for something that Marsden had abandoned several years earlier to the dismay of her first audiences, a philosophy dedicated solely to the feminist perspective, a "vigorous female side." Williams's critique of the androgynous Marsden of the *Egoist* follows the lines of Floyd Dell's masculinist preference for a fighting feminism.

> Instead of recognizing the first element in her argument to be the re-establishment of life in a sterile "philosophy," sterile because entirely male, by bending all her energies to the setting up of a vigorous female side—thus establishing a male and female psychology in vigorous opposition—she has tried to "solve" philosophy: that is, she has tried to deny reality to male psychology because it is not female psychology; she has tried to blend the two sexual concepts in her search for reality. Could she succeed, only one thing would result: death. (111)

It was at this point that Williams trotted out Weininger explicitly in order to comment that the sexologist had also made a similarly mistaken attempt to "obliterate" sexual difference: "having established the fundamental divergence between the sexes, and having discovered a certain trend toward a physical convergence, a blurring of the two, he seeks to discover a third gender as the type to be approached. This proved the despair of his genius" (111). As Dijkstra has previously argued in his "Introduction," this misreading of Weininger conceals Williams's essential convergence with his doctrines. In fact, "The Great Sex Spiral" may be read as a cryptogram of Williams's attempt to resolve his own conflicted sexuality as expressed six years earlier to Viola Baxter and three years earlier in "Transitional." The third-sex concept is properly attributed to Carpenter's writings, to which both Marsden and Williams had presumably paid some close attention. The fact is that Weininger's brief discussions of a "third gender" are primarily a prologue to his lengthy disquisition on the pure sexual types. In Weininger's cosmic polarism, moreover, the negativity of the female is to be ultimately absorbed into the transcendental positivity of male spirit, even at the price of relinquishing sexual generation altogether. That was too much for Williams, whose erotic logic was more Lawrencean: the greater the gender distinction, the stronger the resulting polarity, and thus the more "vital" the sexual circuit between male and female.

The gist of Williams's sexual vitalism is not only to justify a liberated heterosexualism but also to proclaim the morbidity of bisexuality, thereby to counter feelings of androgynous ambivalence and to underwrite his own masculinist investments. Like Lawrence in the *Study of Thomas Hardy*, Williams overlaid a sexist dualism upon a monistic vitalism in his pursuit of positive, or "manly," creativity and in justification of his attitudes toward the instrumentality of the female as providing a "definite point of action" for his own "engendering force." In contrast to Marsden's early example of an androgynous solution that would be replayed in female modernists for the next several decades, Williams's philosophical professions in these passages reconnect with the residual masculinism of aesthetic egoism.

Weininger's popularity in the first two decades of the century has been well documented, if not equally well remembered among recent critical apologists. An accurate accounting of the influence Weininger exerted on early modernism is important, for one thing, in order to distinguish more precisely Dora Marsden's proper position within this milieu. I have argued that Marsden's thought remained crucially distinct from bourgeois or corporatist forms of sexist and racist stereotypification. And I would urge that in balance, and despite Williams's occasional defensive attacks upon it, Marsden's thought was both crucial and salutary for his literary development. If Dijkstra is correct to say that Williams never quite shook off an essentialist masculinism, that cannot be laid at Marsden's door. Moreover, Williams was never so entirely comfortable with his professed sexuality that he left off provoking productive intrigues with female opponents on the model of his early and vigorous reception of Dora Marsden's discourses. In the immediate issue, Williams's early modernist egoism produced discernible poetic payoffs: his total accomplishment in *Spring and All* results to a dramatic degree from its conceptual cultivation within the discourse of the *Egoist*.

Dora Marsden's Philosophic Algebra

Traces of Dora Marsden's linguistic turn occur as early as 1912, for instance, in "Freewomen and Evolution": "The failure of language to advance parallel with the new differentiations of thought presents a problem of increasing dimensions and difficulty. . . . We suggest the gradual compiling of a 'Select Glossary'" (503). In the *New Freewoman*, Marsden's nominalist critiques of abstract ideals are further steps toward the "Lingual Psychology" of the *Egoist*. But she gives most of her attention in 1913 to aesthetic issues such as those prompted by the text of her current subeditor, Ezra Pound. Throughout much of 1914, her leaders and commentaries reflect on the current labor agitation and the Irish home-rule uprising.[39] She seizes on these events to define her egoism as an "archism" devoted to the primacy of the individual power-motive, in distinction to the ineffectual humanitarianism of the political anarchists, whom she castigates as "embargoists" placing conscientious constraints on their own actions in the futile hope that the community as a whole will follow suit. Once the Great War breaks out, Marsden retreats somewhat from the political fray: international military mobilizations do not create an atmosphere conducive to individualistic assertions.

With her leader for January 1, 1915, Marsden musters and regroups anew her discursive forces: "The beginning of the New Year will serve as a sufficient apology for stating afresh the ambitions of this journal and detailing what one considers to be its unique and supremely important task: one for the execution of which we can see no evidence of minds other than our own being forthcoming."[40] In the last of the doctrinal valedictions that began with her departure from the WSPU, she defies the patronizing remnants of her femino-anarchist well-wishers and declares war on the "Verbal Age," initiating her philosophical campaign waged in the *Egoist* for the next five years.

> Let this, then, be the answer to those friends who have been good enough to say that *The Egoist*'s activities are all derailed and are willing to pray that the journal might die, if by dying the "remarkable abilities" of the writer might have a chance of "coming into their own." "Their own": the only task which matches their powers in a Verbal Age like this is—to break the hypnotic spell, to blast the stupefactions of—The Word.

> Our war is with words and in their every aspect: grammar, accidence, syntax: body, blood, and bone. . . . The trying of issues with the forms of language is the next great task of human explorative, power-evidencing, enfranchising genius because words in one half of their activities have grown great and climbed high to secure all the heavenly seats. They are to be torn down. . . . To blast the Word, to reduce it to its function of instrument is the enfranchisement of the human kind: the imminent new assertion of its next reach of power. ("I Am," 1–2)

Marsden's egoistic blinders aside, in hindsight we can see how thoroughly her particular linguistic project resonates with the salient activities of literary modernism: the great philological enterprises coming down from the nineteenth century, Pierce's semiotics and Saussure's semiology, Pound's ideogrammatic sinology, Stein's and Joyce's literary deformations, Dada manifestoes, Lawrence's setting out of a "black tom-cat" to pounce on "the white dove of the Word," and William Carlos Williams's repeated calls for linguistic demolition: "It can't be helped that it's been forgotten what words are made for. It can't be helped that the whole house has to come down."[41]

Marsden's evolution from literal to linguistic insurrection also parallels the modernist transit from the autonomous self to the autonomous text. Ironically, the linguistic turn enables Marsden to reconstitute, albeit in the displaced form of a shareable semiotic system, her abandoned relationship to the political community. For instance, the second installment of "Lingual Psychology" discusses the distinction between numerical and verbal signs, and the tonality of Marsden's remarks on the arbitrary nature of mathematical signifiers is strikingly moderated from the strident egoism of previous years: "Plainly it is not anything in the 'nature of things' which makes $2 + 2 = 4$. It is merely the advisability of keeping compacts and respecting one's own definitions once having agreed upon them."[42] Modulating her discourse to the collaborative task at hand, Marsden sets aside her Stirnerian trumpet and Nietzschean hammer for the more harmonious tones of a philosophical dulcimer, even praising her intellectual forebears in the tradition within which her present discourse seeks entry: "Aristotle's *Logic* is the most impressive monument in the world. In it one great mind faces a subject practically untouched, immensely vast, and in one unflagging and unbroken effort apprehends how chaos may be dominated and dominates it. . . . The syllogism is the relentless vindicator of the underlying linguistic compact" ("Science of Signs," 116). Marsden's particular claim is that the impasse of contemporary philosophy stems not from any imperfection in the logic of propositions but from unresolved problems in the units of language: "In the scrutiny and ultimate redefinition of the primary elements of speech— the verb, the auxiliaries above all, the pronoun, the noun, the adverb and the remaining elemental forms—lie the new hopes and prospects of philosophy" (117).

The next installment makes good on her stated intention to pursue an elemental linguistic analysis of auxiliary verbs and pronouns, and also holds to my mind the first concrete key to an adequate gloss of Williams's cryptic phrase, "Dora Marsden's philosophic algebra." This article begins with a definition of definition that expresses not just the fundamental rationale of Marsden's philosophical project but also her linguistic renewal of social circulation, after a long

period of egoistic absolutism: "We concluded in the last chapter that the function of philosophy was definition. Now definition consists in finding equiva-
lents for a verbal form, or a set of verbal forms, in terms of some other. In effect,
therefore, definition amounts to a mustering of synonyms. It is an exchange and
commerce of words with words."[43] Marsden proceeds to develop an ontological algebra by threshing out the significance of "the great landmark of modern
philosophy . . . Berkeley's definition of the verb '*to be*'" ("'I' and 'Ego,'" 129).
Starting from the Berkeleyan formula *esse* = *percipi* (to be = to be perceived),
Marsden works through a detailed series of stipulations concerning its sense and
comes out with this.

> (3) Let then the "I" of ordinary speech express the normal con-
>   notation of a "WORLD-EXCLUSIVE I" and the term "EGO" the
>   philosophic and "WORLD-INCLUSIVE I."
> (4) Having differentiated between them broadly, their differences
>   in scope can be cited in more detail. Thus the "EGO," addi-
>   tionally to what is connoted by the WORLD-EXCLUSIVE "I,"
>   includes also the rest of the universe, spiritual and material.
>   Therefore from the "EGO" nothing can be discriminated as
>   distinct or separate. It is the Universe in which "ALL" is com-
>   prehended and unified. . . .
> (5) Plainly this "EGO" is a conception not recognized by com-
>   mon language. Its nearest conception in everyday language is
>   "UNIVERSE" . . . . (130)

These are the concerted opening moves of the *Science of Signs*. William
Carlos Williams would contain it within the label "militant female psychology,"
but nevertheless he applied himself to it with more documented rigor of attention than any of his modernist peers. We will not follow in precise detail the
unfolding of this psycholinguistic phenomenology but rather will stand back
from it to make a few basic points. Marsden's fundamental move is to analyze
the cognitive and the imaginary into a combination of the semiotic and the
affective: "Berkeley's famous formula *esse* = *percipi* was an answer to the first
great question which emerges if we adopt the formula that philosophy is the science of the property of signs. That question resolves itself into a demand for the
symbol expressive of the attribute of experience. . . . The formula *esse* = *percipi*
asserts that the required attribute is perception: feeling."[44] Clearly Marsden
develops what we have come to recognize as a "metaphysics of presence,"
founded on an ego-principle granted an ultimacy traditionally reserved to the
divine. However, it makes all the difference that, rather than merely declaiming

that ego through imperative assertion, she has now inscribed it within a system of signs. In other words, the "EGO" in Marsden's mature philosophy is an ego in quotation marks, a relativized ego residing on one side of an equal sign and disposed to existential commerce. Even if the other half of the equation is "the universe," it is a universe that is equally in quotation marks, that is, it is a trope for the ultimate limits of an empirical system.

In *Critic as Scientist*, Ian Bell credits the *Egoist* with a singular intellectual capaciousness. His accurate recognition makes it especially ironic that scholarly attention to the paper has so long been monopolized by the miniaturists of imagism: "To say that *The Egoist*, of all the literary magazines of the period, was most willing to incorporate the discourse of science, is really to say that the articles constituting the editorial column by Dora Marsden from July 1916 to December 1919 were willing to incorporate that discourse. They employed an intensive combination of philosophy, psychology, and the physical sciences to define a material base for the major terms usually associated with abstract speculation: imagination, memory, will and, indeed, knowledge itself" (261). In the further development of the *Science of Signs*, on occasion Marsden explicitly considers the significance of an egoistic epistemology for the methods of science, thereby collaborating in the relativization of cosmology and nuclear physics that we now associate with the names of Einstein and Heisenberg.

As we have noted, a defining feature of early modernism is a discursive adaptation of the vocabularies of physical energies to vitalist paradigms. In the closing articles of the *Science of Signs,* Marsden further refines her algebraic presentation by explicitly folding an electro-polarity model into her description of "the vital universe or ego."[45] She begins by rehearsing once more the Berkeleyan substitutions detailed above.

> The total thus presented by my body, and my external world, I call my *universe* or *ego*. . . .
> Setting out these facts as an equation we get this:—
> My universe = My body *plus* My external world.
> And transposing the items we get:—
> My universe *minus* my body = My external world. ("Philosophy—Truth V," 34)

But now Marsden dynamizes these discrete arithmetic formulas by negating the notion of a self-subsistent world in the absence of a perceiving body or ego. The following lengthy passage presents her supreme algebraic formulation of philosophical egoism, produced by incorporating an electro-vital polarity model inherited from the physico-chemical and dialectical models of the nineteenth century. At this extreme of (re)visionary discourse, subsidiary considerations of modernism, individualism, or gender are submerged in the evocation of a unitary cosmic life force.

> Egoism makes this important alteration upon transporting the terms:—
>
> My universe *minus* My body = o.
>
> or
>
> The scientist's universe *minus* His body = o.
>
> That is, egoism denies the absolute and independent existence of the external world. The kind of question which at once confronts it is obvious. In the first place, egoism needs to say why, if a universe is the sum of two quantities, the abstraction of one should exhaust the whole. And in the second, if such abstraction *does* so exhaust it, what is the nature of the *plus* sign which is supposed to amalgamate the two? Certainly, it cannot be the innocent-seeming arithmetical sign which one at first sight assumes it to be.
>
> 5. Now in accordance with the theory of the vital system we have already laid down, we hold we are on the track towards an explanation of the entire matter when we fix attention upon the nature of this *plus* sign. For though out of the totality of our experience we can discriminate the two items of *organism* and its *surrounding world*, the nature of the relation between the two is not that of simple addition. Rather the nature of the connection between them is like that existing between the two poles of any polarised force with which we are familiar. In such a force the feature is presented of two poles constituting respectively the terminal points of a single and unbroken line of force, the nature of the scheme being such that the absence of either terminus would negate the entire scheme. In relation to such a scheme, describing the poles as north and south respectively, there would be no hesitation in accepting the following description of the relationship of the two opposite poles:—
>
> (N *plus* S) minus S = o.
>
> or
>
> (N *plus* S) minus N = o.
>
> Now this condition of affairs is an exact parallel to that which we get in the case of the vital universe or ego. . . .
>
> In short, we hold that there is no solution of the baffling facts of life and consciousness until we accept this fact: that life throughout its entire range means the polarisation: the dualisation: of a something we call the ego

which is even more basic than life: a something unitary in character which, under its own adequate conditions, begets the dual differentiation known as life. Life represents precisely the introduction of that differentiation and is obtained by the hurling apart of those aspects of the *ego, i.e.,* organism and a spatially-disposed substance, to the end that these, by acting and reacting over against each other, may make more fully manifest the nature of the unitary force inherent in and informing the whole. Death, on the other hand, can only mean the breakdown of the polarising conditions playing upon the basic force, so that the dual elements again become unitary as at the first. ("Philosophy—Truth V," 34)

On the basis of this algebra of cosmic polarity by which life hurls itself into differentiated being out of the primal spring of the ego, Marsden traces the evolution of the forms of space—the extension of matter—and time—the series of causal sequences. She goes on to criticize the epistemological constriction of a science limited to "external nature," in that the scientist's purview falls short of the plenum of existence. The external world to which science devotes its attention is the partial opposite of the universal egoistic circuit and is abstracted to nothing without being polarized by an ego's perception. Thus, the scientist "essays to use time as an argument, but because of his neglect of the science of knowing he has robbed himself of the competence to understand time. On the other hand, the philosophy which has forged a coherent theory of the activity of knowing is rewarded with a coherent theory of time. And this theory and egoism yield one another a mutual support" (38). As the caprice of Harriet Shaw Weaver's editorial construction would have it, immediately following the last sentence cited—the concluding remark of Marsden's crucial article, the balance of page 38 is filled out without any break by a poem by Williams.

THE LATE SINGER
Here it is spring again
and I still a young man.
I am late at my singing. . . .[46]

Spring and All

One of the achievements of Williams's *Spring and All* is its subtle distillation of Dora Marsden's visionary egoism into the concrete substance of literary modernism. We have just seen how Williams may have come to associate Dora Marsden's philosophic algebra with his own vernal lyricizing. In addition, there

is a certain "lateness" both to Marsden's electro-vitalism of 1919 and to
Williams's deployments of vitalist figures in *Spring and All,* in that by 1923 the
melancholy tropes of thermodynamic models had largely supplanted vitalism as
the dominant mode of modernist scientism. The obvious example in this regard
is Eliot's *The Waste Land* with its primary assertion, "April is the cruellest
month."[47] So there is an autumnal resonance to the full text of *Spring and All*
that is not corruption or disillusionment but rather a late summation of or ironic
elegy for an entire aesthetic phase, the spent springtime of early modernism.

The famous poem 1 of the sequence ("By the road to the contagious hos-
pital") is placed just prior to the pivotal phrase that occurs in the next paragraph
of prose—"Dora Marsden's philosophic algebra." Marsden's method of
definition as well as the momentaneous productive flux of her metaphysical life
force ("It") are covertly rendered with wonderful delicacy.

> One by one objects are defined—
> It quickens: clarity, outline of leaf
>
> But now the stark dignity of
> entrance—

(Spring and All, 183)

Placing poem 1 in its implicit Marsdenian frame, we may say that "It quickens"
just because the poet is there "By the road." On the one hand, because the poet
is there, as it were "to witness / and adjust" (219), he can situate himself as the
perceiving ego that completes the creative circuit by naming "it." On the other
hand, the tragedy of Elsie's world in poem 18 ("The pure products of America") is exactly the desolation produced by the lack of an effectual ego. "Somehow / it seems to destroy us," leaving Elsie with "broken / brain," unable to
assume or express her own subjectivity and so "succumbing without / emotion
/ save numbed terror // under some hedge of choke-cherry" (217–19). Here,
"it" defies the poet's desire to use the power of his verbal adjustments literally
to raise up this sad spectacle and release its "degraded prisoners" through the
force of his art. However, the poem Williams produces by confessing that lack,
the insufficiency of his witness, by running a line of force between the positivity of his desire and the negativity of that American scene, is one of the great
lyrics of our century.

In a 1970 essay, even with all five books of *Paterson* extant and the breadth
of the Williams canon evident and complete, Hillis Miller was moved to state
that *Spring and All* is "perhaps the most important single work by Williams."[48]
A decade later Perloff seconded this revisionary critical opinion: "*Spring and All*

is, I think, Williams's most remarkable poetic sequence, a work so far ahead of its time that it was safely ignored until the sixties."[49] Sayre termed that treatment by Perloff "one of the two or three best essays on the book."[50] The arc of interest in Hillis Miller, Perloff, and Sayre is to factor the complexities of *Spring and All* into the milieu of the European avant-garde, off to which so many of Williams's artistic colleagues were running in the early twenties. So Miller cites echoes of Rimbaud's *Illuminations* ("Williams' *Spring and All*," 93). Perloff credits Miller and extends the observation by noting the appearance of the special Francis Picabia number of the *Little Review* for spring 1922: *Spring and All* "is Williams's most 'French' composition. It bears the imprint not only of Apollinaire's aesthetic but also of Dada improvisation, of Gertrude Stein's poetry and fiction, and of Rimbaud" ("Lines Converging," 110). Sayre ups the ante on this line of approach by detailing the range of significant cultural events—the *Salon des Independents*, the Armory Show, the first numbers of important little magazines, and so forth—that had occurred in spring: "for Williams, spring was in fact Dada's season" ("Avant-Garde," 16). For Sayre, then, the spring of *Spring and All* is a synchronizing gesture indicating the author's participation in the seasonal contemporaneity of the artistic moment. While this gambit produces a lively essay with an informative sketch of Williams's wider aesthetic world, I would venture to say that its historical literalism obscures the finer connotations the trope embedded in the title *Spring and All*.

I do not mean to discount the importance of the French connection for Williams or Anglo-American modernism generally. While we are on the topic, however, I would like to point out that "spring" is the first translation provided in my Pocket Book Larousse for the term *élan*, as in Henri Bergson's *élan vital*: "*élan m.* spring, dash, bound; impetus, impulse, outburst." In other words, *Spring and All* may be translated by way of Bergson's vitalism into the idiom of Dora Marsden's egoism. The deepest "spring" in *Spring and All* is the cosmogonic impulse itself, parodically performed at the beginning of the text. In Marsden's terms, this primal "spring" is the leap of the ego into the dual and polarized modalities of temporal life and spatial world. The "All" (which I do not find glossed by other commentaries) is fundamentally the universe thereby constituted and present to the ego from which it springs, "the Universe in which 'ALL' is comprehended and unified" (Marsden, "'I' and 'Ego,'" 130). As Williams was forthright enough to declare, albeit with the probable reflection that very few would be in any position to construe his meaning, this is exactly "Dora Marsden's philosophic algebra." Whereas the impress of Marsden's system is mostly implicit in the lyrics of *Spring and All*, however, it rises strongly to the surface in the prose passages. Here especially I will argue that the stylistic

and thematic influences of Rimbaud, Stein, Picabia, and company are secondary in relation to the philosophical priority of Dora Marsden's "militant
female psychology." Essentially, Williams rewrites Marsden's egoism under the
conveniently effaced coin of the romantic term *Imagination*.[51] Distilling the scientistic ideology of Dora Marsden's philosophy, *Spring and All* both parodies
and preserves the early modernist discourse of evolutionary vitalism.

To begin with, in the July 1919 continuation of the *Science of Signs*, Marsden prefaces her exposition of cosmological algebra by acknowledging that the
typical "scientific" attitude is one of personal insignificance when confronted
with the omnidimensional infinitude of the universe. "How can any balanced
thinker," Marsden declares rhetorically,

> bind himself up with the doctrine that his own organism is the indispens-
> able nucleus of his entire universe, including *substance*, *space* and *time*, when
> he sees himself as a most insignificant speck of substance swallowed up in
> an illimitable space and enduring through only the very briefest moment
> of an illimitable time. . . . It takes all the courage he has to prevent himself
> sinking into utter abasement under the conviction of his own almost com-
> plete spatial and temporal negligibility. . . . This then is the difficulty ego-
> ism must meet to make itself acceptable. ("Philosophy—Truth IV," 34)

The last three installments of the *Science of Signs* are set to this sublime task of
justifying the logical ultimacy of the individual ego in the face of a cosmos both
science and philosophy have declared to be alien and indifferent. In *Spring and
All*, Williams converts Marsden's egoistic solution into his own aesthetic idiom:
"art" must release "life" from its habitual humility by the universal dynamism of
the imagination. The following prose passages have often been cited in
Williams criticism. The fractured grammar around the dangling gendered
reflexive pronoun "himself" lends a curious emphasis to his propositions. But
both the existential problem and its aesthetic solution have been explicitly
adumbrated in Marsden's discourse.

> The inevitable flux of the seeing eye toward measuring itself by the
> world it inhabits can only result in himself crushing humiliation unless the
> individual raise to some approximate co-extension with the universe. This
> is possible by aid of the imagination. Only through the agency of this force
> can a man feel himself moved largely with sympathetic pulses at work—
> (*Spring and All*, 192)

The "seeing eye" is Williams's imagistic pun on Marsden's "I," responding directly to her Berkeleyan algebra equating existence with perception and measuring the ego by the dimensions of the universe. Resting implicitly and profoundly on Marsden's sustained labor of argument throughout the last volumes of the *Egoist*, Williams's prose passages consistently declaim aesthetic variations of her philosophical themes.

Those themes include life, force, imagination, separation, expansion, evolution, words, personality, and values. We can begin with the notion of force, in Marsden's idiom an inexorable quality of the vital ego. In Williams's idiom, "the imagination is an actual force comparable to electricity or steam" (207). In the penultimate article of the *Science of Signs*, Marsden reprises her electro-vitalist description of the ego as a fundamental cosmic force: "The ego is a closed-in universe comprehensive of experience or feeling of every kind. It is the comprehensive description of the entire structure of feeling. It is created out of a unit force existing in a condition of polarisation so that it shows a complex aspect of two opposed reciprocal poles joined together by a neutral line or field of force."[52] The notion of force funding the text of *Spring and All* signifies the interest paid out by Williams's residual investment in philosophical vitalism, an investment he still shares with Dora Marsden. For instance, when Williams remarks, "It is the imagination on which reality rides—It is the imagination— It is a cleavage through everything by a force that does not exist in the mass and therefore can never be discovered by its anatomization" (*Spring and All*, 225), he reiterates the vitalist conviction that the life force eludes the analytical grasp of the physical sciences. It is a point he had made with the utmost emphasis earlier in the text: "we are beginning to discover the truth that in great works of the imagination A CREATIVE FORCE IS SHOWN AT WORK MAKING OBJECTS WHICH ALONE COMPLETE SCIENCE AND ALLOW INTELLIGENCE TO SURVIVE" (199). In her final chapter, Marsden had stated that "there exists *a science of the sciences.*"[53]

We have seen that the scientific ideology of vitalism animates early modernism generally. It then falls into relative disuse or, as co-opted by fascist ideologues, utter disrepute in the decades after the Great War. Vitalism becomes a pejorative label of the first order, as for instance in Bonnie Kime Scott's assertion that D. H. Lawrence "brought his women to kneel in homage to the phallus as part of his anti-modern, vitalist philosophy."[54] And yet, in her introduction to Rebecca West, she will laud that author for her celebration of "the revivifying life force of Molly Bloom" (Scott, *Gender of Modernism*, 567). Can one have it both ways? Is it that male vitalism is repressive whereas female vitalism is "revivifying"? We are reminded that vitalism and gender polarity do not mix well. In *Spring and All*, beneficially for his text and in accordance with Marsden's discourse, Williams suspends the sexist or Weiningerian reading of the vital-polarity model he had advanced in "The Great Sex Spiral."

It is fascinating to notice how the idiom of vitalism persists in modern critical discussion as a kind of rhetorical truism completely detached from the memory of its prior philosophical heyday. Perloff comments about *Spring and All*, "Williams's images—wind, flower, farmer, white, purple—are perfectly transparent; all are nature images, reflecting the sexual energy of the universe, the life force" ("Lines Converging," 131). Similarly, Hillis Miller adjusts Williams's poetic project to the terminology of deconstruction by covertly tapping into the anarchistic vitalism of the text he is discussing: "Williams's universe, unlike the Platonic cosmos, has no center, no reservoir of eternal models. There is only the ubiquitous life force which gives rise to differences in objects appearing side by side or in sequence from an infinity of centers. . . . A poem in *Spring and All* is apposed to the natural objects it names. The same forces flow through it as flow through nature" ("Williams' *Spring and All*," 97, 101).

To continue with our investigation of the thematic congruity between the *Science of Signs* and *Spring and All*, we can take up the notion of *separation*, one of the more obscure terms at play in Williams's text. The negative problematic of separation as an antivital lack of existential immediacy, "divorce . . . from life" (178), is placed at the beginning: "There is a constant barrier between the reader and his consciousness of immediate contact with the world" (177). In his related attack on traditional symbolism, Williams inveighs against "complicated ritualistic forms designed to separate the work from 'reality'" (189). But, as *Spring and All* proceeds, the notion of aesthetic separation also assumes a positive valence, as in Williams's identification of "the modern trend" with abstraction, an attempt "to separate things of the imagination from life" (194), in order to establish and justify their antimimetic, self-referring autonomy and to exploit their inhering material energies. In this vein, then, art "is not a matter of 'representation'—much may be represented actually, but of separate existence" (204). The clues to this polar deployment of separation are the Marsdenian subtexts of the "power to create and apply a sign" ("Philosophy: *Science of Signs* XVIII," 70) and of the doctrine by which phenomena are understood as the manifestations of a "separative" force, by which all "things" emerge along neutral lines within a field of force created by the "condition of polarisation" between organism and world. We can read that egoistic subtext as transposed to the field of *Spring and All* in the following passage.

That is, the imagination is an actual force comparable to electricity or steam, it is not a plaything but a power that has been used from the first to raise the understanding of—it is, not necessary to resort to mysticism—In fact it is this which has kept back the knowledge I seek—

The value of the imagination to the writer consists in its ability to make words. Its unique power is to give created forms reality, actual existence

This separates (207)

In a late reprise of a topic touched on a decade earlier by Pound and Marsden in the *New Freewoman*—"the broad difference between prose and poetry" (Marsden, "Art of the Future," 183)—Williams coordinates the themes of positive separation and the energy of the imagination: "prose has to do with the fact of an emotion; poetry has to do with the dynamization of emotion into a separate form. This is the force of imagination" (*Spring and All*, 219). Marsden's "broad difference" had emerged in the context of her critique of Pound's compositional "mysticism," or, in her satirical characterization, his "coyness, and the vague waving of hands to give the expression of helplessness, in-a-sort, in the grip of some high force" ("Art of the Future," 181). Later in that leader Marsden offered her formula for the aesthetic differentiation between prose and poetry.

The difference is one of brevity, completeness and finish simply because in poetry all the evidence of laboratory work is removed; the creaking of the thinking-machine is not there: it has done its work. Poetry is the expression of the soul-motion: perfect knowledge free both of redundance and hesitancy: it is brief because it is reduced to the exact equivalent: it has reached the completeness of knowledge when its dimensions can be expressed in a formula. It *is* the formula. Anything omitted would make it error; anything added would be confusion and irrelevance. (183)

The immediate continuation of "The Art of the Future" is a nice early example of Marsden's self-deprecating intellectual humor, in that, with the awkward allegorical experiment of "Tales for the Attentive" out of the way, expository prose is in fact her chosen creative medium. However, this passage reprises "Tales" by once again calling out for the overcoming of "thought." And once again it is impossible to think that Williams would not have been profoundly caught up by these formulations in which Marsden adds her own brand of vigor to Pound's poetic modernisms, and in which she, too, like Pound, "rewrites Sidney's 'Defence of Poesy' in the year of grace 1913" (Pound, "The Serious Artist," 161) by taking issue with the Elizabethan courtier's urbane assertion that "the poet nothing affirmeth."

> Prose is the proper place for the half-knowledge, the "I think." It is essentially "essay" work, i.e., trial work. It is honest, it is indispensible, but it is preliminary. It is furzy with opinion and suggestion. It is "interesting," that is, it holds the attention as does any useful uncompleted process. It is ephemeral; it is the fore-runner. It makes straight the way for poetry, the formula which comprehends and supersedes it. That is why a genuine "poem" is beyond the reach of argument. It makes a statement that is to be taken or left. In making statements, the poet takes the very same risks as the scientist: he stands to be discredited. ("Art of the Future," 183)

The interrelation between prose and poetry becomes charged in the early modernist period to a significant degree because of the imagist purge of poetic forms as discursive vehicles.[55] This premium on generic separatism participated in the wider aesthetic project by which media of expression were abstracted from thematic and representational obligations and subjected to formal analysis and reconstruction.[56] The immediate effect of imagistic purifications was to separate literary production into clusters of spare lyrics set against but composed in the textual proximity of orotund aesthetic/cultural manifestoes. The "rhetoric" whose neck the symbolists and their immediate heirs would wring simply shifted its location and flourished anew in the vigorous propagandizing by which the avant-garde justified its new artistic regimens.[57] As a result of these developments, the availability of the little magazine as an organ for the discursive as well as the poetic productions of the early modernists was crucial. In this light the intersection of Ezra Pound's and Dora Marsden's polemical projects was a marriage presided over by the literary zeitgeist. As the imagist doctrines played themselves out, however, the two disunited genres—the purebred lyric and the mongrel manifesto—also struggled to reunite. This dynamic occurred with all the major poetic modernists, whose poetic works gradually coalesced into long, baggy sequences such as the *Cantos* and *Paterson*. But one of the earliest and perhaps the finest discrete example of these specific imagist tensions is immediately available in the composite texture of *Spring and All*.

William may well have felt the potential force of a text containing such emphatic generic shifting simply by reading his file of *Egoists*, especially when his own spare lyrics kept popping up amid the discursive manifestations of Dora Marsden's *Science of Signs,* or, in the final number of the *Egoist,* T. S. Eliot's second installment of "Tradition and the Individual Talent." In the very contextual nature of the little magazine, the lyric or lyric cluster finds itself already enmeshed with, engulfed, or abetted by the circumambient prose content. Dora Marsden's journals regularly produced such effects of radical juxtaposition through the casual but often resonant metonymies of its poetic and discursive content. In *Spring and All* Williams reproduces equivalent effects, by interpolating amid the lyrics "the creaking of the thinking-machine," and in doing so, again in Marsden's phrases, by making "straight the way for poetry, the formula which comprehends and supersedes it." The modernity of *Spring and All* "turns the inside out" like the architecture of a building with its interior structure exposed: the rivets gleam on the girders, the wires dangle from the ceiling, and all the creaking of Williams's poetry machine is there on display.[58]

Williams even names his architectural consultants—Charles Demuth, Dora Marsden, Juan Gris. But it has taken a long time for the finer lines of Marsden's contributions to be appreciated. My discussion here will not exhaust that task. As a starting point for future investigation, we can say that Marsden enabled Williams to see with greater clarity that he could dynamize his own verse by placing his ego or comprehensive imagination at the point of the equal sign between organism and universe. According to the last installment of Marsden's *Science of Signs:* "The organic powers of which the *body* is the expression form an indivisible system with the *outer world* and with *space.* . . . None of these things are independent entities. Each is some aspect of the other. . . . Every point—or pole—in the outer world is connected with its related positive pole in the organism by a line which runs through space" ("Philosophy: Science of Signs XVIII," 68). We catch a late echo of this schema in the preface to *Paterson:* "the city / the man, an identity—it can't be / otherwise—an / interpenetration, both ways" (Williams, *Paterson,* 3). But it also shows up embedded in the perceptional cosmology expounded at the end of the seventh lyric in *Spring and All,* "The rose is obsolete."

. . . .

From the petal's edge a line starts
that being of steel
infinitely fine, infinitely
rigid penetrates
the Milky Way
without contact. . . .

(196)

And on the way through the indivisible, interpenetrating system from the rose petal to the Milky Way that line passes directly through the artist's "seeing eye," the world-inclusive I that has raised itself in imagination "to some approximate co-extension with the universe." Thus this lyric is not simply about cubist painting or the exhaustion and reformulation of symbolic cultural codes like *rose = love*: it also dramatizes the demand of the prose that great art be a trigger for the "enlargement" of the personality. Displacing this theme to our current ideological arena, we might pose Williams's lyric affirmation as the question, what good is a poststructuralism that merely produces a "crushing humiliation" of the personality before the power of the systemic codes that constrain it? If the codes are to change in accordance with emancipatory desires, we would do better to schematize them as contingent upon and bound up in an indivisible system with the selves through which they pass.

Finally, Dora Marsden's philosophic algebra elucidates much of what Williams was most profoundly up to in the introductory destruction of the world that begins *Spring and All*: a dynamizing of Marsden's egoistic vision by raising it into the imagination, satirically honoring the uncanny creativity of Marsden's leap into immortality in the penultimate article of the *Science of Signs*, "Philosophy: The Science of Signs XVII—Truth V: How the Theory of the Ego Requires Us to Construe Death," and her concluding hymn to self-overcoming and self-renewal in the final chapter, "Philosophy: The Science of Signs XVIII: The Egoistic Interpretation of Future Time." Williams cryptically underscores that the destruction and recreation of the world beginning *Spring and All* is his parodic dramatization of Marsden's egoistic apocalypse by intimating that he is continuing on from Marsden's final chapter XVIII. Thus, amid his scrambled chapter headings there is one iterated item: "CHAPTER 19 . . . (more of this in Chapter XIX) . . . CHAPTER XIX" (178–82).

Following the logic of her electro-vitalist premises to the end, Marsden had discovered that the ego or world-inclusive I must be prior to life and that, therefore, if the universe that is indivisibly connected to the organism has a future, then so does the ego, by which death is undone. Moreover, Marsden speculates, the very event of death must produce a refreshing, recuperative effect, which then enhances the reconstitution of the vital ego on the far side of its "point of depolarisation." Thus, Marsden conceives and expounds a supreme antientropic fulfillment, a vitalist apocalypse strikingly reminiscent of the phoenix myth, the notion of renovation by fiery extinction that affected D. H. Lawrence's imagination so profoundly. I will cite the entirety of the crucial section from Marsden's penultimate article of the *Science of Signs*, both for its magnificent mythopoesis, and also to make audible its subtly ironic and heuristic tonality. The point is, this is not mysticism or theosophy; it is discursive poetry rigorously synthesized from a fixed set of syllogistic juxtapositions.

15. Let it be allowed for the sake of argument that life does mean this maintaining apart of the poles of a unitary egoistic force at the extremes of a neutral field of force called space; also, that dying is the drawing in and contracting to a mere point of the spatial zone so that the opposing poles tend to unite in a common point; that death is therefore the depolarisation of the egoistic force. Having gone thus far let us change the complexion of our thought, and instead of regarding death as a collapse of life let us regard it as its fruition. In this way: Just as all organic germs find themselves under the compulsion, to the end of maintaining their life, to perform certain elementary acts such as those of obtaining food and propagating their kind, so may the egoistic life as a whole find itself, reluctantly enough, under compulsion of winding itself up in the living act of dying so as to secure permanence and growth in the egoistic experience as a whole. May not dying constitute life's innate compulsion to put into employ the sole means capable of enabling it, when it has spent itself beyond a point, to renew its youth and vigour in perpetuity? If dying is the coming together of the opposing extremes of a line of force, is it not possible to conceive this very *making of polar contact* the act of refertilisation of the universe of feeling as a whole? May not the extremes touch only to recoil, and this with an even stronger impulsion of life—*i.e.,* of polarisation—than ever owing to the growth in strength of the elements concerned created through their exercising of themselves in an expenditure of feeling while in life? In such case, the point of depolarisation would also be the point of repolarisation. Therefore, while there would be a definite and absolute phenomenon of depolarisation, there would be no *state* of depolarisation: no state of absolute non-existence. The *ego* would continue to manifest perpetually the attribute of polar differentiation. Hence the individual universe of feeling could never actually cease, the point of death being merely the point of transition from one scheme of polarisation to another. The whole round scheme of things would therefore include only life and living activities. Of these last, dying would be the most vitally recuperative even as it was the most drastic. ("Philosophy—Truth V," 52)

Here is certainly a drastic solution to the riddle, "the old unanswerable question," that Williams propounds in the prose of *Spring and All* and to which he then provides the gnomic answer: "Whither? To what end? Each asks the other. Has life its tail in its mouth or its mouth in its tail? Why are we here? Dora Marsden's philosophic algebra" (184). Marsden has supplied Williams's imagination exactly with a scientist myth of cosmic renovation and of the virtual nonentity of annihilation. So in "Chapter 19" of *Spring and All,* beleaguered on all sides by cultural misunderstanding ("Is this what you call poetry? . . . It is the annihilation of life upon which you are bent") and social oppression ("intoxicated by prohibitions"), the poet's mind literalizes those critical figures and "rises to drunken heights to destroy the world. Let it rage, let it kill. The imagination is supreme. . . . Then at last will the world be made anew" (177, 179). As Williams had noted in the prologue to *Kora in Hell,* "It is in the continual and violent refreshing of the idea that love and good writing have their security" (22). Dora Marsden's algebra offered Williams a universal schema for drastic or "violent refreshing." His parodic deployment of Marsden's apocalypse does not subvert her discourse but rather acknowledges its notional character, its proper place beside the poetic imagination.

What skepticism Williams did feel about the ultimate chapter of the *Science of Signs* tells most clearly, I think, in his spoof on evolution as a repetition rather than a higher development, a comic indication of the pervasive postwar disillusion with the millennial progressivisms that had saturated the prewar modernisms of Dora Marsden's London. In this he may have been glancing sardonically at section 13 of that chapter, where Marsden reverted suddenly to the evolutionistic idiom of her *Freewoman* days and reconnected her later philosophical prophecy with her earliest spiritual vision of a progressive cosmic consciousness.

> Man, because he has evolved time finds himself in the clutches of an explaining-instrument which lays him under the compulsion to explain everything whatsoever. . . . This appetite dominates his species and its full satisfaction will mean the over-riding of his species in the production of a higher. . . . In short, a species of super-men whose life is as that of gods-immortal; a life whose shadow seems to fall already upon our labouring human life, but which is in truth existent only in so far as it is projected by our own life, whose labours find their sole meaning in making it conceivable and possible. ("Philosophy: Science of Signs XVIII," 67)

If I have been correct in assuming that Williams came upon Marsden's writings only with the turn away from explicit spiritualism carried out in the *New Freewoman,* this moment of reaffirmation by which Marsden tied together the ends of her journalistic career must have come as something of a shock or a revelation to Williams, her most assiduous of readers.

But, in the full sweep of Marsden's concluding chapter of the *Science of Signs*, section 13 represents at most a kind of uncanny afterthought. The primary emphasis of her remarks has been to annihilate the idea that death holds any ascendancy over the ego. If death is the spatial collapsing upon each other of the poles of organism and universe, that infinitesimal point of depolarisation is immediately followed by a recoil in which the two poles "spring" back to recreate the ego anew. Better yet, according to Marsden's antientropic economy, the more living force we expend during our given lives, the more forceful will be our renewal in the next.

> 20. Hence, when in the *ultimate* stage, the genius of life re-asserts its basic trait: that which knows nothing and will tolerate nothing of spacelessness: which utilises the very force released in the intaking of the spatial canvas to *galvanise* anew the whole scheme by issuing a new space of greater potentiality and range, there is no element of the old life missing. Each is there down to the smallest. . . . What goes in will come out, worked upon and developed by forces of renewal which are none other than those which have accumulated as an effect of expenditure of personal force during our life. The forces of the *ego* have not been dissipated by living. . . . Not a different universe therefore awaits us, but a renewed and further developed one. (69)

In his second "CHAPTER XIX," by bringing back a "miraculous verisimilitude" of the world just at the point in time of depolarisation, the moment of the prior annihilation, by starting off the lyrical content of *Spring and All* from Marsden's unending endpoint, the "spring" of a repolarized and renovated world, Williams is both satirizing and paying homage to Dora Marsden by enacting her egoistic apocalypse in the blink of an eye.

> It is spring! but miracle of miracles a miraculous miracle has gradually taken place during these seemingly wasted eons. Through the orderly sequences of unmentionable time EVOLUTION HAS REPEATED ITSELF FROM THE BEGINNING. . . .

> Now at last that process of miraculous verisimilitude, that great copying which evolution has followed, repeating move for move every move that it made in the past—is approaching the end.

> Suddenly it is at an end. THE WORLD IS NEW. (181–82)

Notes

I.

1. At times these movements crossbred, as in ego-futurism: "Separately from the Russian Cubo-Futurist group, Ego-Futurism developed between 1911 and 1915 around the poet Igor Severianin. . . . Its aesthetics were characterized by the exaltation of 'urbanism' and by extreme individualism, with certain Theosophical components" (Pontus Hulten, ed., *Futurism and Futurisms* [New York: Abbeville, 1986], 470).

2. Mrs. Ward was the author of popular conventional novels on social and religious themes and an advocate of female educational opportunity, but most notoriously she was "a principal figure in the Women's National Anti-Suffrage League" (Lisa Tickner, *The Spectacle of Women: Imagery of the Suffrage Campaign, 1907–14* [Chicago: University of Chicago Press, 1988], 99). Marsden enjoyed flaunting excerpts of Ward's alarmist review of the *Freewoman* published in the London *Times:* "Arguments against the immoral permanence of marriage, complete freedom of union under the guidance of passion between men and women, and other speculations and contentions with regard to the relations between the sexes. . . . Suffragists have no right . . . to ignore this dark and dangerous side of the 'Woman Movement'" ("*The New Freewoman* Thousand Club Membership: Establishment Fund," London, 1913, brochure in the Dora Marsden Collection, quoted with the permission of the Manuscripts Division, Department of Rare Books and Special Collections, Princeton University Libraries).

3. For more on Marsden's role with the WSPU, see Les Garner, *Stepping Stones to Women's Liberty: Feminist Ideas in the Women's Suffrage Movement, 1900–1918* (Rutherford: Fairleigh Dickinson University Press, 1984), 61–62; Les Garner, *A Brave and Beautiful Spirit: Dora Marsden, 1882–1960* (Brookfield, Vt.: Avebury, 1990), 22–50; and Carol Barash, "Dora Marsden's Feminism, the *Freewoman*, and the Gender Politics of Early Modernism," *Princeton University Library Chronicle* 49:1 (Autumn 1987): 31–56. Concerning libertarian, or "anarcho-," feminism, see Marsha Hewitt, "Emma Goldman: The Case for Anarcho-Feminism," in *The Anarchist Papers*, ed. Dimitrios I. Roussopoulos, 167–75 (Buffalo: Black Rose, 1986); and Margaret S. Marsh, *Anarchist Women, 1870–1920* (Philadelphia: Temple University Press, 1981).

4. See Jane Lidderdale and Mary Nicholson, "*The New Freewoman*," in *Dear Miss Weaver: Harriet Shaw Weaver, 1876–1961* (New York: Viking, 1970), 66–81; Louis K.

MacKendrick, "The *New Freewoman:* A Short Story of Literary Journalism," *English Literature in Transition* 15:3 (1972): 180–87; Michael Levenson, "Imagists and Egoists," in *Genealogy of Modernism: A Study of English Literary Doctrine, 1908–1922* (New York: Cambridge University Press, 1984), 63–79; and "*The New Freewoman,* June–December 1913," in Garner, *Brave and Beautiful,* 90–122.

5. Dora Marsden, "Views and Comments," *New Freewoman* 11 (November 15, 1913): 204.

6. Glenn Hughes, *Imagism and the Imagists: A Study in Modern Poetry* (1931; rpt., New York: Humanities Press, 1960).

7. Marjorie Perloff, *The Futurist Moment: Avant-Garde, Avant Guerre, and the Language of Rupture* (Chicago: University of Chicago Press, 1986), 15.

8. My use of the term *scientism* follows David Knight. It denotes a broad cultural investment in science as a foundational discourse and a readiness to extend scientific terms and ideas to heterogeneous areas. "This was the power of scientism, the idea that science is the guide to all reasoning and will provide the answers to all the questions which can reasonably be asked. Behind it lay the faith that the answers given in the sciences were independent of time and place; that they were truths, and that a scientific method led to certitude" (David Knight, *The Age of Science: The Scientific World-view in the Nineteenth Century* [Oxford: Basil Blackwell, 1986], 5).

9. On Pound's several deployments of this figure for the formative force of cultural energies, see Herbert Schneidau, *Ezra Pound: The Image and the Real* (Baton Rouge: Louisiana State University Press, 1969), 150–51. Cf. Ian Bell's discussion of Pound's discursive eclecticism: "Pound's comparison between sexual gnosis and electromagnetism was arguably his most vivid and fertile use of scientific analogy, for the simple reason that it instigates new and suggestive ranges of perception. . . . Pound's deciphering of early medieval sexual mysticism via contemporary electromagnetism thus not only defined his pagan religiosity but was properly the metamorphic vision of the savage in the city which marked primary interstices of psychic and sensual experience" (Ian F. A. Bell, *Critic as Scientist: The Modernist Poetics of Ezra Pound* [New York: Methuen, 1981], 42).

10. Alan Robinson, *Symbol to Vortex: Poetry, Painting and Ideas, 1885–1914* (New York: St. Martin's, 1985), 105.

11. For a related discussion of modernist politics, see Sanford Schwartz, "Bergson and the Politics of Vitalism," in *The Crisis in Modernism: Bergson and the Vitalist Controversy,* ed. Frederick Burwick and Paul Douglas, 277–305 (New York: Cambridge University Press, 1992). Perloff notes: "While it is a truism that the Marinetti of the twenties and thirties had become a confirmed if unorthodox fascist, the Futurism of the *avant guerre* did not, as is often assumed, inevitably point in this direction. . . . Giovanni Lista and others have recently traced the left-wing, anarcho-syndicalist origins of the Italian movement, its anticlericalism, antimonarchism, its opposition to the liberal bourgeoisie" (*Futurist Moment,* 30, 36).

12. Astradur Eysteinsson, *The Concept of Modernism* (Ithaca: Cornell University Press, 1990), 15–16.

13. See Georg Lukács, "The Ideology of Modernism," in *Realism in Our Time* (New York: Harper and Row, 1964), 17–46.

14. T. S. Eliot, "Tradition and the Individual Talent," *Egoist* 6:4 (September 1919): 54–55; T. S. Eliot, "Tradition and the Individual Talent—II," *Egoist* 6:5 (December

1919): 72–73; Dora Marsden, "Philosophy: The Science of Signs XVII—Truth V: How the Theory of the Ego Requires Us to Construe Death," *Egoist* 6:4 (September 1919): 49–53; and Dora Marsden, "Philosophy: The Science of Signs XVIII: The Egoistic Interpretation of Future Time," *Egoist* 6:5 (December 1919): 65–70.

15. Williams registered his aversion to Eliot's poetics as early as September 1918 in the prologue to *Kora in Hell: Improvisations*, in *Imaginations*, ed. Webster Schott, 6–26 (New York: New Directions, 1971).

16. See Wallace Martin, *The New Age under Orage: Chapters in English Cultural History* (New York: Barnes and Noble, 1967), 128–81; and the chapter "Hulme: The Progress of Reaction," in Levenson, *Genealogy of Modernism*, 81–102.

17. Judith Butler, *Gender Trouble: Feminism and the Subversion of Identity* (New York: Routledge, 1990), 14.

18. "The premature insistence on a stable subject of feminism, understood as a seamless category of women, inevitably generates multiple refusals to accept the category. These domains of exclusion reveal the coercive and regulatory consequences of that construction, even when the construction has been elaborated for emancipatory purposes. Indeed, the fragmentation within feminism and the paradoxical opposition to feminism from 'women' whom feminism claims to represent suggest the necessary limits of identity politics" (Butler, *Gender Trouble*, 4).

19. Rachel Blau DuPlessis, *The Pink Guitar: Writing as Feminist Practice* (New York: Routledge, 1990). DuPlessis relates Dora Marsden's *New Freewoman* writing to Mina Loy's "Feminist Manifesto," in "'Seismic Orgasm': Sexual Intercourse, Gender Narratives, and Lyric Ideology in Mina Loy," in *Studies in Historical Change*, ed. Ralph Cohen, 264–91 (Charlottesville: University Press of Virginia, 1992).

20. Charles Altieri, *Painterly Abstraction in Modernist American Poetry: The Contemporaneity of Modernism* (New York: Cambridge University Press, 1989), 7.

21. Gillian Hanscombe and Virginia L. Smyers, *Writing for Their Lives: The Modernist Women, 1910–1940* (Boston: Northeastern University Press, 1987), 172.

22. William Carlos Williams, *Collected Poems of William Carlos Williams*, ed. A. Walton Litz and Christopher MacGowan, 1:184 (New York: New Directions, 1986).

23. Dora Marsden, "Notes of the Week," *Freewoman* 1:1 (November 23, 1911): 3.

24. Floyd Dell, *Women as World Builders: Studies in Modern Feminism* (Chicago: Forbes, 1913), 10.

25. The *"New Freewoman* Thousand Club Membership" brochure that cited Mrs. Humphry Ward also stated Floyd Dell's credentials—editor of the "Friday Literary Review" of the *Chicago Evening Post*—and published his endorsement: "Until *The Freewoman* came, I had to lie about the feminist movement. I lied loyally and hopefully, but I could not have held out much longer. Your paper proves that feminism has a future as well as a past. We needed that assurance."

26. "Men say that there are two unrepresentable things: death and the feminine sex. That's because they need femininity to be associated with death; it's the jitters that gives them a hard-on! for themselves! They need to be afraid of us. Look at the trembling Perseuses moving backwards toward us, clad in apotropes" (Hélène Cixous, "The Laugh of the Medusa," in *The Critical Tradition: Classic Texts and Contemporary Trends,* ed. David H. Richter [New York: St. Martin's, 1989], 1097).

27. See Havelock Ellis, *The New Spirit* (1890; rpt., New York: Houghton Mifflin,

1929), esp. "Whitman" (89–132); Jeffrey Weeks, "Havelock Ellis and the Politics of Sex Reform," in Sheila Rowbotham and Jeffrey Weeks, *Socialism and the New Life: The Personal and Sexual Politics of Edward Carpenter and Havelock Ellis* (London: Pluto, 1977), 139–85; and Carroll Smith-Rosenberg, *Disorderly Conduct: Visions of Gender in Victorian America* (New York: Knopf, 1985), 275–80.

28. The full text of Duncan's remarks is "The Dance of the Future," collected in Isadora Duncan, *The Art of the Dance,* ed. Sheldon Cheney, 54–63 (New York: Theatre Arts, 1928).

29. See David Miller, "Individualist Anarchism," in *Anarchism,* 30–44 (London: J. M. Dent, 1984).

30. Marsden treats Max Stirner, German author of the individualist anarchist classic *The Ego and His Own,* explicitly in "The Growing Ego" (*Freewoman* 2:38 [August 8, 1912]: 221–22). Levenson's assertion in *Genealogy of Modernism* that "The *New Freewoman*'s principal and overriding concern was to trumpet Stirnerian egoism, and the rhetoric was deafening" (66) is overstated; a "deafening trumpet" describes Stirner's book more properly than it does Marsden's journal. But Marsden clearly tended toward Stirner's brand of anarchism. See Max Stirner, *The Ego and His Own: The Case of the Individual Against Authority,* trans. Steven F. Byington (New York: Libertarian Book Club, 1963); Herbert Read, "Max Stirner," *The Tenth Muse: Essays in Criticism* (London: Routledge and Kegan Paul, 1957), 74–82; and Eugene Goodheart, *The Cult of the Ego: The Self in Modern Literature* (Chicago: University of Chicago Press, 1968).

31. James Huneker, *Egoists: A Book of Supermen* (1909; New York: Scribner's, 1913).

32. In England, from 1898 to 1903, *The Eagle and the Serpent: A Journal of Egoistic Philosophy and Sociology* was dedicated to "'the Philosophy of Life Enunciated by Nietzsche, Emerson, Stirner, Thoreau, and Goethe.' . . . The first issue contained a fiery editorial manifesto: 'A race of altruists is necessarily a race of slaves. A race of freemen is necessarily a race of egoists. Freedom cannot be granted. It must be taken. . . . Nietzsche is, perhaps, the greatest prophet of Egoism the world has ever seen'" (David S. Thatcher, *Nietzsche in England, 1890–1914: The Growth of a Reputation* [Toronto: University of Toronto Press, 1970], 55–56).

33. "Now that Arthur Symons is no longer active in English letters, Mr. James Huneker alone represents modernity in criticism. . . . The Egoists are all men—French and German—of highly individual, some of perverse and lunary, genius" (T. S. Eliot, "*Egoists,* by James Huneker," *Harvard Advocate* 88:1 [October 5, 1909]: 16).

34. See David Kadlec, "Pound, *Blast,* and Syndicalism," *ELH* 60 (1993): 1015–31.

35. On Tucker, see Paul Avrich, *Anarchist Portraits* (Princeton: Princeton University Press, 1988), 144–52.

36. Vernon Lee [Violet Paget], *Gospels of Anarchy and Other Contemporary Studies* (1908; New York: Brentano's, 1909). Lee's life and writings are treated in Peter Gunn, *Vernon Lee: Violet Paget, 1856–1935* (New York: Oxford University Press, 1964).

37. See the critiques of Stirner in David Goodway, ed., *For Anarchism: History, Theory, and Practice* (New York: Routledge, 1989): Daniel Guérin, "Marxism and Anarchism," 116–17; and Peter Marshall, "Human Nature and Anarchism," 130–34.

38. His full-length exposition of Whitman's significance may be found in John Addington Symonds, *Walt Whitman: A Study* (London: John C. Nimmo, 1893).

39. For an old approach to Whitman's British reception, see Harold Blodgett, *Walt Whitman in England* (Ithaca: Cornell University Press, 1934); for a current one, see Gregory Woods, "'Still on My Lips': Walt Whitman in Britain," in *The Continuing Presence of Walt Whitman: The Life after the Life,* ed. Robert K. Martin, 129–40 (Iowa City: University of Iowa Press, 1992).

40. For a Whitmanesque instance of optimistic synthesis between religion and science, see John Addington Symonds, "The Philosophy of Evolution," in *Essays Speculative and Suggestive,* 3d ed., 1–26 (New York: Charles Scribner's Sons, 1907).

41. Georges Canguilhem, *Ideology and Rationality in the History of the Life Sciences,* trans. Arthur Goldhammer (Cambridge: MIT Press, 1988).

42. See Michel Foucault, "Introduction," in Georges Canguilhem, *The Normal and the Pathological,* trans. Caroline R. Fawcett, 7–24 (New York: Zone, 1991).

43. This phase of Canguilhem's discussion would seem to replicate a problematic distinction between "pure" science and "applied" technology. Surveying the current status of evolutionism, Canguilhem states: "The theory of evolution has changed since Darwin, but Darwinism is an integral part of the history of the science of evolution. By contrast, evolutionist ideology is merely an inoperative residue in the history of the social sciences" (*Ideology and Rationality,* 37). Canguilhem's historiography is limited here by an academically discipline-bound perspective. For instance, the ambiguous legacy of evolutionist ideology is alive and well in capitalist technoculture—from Levi's Loose 501 jeans' "Everything Basic Evolves" to the cybernetic scenarios of microelectronic "silicon evolution" beyond the carbon creation.

44. Anson Rabinbach, *The Human Motor: Energy, Fatigue, and the Origins of Modernity* (New York: Basic Books, 1990), 5.

45. Jacques Monod, *Chance and Necessity: An Essay on the Natural Philosophy of Modern Biology,* trans. Austryn Wainhouse (New York: Knopf, 1971), xii.

46. David F. Channell, *The Vital Machine: A Study of Technology and Organic Life* (New York: Oxford University Press, 1991), 55.

47. See also Guenter B. Risse, "Kant, Schelling, and the Early Search for a Philosophical 'Science' of Medicine in Germany," *Journal of the History of Medicine and Allied Sciences* 27 (1972): 145–58; and Karl E. Rothschuh, M.D., "The So-called 'Romantic' Interlude in Physiology," in *History of Physiology,* trans. Guenter B. Risse, 155–66 (Huntington, N.Y.: R. E. Krieger, 1973).

48. See Chishichi Tsuzuki, *Edward Carpenter, 1844–1929: Prophet of Human Fellowship* (New York: Cambridge University Press, 1980); and Sheila Rowbotham, "Edward Carpenter: Prophet of the New Life," in Rowbotham and Weeks, *Socialism,* 25–138. On Carpenter in the context of early modernist feminism, see Sandra M. Gilbert and Susan Gubar, *No Man's Land: The Place of the Woman Writer in the Twentieth Century,* vol. 2: *Sexchanges* (New Haven: Yale University Press, 1989), 216–17. The most detailed study of Carpenter in relation to literature is Emile Delavenay, *D. H. Lawrence and Edward Carpenter: A Study in Edwardian Transition* (New York: Taplinger, 1971). See also Ian F. A. Bell, "The Art of Creation," in *Critic as Scientist,* 197–206; Ian F. A. Bell, "'In a Station of the Metro' and Carpenterian Transformations," *Notes and Queries,* n.s., 29:4 (August 1982): 345–46; and Tony Brown, "Figuring in History: The Reputation of Edward Carpenter, 1883–1987: Annotated Secondary Bibliography, I & II," *English Literature in*

Transition 32:1, 2 (1989): 27–32, 170–210. For assorted essays on Carpenter's politics, see Tony Brown, ed., *Edward Carpenter and Late Victorian Radicalism* (London: Frank Cass, 1990). Bound together with the Texas Tech Library's copy of Carpenter's long Whit-manesque poetry sequence, *Towards Democracy*, is a pamphlet by T. H. Bell, "Edward Carpenter: The English Tolstoy," which begins with the declaration, "Edward Carpenter died June, 1929, a great Englishman and the greatest of modern British Anarchists." Rowbotham dates this pamphlet 1932 and credits it to the Los Angeles Libertarian Group (Rowbotham and Weeks, *Socialism*, 122).

49. Edward Carpenter, *Civilisation: Its Cause and Cure and Other Essays*, 12th ed. (London: George Allen, 1912), 1–50.

50. Cf. Whitman, *Song of Myself*, chant 25: "Dazzling and tremendous how quick the sunrise would kill me, / If I could not now and always send sunrise out of me. // We also ascend dazzling and tremendous as the sun" (Walt Whitman, *Leaves of Grass: The First (1855) Edition*, ed. Malcolm Cowley [New York: Viking, 1961], 50). Notice, too, the titling of a Whitman study with a phrase taken from D. H. Lawrence's *Apocalypse*: James E. Miller, Jr., Karl Shapiro, and Bernice Slote, *Start with the Sun: Studies in the Whitman Tradition* (Lincoln: University of Nebraska Press, 1960).

51. Cf. this discussion of the "lingering character" of Whitman's death: "In some ways this was in consonance with his physical temperament—his extraordinarily volu-minous hold on life, all phases of it, his extreme tenacity, his strong implication in the life of the body and the senses, his affectionate and unceasing love towards his friends, and his marked and obdurate egoism—all things which held him to life, and needed a long process of disentanglement, fibre by fibre as it were, before he could be released" (Edward Carpenter, *Days with Walt Whitman, With Some Notes on His Life and Work* [London: George Allen, 1896], 45).

52. Edward Carpenter, *The Art of Creation: Essays on the Self and Its Powers*, new and enlarged ed. (London: George Allen, 1907), 37.

53. William Thomson (Lord Kelvin), "On a Universal Tendency in Nature to the Dissipation of Mechanical Energy," *Mathematical and Physical Papers* (Cambridge: Cambridge University Press, 1882), 1:514. "Thermodynamics is sometimes called the science of imperialism. To Kelvin and his fellow thermodynamicists, entropy represented the tendency of the universe to run down, despite the best efforts of British rectitude to prevent it from doing so. In Kelvin's prose, the rhetoric of imperialism confronts the inescapability of failure. In this context entropy represents an apparently inescapable limit on the human will to control" (N. Katherine Hayles, *Chaos Bound: Orderly Disorder in Contemporary Literature and Science* [Ithaca: Cornell University Press, 1990], 40). "The very slight margin of escape Kelvin allowed himself in his prediction was well advised," Hayles adds, because in 1859 James Clerk Maxwell lay the groundwork for the recognition that "thermodynamic laws are statistical generalizations rather than laws in an absolute sense" (40). Carpenter's daemonic evolutionism parallels Maxwell's "Demon": they both represent heuristic attempts to seize the margin of "escape" from Kelvin's entropic scenario.

54. "So when this intimacy continues and the lover comes near and touches the beloved in the gymnasia and elsewhere, then the fountain of that stream, which Zeus, when he was in love with Ganymede, called the 'flood of passion,' pours abundantly upon the lover. . . . So the stream of beauty flows back again into the beautiful beloved

through his eyes, the natural inlet to the soul. There it comes and excites the soul, watering the outlets of the wings and quickening them to sprout" (Plato, *Phaedrus*, trans. W. C. Helmbold and W. G. Rabinowitz [Indianapolis: Bobbs-Merrill, 1956], 40).

55. Walt Whitman, *Democratic Vistas*, in *Prose Works, 1892*, vol. 2: *Collect and Other Prose*, ed. Floyd Stovall (New York: New York University Press, 1964), 374.

56. On Whitman's use of scientific sources in general and Robert Chambers's *Vestiges of Creation* in particular, see Robert J. Scholnick, "'The Password Primeval': Whitman's Use of Science in 'Song of Myself,'" in *Studies in the American Renaissance 1986*, ed. Joel Myerson, 385–425 (Charlottesville: University Press of Virginia, 1986); and Judith Kent Green, "A Note on Walt Whitman's Probable Reading of Robert Chambers," *Walt Whitman Quarterly Review* 3:3 (Winter 1986): 23–28. Thanks to Sherry Ceniza and M. Jimmie Killingsworth.

57. Kathryne V. Lindberg, "Whitman's 'Convertible Terms': America, Self, Ideology," in *Theorizing American Literature: Hegel, the Sign, and History*, ed. Bainard Cowan and Joseph G. Kronick, 233–68 (Baton Rouge: Louisiana State University Press, 1991). On the vogue for idealism, Hegelian and other, in late Victorian and Edwardian culture, see Tom Gibbons, *Rooms in the Darwin Hotel: Studies in English Literary Criticism and Ideas, 1880–1920* (Nedlands: University of Western Australia Press, 1973), 1–38; and Jonathan Rose, *The Edwardian Temperament, 1895–1919* (Athens: Ohio University Press, 1986), 4–39.

58. Citing Kojève's reading of the *Phenomenology*, Lindberg acknowledges that "only recently, after several crossings of influence, including those of Emerson and Nietzsche and back through French readings of Hegel, has the full logical and existential negativity of the dialectic been appreciated" ("Whitman's Terms," 245).

59. For a largely sympathetic treatment of Whitman's individualism, see M. Jimmie Killingsworth, "Tropes of Selfhood: Whitman's 'Expressive Individualism,'" in R. Martin, *Continuing Presence*, 39–52.

60. G. W. F. Hegel, *The Phenomenology of Mind*, trans. J. B. Baillie, intro. George Lichtheim (New York: Harper and Row, 1967), 93.

61. Edward Carpenter, "Exfoliation: Lamarck *versus* Darwin," in Carpenter, *Civilisation*, 129–47. The epigraph is from Walt Whitman, "The Great Unrest of Which We Are Part," a brief passage in *Specimen Days* (in Walt Whitman, *Leaves of Grass and Selected Prose*, ed. Lawrence Buell [New York: Modern Library, 1981], 750).

62. "Much like Whitman, Carpenter used the term 'desire' for the Lamarckian expression, 'avoir besoin de'" (Harry Gershenowitz, "Two Lamarckians: Walt Whitman and Edward Carpenter," *Walt Whitman Quarterly Review* 2:1 [Summer 1984]: 38). That is, these two Lamarckian ideologists conflated the biological level of need with the psychological and cultural level of desire.

63. Dora Marsden, "The New Morality," *Freewoman* 1:4 (December 14, 1911): 61–62.

2.

1. *Blast: Review of the Great English Vortex*, ed. Wyndham Lewis (London), no.1 (June 1914), no.2 (July 1915). "The Vorticists felt that the only way to disturb public apathy to art was to resort to shock tactics, in a deliberately provocative form of intellec-

tual terrorism" (Robinson, *Symbol to Vortex*, 195). Some "bomb-throwing anarchists" did exist, but they were largely media stereotypes of the time, deflecting public notice from the more common anarchist profiles of trade unionist (syndicalist), educationalist, and propagandist (see Avrich, *Anarchist Portraits;* and Goodway, *For Anarchism*). A global survey of the connections between anarchism and literature has yet to be undertaken. For some examples of that connection, see Arthur Efron, "War Is the Health of the State: An Anarchist Reading of *Henry IV, Part One*," *Works and Days* 10:1 (Spring 1992): 7–75; and the other essays in that number of *Works and Days*. See also Richard Nickson, "Shaw and Anarchism: Among the Leftists," *The Independent Shavian* 26:1–2 (1988): 3–13; and Eileen Sypher, "Anarchism and Gender: James's *The Princess Casamassima* and Conrad's *The Secret Agent*," *Henry James Review* 9:1 (Winter 1988): 1–16.

2. The spotty political career of the futurist movement is succinctly treated in the entry on "Ideology" in the "Dictionary of Futurism" provided in Hulten, *Futurism*, 488–92. Perloff's definition of the "futurist moment" overlaps precisely with Dora Marsden's London as "the brief utopian phase of early Modernism when artists felt themselves to be on the verge of a new age that would be more exciting, more promising, more inspiring than any preceding one" (*Futurist Moment*, 36).

3. "In her previous work, for the suffragettes, Dora had passed from one crisis to another. She was a compelling speaker and a very successful demonstrator—but she was not an accomplished organizer" (Lidderdale and Nicholson, *Dear Miss Weaver*, 54). For more on Marsden's role with the WSPU, see Garner, *Stepping Stones*, 61–62; Garner, *Brave and Beautiful*, 22–50; and Barash, "Dora Marsden's Feminism," 37–40. See also Elaine Showalter, *A Literature of Their Own: British Women Novelists from Brontë to Lessing* (Princeton: Princeton University Press, 1977), 216–39.

4. Dora Marsden, "Views and Comments," *Egoist* 1:12 (June 15, 1914): 223.

5. Susan Kingsley Kent, *Sex and Suffrage in Britain, 1860–1914* (Princeton: Princeton University Press, 1987), examines the long quest for the vote in Britain against the cultural backdrop of wider feminist concerns. In *Spectacle of Women*, Tickner criticizes the rhetorical strategies of both the suffrage and the antisuffrage campaigns by recovering the posters, cartoons, postcards, banners, and murals of the day. See also Andrew Rosen, *Rise Up, Women! The Militant Campaign of the Women's Social and Political Union, 1903–1914* (Boston: Routledge and Kegan Paul, 1974); and Antonia Raeburn, *The Militant Suffragettes* (London: Michael Joseph, 1973).

6. Emily Wilding Davison died after being trampled at Derby on June 3, 1913, while disrupting a race by waving the WSPU colors before the horses (see Rosen, *Rise Up*, 198–99). Dora Marsden's "The Lean Kind" (*New Freewoman* 1 [June 15, 1913]: 1–2), and "Views and Comments" (*New Freewoman* 1 [June 15, 1913]: 3–5) may be read as a composite requiem for her WSPU colleague Davison.

7. Emmeline Pethick-Lawrence to Dora Marsden, October 6, 1909, Dora Marsden Collection, Princeton University Libraries.

8. "Extraordinary Charges at Manchester," *Votes for Women* 3:83 (October 8, 1909): 27.

9. For a discussion of others who left the organization, see Garner, *Stepping Stones*, 47.

10. Dora Marsden, "Commentary on Bondwomen," *Freewoman* 1:2 (November 30, 1911): 22.

11. Emmeline Pethick-Lawrence to Dora Marsden, December 1, 1909, Dora Marsden Collection, Princeton University Libraries.

12. See Tickner's illustrations nos. 13, 33, and 87 for examples of the "angel" motif in suffragist allegory *(Spectacle of Women)*. Garner quotes from Sylvia Pankhurst's memoir of Marsden's exploit: "peering through one of the great porthole openings in the slope of the ceiling, was seen a strange elfin form with wan, childish face, broad brow and big grey eyes, looking like nothing real or earthly but a dream waif. But for the weary paleness of her, she might have been one of those dainty little child angels the old Italian painters loved to show peeping down from the tops of high clouds" (*Brave and Beautiful*, 39).

13. Gertrude Colmore, *Suffragette Sally* (London: Stanley, Paul, 1911), 251. Thanks to Vicki Hill for bringing this novel to my attention. It has been republished as *Suffragettes: A Story of Three Women* (London: Pandora, 1984). See Shirley Peterson, "The Politics of a Moral Crusade: Gertrude Colmore's *Suffragette Sally*," in *Rediscovering Forgotten Radicals: British Women Writers, 1889–1939*, ed. Angela Ingram and Daphnae Patai, 101–17 (Chapel Hill: University of North Carolina Press, 1993).

14. "The Lancashire Protest Campaign," *Votes for Women* 3:92 (December 10, 1909): 164.

15. Garner reports that Marsden's article on the Huddersfield rally, in *Votes for Women*, October 1, 1908, was probably her first publication (*Brave and Beautiful, 29*). After that, she contributed occasional reports from the front lines of the militant campaign.

16. "Lancashire Protest," 164.

17. Dora Marsden, "The Over-and-Above in Life," *Freewoman* 1:11 (February 1, 1912): 201.

18. "Very little news has reached us except scanty accounts in the paper of your exploit at Southport on Saturday, but we know quite enough to be able to appreciate and very much admire the wonderful resources and immense courage shown by you and your friends. . . . We were delighted, of course, to get your telegram saying that the case against you had been dismissed. It was a surprise, of course, to know that you had engaged counsel. I want to hear more particulars. Will you tell me whether you have incurred any legal expenses?" (Emmeline Pethick-Lawrence to Dora Marsden, December 7, 1909, Dora Marsden Collection, Princeton University Libraries).

19. Emmeline Pethick-Lawrence to Dora Marsden, December 8, 1909, Dora Marsden Collection, Princeton University Libraries.

20. In *Brave and Beautiful*, Garner sifts at length through the matter of Marsden and forcible feeding without coming to a definitive conclusion. Raeburn quotes Dorothy Pethick at length on her experiences in prison after the Newcastle stone-throwing protest during Lloyd George's appearance at the Palace Theatre on October 9, 1909. Curiously, Pethick incorrectly includes Dora Marsden in her reminiscences, whereas Marsden still would have been in Manchester shortly after her Victoria University protest: "We were still being forcibly fed. . . . It was not until within four days of my release, when the nasal passages were very much swollen and inflamed, that the tube was dipped in glycerine to facilitate its passage and relieve the agonising pain. They were unnecessarily violent, and when the feeding was over, they just left you in a kind of half sobbing condition. . . . There was an awful old chaplain. He had a long white beard

which swung in front of his greasy old waistcoat, and he stood over me lying on the plank bed, and said how sorry he was to see me in such a condition. . . . But when he began moithering on like this to Dora Marsden, she eyed him without a word, until at last she said: 'If you're not out of my cell within half a minute, you'll find yourself outside'" (*Militant Suffragettes*, 124). It would seem reasonable to interpret Pethick's mistake as evidence for Marsden's having earned her reputation among the suffragettes as a powerful and inviolable personality.

21. Dora Marsden, "Views and Comments," *Egoist* 1:12 (June 15, 1914): 223.

22. Christabel Pankhurst to Dora Marsden, June 25, 1910, Dora Marsden Collection, Princeton University Libraries.

23. Christabel Pankhurst to Dora Marsden, November 14, 1910, Dora Marsden Collection, Princeton University Libraries.

24. Emmeline Pethick-Lawrence to Dora Marsden, December 22, 1910, Dora Marsden Collection, Princeton University Libraries.

25. Dora Marsden to Emmeline Pethick-Lawrence, January 9, 1911, Dora Marsden Collection, Princeton University Libraries. Cf. Garner, *Brave and Beautiful*, 44–48.

26. Constance Tite to Dora Marsden, April 26, 1911, Dora Marsden Collection, Princeton University Libraries. However, Tite published a letter sympathetic to Marsden's critiques of the WSPU in the *Freewoman*, December 21, 1911.

27. Henry Bryan Binns to Dora Marsden, July 30, 1912, Dora Marsden Collection, box 2, folder 26, Princeton University Libraries. Binns was an occasional contributor of poems and letters to the *New Age* as well as to the *Freewoman*. See Henry Bryan Binns, "The Spanish Gypsy," *New Age* (May 5, 1910): 14; and Henry Bryan Binns, "A Free Woman," *Freewoman* 2:32 (June 27, 1912): 112. The last stanza of "A Free Woman" runs: "She is the enemy / Of our accomplished good, / Our comfort and complacency: / Her unenfranchised womanhood / Laughs at our freedom; and it would / Methinks have set us free, / For it is nearer far / To manhood than are we."

28. The two volumes of the *Freewoman* ran weekly from November 23, 1911, to October 10, 1912. The *Freewoman* was not extensively covered in Lidderdale and Nicholson's 1970's account of Dora Marsden in *Dear Miss Weaver*, because Harriet Shaw Weaver's close association with Marsden began only with the planning for the *New Freewoman*. In "Dora Marsden's Feminism," Barash traced some of the tensions constellated by Marsden between feminist strategies and literary pressures. Hanscombe and Smyers survey the span of Marsden's journalistic projects in the context of the literary connections of female modernists *(Writing for Their Lives).*

29. Dora Marsden, *The Definition of the Godhead* (London: Egoist Press, 1928). Aspects of this debate may be traced through Hilary Simpson, *D. H. Lawrence and Feminism* (DeKalb: Northern Illinois University Press, 1982), 23; Hanscombe and Smyers, *Writing for Their Lives*, 12–13, 170–72; Barash, "Dora Marsden's Feminism," 53–56; and Garner, *Brave and Beautiful*, 197.

30. Cf. Andrew Thacker, "Dora Marsden and *The Egoist*: 'Our War Is With Words,'" *English Literature in Transition: 1880–1920* 36:2 (1993): 178–96.

31. See Nick Rider, "The Practice of Direct Action: The Barcelona Rent Strike of 1931," in Goodway, *For Anarchism*, 79–105; and David Miller, "Revolutionary Organization and Strategy," in *Anarchism*, 94–108 (London: J. M. Dent, 1984).

32. This format is reminiscent of the *New Age;* see Wallace Martin, *The New Age Under Orage: Chapters in English Cultural History* (New York: Barnes and Noble, 1967). From 1907 to 1922, the *New Age* turned away from its Fabian origins to become an influential independent socialist review of political and literary culture. Its mixture of topical commentary and cultural debate provided a salutary model for Marsden's own journals.

33. Dora Marsden, "Bondwomen," *Freewoman* 1:1 (November 23, 1911): 1–2; Dora Marsden, "Notes of the Week," *Freewoman* 1:1 (November 23, 1911): 3–4; Dora Marsden, "Commentary on Bondwomen," *Freewoman* 1:2 (November 30, 1911): 21–22. A reprint of parts of "Bondwomen" and "Commentary on Bondwomen" was published in New York in August 1912 by the National American Woman Suffrage Association. This particular manifesto is still perhaps the best-known of Marsden's writings.

34. Otto Weininger, *Sex and Character* (New York: G. P. Putnam's Sons, 1906).

35. Allan Janik writes sardonically: "Weininger is such a focal point in the cultural life of *Alt Wein* that I am surprised that no one has yet written a book called *Weininger's Vienna*" ("Therapeutic Nihilism: How Not to Write about Otto Weininger," in *Structure and Gestalt: Philosophy and Literature in Austro-Hungary and Her Successor States*, ed. Barry Smith [Amsterdam: John Benjamins, 1981], 263). See also Viola Klein, "The Philosophical Approach: Otto Weininger," in *The Feminine Character: History of an Ideology*, 53–70 (New York: International Universities Press, 1949); Emile Delavenay, "Lawrence, Otto Weininger and 'Rather Raw Philosophy,'" in *D. H. Lawrence: New Studies*, ed. Christopher Heywood, 137–57 (New York: St. Martin's, 1987); and Sandra M. Gilbert and Susan Gubar, *No Man's Land: The Place of the Woman Writer in the Twentieth Century*, vol. 1: *The War of the Words* (New Haven: Yale University Press, 1988), 22.

36. Dora Marsden, "Views and Comments," *New Freewoman* 5 (August 15, 1913): 84.

37. For incisive discussions of the use and abuse of biomedical sciences to enforce patriarchy and resist female emancipation, see "The Doctors," in Kent, *Sex and Suffrage*, 114–39; and Tickner, *Spectacle of Women*, 192–205.

38. Selwyn Weston, "Millennium," *Freewoman* 1:8 (January 11, 1912): 148.

39. E. M. White, "Militancy in Women," *Freewoman* 1:8 (January 11, 1912): 159.

40. For some feminist literary applications of poststructural and psychoanalytical concepts to the critique of patriarchy as an ideological system and psychical structure, see Cixous, "Laugh of the Medusa"; Jane Gallop, *The Daughter's Seduction: Feminism and Psychoanalysis* (Ithaca: Cornell University Press, 1982); Kaja Silverman, "The Subject," in *The Subject of Semiotics*, 126–93 (New York: Oxford University Press, 1983); and Kaja Silverman, *Male Subjectivity at the Margins* (New York: Routledge, 1992). Toril Moi discusses a "libertarian" turn in Julia Kristeva's writings, reminiscent of Marsden's development, in "Feminism, Marxism, Anarchism," in *Sexual/Textual Politics: Feminist Literary Theory*, 167–73 (New York: Methuen, 1985).

41. The first person other than Marsden was the nominal coeditor, invalided suffragette Mary Gawthorpe, who led off the third number of the *Freewoman* in order to respond to the outrage over its criticisms of the WSPU. The *Herald of Revolt* was edited by Guy Aldred, about whom we shall hear more shortly. On Aldred and British anarchism generally, see John Quail, *The Slow Burning Fuse: The Lost History of the British*

Anarchists (New York: Granada, 1978); and Hermia Oliver, *The International Anarchist Movement in Late Victorian London* (New York: St. Martin's, 1983).

42. Rebecca West to Dora Marsden, n.d. [ca. June 1912], Dora Marsden Collection, box 1, folder 26, Princeton University Libraries. On the Freewoman Discussion Circle, see below. An anarchist in deed as well as word, it seems that later in 1912 Weston appropriated some capital from the Freewoman Discussion Circle treasury: "I had a very lengthy, very rambling, very repentant letter from S. Weston, confessing his sins (in using the Circle monies) & promising to repay the moment he had any money— at present he is penniless" (Barbara Low to Dora Marsden, December 7 [1912], Dora Marsden Collection, Princeton University Libraries).

43. Selwyn Weston, "A Gospel of Goodwill," *Freewoman* 1:5 (December 21, 1911): 81–82.

44. Sheila Jeffreys, *The Spinster and Her Enemies: Feminism and Sexuality, 1880–1930* (London: Pandora, 1985), 93–99.

45. "Embodied as a legal enactment, or postulated as a strict morality affecting people of every range of temperament, [indissoluble matrimony] is an unjustifiable tyranny, and psychologically monstrous and morally dangerous. . . . Passion will last, and will only last, as long as continued communion has something new to offer to the mind. When the store has run out, then it comes to an end. And very rightly so. For nothing justifies the exclusive attention which passion demands, except that passion provide something continuously worthy of attention. Even our virtues carry their own egotism" (Dora Marsden, "The New Morality—III," *Freewoman* 1:7 [January 4, 1912]: 122).

46. Dora Marsden, "The New Morality—II," *Freewoman* 1:6 (December 28, 1911): 101–2.

47. Cf. Alice Ruth Wexler's "Emma Goldman and Women" (in Roussopoulos, *Anarchist Papers*, 151–66) on Goldman's criticism of the "social purity" politics of mainstream suffragism and feminism. I have found no mention of Goldman in Marsden's writings. Marsden's closest American counterpart, so to speak, was Margaret Anderson, who brought anarchist ideals and literary activity together as the editor of the *Little Review*. See Margaret Anderson, "Challenge of Emma Goldman," *Little Review* 1 (May 1914): 5–9.

48. Cf. the excellent and eye-opening account in Quail, *Slow Burning Fuse*.

49. Selwyn Weston, "Millennium," *Freewoman* 1:8 (January 11, 1912): 148–49. "Millennium" had been previously published in the October 1911 number of the *Herald of Revolt*.

50. See Guérin, "Marxism and Anarchism," 109–26. Theoretically, as an antiparliamentary, antistatist attitude, anarchism transcends the politics of "wings," literally, seating positions in a state house. But divisions into left and right or communist and individualist varieties are standard ways of cataloguing anarchisms. See David DeLeon, *The American as Anarchist: Reflections on Indigenous Radicalism* (Baltimore: Johns Hopkins University Press, 1978), 61–101; and D. Miller, *Anarchism*, 30–59.

51. Dora Marsden, "The New Morality—V," *Freewoman* 1:9 (January 18, 1912): 162.

52. Guy Aldred, "The Freewoman," *Freewoman* 1:9 (January 18, 1912): 179.

53. Selwyn Weston, "Anarchy in Art," *Freewoman* 1:10 (January 25, 1912): 194. A

previous version of this article, "Revolt in Relation to Art," appeared in the June 1911 number of the *Herald of Revolt*.

54. Dora Marsden, "Creation and Immortality," *Freewoman* 1:19 (March 28, 1912): 362.

55. Dora Marsden, "Interpretations of Sex—IV," *Freewoman* 2:27 (May 23, 1912): 1.

56. Letter to the *Freewoman*, no signature, perhaps fragmentary, Dora Marsden Collection, Princeton University Libraries.

57. Barbara Low to Dora Marsden, February 4, 1912, Dora Marsden Collection, Princeton University Libraries. The original Discussion Circle seems to have lapsed in the spring of 1913. In the *New Freewoman* of October 15, 1913, a proposal to restart the Discussion Circle included among its signatories Barbara Low and another early British Freudian, J. C. Flügel (166). Around that time Low met D. H. Lawrence, whose *Sons and Lovers* was eagerly seized upon by the psychoanalytically minded; her numerous letters from Lawrence may be consulted in D. H. Lawrence, *The Letters of D. H. Lawrence*, vol. 2: *June 1913–October 1916*, ed. George Zytaruk and James T. Boulton (New York: Cambridge University Press, 1981).

58. Guy Aldred to Dora Marsden, February 9, 1912, Dora Marsden Collection, box 2, folder 25, Princeton University Libraries. Aldred's memoirs are *No Traitor's Gait* (Glasgow: Strickland, 1956).

59. Dora Marsden to Mary Gawthorpe, March 8, 1912, Dora Marsden Collection, Princeton University Libraries.

60. Dora Marsden to Charles Granville, April 29, 1912, Dora Marsden Collection, Princeton University Libraries.

61. Dora Marsden, "Freewomen and Evolution," *Freewoman* 1:26 (May 16, 1912): 503–4.

62. See also Edward Carpenter, *The Intermediate Sex: A Study of Some Transitional Types of Men and Women* (New York: Mitchell Kennerly, 1912). Carpenter placed one article with Marsden, "The Status of Women in Early Greek Times" (*New Freewoman* 4 [August 1, 1913]: 68–69).

63. "Sex is fundamental, lies deeper than culture, cannot be ignored or defied with impunity. . . . If the attempt to do so be seriously and persistently made, the result may be a monstrosity—something which having ceased to be woman is not yet man" (Henry Maudsley, M.D., "Sex and Mind in Education," *Fortnightly Review* 15 [1874], cited in Kent, *Sex and Suffrage*, 44).

64. Bram Dijkstra, "The Androgyne in Nineteenth-Century Art and Literature," *Comparative Literature* 26:1 (Winter 1974): 63.

65. See *Women's Studies* 2:2 (1974) for a round table on feminism and androgyny in the context of the recent publication of Carolyn Heilbrun's *Toward a Recognition of Androgyny* (New York: Knopf, 1973). Gilbert and Gubar review the problematics of androgyny in male and female modernist literature in "Cross-Dressing and Re-Dressing: Transvestism as Metaphor" in *No Man's Land*, 2:324–76, esp. 362–69. Marsden's androgyny is more nearly related to the deconstructive feminism of Kristeva and Cixous. Moi discusses Kristeva's deconstruction of gender in *Sexual/Textual Politics* (13–15); cf. Cixous, "Laugh of the Medusa," on the "other bisexuality" (1096).

66. Carroll Smith-Rosenberg, *Disorderly Conduct: Visions of Gender in Victorian America* (New York: Knopf, 1985), 287–88.

67. See Jane Marcus, *The Young Rebecca: Writings of Rebecca West, 1911–1917* (New York: Viking, 1982), 3–79, for selected texts of and commentary on West's contributions to the *Freewoman* and the *New Freewoman* between 1911 and 1913. In 1926, West stated that the *Freewoman* "was coming to an end psychically when it came to an end physically. Its psychic death was due to the fact that Dora Marsden started on a train of thought which led her to metaphysics" ("The Freewoman," 649). However, Marsden's "metaphysics" were already full-blown in "Bondwomen," the first leader of the first *Freewoman*, and West herself aided in the services by which this demise led to the rebirth of the *New Freewoman*, parting company for good only when that incarnation was turning into the *Egoist*. See the introduction to West in Bonnie Kime Scott, ed., *The Gender of Modernism: A Critical Anthology* (Bloomington: Indiana University Press, 1990), 560–68.

68. Rebecca West to Dora Marsden, n.d. [ca. winter 1913], Dora Marsden Collection, box 1, folder 26, Princeton University Libraries. See Hugo Dick, "War and—Manure," *Herald of Revolt* 3:1 (February 1913): 10.

69. Harry J. Birnstingl, "'Uranians,'" *Freewoman* 1:7 (January 4, 1912): 127. Carpenter's *Intermediate Sex* has an epigraph from Weininger preceding the table of contents: "There are transitional forms between the metals and non-metals. . . . The improbability may henceforth be taken for granted of finding in Nature a sharp cleavage between all that is masculine on the one side and all that is feminine on the other." Carpenter's endorsement indicates how for many readers of the *Freewoman* Weininger's theories were broadly granted the credibility of scientific discourse.

70. Charles J. Whitby, "Tertium Quid," *Freewoman* 1:9 (January 18, 1912): 167.

71. See Tickner, *Spectacle of Women*, 185–86, for more discussion of the relation of medicine to the British women's movement of Marsden's day. Compared to the medical misogyny of Sir Almroth Wright, for instance, Whitby is a very liberal specimen.

72. Harry J. Birnstingl, "Uranians—II," *Freewoman* 1:10 (January 25, 1912): 190.

73. Charles J. Whitby, "A Matter of Taste," *Freewoman* 1:11 (February 1, 1912): 215.

74. Harry J. Birnstingl, "The Human Minority," *Freewoman* 1:12 (February 8, 1912): 235.

75. In 1918, Hueffer (Ford Madox Ford) reminisced mordantly about the Weininger craze half a generation earlier: "being naive and ingenuous I really believed my Young Liberal friends when they assured me that 'Sex and Character' was a scientific work" ("Women and Men II," 43); "for years and years they had had, as Liberal minded men, to live up to the idea that women should have justice done to them. Now Dr. Weininger had come along and proved that women were inferior animals. He had proved it by all the sciences that are open to a very very young German doctor of medicine" (42).

76. Dora Marsden, "The Emancipation of Man," *Freewoman* 1:20 (April 4, 1912): 381–83.

77. For another topical response to Wright's diatribe, see May Sinclair, *Feminism* (London: Women Writers Suffrage League, 1912), dated by the author as having been composed on March 31, 1912. Concerning "hysteria" as a counter in antisuffrage argu-

ment, with numerous references to Almroth Wright, see Tickner, *Spectacle of Women*, 192–213.

78. Otto Weininger, "Woman and Mankind: Chapter XIV of Weininger's 'Sex and Character,'" *Freewoman* 1:23 (April 25, 1912): 452–55, and Otto Weininger, "Woman and Mankind: Chapter XIV of Weininger's 'Sex and Character'—II," *Freewoman* 1:24 (May 2, 1912): 470–73. The Dora Marsden Collection preserves a letter from the publisher of the English translation of *Sex and Character* granting her permission to publish excerpts.

79. Hueffer described Weininger's "trick" this way: "With an admirable cunning he wraps up a truism in scientific language that may awe the simple-minded and comfort the erudite. . . . When he has proved to his own satisfaction that he is learned, balanced, thoughtful and scientific he makes a statement from quite another department of knowledge and trusts that his former erudition may carry him over. This is Dr. Weininger's one technical trick and he uses it with such consummate skill that he certainly hoodwinked a large portion of the world of his day. . . . He was nothing more or less than a conscientious book-worm and an absolutely unscrupulous theorist, these characteristics going so often hand in hand" ("Women and Men II," 47).

80. Charles J. Whitby, "A Sex Heresy," *Freewoman* 1:26 (May 16, 1912): 505.

81. Whitby, "Sex Heresy," 507. However, Whitby himself slipped into a form of masculine condescension, the common "complementarity" argument, at the end of his article: "Reason without love is form without substance; love without reason is substance without form. This, and not Weininger's opposition of existence and nonentity, is the true antithesis of the male and the female. It is a complementary, not a contradictory relation" (507). "Complementarity" between masculine reason and feminine love is not especially complimentary, as it amounts to a sentimentalized restatement of Weininger's Neoplatonic distinction between masculine form and feminine matter.

82. True Womanhood, "An Estimation of Weininger," *Freewoman* 2:28 (May 30, 1912): 38.

83. A.H. to Dora Marsden, n.d., Dora Marsden Collection, Princeton University Libraries. Presumably this was written in late 1911 or early 1912 by Amy Haughton, author of a series of articles on "Feminism in the Republic and the Early Empire" that ran through the first eight numbers of the *Freewoman*. Barash has identified Haughton as a friend of Marsden's from Owen College in Manchester, then part of Victoria University ("Dora Marsden's Feminism," 37–38).

84. Dora Marsden, "Sex and Character," *Freewoman* 2:30 (June 13, 1912): 63.

85. Even on his own terms, the drift of Weininger's logic led in his last chapter to statements that, taken out of context, could be mistaken for profeminist remarks. I assume that Marsden was alert to these ironies. I cite from the text of Weininger's chapter 14 as reprinted in the *Freewoman*: "Woman must be looked upon as an individual and as if she were a free individual, not as one of a species, not as a sort of creation from the various wants of man's nature" ("Woman and Mankind," 455); "If any one should think it a high-flown idea that man should respect woman as an entity, a real existence, and not use her merely as a means to an end, that he should recognise in her the same rights and the same duties (those of building up one's own moral personality) as his own, then he must reflect that man cannot solve the ethical problem in his own case, if he contin-

ues to lower the idea of humanity in the women [*sic*] by using her simply for his purposes" (471).

86. Mary Gawthorpe to Dora Marsden, September 29, 1912, Dora Marsden Collection, box 2, folder 1, Princeton University Libraries. For more on Marsden's relationship with Gawthorpe, see Garner, *Brave and Beautiful*, 58–72; and Barash, "Dora
Marsden's Feminism," 35–41.

87. See Mary Gawthorpe, *Up Hill to Holloway* (Penobscot, Maine: Traversity,
1962), 191–202, for an engaging memoir of her early association with Orage and the
Leeds Art Club. For more on Orage's career prior to his association with the *New Age,*
see Tom Steele, *Alfred Orage and the Leeds Art Club, 1893–1923* (Brookfield, Vt.: Scolar,
1990).

88. Allen Upward, *The Divine Mystery: A Reading of the History of Christianity Down
to the Time of Christ* (1914; rpt., with an introduction by Robert Duncan, Santa Barbara:
Ross-Erikson, 1976); Allen Upward, *The New Word: An Open Letter addressed to the
Swedish Academy in Stockholm on the Meaning of the word IDEALIST* (New York: Mitchell
Kennerly, 1910).

3.

1. Rebecca West to Dora Marsden, n.d. [ca. February 1913], Dora Marsden Collection, box 1, folder 26, Princeton University Libraries. E. H. Visiak's undistinguished
poetry appeared throughout the *Freewoman* and occasionally in the *New Age.*

2. For other accounts of West's involvement with Dora Marsden's projects, see
Garner, *Brave and Beautiful;* Lidderdale and Nicholson, *Dear Miss Weaver,* 56–68; Marcus,
Young Rebecca, 4–6; and Scott, *Gender of Modernism,* 560–69.

3. Rebecca West to Dora Marsden, n.d. [ca. fall 1913], Dora Marsden Collection,
box 1, folder 26, Princeton University Libraries.

4. Hughes's further claim that Marsden's writings were "studiously overlooked by
most readers" (32) presumably captures the particular distaste of the imagist faction but
still distorts the overall record. Cf. Allen Upward's remarks on Marsden: "I do not always
find myself in full agreement with the Editor of *The Egoist*. But I want to read her, and
agree with as much as I can" ("The Plain Person," *Egoist* 1:3 [February 2, 1914]: 49).

5. H.D.'s [Hilda Doolittle's] letter to Lowell is dated April 27, 1915. On the matter of imagist unhappiness with the *Egoist*'s Special Imagist Number: "Miss Lowell was
infuriated. . . . First, there was the presence on the front page of an article [of Marsden's]
continued from the previous number, which hurt the effect of an Imagist number. Second, there was the hostility of Harold Monro's criticism. Third, there was Lawrence's
poem ["Eloi, Eloi, Lama Sabachthani?"], which, she said, 'for pure, farfetched indecency
beats anything I have ever seen'" (E. W. Tedlock, Jr., "A Forgotten War Poem by
D. H. Lawrence," *Modern Language Notes* 67 [June 1952]: 410–11). See also Charles
Doyle, *Richard Aldington: A Biography* (Carbondale: Southern Illinois University Press,
1989), 44.

6. Timothy Rogers, "Introduction," in *Georgian Poetry, 1911–1922: The Critical
Heritage,* ed. Timothy Rogers (Boston: Routledge and Kegan Paul, 1977), 32 .

7. Dora Marsden, "Views and Comments," *New Freewoman* 11 (November 15,
1913): 204.

8. "There has probably been no more illustrious proponent of a metaphysical vitalism than Henri Bergson. . . . This philosophy . . . rests entirely upon a certain idea of life conceived as an *élan*, a 'current,' absolutely distinct from inanimate matter but contending with it, 'traversing' it so as to force it into organized form. Contrary to almost all other vitalisms and animisms, that of Bergson predicates no ultimate goal: it refuses to put life's essential spontaneity in bondage to any kind of predetermination. Evolution, identified with the *élan vital* itself, can therefore have neither final nor efficient causes" (Monod, *Chance and Necessity*, 26).

9. Dora Marsden, "The Heart of the Question," *New Freewoman* 4 (August 1, 1913): 61–64.

10. Dora Marsden, "The Lean Kind," *New Freewoman* 1 (June 15, 1913): 1–2.

11. Dora Marsden, "Views and Comments," *New Freewoman* 1 (June 15, 1913): 3.

12. West's "Life of Davison" emphasizes the contributing factor of Davison's broken health, the result of her having thrown herself down a prison stairwell and undergone forcible feedings. Her longing to die was thus related to a life of physical misery incurred by, in Marsden's terms, "acting out her beliefs in her own person."

13. Dora Marsden, "Intellect and Culture," *New Freewoman* 2 (July 1, 1913): 21.

14. Dora Marsden, "Views and Comments," *New Freewoman* 9 (October 15, 1913): 165.

15. Dora Marsden, "Views and Comments," *New Freewoman* 11 (November 15, 1913): 203.

16. Ezra Pound, "The Serious Artist," *New Freewoman* 9 (October 15, 1913): 161–63; 10 (November 1): 194–95; 11 (November 15): 213–14.

17. Ezra Pound to Dora Marsden, n.d. [ca. summer 1913], Dora Marsden Collection, box 1, folder 23, Princeton University Libraries.

18. Ezra Pound to Dora Marsden, n.d. [ca. summer 1913], Dora Marsden Collection, box 1, folder 23, Princeton University Libraries.

19. Wyndham Lewis, "Long Live the Vortex!" *Blast* 1 (June 20, 1914): 7–8.

20. Ezra Pound, "Edward Wadsworth, Vorticist," *Egoist* 1:16 (August 15, 1914): 306.

21. Allen Upward, "The Order of the Seraphim—I," *New Age* (February 10, 1910): 349. This series of articles is included in Upward, *Divine Mystery*, 333–55.

22. Ezra Pound to Dora Marsden, n.d. [ca. summer 1913], Dora Marsden Collection, box 1, folder 23, Princeton University Libraries.

23. Ezra Pound, "The Contemporania of Ezra Pound," *New Freewoman* 5 (August 15, 1913): 87–88. See Bruce Fogelman, "The Evolution of Ezra Pound's 'Contemporania,'" *Journal of Modern Literature* 15:1 (Summer 1988): 93–103. However, Fogelman treats only the *Poetry* appearance of the sequence.

24. Ezra Pound, "In Metre," *New Freewoman* 6 (September 1, 1913): 113.

25. Ezra Pound to Dora Marsden, n.d. [ca. summer 1913], Dora Marsden Collection, box 1, folder 23, Princeton University Libraries.

26. Curiously but symptomatically, in his footnote Eliot misstates the source of the essay: "From *The Egoist* A.D. 1913" (Pound, *Literary Essays*, 41).

27. The history of critical commentary on "The Serious Artist" shows an unstable play between the poles of mysticism and empiricism. For a magisterial treatment of both aspects of that dialectic, see I. Bell, *Critic as Scientist*. Patricia Rae discusses this basic

ambivalence in terms of a "tensional relation" at large in Pound and vorticism in "From Mystical Gaze to Pragmatic Game: Representations of Truth in Vorticist Art," *ELH* 56:3 (Fall 1989): 689–720. On the one hand, "The Serious Artist" addresses Pound's imagistic advocacy of empirical discipline and poetic "efficiency": it is "full of praise for a kind of scientific accuracy in art" (Schneidau, *Ezra Pound: Image and Real*, 25). On the basis of "The Serious Artist," Alan Durant concludes: "Pound's general epistemology, then, is an empiricist one" (*Ezra Pound, Identity in Crisis* [Totowa, N.J.: Barnes and Noble, 1981], 21). On the other hand, Robinson has argued that, here as elsewhere, Pound's use of scientistic rhetoric was a cover for matters that were rather more medieval and mystical in origin: "I noted Pound's conception in 1911–12 of the artist as channeller of psychic energy or *virtù*; this emphasis on poetry as the transfer of force was reiterated in November 1913 in 'The Serious Artist.' It seems likely that by this stage Pound's reading of the Fenollosa papers, which presented language as activity or the transference of force, had confirmed his Stilnovist hermeticism" (*Symbol to Vortex*, 212). But Robinson's surmise runs counter to Pound's own memory of the advent of Fenollosa's influence: "example of ideogrammic method used by E. P. in *The Serious Artist* in 1913 before having access to the Fenollosa papers" (Ezra Pound, *ABC of Reading* [New York: New Directions, 1960], 96). On the matter of science versus mysticism—or material versus immaterial forces—see also Martin Kayman, "A Model for Pound's Use of 'Science,'" in I. Bell, *Ezra Pound: Tactics for Reading*, 121–47. Kathryne V. Lindberg relates Pound's tropes for reading to "a series of metaphors drawn from the 'new sciences' of electromagnetism and telecommunications," in *Reading Pound Reading: Modernism After Nietzsche* (New York: Oxford University Press, 1987), 35.

28. Levenson traces Pound's line to Max Stirner's egoism not through Marsden but through Upward: "Several of Upward's notions found their way into Pound's thought, but unquestionably the most important was the urbane, if nonetheless extreme, version of the egoist position. Where Pound kept at a distance from Dora Marsden's more technical polemics, he became a doting admirer of Upward" (*Genealogy of Modernism*, 72). For two sympathetic accounts, see Robert Duncan's "Introduction" to Upward, *Divine Mystery*, ix–xxvii; and Kenneth Cox, "Allen Upward," *Agenda* 16:3–4 (Autumn/Winter 1978–79): 87–121.

29. David Kadlec's unpublished essay on the economic contexts of early modernist radicalism, "Imagism and the Gold Standard," argues that Pound's poetics were mediated by an antistatist, "underconsumptionist" discourse espoused by Arthur Kitson in a series of articles in the *Freewoman*, a series Marsden seconded and critiqued in her own leaders. Thus, Marsden also becomes a relay in Pound's absorption of radical economics a decade before his investment in Major C. H. Douglas's "social credit" theories. See also Leon Surette, "Ezra Pound and British Radicalism," *English Studies in Canada* 9:4 (December 1983): 435–51.

30. Ezra Pound to Dora Marsden, n.d. [ca. September 1913], Dora Marsden Collection, box 1, folder 23, Princeton University Libraries.

31. Ezra Pound to Dora Marsden, n.d. [ca. September 1913], Dora Marsden Collection, box 1, folder 23, Princeton University Libraries.

32. Noel Stock, *The Life of Ezra Pound*, expanded ed. (San Francisco: North Point, 1982), 141.

33. "The conjunction of mathematics and magic was . . . crucial to the epistemology of Pound's modernity. . . . Such correspondence was essential for a poet whose

residual tastes always sought sustenance from the mystifications of Provençal and medieval poetics of love, from works that testified to the vitality of a divinely ordered world which hitherto had had only myth, magic and metaphor as its modes of articulation" (I. Bell, *Critic as Scientist*, 39); "This 'chivalric' poetry" was "a veiled symbolic expression for his private spiritual experience . . . an instinctive defence-mechanism" (Robinson, *Symbol to Vortex*, 165).

34. Dora Marsden, "Views and Comments," *New Freewoman* 9 (October 15, 1913): 163–66.

35. Friedrich Nietzsche, *Basic Writings of Nietzsche*, trans. and ed. Walter Kaufmann (New York: Modern Library, 1968), 481; William Carlos Williams, *Paterson* (New York: New Directions, 1963), 6.

36. One might read in Pound's recourse to the ineffable an unwillingness to divulge, to Marsden in particular, that the roots of his attitude lay in the realm of his "mythic" experiences. If that was the case, it was unfortunate, since Marsden was no stranger to the visionary mode and was herself open to Orphic rationales (see the subsection, "Passion and Duration," below).

37. Dora Marsden, "The Art of the Future," *New Freewoman* 10 (November 1, 1913): 181.

38. Ezra Pound, *The Letters of Ezra Pound: 1907–1941*, ed. D. D. Paige (New York: Harcourt, Brace, 1950), 27–28.

39. William Carlos Williams, "The Great Sex Spiral: A Criticism of Miss Marsden's 'Lingual Psychology,' Chapter I," *Egoist* 4:3 (April 1917): 46.

40. These bracketed remarks are crossed out in pencil.

41. Ezra Pound to Dora Marsden, n.d. [ca. September 1913], Dora Marsden Collection, box 1, folder 23, Princeton University Libraries.

42. Dora Marsden Collection, Princeton University Libraries.

43. Richard Maurice Bucke, M.D., *Cosmic Consciousness: A Study in the Evolution of the Human Mind* (1901; rpt., New York: E. P. Dutton, 1923).

44. Isabelle M. Pagan to Dora Marsden, August 5, 1913, Dora Marsden Collection, Princeton University Libraries. Pagan is listed on the summer school syllabus.

45. Dora Marsden, "Interpretation of Sex—II," *Freewoman* 1:25 (May 9, 1912): 481–82.

46. My confidence in attributing this experience to Marsden herself is also based on the mention of headaches, which malaise continued for the rest of her life. In an undated letter written during the *Freewoman* period, "A.H." implored: "My dear Dora, Do get that headache better. It quite worries me to think that you have it so often. Why not spend a fraction of the salary on seeing that doctor of yours & getting a remedy?" (A.H. to Dora Marsden, n.d., Dora Marsden Collection, Princeton University Libraries).

47. May Sinclair, *The Tree of Heaven* (1917; New York: Macmillan, 1919).

48. Francis Grierson, "Women's New Era," *New Freewoman* 1 (June 15, 1913): 11.

49. Harriet Shaw Weaver to Grace Jardine, August 1, 1913, Dora Marsden Collection, box 4, folder 1A, Princeton University Libraries.

50. Dora Marsden to Harriet Shaw Weaver, September 2, 1913, Harriet Shaw Weaver Papers, MS. 57354, British Library.

51. Dora Marsden, "Beauty and the Senses," *New Freewoman* 11 (November 15, 1913): 201–3.

52. "Thermodynamics conceived of nature as a vast machine capable of producing

mechanical work or, as von Helmholtz called it, 'labor power' *[Arbeitskraft]*. Initially a measurement of the force of machines, 'labor power' became after the discovery of energy conservation the basis of all matter and motion in the physical world. . . . For physiologists armed with the principles of thermodynamics, the energy of the body was not merely analogous to other natural physical forces, it became one among them. . . . Especially striking in the reconceptualization of the body as a thermodynamic machine is that work became a universal concept, a conversion of energy into use" (Rabinbach, *Human Motor*, 46).

53. On the wide cultural dissemination of degeneration scenarios, see J. Edward Chamberlin and Sander L. Gilman, ed., *Degeneration: The Dark Side of Progress* (New York: Columbia University Press, 1985).

54. Rebecca West, "Imagisme," *New Freewoman* 5 (August 15, 1913): 86.

55. For a study of Anglo-American modernism in relation to the "science of work," see James F. Knapp, *Literary Modernism and the Transformation of Work* (Evanston: Northwestern University Press, 1988): "Taylorism's fragmentation of the human subject, and modernism's equally radical dislocations of literary form . . . call into question the view that modernist writing tended to suppress historical reference and engagement" (14). Knapp focuses his analyses on Pound, Lawrence, and Williams.

56. Dora Marsden, "Tales for the Attentive," *New Freewoman* 8 (October 1, 1913): 141.

57. James Joyce, "A Portrait of the Artist as a Young Man: Chapter V (continued)," *Egoist* 2:9 (September 1, 1915): 146.

58. Greg Myers, in "Nineteenth-Century Popularizations of Thermodynamics and the Rhetoric of Social Prophecy," in *Energy and Entropy: Science and Culture in Victorian Britain*, ed. Patrick Brantlinger (Bloomington: Indiana University Press, 1989), aptly describes the social moralization of Lord Kelvin's thermodynamic contrast between the first law's eternal conservation of energy and the second law's temporal dissipation: "The contrast between eternity and temporality is explicit; the earth shall pass away in entropy, dissipation, and sin, but righteousness, salvation, and energy shall not be abolished. Thomson recalls the Old Testament vision of decline in order to preserve a conservative, natural theological sense of the power of the Creator over nature. . . . Prophets through the ages have predicted the end of the earth; Thomson gives a formula for its final temperature" (318).

59. Dora Marsden, "Views and Comments," *New Freewoman* 13 (December 15, 1913): 244.

60. Harriet Shaw Weaver to Dora Marsden, September 15, 1913, Dora Marsden Collection, box 4, folder 1A, Princeton University Libraries.

61. Raymond Williams, *Culture and Society, 1780–1950* (New York: Columbia University Press, 1983), 212.

62. D. H. Lawrence, "Education of the People," in *Reflections on the Death of a Porcupine and Other Essays*, ed. Michael Herbert (New York: Cambridge University Press, 1988), 113–14.

63. Dora Marsden, "Views and Comments," *Egoist* 1:7 (April 1, 1914): 125.

64. Peter Kropotkin, *Modern Science and Anarchism* (London: Freedom Press, 1912), 45.

4.

1. Richard Aldington to Dora Marsden, n.d. [December 1913?], Dora Marsden Collection, box 1, folder 12, Princeton University Libraries.

2. *Pound/The Little Review: The Letters of Ezra Pound to Margaret Anderson: The Little Review Correspondence,* ed. Thomas L. Scott, Melvin J. Friedman, and Jackson R. Bryer (New York: New Directions, 1988), 10.

3. Richard Aldington to Dora Marsden, n.d. [late December 1913?], Dora Marsden Collection, box 1, folder 12, Princeton University Libraries.

4. Ezra Pound to Grace Jardine, n.d. [fall 1913?], Dora Marsden Collection, box 1, folder 23, Princeton University Libraries.

5. Henri Bergson, "The Philosophy of Ideas," *New Freewoman* 13 (December 15, 1913): 246–48.

6. James Stephens to Dora Marsden, January 7, 1914, Dora Marsden Collection, Princeton University Libraries. Stephens received the Polignac Prize presumably for a collection of poems, *The Hill of Vision* (London: Maunsel, 1912). In a letter to Henry Savage of December 2, 1913, Lawrence offers a long critique of James Stephens's novel *The Crock of Gold* (Lawrence, *Letters,* 114–15). For another contemporary review of Stephens's work, see West, "Two Poets."

7. Mary Gawthorpe to Dora Marsden, September 29, 1912, Dora Marsden Collection, box 2, folder 1, Princeton University Libraries.

8. Cf. I. Bell's close reading of modernist irony in Marsden's *New Freewoman* leader "The Art of the Future" (*Critic as Scientist,* 66).

9. Harriet Shaw Weaver to Grace Jardine, November 1 (or 9), 1914, Dora Marsden Collection, box 4, folder 1A, Princeton University Libraries.

10. C. H. Bechhöfer, "More Contemporaries—V—*Egoist,*" *New Age* (June 15, 1914): 186. Ellipses in the original.

11. Harriet Shaw Weaver to Dora Marsden, August 5, 1914, Dora Marsden Collection, box 4, folder 1A, Princeton University Libraries.

12. Huntly Carter, "Poetry versus Imagism," *Little Review* 2:6 (September, 1915): 27.

13. See Pound, *Letters to Anderson,* on the history of lax proofreading at the *Little Review;* and cf., below, D. H. Lawrence's displeasure with the *Egoist* on the same score.

14. Hilary Simpson, *D. H. Lawrence and Feminism* (DeKalb: Northern Illinois University Press, 1982), 23.

15. See Delavenay, *Lawrence and Carpenter.* My work is indebted to Delavenay's pioneering cultural studies. The problem one encounters with Delavenay is essentially historical: his sensibility is so bound up with the cataclysms of the 1930s and 1940s that he tends to collapse them too entirely upon his subjects.

16. Speaking of Carpenter, Delavenay sketches a particular example of this volatile complex: "personal revolt against the more crushing aspects of Victorian life—and . . . longing for a new, freer, more human society—combined with a deeply religious and mystical temperament, produced this original synthesis of libertarian anarchism and Fabian socialism: a precarious compound, containing in itself the potentialities of its own destruction" (*Lawrence and Carpenter,* 44).

17. See Kim A. Herzinger, *D. H. Lawrence in His Time: 1908–1915* (Lewisburg: Bucknell University Press, 1982).

18. See Herzinger, *Lawrence in His Time*, 140–57; Warren Roberts, "London 1908: Lawrence and Pound," *Helix* 13–14 (1983): 45–49; A. Walton Litz, "Lawrence, Pound, and Early Modernism," in *D. H. Lawrence: A Centenary Consideration*, ed. Peter Balbert and Phillip L. Marcus, 15–28 (Ithaca: Cornell University Press, 1985); and David Roessel, "Pound, Lawrence, and 'The Earthly Paradise,'" *Paideuma* 18:1–2 (Spring/Fall 1989): 227–30.

19. See Lawrence's letter of July 31, 1914, to Harriet Monroe, the editor of *Poetry*, responding to her decisions about publishing some of his poems and giving his impressions of the Berkeley Hotel dinner (Lawrence, *Letters*, 203). Lawrence's relations with the imagist faction—Aldington, H.D., and Lowell—have been given careful attention by Paul Delany in *D. H. Lawrence's Nightmare: The Writer and His Circle in the Years of the Great War* (New York: Basic Books, 1978); E. Claire Healey and Keith Cushman, ed., *The Letters of D. H. Lawrence and Amy Lowell, 1914–1925* (Santa Barbara: Black Sparrow, 1985); and Doyle, *Richard Aldington*.

20. Lerici and Fiascherino are two neighboring villages on the Gulf of Spezia, on the Ligurian Sea, west of Florence. Lawrence and Frieda lived in one or the other town from September 28, 1913, to June 8, 1914.

21. In a letter to Edward Garnett written four days after the one to Pound, asking Garnett to forward copies of *Love Poems and Others* to Pound for submission to the Polignac competition, Lawrence echoed Stephens's phrase "the Pound-Hueffer group" in referring to the "Hueffer-Pound faction" (Lawrence, *Letters*, 132–33).

22. Ezra Pound to Dora Marsden, n.d. [ca. January 1914], Dora Marsden Collection, box 1, folder 23, Princeton University Libraries. "Wright" was the editor of the *Smart Set*.

23. One can find evidence in the whole span of Dora Marsden's journals for the quickness with which Lawrence's writings were received and appreciated, at least by London's more radical literati. In the *Freewoman*, reviewing several novels under the heading "Spinsters and Art," Rebecca West singled out *The Trespasser* for a lengthy commentary: "Last year Mr. Lawrence published 'The White Peacock,' in which there was some imagination, but much more fancy, which had within therefore the seeds of both genius and decay. Mr. Lawrence has conquered. This book is magic" (*Freewoman* 2:34 [July 11, 1912]: 147).

24. Ezra Pound, "D. H. Lawrence," in Pound, *Literary Essays*, 387–88.

25. Ezra Pound, "In Metre," *New Freewoman* 6 (September 1, 1913): 113. John Masefield had won the Polignac Prize for 1912.

26. Rebecca West to Dora Marsden, n.d. [ca. February 1913], Dora Marsden Collection, box 1, folder 26, Princeton University Libraries.

27. Concerning the identity of Fletcher as Pound's money man, see Lidderdale and Nicholson, *Dear Miss Weaver*, 67. See also John Gould Fletcher, "'Amores' by D. H. Lawrence," *Egoist* 3:12 (December 1916): 182.

28. D. H. Lawrence, "Poems," *Egoist* 1:7 (April 1, 1914): 134–35: "A Winter's Tale," "Song," "Early Spring," "Honeymoon," and "Fooled." Most were revised and renamed when included in later collections (see Warren Roberts, *A Bibliography of D. H.*

Lawrence [London: Rupert Hart-Davis, 1963], 252). His other appearances in the *Egoist* were "Eloi, Eloi, Lama Sabachthani?" *Egoist* 2:5 (May 1, 1915): 75–76; "Street Lamps," *Egoist* 4:1 (January 1917): 9; and "Autumn Rain," *Egoist* 4:2 (February 1917): 22.

29. Leigh Henry, "Liberations: Studies of Individuality in Contemporary Music—I. Prelude," *Egoist* 1:7 (April 1, 1914): 121–23. For instance, "if art is to be of any avail . . . it must be a record of its epoch, not an inert sentimentalism stagnant with out-worn tradition" (121); or, again, "the forms which sufficed for purely objective incidents have become inadequate to express the more subjective trend of modern thought. As the novel evolved from a mere depiction of externals to a study of psychology, so with music" (122).

30. James Joyce, "A Portrait of the Artist as a Young Man (Chapter I—continued)," *Egoist* 1:7 (April 1, 1914): 132–34.

31. Dora Marsden, "Views and Comments," *Egoist* 1:7 (April 1, 1914): 126.

32. The extremism abroad in English society and culture during 1910–14 is economically evoked in Wees, *Vorticism*, 9–35.

33. Richard Aldington, "Imitations of Lucian: Dialogues of the Dead," *Egoist* 1:7 (April 1, 1914): 128.

34. "Futurist free verse is the dynamism of our malleable consciousness fully realised: the integral ego, sung, painted, sculptured indefinitely in its perpetual aggressive evolution," from *I Poeti Futuristi*, cited, with translation, in Vivian de Sola Pinto's introduction to D. H. Lawrence, *The Complete Poems of D. H. Lawrence*, ed. Vivian de Sola Pinto and F. Warren Roberts (New York: Viking, 1971), 9. See also Emile Delavenay, "Lawrence and the Futurists," in *The Modernists: Studies in a Literary Phenomenon*, ed. Lawrence B. Gamache and Ian S. MacNiven, 140–62 (Rutherford: Fairleigh Dickinson University Press, 1987).

35. D. H. Lawrence, "We Need One Another," in *Phoenix: The Posthumous Papers of D. H. Lawrence*, ed. Edward D. McDonald (1936; rpt., New York: Viking, 1968), 188.

36. Michael Bentley, "Lawrence's Political Thought: Some English Contexts, 1906–19," in Heywood, *Lawrence: New Studies*, 76.

37. D. H. Lawrence, *Study of Thomas Hardy*, in *Study of Thomas Hardy and Other Essays*, ed. Bruce Steele, 7–128 (New York: Cambridge University Press, 1985).

38. "New Heaven and Earth" was first published in a somewhat shorter version as "Terra Nuova" in *Some Imagist Poets 1917: An Annual Anthology*, 69–75 (New York: Houghton Mifflin, 1917; rpt., New York: Kraus, 1969).

39. D. H. Lawrence, "Poetry of the Present," in *Complete Poems*, 184, 182.

40. Knapp, *Literary Modernism*, 69.

41. Friedrich Nietzsche, "On Truth and Lie in an Extra-Moral Sense," in *Deconstruction in Context: Literature and Philosophy*, ed. Mark C. Taylor (Chicago: University of Chicago Press, 1986), 216.

42. "As Darwin revealed the mechanisms that governed the transformations of natural history, and perhaps human populations as well, so too, thermodynamics revealed those that governed nature and the deployment of labor power. And, as Darwin's writings left open the social implications of evolutionary doctrine—giving credence to conservative, liberal, as well as socialist versions of 'Darwinism'—thermodynamics permitted an equally broad range of interpretations from progressive social reform to the more

apocalyptic conclusions of Nietzsche's image of history" (Rabinbach, *Human Motor*, 69).

43. See Stephen G. Brush, *The Temperature of History: Phases of Science and Culture in the Nineteenth Century* (New York: Burt Franklin, 1978); and Myers, "Nineteenth-Century Popularizations."

44. The impetus recently given literary studies by developments in chaos theory and other nonlinear dynamical systems theories has led to an upsurge in the interrelation of thermodynamic models to literary texts. See Michel Serres, *Hermes: Literature, Science, Philosophy*, ed. Josué V. Harari and David F. Bell (Baltimore: Johns Hopkins University Press, 1982); William R. Paulson, *The Noise of Culture: Literary Texts in a World of Information* (Ithaca: Cornell University Press, 1988); and N. Katherine Hayles, "Self-Reflexive Metaphors in Maxwell's Demon and Shannon's Choice: Finding the Passages," in *Chaos Bound*, 31–60. A more traditional approach to the connection between literature and thermodynamics is J. Edward Chamberlin, "Images of Degeneration: Turnings and Transformations," in Chamberlin and Gilman, *Degeneration*, 263–89.

45. James Clerk Maxwell, *Theory of Heat*, 9th ed. (New York: Longmans, Green, 1888), 328–29.

46. D. H. Lawrence, *Women in Love*, ed. David Farmer, Lindeth Vasey, and John Worthen (New York: Cambridge University Press, 1987), 128. Lawrence completed the novel in 1916 but was unable to publish it until 1921.

47. On the presence of Xavier Bichat's physiology within the text of *Women in Love*, see Christopher Heywood, "'Blood-Consciousness' and the Pioneers of the Reflex and Ganglionic Systems," in Heywood, *Lawrence: New Studies*, 104–36.

48. D. H. Lawrence, "Apropos of 'Lady Chatterley's Lover,'" in *Phoenix II*, ed. Warren Roberts and Harry T. Moore (New York: Viking, 1968), 507–8.

49. Roger Ebbatson has discussed the thermodynamic scenario in *Women in Love* from the perspective of Herbert Spencer's notion of dissolution. See "Gerald's Sense of an Ending," in *The Evolutionary Self: Hardy, Forster, Lawrence*, 96–112 (Totowa, N.J.: Barnes and Noble, 1982).

50. For detailed readings of *Women in Love* in the context of Taylor's system of scientific management, see Knapp, *Literary Modernism*, 59–73; and Hubert Zapf, "Taylorism in D. H. Lawrence's *Women in Love*," *D. H. Lawrence Review* 15:1–2 (Spring/Summer 1982): 129–39.

51. "In 1858 Herbert Spencer . . . wrote to [physicist John] Tyndall, shaken by Tyndall's exposition to him of the second law of thermodynamics: 'That which was new to me in your position . . . was that equilibration was death. . . . Your assertion that when equilibration was reached, life must cease, staggered me'" (cited in Gillian Beer, "Wave Theory and the Rise of Literary Modernism," in *Realism and Representation: Essays on the Problem of Realism in Relation to Science, Literature, and Culture*, ed. George Levine [Madison: University of Wisconsin Press, 1993], 197).

52. "By the beginning of the nineteenth century, it was becoming more and more popular to associate the vital principle with electricity. . . . Throughout much of the nineteenth century it was an open question whether electricity was a material phenomenon or the result of some unknown force similar to gravity" (Channell, *Vital Machine*, 56–57). For another approach to Lawrence's electro-vitalism with explicit reference to Clerk Maxwell, see N. Katherine Hayles, "Evasion: The Field of the Unconscious in

D. H. Lawrence," in *The Cosmic Web: Scientific Field Models and Literary Strategies in the Twentieth Century*, 85–110 (Ithaca: Cornell University Press, 1984).

53. John Palattella, "'In the Midst of Living Hell'": The Great War, Masculinity, and Maternity in Williams' *Kora in Hell: Improvisations* and 'Three Professional Studies,'" *William Carlos Williams Review* 17:2 (Fall 1991): 13–19.

54. For other ramifications of the Lawrence/Williams relation, see my essays "The Fall of Montezuma: Poetry and History in William Carlos Williams and D. H. Lawrence," *William Carlos Williams Review* 12:1 (Spring 1986): 1–12; and "The Melancholy Serpent: Body and Landscape in Lawrence and William Carlos Williams," in *D. H. Lawrence's Literary Inheritors*, ed. Keith Cushman and Dennis Jackson, 188–210 (New York: St. Martin's, 1991).

55. "Despite the unmitigated optimism of a synthesis between evolution and thermodynamics, the principle of entropy still lurked" (Rabinbach, *Human Motor*, 68).

56. Garrett Stewart remarks on the narrator's delivery in this passage: "Armed with the hyperbole of his own verbal arsenal, the narrator now launches by counter-example a frontal assault on the spurious syntax of personal subject and object [i.e., the previous subject positions constructed from gender polarity] in one of the finest, most supple runs of abstract lyric writing in Lawrence's fiction" ("Lawrence, 'Being,' and the Allotropic Style," *Novel: A Forum on Fiction* [Spring 1976]: 238).

57. Michael Ragussis, *The Subterfuge of Art: Language and the Romantic Tradition* (Baltimore: Johns Hopkins University Press, 1978), 201–5.

5.

1. William Carlos Williams, *The Collected Poems of William Carlos Williams*, ed. A. Walton Litz and Christopher MacGowan, vol. 1 (New York: New Directions, 1986), 184.

2. See Patrick Moore, "Ten Unpublished Letters from William Carlos Williams to Viola Baxter Jordan," *William Carlos Williams Review* 14:2 (Fall 1988): 30–60; and Palattella, "Midst of Hell."

3. Mike Weaver, *William Carlos Williams: The American Background* (Cambridge: Cambridge University Press, 1971), 23.

4. Carl Rapp, *William Carlos Williams and Romantic Idealism* (Hanover, N.H.: University Press of New England, 1984).

5. See especially "Idealism and the Vision of 'The Wanderer,'" in Rapp, *Williams and Idealism*, 1–30.

6. William Carlos Williams, "Postlude," *New Freewoman* 6 (September 1, 1913): 114.

7. Ezra Pound, "Reviews," *New Freewoman* 12 (December 1, 1913): 227.

8. Dora Marsden, "Thinking and Thought," *New Freewoman* 5 (August 15, 1913): 82.

9. In the same number, Huntly Carter touches on a similar matter and names the probable primary source for Marsden's artist baiting, Nietzsche's critique of artists as panders to the bourgeois establishment. Carter comments: "It seems that Neitzsche [*sic*] has referred somewhere to Art as the Arch-seducer. He was aware that the deadly formalism

and fallacies arising from the artist-fetish had bred a race of intermediaries called profes-sional artists" ("The Rape of the Drama," *New Freewoman* 5 [August 15, 1913]: 94). Per-haps Carter's source (among the *New Age* Nietzscheans?) was referring to the following of Nietzsche's remarks in *On the Genealogy of Morals:* artists "always need at the very least protection, a prop, an established authority: artists never stand apart. . . . Nothing is more easily corrupted than an artist" (538, 590).

10. In addition to the two "Great Sex Spiral" letters of 1917, these items are: "The Wanderer: A Rococo Study," *Egoist* 1:6 (March 16, 1914): 109–11; "Invocations" ["1. At Dawn," "2. Rendezvous," "3. (My Townspeople)," "4. To the Outer World," "La Flor," "Offering," "A La Lune," "In Harbour," "The Revelation"], *Egoist* 1:16 (August 15, 1914): 307–8; "Poems" ["Woman Walking," "Transitional," "Invitation," "Aux Imagistes," "Peace"], *Egoist* 1:23 (December 1, 1914): 444; "The Great Opportunity," *Egoist* 3:9 (September 1916): 137; "March," *Egoist* 3:10 (October 1916): 148–49; "The Delicacies," *Egoist* 4:9 (October 1917): 137–38; "A Celebration," *Egoist* 5:5 (May 1918): 73–74; "The Late Singer," *Egoist* 6:3 (July 1919): 38; and "Chicago," *Egoist* 6:5 (Decem-ber 1919): 73.

11. As we have argued, the *New Freewoman* represents Marsden's transitional period of testing out her own literary leanings. The last Gawthorpe letter in Dora Marsden's papers offers Gawthorpe's response to "Tales for the Attentive," which she refers to as "the 'Mind' allegory." This letter could be said to close the chapter in Marsden's devel-opment that began with the planning for the *Freewoman:* "I ought to have acknowledged the receipt of the *New Freewoman* for Oct 1st days ago. I am very grateful for the kind offer to put me in the 'free list'; and for the present I should like to accept. . . . I found myself quite at home with the 'Mind' allegory. Perhaps I liked it best of all. Many other things I don't care for, except in the sense that they're very necessary for intellectual clar-ity and mastery. Good luck always. As ever—just as ever, at bottom" (Mary Gawthorpe to Dora Marsden, October 12, 1913, Dora Marsden Collection, box 2, folder 1, Prince-ton University Libraries).

12. Paul Mariani gives examples from Williams's Keatsian phase in *William Carlos Williams: A New World Naked* (New York: McGraw-Hill, 1981), 54, 70. He writes about "The Wanderer": "Finally, here, Keats was submerged in order that Whitman's presence might surface" (113). More precisely, Keatsian versification was submerged so that a Whitmanian line was enabled to work over a Keatsian occasion. Cf. Stuart Peterfreund, "Vision and Revision in Keats and Williams," *Lamar Journal of the Humanities* 5:2 (1978): 28–39. On "The Wanderer," Peterfreund writes: "If Williams' symbolic immersion in the river of the present marks a triumph in the struggle with Keats, one of his poetic 'fathers,' it should be realized that the triumph proves a temporary one and must be enacted over and over again" (32).

13. See Kerry Driscoll, *William Carlos Williams and the Maternal Muse* (Ann Arbor: UMI Research Press, 1987).

14. For more on the political contexts of "The Wanderer," see Andrew Lawson, "Divisions of Labor: William Carlos Williams's 'The Wanderer' and the Politics of Mod-ernism," *William Carlos Williams Review* 20:1 (Spring 1994): 1–23.

15. Weaver reports having to calculate the date of this letter from other evidence, whereas the date as the collection is currently catalogued appears to be unambiguously June, not July, 1914.

16. Ezra Pound to Viola Baxter, July [?] 1909, Beinecke Library, Yale University.

17. Ezra Pound to Viola Baxter, n.d. [ca. 1909–10], Beinecke Library, Yale University.

18. William Carlos Williams to Viola Baxter, October 26, 1911, Beinecke Library, Yale University.

19. Ezra Pound to Viola Baxter, April 17, 1914, Beinecke Library, Yale University.

20. Ezra Pound to Viola Baxter, n.d. [ca. fall 1911], Beinecke Library, Yale University.

21. William Carlos Williams to Viola Baxter, April 29, 1914, Beinecke Library, Yale University.

22. William Carlos Williams to Viola Baxter, June 7, 1914, Beinecke Library, Yale University. For the whole text of this letter, see Moore, "Ten Letters."

23. H.D. [Hilda Doolittle], "Hermes of the Ways," *Egoist* 3:1 (February 2, 1914): 54–55; Bastien von Helmholtz [Ezra Pound], "The Bourgeois" and "John Synge," *Egoist* 3:1 (February 2, 1914): 53, 53–54.

24. William Carlos Williams, "Transitional," in "Poems," *Egoist* 1:23 (December 1, 1914): 444.

25. Driscoll does cite the entire poem later in the book, but, again, without close reading and in support of the same point, Williams's positive "fascination" with the "androgynous character of the artist" (*Williams and the Maternal Muse*, 86). The positivity of Driscoll's reading mutes the negative crosscurrents of what was clearly a difficult topic for Williams, a zone of ambivalence and resistance.

26. On Williams's confession of desperation in firing off letters, for instance, on one occasion to D. H. Lawrence, see Clarke, "Melancholy Serpent," 203–4.

27. Henri Gaudier-Brzeska, "VORTEX GAUDIER-BRZESKA (Written from the Trenches)," *Blast* 2 (July 1915): 33–34.

28. Henri Gaudier-Brzeska, "VORTEX. GAUDIER BRZESKA," *Blast* 1 (June 20, 1914): 155–58.

29. Ezra Pound, *Gaudier-Brzeska: A Memoir* (1916; rpt., New York: New Directions, 1960).

30. William Carlos Williams, *Kora in Hell: Improvisations,* in *Imaginations,* ed. Webster Schott (New York: New Directions, 1971), 16.

31. This title, an explicit imitation of Gaudier-Brzeska, appears on one of the typescripts of "Vortex," item C147 of the Williams materials in the Poetry/Rare Books Collection, State University of New York, Buffalo.

32. Bryce Conrad has demonstrated an equivalent operation in the composition of *In the American Grain,* wherein "Williams' whole book seems to be structurally patterned" on a "reprint series—the *Old South Leaflets* issued from 1895 to 1922" (*Refiguring America: A Study of William Carlos Williams'* In the American Grain [Urbana: University of Illinois Press, 1990], 163).

33. J. Hillis Miller, *Poets of Reality: Six Twentieth-Century Writers* (New York: Atheneum, 1974), 7–8.

34. William Carlos Williams, "The Great Sex Spiral: A Criticism of Miss Marsden's 'Lingual Psychology,' Chapter I," *Egoist* 4:3 (April 1917): 46; 4:7 (August 1917): 110–11.

35. Dora Marsden, "Lingual Psychology: A New Conception of the Function of Philosophic Inquiry," *Egoist* 3:7 (July 1, 1916): 97–102. Palattella notes the simultaneity

of the publication of Williams's first "Great Sex Spiral" letter and his initiation of the improvisations for *Kora in Hell* and properly underlines Williams's particular interest in gender issues: "Williams first wrote about Marsden the same month that he started improvising, April 1917. Williams was indeed interested in Marsden's work before the war, but the war's effect on Williams forced him to consolidate his views about Marsden in terms of masculinity" ("Midst of Hell," 19). However, archival evidence I cite below shows that Williams composed the first part of his Marsden correspondence no later than early February 1917.

36. The case of Weininger is a sore issue in Williams criticism. In *Williams and the Maternal Muse*, Driscoll made no mention of him whatsoever. Palattella ("Midst of Hell"), while cognizant of the Weininger connection and critical of the sexism in the documents it examines, discounts Dijkstra's presentation of "The Great Sex Spiral" as evidence of the mark Weininger's system left throughout Williams's work: "Caught early, like many of his generation, in an uncritical fascination with Weininger's rabidly anti-feminist, anti-woman, pseudo-scientific psychologism, Williams never managed to shake the sexist dualism conveniently formulated for him in *Sex and Character*" (Dijkstra, "Introduction," 32). Dijkstra situates Weininger's masculinism in terms that resonate with Williams's appreciation of Marsden's egoism: "Eternally inimical to individualism, woman was forever scheming to prevent man from progressing to that realm of individualist consciousness which would allow him to transcend the material limitations of the woman's world" (32). Moreover, Palattella's charge that Weaver's *William Carlos Williams* "obfuscates Williams's reaction to Marsden and *Lingual Psychology*" (19) misleadingly deflects attention from Weaver's perspicuous and proper insistence on the significance of the Williams/Weininger connection beginning as early as 1906 when the bookish medical student would have first come into contact with the English translation of *Sex and Character*.

37. Harriet Shaw Weaver to William Carlos Williams, item F706, Poetry/Rare Books Room, State University of New York, Buffalo.

38. Dora Marsden, "Mainly Anent the Decalogue," *Egoist* 1:4 (February 16, 1914): 62.

39. Wees lists some of the sources of the British social malaise that crested in 1914, concurrently with the publication of *Blast*: "The passage of the Parliament Act of 1911, after two years of the bitterest political rancour and class strife, the emergence of a fanatically militant women's suffrage movement, the sinister blustering of Sir Edward Carson and the Orangemen of Ulster and their open preparations for civil war with England, the tremendously intensified labour strife which could have led to a syndicalist-style general strike in September 1914 had war not broken out in August" (*Vorticism*, 14).

40. Dora Marsden, "I Am," *Egoist* 2:1 (January 1, 1915): 1.

41. Quoted from Lawrence, "The Novel," in *Study of Thomas Hardy and Other Essays*, 181; and William Carlos Williams, "A 1 Pound Stein," in *Selected Essays of William Carlos Williams* (New York: New Directions, 1969), 163.

42. Dora Marsden, "The Science of Signs," *Egoist* 3:8 (August 1916): 115. Marsden's unified philosophical project began with the title "Lingual Psychology"; the article "The Science of Signs" comprised the second installment of that initial series. But to indicate the internal consistency of the project, I refer to the entire series that began with

"Lingual Psychology" (July 1, 1916) and ended with "Philosophy: Science of Signs XVIII" (December 1919) as the *Science of Signs*.

43. Dora Marsden, "The 'I' and the 'Ego': A Differentiation," *Egoist* 3:9 (September 1916): 129.

44. Dora Marsden, "Philosophy: The Science of Signs XV—Two Rival Formulas," *Egoist* 5:4 (April 1918): 51.

45. Dora Marsden, "Philosophy: The Science of Signs XVII—Truth IV: The Measure of Authority Which Egoism Allows to the Science of External Nature," *Egoist* 6:3 (July 1919): 34.

46. William Carlos Williams, "The Late Singer," *Egoist* 6:3 (July 1919): 38.

47. T. S. Eliot, *The Waste Land and Other Poems* (New York: Harcourt, Brace, and World, 1962), 29.

48. J. Hillis Miller, "Williams' *Spring and All* and the Progress of Poetry" (1970), reprinted in *Tropes, Parables, Performatives: Essays on Twentieth-Century Literature* (Durham: Duke University Press, 1991), 88.

49. Marjorie Perloff, "'Lines Converging and Crossing': The 'French' Decade of William Carlos Williams," in *The Poetics of Indeterminacy: Rimbaud to Cage* (Princeton: Princeton University Press, 1981), 110.

50. Henry M. Sayre, "Avant-Garde Dispositions: Placing *Spring and All* in Context," *William Carlos Williams Review* 10:2 (Fall 1984): 17.

51. For a treatment critical of the "romanticism" of *Spring and All*, see Brian A. Bremen, *William Carlos Williams and the Diagnostics of Culture* (New York: Oxford University Press, 1993).

52. Dora Marsden, "Philosophy: The Science of Signs XVII—Truth V: How the Theory of the Ego Requires Us to Construe Death," *Egoist* 6:4 (September 1919): 50.

53. Dora Marsden, "Philosophy: The Science of Signs XVIII: The Egoistic Interpretation of Future Time," *Egoist* 6:5 (December 1919): 67.

54. Bonnie Kime Scott, *Joyce and Feminism* (Bloomington: Indiana University Press, 1984), 236.

55. See John T. Gage, *In the Arresting Eye: The Rhetoric of Imagism* (Baton Rouge: Louisiana State University Press, 1981); and "Ezra Pound and 'The Prose Tradition in Verse,'" in Perloff, *Futurist Moment*, 162–93.

56. See Altieri, *Painterly Abstraction*. Altieri's critical rhetoric invokes the vocabulary of energetics first bequeathed to literary discussion by the early modernists—for instance, Pound, Williams, and Marsden—thus his subtitle "The Contemporaneity of Modernism." Here he discusses the "synthetic role of form": "Form becomes that foregrounding of the compositional energies which gives the composing power external expression and thus defines those capacities of spirit inviting the audience's provisional identifications. . . . By grasping the abstract contours of the scene, one in effect gains a hold on the relation between natural and psychic constitutive energies that actually compose what we come to see" (403).

57. In Perloff's discussion in *The Futurist Moment*, "the autumn of 1913" was "the height of the manifesto fever that swept across Europe in the years preceding the First World War"; the futurist manifesto was "essentially a new literary genre, a genre that might meet the needs of a mass audience even as, paradoxically, it insisted on the avant-

garde, the esoteric, the antibourgeois. The Futurist manifesto marks the transformation of what had traditionally been a vehicle for political statement into a literary, one might say, a quasi-poetic construct" (81–82). The prose of *Spring and All* is a late outbreak of that same "manifesto fever."

58. In *Kora in Hell*, Williams remarks: "*It is nearly pure luck that gets the mind turned inside out in a work of art*" (75). In book 3 of *Paterson*, an image of inversion recurs again as a kind of recuperative strategy: "But somehow a man must lift himself / again— / again is the magic word . / turning the in out : / Speed against the inundation" (135). One of the earliest examples of this "inversion" theme occurs in a letter Williams wrote to Viola Baxter in 1911: "What am I? I am to a man what you are to a woman—one might say an auto glove inverted; the inside, skin-side, outside" (cited in Weaver, *William Carlos Williams*, 22).

Bibliography

Aldington, Richard. "Imitations of Lucian: Dialogues of the Dead." *Egoist* 1:7 (April 1, 1914): 126–28.

Aldred, Guy. "Freewoman." *Freewoman* 1:9 (January 18, 1912): 178–79.

———. *No Traitor's Gait*. Glasgow: Strickland, 1956.

Altieri, Charles. *Painterly Abstraction in Modernist American Poetry: The Contemporaneity of Modernism*. New York: Cambridge University Press, 1989.

Anderson, Margaret. "Challenge of Emma Goldman." *Little Review* 1 (May 1914): 5–9.

Avrich, Paul. *Anarchist Portraits*. Princeton: Princeton University Press, 1988.

Barash, Carol. "Dora Marsden's Feminism, the *Freewoman*, and the Gender Politics of Early Modernism." *Princeton University Library Chronicle* 49:1 (Autumn 1987): 31–56.

Bechhöfer, C. H. "More Contemporaries—V.—*Egoist*." *New Age* (June 15, 1914): 186.

Beer, Gillian. "Wave Theory and the Rise of Literary Modernism." In *Realism and Representation: Essays on the Problem of Realism in Relation to Science, Literature, and Culture*. Ed. George Levine, 193–213. Madison: University of Wisconsin Press, 1993.

Bell, Ian F. A. *Critic as Scientist: The Modernist Poetics of Ezra Pound*. New York: Methuen, 1981.

———. "'In a Station of the Metro' and Carpenterian Transformations." *Notes and Queries*, n.s., 29:4 (August 1982): 345–46.

———, ed. *Ezra Pound: Tactics for Reading*. Totowa, N.J.: Barnes and Noble, 1982.

Bell, T. H. "Edward Carpenter: The English Tolstoy." Los Angeles: Los Angeles Libertarian Group, 1932. Pamphlet.

Bentley, Michael. "Lawrence's Political Thought: Some English Contexts, 1906–19." In Heywood, *Lawrence: New Studies*, 59–83.

Bergson, Henri. "Philosophy of Ideas." *New Freewoman* 13 (December 15, 1913): 246–48.

Binns, Henry Bryan. "A Free Woman." *Freewoman* 2:32 (June 27, 1912): 112.

———. "The Spanish Gypsy." *New Age* (May 5, 1910): 14.

Birnstingl, Harry J. "'Uranians.'" *Freewoman* 1:7 (January 4, 1912): 127–28.

———. "Uranians—II." *Freewoman* 1:10 (January 25, 1912): 189–90.

———. "Human Minority." *Freewoman* 1:12 (February 8, 1912): 235.

Blast: Review of the Great English Vortex. Ed. Wyndham Lewis. London. No.1 (June 20, 1914); no.2 (July 1915).

Blatt, Martin Henry. *Free Love and Anarchism: The Biography of Ezra Heywood*. Chicago: University of Illinois Press, 1989.

Blodgett, Harold. *Walt Whitman in England*. Ithaca: Cornell University Press, 1934.

Bremen, Brian A. *William Carlos Williams and the Diagnostics of Culture*. New York: Oxford University Press, 1993.

Brown, Tony. "Figuring in History: The Reputation of Edward Carpenter, 1883–1987: Annotated Secondary Bibliography, I & II." *English Literature in Transition* 32:1 (1989): 27–32; 32:2 (1989): 170–210.

———, ed. *Edward Carpenter and Late Victorian Radicalism*. London: Frank Cass, 1990.

Brush, Stephen G. *The Temperature of History: Phases of Science and Culture in the Nineteenth Century*. New York: Burt Franklin, 1978.

Bucke, Richard Maurice, M.D. *Cosmic Consciousness: A Study in the Evolution of the Human Mind*. 1901; rpt. New York: E. P. Dutton, 1923.

Burwick, Frederick, and Paul Douglass, eds. *The Crisis in Modernism: Bergson and the Vitalist Controversy*. New York: Cambridge University Press, 1992.

Butler, Judith. *Gender Trouble: Feminism and the Subversion of Identity*. New York: Routledge, 1990.

Canguilhem, Georges. *Ideology and Rationality in the History of the Life Sciences*. Trans. Arthur Goldhammer. Cambridge: MIT Press, 1988.

———. *The Normal and the Pathological*. Trans. Caroline R. Fawcett. New York: Zone, 1991.

Carpenter, Edward. *The Art of Creation: Essays on the Self and Its Powers*. New and enlarged ed. London: George Allen, 1907.

———. "Civilisation: Its Cause and Cure." In *Civilisation: Its Cause and Cure*, 1–50.

———. *Civilisation: Its Cause and Cure and Other Essays*. 12th ed. London: George Allen, 1912.

———. *Days with Walt Whitman, With Some Notes on His Life and Work*. London: George Allen, 1896.

———. "Exfoliation: Lamarck *versus* Darwin." In *Civilisation: Its Cause and Cure*, 129–47.

———. *The Intermediate Sex: A Study of Some Transitional Types of Men and Women*. New York: Mitchell Kennerly, 1912.

———. "The Status of Women in Early Greek Times." *New Freewoman* 4 (August 1, 1913): 68–69.

Carter, Huntly. "The Golden Age." *New Freewoman* 1 (June 15, 1913): 16–17.

———. "Poetry Versus Imagism." *Little Review* 2:6 (September 1915): 27–37.

———. "The Rape of the Drama." *New Freewoman* 5 (August 15, 1913): 94–96.

Chamberlin, J. Edward. "Images of Degeneration: Turnings and Transformations." In *Degeneration: The Dark Side of Progress*. Ed. J. Edward Chamberlin and Sander L. Gilman, 263–89. New York: Columbia University Press, 1985.

Channell, David F. *The Vital Machine: A Study of Technology and Organic Life*. New York: Oxford University Press, 1991.

Cixous, Hélène. "The Laugh of the Medusa." In *The Critical Tradition: Classic Texts and Contemporary Trends*. Ed. David H. Richter, 1090–1102. New York: St. Martin's, 1989.

Clarke, Bruce. "The Fall of Montezuma: Poetry and History in William Carlos Williams and D. H. Lawrence." *William Carlos Williams Review* 12:1 (Spring 1986): 1–12.

———. "The Melancholy Serpent: Body and Landscape in Lawrence and William Carlos Williams." In *D. H. Lawrence's Literary Inheritors*. Ed. Keith Cushman and Dennis Jackson, 188–210. New York: St. Martin's, 1991.

Colmore, Gertrude. *Suffragette Sally*. London: Stanley, Paul, 1911; rpt. *Suffragettes: A Story of Three Women*. London: Pandora, 1984.

Conrad, Bryce. *Refiguring America: A Study of William Carlos Williams'* In the American Grain. Urbana: University of Illinois Press, 1990.

Cox, Kenneth. "Allen Upward." *Agenda* 16:3–4 (Autumn/Winter 1978–79): 87–121.

Davie, Donald. *Ezra Pound*. Chicago: University of Chicago Press, 1975.

Delany, Paul. *D. H. Lawrence's Nightmare: The Writer and His Circle in the Years of the Great War*. New York: Basic Books, 1978.

Delavenay, Emile. *D. H. Lawrence and Edward Carpenter: A Study in Edwardian Transition*. New York: Taplinger, 1971.

———. "Lawrence and the Futurists." In *The Modernists: Studies in a Literary Phenomenon*. Ed. Lawrence B. Gamache and Ian S. MacNiven, 140–62. Rutherford: Fairleigh Dickinson University Press, 1987.

———. "Lawrence, Otto Weininger and 'Rather Raw Philosophy.'" In Heywood, *Lawrence: New Studies*, 137–57.

DeLeon, David. *The American as Anarchist: Reflections on Indigenous Radicalism*. Baltimore: Johns Hopkins University Press, 1978.

Dell, Floyd. *Women as World Builders: Studies in Modern Feminism*. Chicago: Forbes, 1913.

Des Imagistes: An Anthology. New York: Albert and Charles Boni, 1914.

Dick, Hugo. "War and—Manure." *Herald of Revolt* 3:1 (February 1913): 10.

Dijkstra, Bram. "The Androgyne in Nineteenth-Century Art and Literature." *Comparative Literature* 26:1 (Winter 1974): 62–73.

———. *Cubism, Stieglitz, and the Early Poetry of William Carlos Williams*. Princeton: Princeton University Press, 1969.

———. *Idols of Perversity: Fantasies of Feminine Evil in Fin-de-Siècle Culture*. New York: Oxford University Press, 1986.

———. "Introduction." *A Recognizable Image: William Carlos Williams on Art and Artists*. Ed. Bram Dijkstra, 1–46. New York: New Directions, 1978.

Doolittle, Hilda [H.D.]. "Hermes of the Ways." *Egoist* 3:1 (February 2, 1914): 54–55.

Doyle, Charles. *Richard Aldington: A Biography*. Carbondale: Southern Illinois University Press, 1989.

Driscoll, Kerry. *William Carlos Williams and the Maternal Muse*. Ann Arbor: UMI Research Press, 1987.

Duncan, Isadora. *The Art of the Dance*. Ed. Sheldon Cheney. New York: Theatre Arts, 1928.

DuPlessis, Rachel Blau. *The Pink Guitar: Writing as Feminist Practice*. New York: Routledge, 1990.

———. "'Seismic Orgasm': Sexual Intercourse, Gender Narratives, and Lyric Ideology in Mina Loy." In *Studies in Historical Change*. Ed. Ralph Cohen, 264–91. Charlottesville: University Press of Virginia, 1992.

Durant, Alan. *Ezra Pound: Identity in Crisis*. Totowa, N.J.: Barnes and Noble, 1981.

Ebbatson, Roger. *The Evolutionary Self: Hardy, Forster, Lawrence*. Totowa, N.J.: Barnes and Noble, 1982.

―――. "A Spark Beneath the Wheel: Lawrence and Evolutionary Thought." In Heywood, *Lawrence: New Studies*, 90–103.

Efron, Arthur. "War Is the Health of the State: An Anarchist Reading of *Henry IV, Part One*." *Works and Days* 10:1 (Spring 1992): 7–75.

Egoist. Ed. Dora Marsden and Harriet Shaw Weaver. London. January 1, 1914–December 1919.

Eliot, T. S. "*Egoists*, by James Huneker." *Harvard Advocate* 88:1 (October 5, 1909): 16.

―――. "Tradition and the Individual Talent." *Egoist* 6:4 (September 1919): 54–55; 6:5 (December 1919): 72–73.

―――. *The Waste Land and Other Poems*. New York: Harcourt, Brace, and World, 1962.

Ellis, Havelock. *The New Spirit*. 1890; rpt. New York: Houghton Mifflin, 1929.

"Extraordinary Charges at Manchester." *Votes for Women* 3:83 (October 8, 1909): 27.

Eysteinsson, Astradur. *The Concept of Modernism*. Ithaca: Cornell University Press, 1990.

Fletcher, John Gould. "'Amores' by D. H. Lawrence." *Egoist* 3:12 (December 1916): 182.

Fogelman, Bruce. "The Evolution of Ezra Pound's 'Contemporania.'" *Journal of Modern Literature* 15:1 (Summer 1988): 93–103.

Foucault, Michel. "Introduction." In Canguilhem, *Normal and Pathological*, 7–24.

Freewoman. Ed. Dora Marsden and Mary Gawthorpe. London. November 23, 1911–October 10, 1912.

Gage, John T. *In the Arresting Eye: The Rhetoric of Imagism*. Baton Rouge: Louisiana State University Press, 1981.

Gallop, Jane. *The Daughter's Seduction: Feminism and Psychoanalysis*. Ithaca: Cornell University Press, 1982.

Garner, Les. *A Brave and Beautiful Spirit: Dora Marsden, 1882–1960*. Brookfield, Vt.: Avebury, 1990.

―――. *Stepping Stones to Women's Liberty: Feminist Ideas in the Women's Suffrage Movement, 1900–1918*. Rutherford: Fairleigh Dickinson University Press, 1984.

Gaudier-Brzeska, Henri. "VORTEX. GAUDIER BRZESKA." *Blast* 1 (June 20, 1914): 155–58.

―――. "VORTEX GAUDIER-BRZESKA (Written from the Trenches)." *Blast* 2 (July 1915): 33–34.

Gawthorpe, Mary. *Up Hill to Holloway*. Penobscot, Maine: Traversity, 1962.

Gershenowitz, Harry. "Two Lamarckians: Walt Whitman and Edward Carpenter." *Walt Whitman Quarterly Review* 2:1 (Summer 1984): 35–38.

Gibbons, Tom. *Rooms in the Darwin Hotel: Studies in English Literary Criticism and Ideas, 1880–1920*. Nedlands: University of Western Australia Press, 1973.

Gilbert, Sandra, and Susan Gubar. *No Man's Land: The Place of the Woman Writer in the Twentieth Century*. Vol. 1: *The War of the Words*. New Haven: Yale University Press, 1988.

―――. *No Man's Land: The Place of the Woman Writer in the Twentieth Century*. Vol. 2: *Sexchanges*. New Haven: Yale University Press, 1989.

Godden, Richard. "Icons, Etymologies, Origins and Monkey Puzzles in the Languages of Upward and Fenollosa." In I. Bell, *Ezra Pound: Tactics for Reading*, 221–44.

Goodheart, Eugene. *The Cult of the Ego: The Self in Modern Literature*. Chicago: University of Chicago Press, 1968.

Goodway, David, ed. *For Anarchism: History, Theory, and Practice.* New York: Routledge, 1989.

de Gourmont, Remy. *The Horses of Diomedes. New Freewoman* 5 (August 15, 1913)–*Egoist* 1:5 (March 2, 1914).

Green, Judith Kent. "A Note on Walt Whitman's Probable Reading of Robert Chambers." *Walt Whitman Quarterly Review* 3:3 (Winter 1986): 23–28.

Grierson, Francis. "Women's New Era." *New Freewoman* 1 (June 15, 1913): 10–11.

Grover, Philip, ed. *Ezra Pound: The London Years, 1908–1920.* New York: AMS, 1978.

Guérin, Daniel. "Marxism and Anarchism." In Goodway, *For Anarchism*, 109–26.

Gunn, Peter. *Vernon Lee: Violet Paget, 1856–1935.* New York: Oxford University Press, 1964.

Hanscombe, Gillian, and Virginia L. Smyers. *Writing for Their Lives: The Modernist Women, 1910–1940.* Boston: Northeastern University Press, 1987.

Hayles, N. Katherine. *Chaos Bound: Orderly Disorder in Contemporary Literature and Science.* Ithaca: Cornell University Press, 1990.

———. *The Cosmic Web: Scientific Field Models and Literary Strategies in the Twentieth Century.* Ithaca: Cornell University Press, 1984.

Healey, E. Claire, and Keith Cushman, eds. *The Letters of D. H. Lawrence and Amy Lowell 1914–1925.* Santa Barbara: Black Sparrow, 1985.

Hegel, G. W. F. *The Phenomenology of Mind.* Trans. J. B. Baillie. Intro. George Lichtheim. New York: Harper and Row, 1967.

Heilbrun, Carolyn. *Toward a Recognition of Androgyny.* New York: Knopf, 1973.

Henry, Leigh. "Liberations: Studies of Individuality in Contemporary Music—I. Prelude." *Egoist* 1:7 (April 1, 1914): 121–23.

Herzinger, Kim A. *D. H. Lawrence in His Time: 1908–1915.* Lewisburg: Bucknell University Press, 1982.

Hewitt, Marsha. "Emma Goldman: The Case for Anarcho-Feminism." In Roussopoulos, *Anarchist Papers*, 167–75.

Heywood, Christopher. "'Blood-Consciousness' and the Pioneers of the Reflex and Ganglionic Systems." In Heywood, *Lawrence: New Studies*, 104–36.

———, ed. *D. H. Lawrence: New Studies.* New York: St. Martin's, 1987.

Hueffer [Ford], Ford Madox. "Women and Men II." *Little Review* (March 1918): 36–51.

Hughes, Glenn. *Imagism and the Imagists: A Study in Modern Poetry.* 1931; rpt. New York: Humanities Press, 1960.

Hulten, Pontus, ed. *Futurism and Futurisms.* New York: Abbeville, 1986.

Huneker, James. *Egoists: A Book of Supermen.* 1909; New York: Scribner's, 1913.

Imagist Anthology, 1930. London: Chatto and Windus, 1930.

Jacob, François. *The Logic of Life: A History of Heredity.* Trans. Betty E. Spillmann. New York: Pantheon, 1973.

Janik, Allan. "Therapeutic Nihilism: How Not to Write about Otto Weininger." In *Structure and Gestalt: Philosophy and Literature in Austro-Hungary and Her Successor States.* Ed. Barry Smith, 263–92. Amsterdam: John Benjamins, 1981.

Jeffreys, Sheila. *The Spinster and Her Enemies: Feminism and Sexuality, 1880–1930.* London: Pandora, 1985.

Joyce, James. "A Portrait of the Artist as a Young Man. (Chapter I.—continued)." *Egoist* 1:7 (April 1, 1914): 132–34.

———. "A Portrait of the Artist as a Young Man. Chapter V (continued)." *Egoist* 2:9 (September 1, 1915): 144–47.

Kadlec, David. "Imagism and the Gold Standard." Typescript.

———. "Pound, *Blast,* and Syndicalism." *ELH* 60 (1993): 1015–31.

Kayman, Martin A. "A Model for Pound's Use of 'Science.'" In I. Bell, *Ezra Pound: Tactics for Reading,* 121–47.

Kenner, Hugh. *The Pound Era.* Berkeley: University of California Press, 1971.

Kent, Susan Kingsley. *Sex and Suffrage in Britain, 1860–1914.* Princeton: Princeton University Press, 1987.

Killingsworth, M. Jimmie. "Tropes of Selfhood: Whitman's 'Expressive Individualism.'" In R. Martin, *Continuing Presence,* 39–52.

Klein, Viola. "The Philosophical Approach: Otto Weininger." In *The Feminine Character: History of an Ideology,* 53–70. New York: International Universities Press, 1949.

Knapp, James F. *Literary Modernism and the Transformation of Work.* Evanston: Northwestern University Press, 1988.

Knight, David. *The Age of Science: The Scientific World-view in the Nineteenth Century.* Oxford: Basil Blackwell, 1986.

Kropotkin, Peter. *Modern Science and Anarchism.* London: Freedom Press, 1912.

"The Lancashire Protest Campaign." *Votes for Women* 3:92 (December 10, 1909): 164–65.

Lawrence, D. H. "A Propos of 'Lady Chatterley's Lover.'" In *Phoenix II,* 487–515.

———. "Autumn Rain." *Egoist* 4:2 (February 1917): 22.

———. *The Complete Poems of D. H. Lawrence.* Ed. Vivian de Sola Pinto and F. Warren Roberts. New York: Viking, 1971.

———. "The Crown." In *Reflections,* 251–306.

———. "Education of the People." In *Reflections,* 87–166.

———. "Eloi, Eloi, Lama Sabachthani?" *Egoist* 2:5 (May 1, 1915): 75–76.

———. *The Letters of D. H. Lawrence.* Vol. 2: *June 1913–October 1916.* Ed. George Zytaruk and James T. Boulton. New York: Cambridge University Press, 1981.

———. "New Heaven and Earth." In *Complete Poems,* 256–61.

———. "The Novel." In *Study of Thomas Hardy and Other Essays,* 179–90.

———. *Phoenix: The Posthumous Papers of D. H. Lawrence.* Ed. Edward D. McDonald. 1936; rpt. New York: Viking, 1968.

———. *Phoenix II.* Ed. Warren Roberts and Harry T. Moore. New York: Viking, 1968.

———. "Poems." *Egoist* 1:7 (April 1, 1914): 134–35.

———. "Poetry of the Present." In *Complete Poems,* 181–86.

———. *Reflections on the Death of a Porcupine and Other Essays.* Ed. Michael Herbert. New York: Cambridge University Press, 1988.

———. "Street Lamps." *Egoist* 4:1 (January 1917): 9.

———. *Study of Thomas Hardy.* In *Study of Thomas Hardy and Other Essays,* 7–128.

———. *Study of Thomas Hardy and Other Essays.* Ed. Bruce Steele. New York: Cambridge University Press, 1985.

———. "We Need One Another." In *Phoenix,* 188–95.

———. *Women in Love.* Ed. David Farmer, Lindeth Vasey, and John Worthen. New York: Cambridge University Press, 1987.

Lawson, Andrew. "Divisions of Labor: William Carlos Williams's 'The Wanderer' and the Politics of Modernism." *William Carlos Williams Review* 20:1 (Spring 1994): 1–23.

Lee, Vernon [Violet Paget]. *Gospels of Anarchy and Other Contemporary Studies.* New York: Brentano's, 1909.

Leisenring, Winnifred W. "A Race of Individuals." *New Freewoman* 2 (July 1, 1913): 34–35.

Levenson, Michael. *A Genealogy of Modernism: A Study of English Literary Doctrine, 1908–1922.* New York: Cambridge University Press, 1984.

Lewis, Wyndham. "The Cubist Room." *Egoist* 1:1 (January 1, 1914): 8–9.

———. "Long Live the Vortex!" *Blast* 1 (June 20, 1914): 7–8.

Lidderdale, Jane, and Mary Nicholson. *Dear Miss Weaver: Harriet Shaw Weaver, 1876–1961.* New York: Viking, 1970.

Lindberg, Kathryne V. *Reading Pound Reading: Modernism After Nietzsche.* New York: Oxford University Press, 1987.

———. "Whitman's 'Convertible Terms': America, Self, Ideology." In *Theorizing American Literature: Hegel, the Sign, and History.* Ed. Bainard Cowan and Joseph G. Kronick, 233–68. Baton Rouge: Louisiana State University Press, 1991.

Litz, A. Walton. "Lawrence, Pound, and Early Modernism." In *D. H. Lawrence: A Centenary Consideration.* Ed. Peter Balbert and Phillip L. Marcus, 15–28. Ithaca: Cornell University Press, 1985.

Lukács, Georg. *Realism in Our Time: Literature and the Class Struggle.* New York: Harper and Row, 1964.

MacKendrick, Louis K. "*New Freewoman:* A Short Story of Literary Journalism." *English Literature in Transition* 15:3 (1972): 180–87.

Marcus, Jane, ed. *The Young Rebecca: Writings of Rebecca West, 1911–1917.* New York: Viking, 1982.

Mariani, Paul. *William Carlos Williams: A New World Naked.* New York: McGraw-Hill, 1981.

Marsden, Dora. "The Art of the Future." *New Freewoman* 10 (November 1, 1913): 181–83.

———. "Beauty and the Senses." *New Freewoman* 11 (November 15, 1913): 201–3.

———. "Bondwomen." *Freewoman* 1:1 (November 23, 1911): 1–2.

———. "Commentary on Bondwomen." *Freewoman* 1:2 (November 30, 1911): 21–22.

———. "Creation and Immortality." *Freewoman* 1:19 (March 28, 1912): 361–62.

———. *The Definition of the Godhead.* London: Egoist Press, 1928.

———. "The Emancipation of Man." *Freewoman* 1:20 (April 4, 1912): 381–83.

———. "Freewomen and Evolution." *Freewoman* 1:26 (May 16, 1912): 503–4.

———. "The Growing Ego." *Freewoman* 2:38 (August 8, 1912), 221–22.

———. "The Heart of the Question." *New Freewoman* 4 (August 1, 1913): 61–64.

———. "I Am." *Egoist* 2:1 (January 1, 1915): 1–4.

———. "The 'I' and the 'Ego': A Differentiation." *Egoist* 3:9 (September 1916): 129–31.

———. "Intellect and Culture." *New Freewoman* 2 (July 1, 1913): 21–23.

———. "Interpretation of Sex—II." *Freewoman* 1:25 (May 9, 1912): 481–82.

———. "Interpretations of Sex—IV." *Freewoman* 2:27 (May 23, 1912): 1–2.

———. "The Lean Kind." *New Freewoman* 1 (June 15, 1913): 1–2.

———. "Lingual Psychology: A New Conception of the Function of Philosophic Inquiry." *Egoist* 3:7 (July 1, 1916): 97–102.

———. "Mainly Anent the Decalogue." *Egoist* 1:4 (February 16, 1914): 61–65.

———. "The New Morality." *Freewoman* 1:4 (December 14, 1911): 61–62.

———. "The New Morality—II." *Freewoman* 1:6 (December 28, 1911): 101–2.

———. "The New Morality—III." *Freewoman* 1:7 (January 4, 1912): 121–22.

———. "The New Morality—V." *Freewoman* 1:9 (January 18, 1912): 161–62.

———. "Notes of the Week." *Freewoman* 1:1 (November 23, 1911): 3–4.

———. "The Over-and-Above in Life." *Freewoman* 1:11 (February 1, 1912): 201–2.

———. "Philosophy: The Science of Signs XV—Two Rival Formulas." *Egoist* 5:4 (April 1918): 49–54.

———. "Philosophy: The Science of Signs XVII—Truth IV: The Measure of Authority Which Egoism Allows to the Science of External Nature." *Egoist* 6:3 (July 1919): 33–38.

———. "Philosophy: The Science of Signs XVII—Truth V: How the Theory of the Ego Requires Us to Construe Death." *Egoist* 6:4 (September 1919): 49–53.

———. "Philosophy: The Science of Signs XVIII: The Egoistic Interpretation of Future Time." *Egoist* 6:5 (December 1919): 65–70.

———. "The Science of Signs." *Egoist* 3:8 (August 1916): 113–17.

———. "Sex and Character." *Freewoman* 2:30 (June 13, 1912): 61–63.

———. "Tales for the Attentive." *New Freewoman* 8 (October 1, 1913): 141–44.

———. "Thinking and Thought." *New Freewoman* 5 (August 15, 1913): 81–83.

———. "Views and Comments." *Egoist* 1:3 (February 2, 1914): 44–46.

———. "Views and Comments." *Egoist* 1:7 (April 1, 1914): 123–26.

———. "Views and Comments." *Egoist* 1:12 (June 15, 1914): 223–26.

———. "Views and Comments." *New Freewoman* 1 (June 15, 1913): 3–5.

———. "Views and Comments." *New Freewoman* 2 (July 1, 1913): 23–25.

———. "Views and Comments." *New Freewoman* 5 (August 15, 1913): 83–85.

———. "Views and Comments." *New Freewoman* 9 (October 15, 1913): 163–66.

———. "Views and Comments." *New Freewoman* 11 (November 15, 1913): 203–5.

———. "Views and Comments." *New Freewoman* 13 (December 15, 1913): 244–45.

Marsh, Margaret S. *Anarchist Women, 1870–1920*. Philadelphia: Temple University Press, 1981.

Marshall, Peter. "Human Nature and Anarchism." In Goodway, *For Anarchism*, 127–49.

Martin, Robert K, ed. *The Continuing Presence of Walt Whitman: The Life After the Life*. Iowa City: University of Iowa Press, 1992.

Martin, Wallace. *The New Age Under Orage: Chapters in English Cultural History*. New York: Barnes and Noble, 1967.

Maxwell, James Clerk. *Theory of Heat*. 9th ed. New York: Longmans, Green, 1888.

Miller, David. *Anarchism*. London: Dent, 1984.

Miller, J. Hillis. *Poets of Reality: Six Twentieth-Century Writers*. New York: Atheneum, 1974.

———. "Williams' *Spring and All* and the Progress of Poetry." 1970; rpt. in *Tropes, Parables, Performatives: Essays on Twentieth-Century Literature*, 79–105. Durham: Duke University Press, 1991.

Miller, James E., Jr., Karl Shapiro, and Bernice Slote. *Start with the Sun: Studies in the Whitman Tradition*. Lincoln: University of Nebraska Press, 1960.

Moi, Toril. *Sexual/Textual Politics: Feminist Literary Theory*. New York: Methuen, 1985.

Monod, Jacques. *Chance and Necessity: An Essay on the Natural Philosophy of Modern Biology*. Trans. Austryn Wainhouse. New York: Knopf, 1971.

Moore, Patrick. "Ten Unpublished Letters from William Carlos Williams to Viola Baxter Jordan." *William Carlos Williams Review* 14:2 (Fall 1988): 30–60.

Myers, Greg. "Nineteenth-Century Popularizations of Thermodynamics and the Rhetoric of Social Prophecy." In *Energy and Entropy: Science and Culture in Victorian Britain*. Ed. Patrick Brantlinger, 307–38. Bloomington: Indiana University Press, 1989.

New Freewoman. Ed. Dora Marsden. London. June 15–December 15, 1913.

"*The New Freewoman* Thousand Club Membership: Establishment Fund." London, 1913.

Nickson, Richard. "Shaw and Anarchism: Among the Leftists." *The Independent Shavian* 26:1–2 (1988): 3–13.

Nietzsche, Friedrich. *On the Genealogy of Morals*. In *Basic Writings of Nietzsche*. Trans. and ed. Walter Kaufmann, 449–599. New York: Modern Library, 1968.

———. "On Truth and Lie in an Extra-Moral Sense." In *Deconstruction in Context: Literature and Philosophy*. Ed. Mark C. Taylor, 216–19. Chicago: University of Chicago Press, 1986.

Oliver, Hermia. *The International Anarchist Movement in Late Victorian London*. New York: St. Martin's, 1983.

Palattella, John. "'In the Midst of Living Hell': The Great War, Masculinity, and Maternity in Williams' *Kora in Hell: Improvisations* and 'Three Professional Studies.'" *William Carlos Williams Review* 17:2 (Fall 1991): 13–38.

Paulson, William R. *The Noise of Culture: Literary Texts in a World of Information*. Ithaca: Cornell University Press, 1988.

Perloff, Marjorie. *The Futurist Moment: Avant-Garde, Avant Guerre, and the Language of Rupture*. Chicago: University of Chicago Press, 1986.

———. "'Lines Converging and Crossing': The 'French' Decade of William Carlos Williams." *The Poetics of Indeterminacy: Rimbaud to Cage*, 109–54. Princeton: Princeton University Press, 1981.

Peterfreund, Stuart. "Vision and Revision in Keats and Williams." *Lamar Journal of the Humanities* 5:2 (1978): 28–39.

Peterson, Shirley. "The Politics of a Moral Crusade: Gertrude Colmore's *Suffragette Sally*." In *Rediscovering Forgotten Radicals: British Women Writers, 1889–1939*. Ed. Angela Ingram and Daphnae Patai, 101–17. Chapel Hill: University of North Carolina Press, 1993.

Plato. *Phaedrus*. Trans. W. C. Helmbold and W. G. Rabinowitz. Indianapolis: Bobbs-Merrill, 1956.

Pound, Ezra. *ABC of Reading*. New York: New Directions, 1960.

———. [Bastien von Helmholtz]. "The Bourgeois." *Egoist* 3:1 (February 2, 1914): 53.

———. "The Contemporania of Ezra Pound." *New Freewoman* 5 (August 15, 1913): 87–88.

———. "D. H. Lawrence." In *Literary Essays*, 387–88.

————. "Edward Wadsworth, Vorticist." *Egoist* 1:16 (August 15, 1914): 306–7.

————. *Gaudier-Brzeska: A Memoir.* 1916; rpt. New York: New Directions, 1960.

————. "In Metre." *New Freewoman* 6 (September 1, 1913): 113.

————. [Bastien von Helmholtz]. "John Synge." *Egoist* 3:1 (February 2, 1914): 53–54.

————. *The Letters of Ezra Pound: 1907–1941.* Ed. D. D. Paige. New York: Harcourt, Brace, 1950.

————. *The Letters of Ezra Pound to Margaret Anderson: The Little Review Correspondence.* Ed. Thomas L. Scott, Melvin J. Friedman, and Jackson R. Bryer. New York: New Directions, 1988.

————. *Literary Essays of Ezra Pound.* Ed. T. S. Eliot. New York: New Directions, 1968.

————. "The New Sculpture." *Egoist* 1:4 (February 16, 1914): 67–68.

————. "Reviews." *New Freewoman* 12 (December 1, 1913): 227.

————. "The Serious Artist." *New Freewoman* 9 (October 15, 1913): 161–63; 10 (November 1, 1913): 194–95; 11 (November 15, 1913): 213–14.

Quail, John. *The Slow Burning Fuse: The Lost History of the British Anarchists.* New York: Granada, 1978.

Rabinbach, Anson. *The Human Motor: Energy, Fatigue, and the Origins of Modernity.* New York: Basic Books, 1990.

Rae, Patricia. "From Mystical Gaze to Pragmatic Game: Representations of Truth in Vorticist Art." *ELH* 56:3 (Fall 1989): 689–720.

Raeburn, Antonia. *The Militant Suffragettes.* London: Michael Joseph, 1973.

Ragussis, Michael. *The Subterfuge of Art: Language and the Romantic Tradition.* Baltimore: Johns Hopkins University Press, 1978.

Rapp, Carl. *William Carlos Williams and Romantic Idealism.* Hanover, N.H.: University Press of New England, 1984.

Read, Herbert. *The Tenth Muse: Essays in Criticism.* London: Routledge and Kegan Paul, 1957.

Rider, Nick. "The Practice of Direct Action: The Barcelona Rent Strike of 1931." In Goodway, *For Anarchism*, 79–105.

Risse, Guenter B. "Kant, Schelling, and the Early Search for a Philosophical 'Science' of Medicine in Germany." *Journal of the History of Medicine and Allied Sciences* 27 (1972): 145–58.

Roberts, Warren. *A Bibliography of D. H. Lawrence.* London: Rupert Hart-Davis, 1963.

————. "London 1908: Lawrence and Pound." *Helix* 13–14 (1983): 45–49.

Robinson, Alan. *Symbol to Vortex: Poetry, Painting and Ideas, 1885–1914.* New York: St. Martin's, 1985.

Roessel, David. "Pound, Lawrence, and 'The Earthly Paradise.'" *Paideuma* 18:1–2 (Spring/Fall 1989): 227–30.

Rogers, Timothy. "Introduction." In *Georgian Poetry, 1911–1922: The Critical Heritage.* Ed. Timothy Rogers, 1–48. Boston: Routledge and Kegan Paul, 1977.

Rose, Jonathan. *The Edwardian Temperament, 1895–1919.* Athens: Ohio University Press, 1986.

Rosen, Andrew. *Rise Up, Women! The Militant Campaign of the Women's Social and Political Union, 1903–1914.* Boston: Routledge and Kegan Paul, 1974.

Rothschuh, Karl E., M.D. "The So-called 'Romantic' Interlude in Physiology." In *His-*

tory of Physiology. Trans. Guenter B. Risse, 155–66. Huntington, N.Y.: Krieger, 1973.

Roussopoulos, Dimitrios I., ed. *The Anarchist Papers.* Buffalo: Black Rose, 1986.

Rowbotham, Sheila. *A New World for Women—Stella Browne: Socialist Feminist.* London: Pluto, 1977.

Rowbotham, Sheila, and Jeffrey Weeks. *Socialism and the New Life: The Personal and Sexual Politics of Edward Carpenter and Havelock Ellis.* London: Pluto, 1977.

Sayre, Henry M. "Avant-Garde Dispositions: Placing *Spring and All* in Context." *William Carlos Williams Review* 10:2 (Fall 1984): 13–24.

Schneidau, Herbert N. *Ezra Pound: The Image and the Real.* Baton Rouge: Louisiana State University Press, 1969.

Scholnick, Robert J. "'The Password Primeval': Whitman's Use of Science in 'Song of Myself.'" In *Studies in the American Renaissance 1986.* Ed. Joel Myerson, 385–425. Charlottesville: University Press of Virginia, 1986.

Schwartz, Sanford. "Bergson and the Politics of Vitalism." In Burwick and Douglass, *Crisis in Modernism*, 277–305.

Scott, Bonnie Kime. *Joyce and Feminism.* Bloomington: Indiana University Press, 1984.

———, ed. *The Gender of Modernism: A Critical Anthology.* Bloomington: Indiana University Press, 1990.

Serres, Michel. *Hermes: Literature, Science, Philosophy.* Ed. Josué V. Harari and David F. Bell. Baltimore: Johns Hopkins University Press, 1982.

Shatz, Marshall S., ed. *The Essential Works of Anarchism.* New York: Quadrangle, 1972.

Sheldon, Michael. "Allen Upward: Some Biographical Notes." *Agenda* 16:3–4 (Autumn/Winter 1978–79): 109–21.

Showalter, Elaine. *A Literature of Their Own: British Women Novelists from Brontë to Lessing.* Princeton: Princeton University Press, 1977.

Siegel, Carol. *Lawrence among the Women: Wavering Boundaries in Women's Literary Traditions.* Charlottesville: University Press of Virginia, 1991.

Silverman, Kaja. *Male Subjectivity at the Margins.* New York: Routledge, 1992.

———. *The Subject of Semiotics.* New York: Oxford University Press, 1983.

Simpson, Hilary. *D. H. Lawrence and Feminism.* DeKalb: Northern Illinois University Press, 1982.

Sinclair, May. *Feminism.* London: Women Writers Suffrage League, 1912.

———. *The Tree of Heaven.* 1917; New York: Macmillan, 1919.

Smith-Rosenberg, Carroll. *Disorderly Conduct: Visions of Gender in Victorian America.* New York: Knopf, 1985.

Some Imagist Poets, 1917: An Annual Anthology. New York: Houghton Mifflin, 1917; rpt. New York: Kraus, 1969.

Steele, Tom. *Alfred Orage and the Leeds Art Club, 1893–1923.* Brookfield, Vt.: Scolar Press, 1990.

Stephens, James. *The Hill of Vision.* London: Maunsel, 1912.

Stewart, Garrett. "Lawrence, 'Being,' and the Allotropic Style." *Novel: A Forum on Fiction* (Spring 1976): 217–42.

Stirner, Max. *The Ego and His Own: The Case of the Individual Against Authority.* Trans. Steven T. Byington. New York: Libertarian Book Club, 1963.

Stock, Noel. *The Life of Ezra Pound*. Expanded ed. San Francisco: North Point, 1982.

Surette, Leon. "Ezra Pound and British Radicalism." *English Studies in Canada* 9:4 (December 1983): 435–51.

Symonds, John Addington. *Essays Speculative and Suggestive*. 3d ed. New York: Charles Scribner's Sons, 1907.

———. *Walt Whitman: A Study*. London: John C. Nimmo, 1893.

Sypher, Eileen. "Anarchism and Gender: James's *The Princess Casamassima* and Conrad's *The Secret Agent*." *Henry James Review* 9:1 (Winter 1988): 1–16.

Tedlock, E. W., Jr. "A Forgotten War Poem by D. H. Lawrence." *Modern Language Notes* 67 (June 1952): 410–13.

Thacker, Andrew. "Dora Marsden and *The Egoist*: 'Our War Is with Words.'" *English Literature in Transition: 1880–1920* 36:2 (1993): 179–96.

Thatcher, David S. *Nietzsche in England, 1890–1914: The Growth of a Reputation*. Toronto: University of Toronto Press, 1970.

Thomson, William (Lord Kelvin). "On a Universal Tendency in Nature to the Dissipation of Mechanical Energy." In *Mathematical and Physical Papers*, 1:511–14. 5 vols. Cambridge: Cambridge University Press, 1882.

Tickner, Lisa. *The Spectacle of Women: Imagery of the Suffrage Campaign, 1907–14*. Chicago: University of Chicago Press, 1988.

True Womanhood. "An Estimation of Weininger." *Freewoman* 2:28 (May 30, 1912): 38.

Tsuzuki, Chishichi. *Edward Carpenter, 1844–1929: Prophet of Human Fellowship*. New York: Cambridge University Press, 1980.

Upward, Allen. *The Divine Mystery: A Reading of the History of Christianity Down to the Time of Christ*. 1914; rpt. with an introduction by Robert Duncan. Santa Barbara: Ross-Erikson, 1976.

———. *The New Word: An Open Letter Addressed to the Swedish Academy in Stockholm on the Meaning of the Word IDEALIST*. New York: Mitchell Kennerly, 1910.

———. "The Order of the Seraphim—I." *New Age* (February 10, 1910): 349–50.

———. "The Plain Person." *Egoist* 1:3 (February 2, 1914): 47–49.

Weaver, Mike. *William Carlos Williams: The American Background*. Cambridge: Cambridge University Press, 1971.

Wees, William C. *Vorticism and the English Avant-Garde*. Toronto: University of Toronto Press, 1972.

Weininger, Otto. *Sex and Character*. New York: G. P. Putnam's Sons, 1906.

———. "Woman and Mankind: Chapter XIV. of Weininger's 'Sex and Character.'" *Freewoman* 1:23 (April 25, 1912): 452–55.

———. "Woman and Mankind: Chapter XIV. of Weininger's 'Sex and Character'—II." *Freewoman* 1:24 (May 2, 1912): 470–73.

West, Rebecca. "The Freewoman." *Time and Tide* (July 16, 1926): 648–49.

———. "Imagisme." *New Freewoman* 5 (August 15, 1913): 86–87.

———. "The Life of Emily Davison." In Marcus, *Young Rebecca*, 178–83.

———. "Spinsters and Art." *Freewoman* 2:34 (July 11, 1912): 147–49.

———. "Two Poets." *Freewoman* 1:25 (May 9, 1912): 486–88.

Weston, Selwyn. "Anarchy in Art." *Freewoman* 1:10 (January 25, 1912): 193–94.

———. "A Gospel of Goodwill." *Freewoman* 1:5 (December 21, 1911): 81–82.

————. "Millennium." *Freewoman* 1:8 (January 11, 1912): 148–49.

Wexler, Alice Ruth. "Emma Goldman and Women." In Roussopoulos, *Anarchist Papers*, 151–66.

Whitby, Charles J. "A Matter of Taste." *Freewoman* 1:11 (February 1, 1912): 215–16.

————. "A Sex Heresy." *Freewoman* 1:26 (May 16, 1912): 505–7.

————. "Tertium Quid." *Freewoman* 1:9 (January 18, 1912): 167–69.

White, E. M. "Militancy in Women." *Freewoman* 1:8 (January 11, 1912): 158–59.

Whitman, Walt. *Democratic Vistas*. In *Prose Works, 1892*. Vol. 2: *Collect and Other Prose*. Ed. Floyd Stovall, 361–426. New York: New York University Press, 1964.

————. *Leaves of Grass: The First (1855) Edition*. Ed. Malcolm Cowley. New York: Viking, 1961.

————. *Leaves of Grass and Selected Prose*. Ed. Lawrence Buell. New York: Modern Library, 1981.

Williams, Raymond. *Culture and Society, 1780–1950*. New York: Columbia University Press, 1983.

Williams, William Carlos. "A 1 Pound Stein." In *Selected Essays*, 162–66.

————. *Collected Poems of William Carlos Williams*. Ed. A. Walton Litz and Christopher MacGowan. Vol. 1. New York: New Directions, 1986.

————. "A Celebration." *Egoist* 5:5 (May 1918): 73–74.

————. "Chicago." *Egoist* 6:5 (December 1919): 73.

————. "The Delicacies." *Egoist* 4:9 (October 1917): 137–38.

————. "The Great Opportunity." *Egoist* 3:9 (September 1916): 137.

————. "The Great Sex Spiral: A Criticism of Miss Marsden's 'Lingual Psychology,' Chapter I." *Egoist* 4:3 (April 1917): 46; 4:7 (August 1917): 110–11.

————. *Imaginations*. Ed. Webster Schott. New York: New Directions, 1971.

————. "Invocations." *Egoist* 1:16 (August 15, 1914): 307–8.

————. *Kora in Hell: Improvisations*. In *Imaginations*, 6–82.

————. "The Late Singer." *Egoist* 6:3 (July 1919): 38.

————. "March." *Egoist* 3:10 (October 1916): 148–49.

————. *Paterson*. New York: New Directions, 1963.

————. "Poems." *Egoist* 1:23 (December 1, 1914): 444.

————. "Postlude." *New Freewoman* 6 (September 1, 1913): 114.

————. *Selected Essays of William Carlos Williams*. New York: New Directions, 1969.

————. *Spring and All*. In *Collected Poems*, 1:177–236.

————. "Transitional." In "Poems," 444.

————. "Vortex." In Dijkstra, *A Recognizable Image*, 57–59.

————. "The Wanderer: A Rococo Study." *Egoist* 1:6 (March 16, 1914): 109–11.

Woodcock, George. *Anarchism: A History of Libertarian Ideas and Movements*. New York: Meridian, 1962.

Woods, Gregory. "'Still on My Lips': Walt Whitman in Britain." In R. Martin, *Continued Presence*, 129–40.

Zapf, Hubert. "Taylorism in D. H. Lawrence's *Women in Love*." *D. H. Lawrence Review* 15:1–2 (Spring/Summer 1982): 129–39.

Index

Huntly; Lawrence, D. H.; Marsden, Dora; Pound, Ezra; Stirner,
Max; Williams, William Carlos
Egoist
and Richard Aldington, 137–39
and Huntly Carter, 141–46
editing of, 3, 137–46
and gender, 63
and the imagists, 144–45
and James Joyce, 71
and D. H. Lawrence, 146–53
and the London avant–garde, 1, 3
Special Imagist Number, 97, 144,
234n.5
and James Stephens, 139–41
and William Carlos Williams, 173–74,
176, 180, 182–84, 192–99
Egoist, The (George Meredith), 67
Egoists: A Book of Supermen (James
Huneker), 12, 19–22, 142
Élan vital, 195, 207, 235n.8
Eliot, T. S.
and the *Egoist,* 1, 147
and Ezra Pound, 109
and James Huneker, 19, 222n.33
and later modernism, 4, 6–7
and politics, 7
works of
"*Egoists,* by James Huneker,"
222n.33
"Tradition and the Individual Talent," 7, 213
Waste Land, The, 4, 206
Elitism, 19, 108
Ellis, Havelock, 8, 15, 68, 83
Emerson, Ralph Waldo, 1, 22, 174
Energetics, 27, 125–28, 136, 159, 163
English Review, 146
Entropy
and heat death, 36–38, 127, 136
and the second law of thermodynamics, 35
and social energetics, 125
and vitalism, 135, 156–57, 214, 217
in *Women in Love,* 161–71
Eugenics, 15, 24, 63, 85

Evolution. *See* Science
Evolutionism
in Edward Carpenter, 32–33, 35–38,
43–46, 65, 78
and feminism, 15
and futurism, 153
in Dora Marsden, 50, 60, 64, 78, 99,
118, 120–22, 216
and modernism, 7
mystic, 23, 44, 64, 120, 122
progressive, 162
reactionary, 162
as scientific ideology, 26, 223n.43
secular, 23
in Herbert Spencer, 27–28, 158
in *Study of Thomas Hardy,* 155, 157
in Vernon Lee, 22–23
in Walt Whitman, 39, 67
See also Lamarck, Jean Baptiste
Expressionism, 2
Eysteinsson, Astradur, 6

Fascism, 24, 42–43
Feminism. *See* Gender
Fletcher, John Gould, 149, 240n.27
Flint, F. S., 2, 129, 138, 140
Ford (Hueffer), Ford Madox, 1, 109,
140–42, 232n.74, 233n.79
Freewoman
anarchism in, 66–73
boycott of, 3, 91
content of, 2–4, 9, 11, 95, 118
dates of publication of, 228n.28
Floyd Dell on, 16–18
and feminism, 1, 155
and Dora Marsden, 55–61, 63–66,
69–73, 76–81, 86–93
transition to the *New Freewoman,* 3,
16–17, 91–93, 118, 122–24
Freewoman Discussion Circle, 66, 73–81,
230n.42, 231n.57
Frost, Robert, 109, 138, 174
Futurism, 2, 153, 226n.2

Garner, Les, 56, 107, 227n.20
Garnett, Edward, 153